PRINCIPLES OF MARKETING

PRINCIPLES OF MARKETING

Jay Diamond
Professor and Chairman
Marketing and Retailing Department
Nassau Community College

Gerald Pintel, Ph.D.
Professor
Business Administration Department
Nassau Community College

PRENTICE-HALL, INC., ENGLEWOOD CLIFFS, NEW JERSEY

Library of Congress Cataloging in Publication Data

DIAMOND, JAY.
    Principles of marketing. ·

    Includes bibliographies.
        1. Marketing.   I. Pintel, Gerald, joint author.
II. Title.
HF5415.D4847   658.8   70-37781
ISBN   0-13-701474-0

© 1972 by PRENTICE-HALL, INC.
    Englewood Cliffs, New Jersey

10 9

Printed in the United States of America

PRENTICE-HALL INTERNATIONAL, INC., *London*
PRENTICE-HALL OF AUSTRALIA, PTY. LTD., *Sydney*
PRENTICE-HALL OF CANADA, LTD., *Toronto*
PRENTICE-HALL OF INDIA PRIVATE LIMITED, *New Delhi*
PRENTICE-HALL OF JAPAN, INC., *Tokyo*

CONTENTS

PREFACE

Principles of Marketing was written to introduce students to the various activities in the field of marketing and to provide the technical and theoretical knowledge necessary for employment for graduates and even those with work experience. Typical of the jobs at this level are middle management, executive assisting, or executive training.

An overview of marketing is presented, which includes such vital areas as channels of distribution, transportation and warehousing, consumer and industrial goods, and pricing and product development.

Much of the material included in the text reflects the actual practices of the leading marketers in the United States. Their procedures and recommendations have been incorporated to insure that the student entering the field will be able to apply what he has learned through formal study.

Significantly important today and perhaps even more so in the future are the areas of research, consumerism, and electronic data processing in marketing. Separate chapters are devoted to these units.

Included in each chapter are review questions and simple cases that require the application of marketing theory. For those entering the field, or merely surveying marketing, the textbook provides the maximum information needed for employment in marketing positions.

Although the traditional marketing textbook is somewhat longer than this one, the brevity is intentional. In most colleges the introductory marketing course runs for one semester and the abundance of material offered in most marketing texts cannot be covered in this time period. In this text all the major topics are discussed in a fashion that permits completion of the text in one semester.

To assist students an outline for student notes has been included in each chapter and a brief summary of key points is at the end of each chapter.

A teacher's manual that provides answers to problems and cases and sample tests is available.

Special thanks to Professor Joseph Reihing of Nassau Community College for his valuable help in gathering and providing information for Chapters 18 and 19, MARKETING MISTAKES and A MARKETING APPLICATION.

PRINCIPLES OF MARKETING

THE NATURE OF MARKETING

1

INTRODUCTION

In a primitive society, marketing is limited and simple because most primitive people are nearly self-sufficient and goods and services need rarely to be exchanged. Where exchanges are required, surplus goods are usually taken to a neighbor or neighboring village and bartered (traded) for the neighbor's surplus. As the society evolves toward a more technical economic level, specialization occurs. Certain individuals may become toolmakers, others farmers, and still others become healers. The exchange of goods and services then becomes a necessity, since the toolmaker's only means of securing food and clothing is by marketing his tools in exchange for the surpluses being offered by the farmer, the hunter, and other specialists.

The more the society progresses, the more workers become specialized. The toolmaker no longer hunts or farms and marketing gains steadily in importance. At this point the exchange of goods and services becomes indispensable. The producer must offer his products at the market to obtain the means of acquiring these goods and services that he needs for his production.

THE MARKET

The term *market* is used in many ways and, consequently, cannot be simply defined. When the term *market* is used to express the exchange of goods, the American Marketing Association suggests the following definition:

> The aggregate of forces or conditions within which buyers and sellers make decisions that result in the transfer of goods and services.

When the term *market* is used to represent a demand for a product, the American Marketing Association suggests this definition:

> The aggregate demand of the potential buyers of a commodity or service.

Frequently the word *market* is used to define a specific geographical area. In that case, the following definition is appropriate:

> The place or area in which buyers and sellers function.

The word *market* may also be used as a verb, that is, to define an activity. To market is:

> To perform business activities that direct the flow of goods and services from the producer to the consumer or user.

Obviously, since the term *market* may be used correctly in many ways, there is no single definition that can be entirely suitable. A reasonable working definition that combines the main features of the first three listed above is as follows:

> A market is an area in which the aggregate of forces or conditions result in decisions that satisfy demand by the transfer of goods and services.

MARKETING

Since the market is an absolute requirement of all but the most primitive, self-sufficient societies, the problem of getting goods to the market, or more properly, from the producer to the user, becomes basic. Because great distances and competing products may be involved, it becomes highly complicated and essential for the successful operation of a business. The American Marketing Association's committee on definitions describes marketing in this way:

> The performance of business activities that direct the flow of goods and services from the producer to the consumer or user.

It would seem from the above definition that marketing covers all business activities. This is not the case. The key to the decision of whether or not marketing is involved in a particular business activity is the use of the word *direct* in the definition. Thus, tasks that significantly change the product such as manufacturing, mining, and agriculture are not included in the term *marketing,* although they are directed by marketers. Activities such as market research, product planning, and product design are the responsibility of the marketing division. The marketing manager is not concerned with the manufacturing process, but he is responsible for the type of goods that are produced and for the time of their production. Similarly, although not involved with accounting, the marketing function must direct pricing and credit policies. The marketing division, therefore, is involved in almost every activity of the firm. It is directly responsible for activities such as selling, advertising, transportation, and promotion, and indirectly for production and accounting.

Historical Aspects

Prior to the Industrial Revolution, marketing was of relatively little importance to American business. The early farming communities were comparatively self-sufficient. The people raised their own crops, made their own clothes, and required very little of the outside world. With the passing of time, individuals began to concentrate on the production of goods most appropriate for their abilities. A farmer, rather than planting all the food-stuffs he required, concentrated all his energies on the particular crop for which he and his land were best suited. This created the two things that are the basis of marking: a surplus of the product produced and a demand for the necessities no longer produced.

In early colonial times, the population was clustered around the great ports of the eastern seaboard. The colonists produced raw materials for the European economy and were, themselves, a market for European finished products. As the population moved westward, there was a beginning of domestic manufacturing, which resulted in a decrease of the dependence of the colonists upon foreign markets. The Revolutionary War and the War of 1812 added impetus to this development by reducing European trade and placing domestic production in a preferred competitive position. At this point marketing was still a relatively minor business function because surpluses were minimal and easily distributed, since the demand generally exceeded the supply.

The Industrial Revolution resulted in a growth of urban areas at the expense of the rural population. This accelerated marketing growth by increasing the effect of the two factors most important to the distribution of goods: the demand of the urban centers for the necessities of their people and raw materials for production, and the surplus production of their factories. The extension of the railroad network after the Civil War provided a means for transporting goods into and out of the urban centers and facilitated the movement of the manufacturing centers away from the eastern seaboard. As of the late 1800s the supply (surplus) began to catch up with the demand. Until this time, marketing was little more than trans-portation. Now competition began to take on importance. This led to styling and packaging changes, to the beginning of advertising, and even to the use of drummers (salesmen).

It was not until the close of World War I and the emergence of mass production as a factor in American industry that the importance of market-ing was established. Until then, the demand for goods had exceeded the supply and expensive marketing systems were not required. With mass production, the supply of goods is almost unlimited, whereas the demand for goods, though growing, lags behind. In the 1920s, for the first time in American history, surplus goods suddenly exceeded demand. This resulted in a buyer's market (more goods available than purchasing power) rather than a seller's market (more purchasing power available than goods). Such conditions lead to fierce competition among producers to increase their share of the market.

One way of increasing sales is to give the customer what he wants, when he wants it, where he wants it, and at a fair price that he is willing to pay. This is another way of saying that the answer to overproduction is improved marketing.

The Utilities of Marketing

To operate successfully, a business must perform four basic utilities: form, place, time, and ownership. The value of goods is determined by the creation of one or more of these utilities.

Form is created by extracting goods from nature and changing them to satisfy human needs. It refers to manufacturing and production. Although marketing is not concerned with the manufacturing process, it directs production into the areas that will satisfy consumer demand. In other words, the milling of wheat into flour and the baking of bread are not the concern of marketers, but the types of bread to be made and the quantities of each category to be produced must be directed by the marketing division. The marketing manager must see to it that the form goods take is keyed to customer demand.

Place is created by moving the goods from the facility at which they are produced, through intermediary places such as the wholesaler's, to the location at which the customers will buy them. Place is very much the utility of the marketing division. It requires selection of various transportation systems as well as channels of distribution, which are routes (through the hands of various wholesalers and other middlemen) by which goods flow from the producer to the consumer.

Time is created by storing goods until they are required by the consumer. It entails the use of warehousing and storage facilities that are usually selected and supervised by the marketing division.

Ownership is created by getting the goods into the hands of consumers (wholesale or retail).

The utilities listed above are so interrelated that it is impossible to evaluate their individual importance. They are equally important and all must be performed efficiently if a business is to operate successfully. If bread is to be supplied to a customer, it is as important to ship the wheat to the miller and baker, keep the wheat until the customer wants it and have it where he needs it, as it is for the wheat to be grown and milled into flour.

The Functions of Marketing

There are eight specialized activities or functions involved in marketing. These are:

Buying.   This requires the recognition of the needs of an enterprise; the selection of the best source of supply; and the negotiation of price, shipping dates, and other matters.

Selling.   This is a function that requires the creation of customer demand the discovery of buyers, and negotiation.

Transportation.   The place utility arises as a result of the function of transportation. It involves the physical movement of goods from the producer to the user.

Storage.   The time utility arises through storage. It involves the holding and preserving of goods until they are required by the users.

Grading.   Agricultural and extractive (lumber, mining, and so on) industries require definite standards of quality and the sorting of goods into standardized grades. Only in this way can a buyer be certain of what he is buying.

Financing.   This function is concerned with the management of the money and credit required from the producer to the ultimate consumer. (The financial transactions arising from production are *not* considered part of the financing function of *marketing.*)

Risk Taking.   The marketing of goods and services involves a considerable amount of risk taking. Minimizing such risks is an important function of marketing.

Market Information.   Increasingly, managerial decision making has become more dependent on comprehensive market information. As the growth of an institution increases the distance between the decision makers and the market, information becomes more important. This is the prime reason for the significance of the computer, essentially an information producer, to industry.

The Importance of Marketing

The importance of marketing to an industrial economy can be pointed out in many ways. Among these are: the cost, the number of people employed, the effect on the standard of living, and the importance to the individual firm.

COST.   In our complex, dispersed, highly competitive society, marketing costs are extremely high. A 1948 estimate stated that it cost almost as much to market goods as to produce them. There is little doubt that since that time marketing costs have increased relative to production costs. The relationship of marketing costs to total costs varies considerably from industry to industry. For example, agricultural products that require little or no processing between producer and consumer frequently have marketing costs in excess of 70 percent of the retail price. Automobiles and heavy farming equipment, on the other hand, are marketed at a cost of about 35 percent, whereas ladies' apparel requires about 60 percent of the retail price for distribution from the manufacturer to the consumer.

PEOPLE EMPLOYED.   Although it is difficult to estimate the number of people employed in marketing jobs, most experts agree that between one-quarter and one-third of the total population is engaged in marketing activities. Included in these figures are all persons employed in retailing, wholesaling, transportation, warehousing, and communications industries, as well as those involved in the marketing functions of manufacture, finance, service, agriculture, and other business activities that are not classified as essentially marketing. Another interesting employment statistic is that during the last hundred years there has been a threefold advance in total employment, whereas retailing and wholesaling jobs have increased twelve times. There is reason to believe that the proportion of market jobs to total employment will continue to increase.

EFFECT ON THE STANDARD OF LIVING.   Ours has been described as an economy of affluence. This means that we produce and consume far in excess of our basic needs. We are not forced to consume all that is produced, but not to do so would result in serious economic disorder. It is the function of marketing to convince us to consume the mass of products turned out. Where marketing is able to successfully build a high demand, new jobs are created and both the individual and national standard of living are increased. This does not mean that the economic health of the United States is dependent upon marketing alone, but rather that inefficient distribution can lead to economic problems. Companies that can enlarge their profits through effective marketing are able to raise the standard of living of their owners and their employees and to hire new employees.

IMPORTANCE TO THE INDIVIDUAL FIRM.   As our technological capabilities grow, our production facilities are able to turn out ever larger surpluses of goods. The gap between necessities and output constantly widens. To dispose of the surplus at a profitable level becomes more difficult and complicated. Product lines are expanding and competition, both from similar products and substitutes, is growing keener. As a result, effective marketing is becoming steadily more important to the individual firm. The National Association of Manufacturers put it this way:

In this exciting age of change, marketing is the beating heart of many operations. It must be considered a principal reason for corporate existence. The modern concept of marketing recognizes its role as a direct contributor to profits as well as sales volume.

No longer can a company just figure out how many widgets it can produce and then go ahead and turn them out. To endure in this highly competitive, change-infested market, a company must first determine what it can sell, how much it can sell, and what approaches must be used to entice the wary customer. The president cannot plan; the production manager cannot manage; the purchasing agent cannot purchase; the chief financial officer cannot budget; and the engineer and designer cannot design until the basic market determinations have been made.

Marketing must be understood to be a dynamic operation requiring the efforts and skills of a *team* of specialists.

The Development of Marketing Management

As American industry poured an ever increasing surplus of goods into a highly competitive market, the function of marketing gained in importance. This has resulted in improved organization and management within the marketing division as well as in a more important position of the marketing manager in the overall operation of the company. The development of marketing from its rudimentary, relatively unimportant stage to its present far-reaching level of importance has been traced by the executive vice-president of the Pillsbury Company into four evolutionary stages that are typical of the growth in significance of marketing management.

PRODUCTION STAGE. When Pillsbury began milling fine flour in 1869, it found itself in a seller's market. That is, the demand for its product far exceeded its production capabilities. Since sales and distribution offered no problems, the company's management was primarily concerned with the improvement, expansion, and efficiency of production. The company employed salesmen but they were not very important.

SALES STAGE. By 1930 the steadily increasing production of flour by Pillsbury and its competitors had changed the seller's market to a buyer's market. At that time there was a greater supply of flour on the market than was necessary to satisfy customer demand. Competition became very keen and selling rivaled production in importance. The organization of a company at this stage of development may be seen in Figure 1–1.

An examination of Figure 1–1 discloses that the functions of marketing are split up among many divisions. However, the importance of the sales area has been established, as indicated by the fact that the sales manager is equal to the other division managers. Note that the marketing execu-

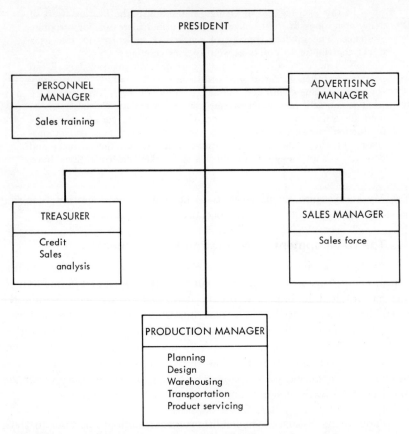

Figure 1–1   Organization chart of a sales-oriented firm, showing the responsibility for marketing functions.

tive is called sales manager and is responsible for none of the marketing functions beyond that of sales.

MARKET-PLANNING STAGE.   By the 1950s, Pillsbury began to put out products other than simple flour. The company sought to improve its position in a highly competitive flour market by making convenience baking products, such as a variety of cake, biscuit, and roll mixes. Since the success of such products required a comprehensive understanding of the market, the marketing function increased in importance. Figure 1–2 depicts the organization of a company at the market-planning stage of development.

Figure 1–2 indicates an improvement in the relative importance of the marketing function in a company at the market-planning stage of development. Since his responsibility is no longer limited to selling, the

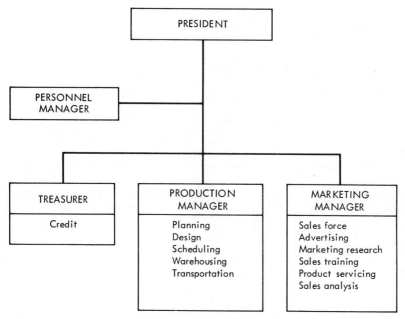

Figure 1–2   Organization chart of a market-oriented company, showing the responsibility for marketing functions.

department manager's title has been changed from sales manager to marketing manager. Recognition has been given to the fact that efficient performance of the marketing function requires that many of the marketing activities, such as advertising, marketing research, sales analysis, and the training of sales personnel have been transferred to the responsibility of the marketing division. At the market-planning stage, the marketing manager's importance to the firm has increased to the point at which he is equal to the production manager.

MARKET-CONTROL STAGE.   The market-control stage at Pillsbury has the total company effort guided by marketing concepts. This entails a recognition of the fact that corporate success may be measured by the manner in which the company satisfies its consumer market. Since customer satisfaction is clearly a marketing function, the marketing division becomes, of necessity, the most significant of the company's functions and is responsible for the control and direction of all the company's efforts, including such nonmarketing areas as production and finance. Figure 1–3 indicates the organization of a marketing-oriented company with a fully integrated marketing division in which the marketing manager is directly responsible for all the marketing functions.

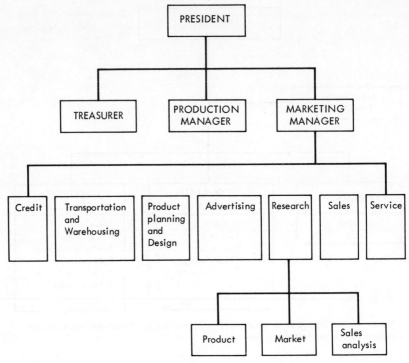

Figure 1–3   Organization chart of a company with a fully integrated marketing division.

The Marketing Mix

It is apparent from the previous discussion that the evolution of marketing will result in directing all the company's efforts toward giving customer satisfaction at a price that will bring in maximum profits. Under this system it is the marketer's responsibility to estimate the size and demand of the market and then to direct the company's efforts toward the profitable satisfaction of such demand. This represents a complete turnabout from the relatively competition-free situation a century ago, in which the emphasis was on production with marketing filling a simple, unimportant role.

In order to fulfill his responsibility, the marketing manager must first estimate his target market. This is done by selecting a particular segment of the market (college girls, housewives, and so on), and then fitting the marketing plans of the company to the satisfaction of this particular group. It is important for the marketing student to understand that the reason for the marketing division's growth to encompass almost all of a company's efforts is that, on today's market, the satisfaction of consumer demand requires a totally integrated company effort.

Considering the wide variety of ways in which goods can be designed and sold (color, style, quality, various advertising media and distribution methods, and so on), market planning is an extremely complicated problem.

A careful study of the marketing problem indicates that it consists of four areas that must be blended together to achieve marketing success. These are known as the marketing mix and consist of:

Product
Place
Promotion
Price

Good market planning requires that the marketing mix be under continuous study and that the individual factors be constantly altered to adjust to a changing market. This may include changed product design, promotional and selling methods, distribution channels, or price adjustments. This regular review is as important to successful as to unsuccessful products. Perhaps the greatest error in American marketing history was Ford's refusal to alter the enormously successful Model T to meet the changed demand that was forced by General Motors' streamlining.

Each element of the marketing mix will have one or more chapters devoted to it later in the text. However, a brief overview at this point will be helpful.

PRODUCT.   Generally speaking, the companies that are growing most quickly are those that are spending the most money for product research and development. A short time ago the average life of a food product was about ten years. Presently marketers are delighted to have a product with a life of more than three years. The success of a company's product line depends upon decisions in the following areas: selecting the right product, knowing when to add new products to the line, dropping products from the line at the right time, and branding and packaging (note that in marketing, branding and packaging are considered part of the product).

PLACE.   In marketing, the term "place" is used to indicate the method used to get the goods to the target market. The choices are very great. Some of the questions that must be answered in solving the problem of place are:

1. What sort of wholesale and retail institutions should be used?

2. Should the goods be marketed through multiple outlets or, in the case of consumer goods, through a few exclusive stores?

3. Where should the outlets be located?

4. Would a consumer product do best in discount, low-priced stores, or in high-prestige, well-serviced stores?

5. How should the goods be shipped and warehoused to insure their availability when the customer wants them?

PROMOTION.   Promotion involves communicating with the target market about the product, place, and price of the goods. There are many ways in which this information can be directed to the consumer and the marketing division must select the media that are best suited to the particular marketing mix. Sales promotion, advertising, and personal selling are the elements that must be considered in the determination of a promotion policy.

PRICE.   In addition to product, place, and promotion, the marketer must also select the proper price at which the goods must be sold. Some of the factors involved in this decision are: competitors' action, existing practices on markdowns and discounts, target profits, and legal restrictions.

All four elements of the marketing mix are so closely interrelated that it is impossible to consider one more important than the others. The success of an institution's marketing program depends upon the effectiveness of each and all of the elements of the marketing mix. The continued success of the program depends upon the ease and rapidity with which the institution adjusts its marketing mix to the constantly changing consumer market.

Careers in Marketing

The trend in America over the last twenty years has been for marketing to become the most important single factor in a business enterprise. Unquestionably, this trend will continue. Some time ago, the American Marketing Association went so far as to say, "Every company president elected from 1965 on will be a marketing man." This is certainly an overstatement, but it is probably close to the truth.

Newcomers to many jobs receive higher starting salaries than marketing graduates, but marketers generally catch up and pass them over a number of years. One author, comparing the earnings of graduates in business and industry in the fields of engineering, accounting, marketing, and general business, found the marketing graduates' earnings to be equal to the others after five years, and to exceed the others after ten years.

Educational requirements have become increasingly stringent in business and industry. It is presently very difficult to find a job in a training position for a mid-management position without a minimum of an associate's degree. Holders of bachelor's degrees and masters of business administration have a decided advantage in the competition for top-level management positions.

The recent growth of management to a total business function has vastly broadened the variety of jobs available in marketing. These include: retailing, wholesaling, sales management, advertising, and industrial procurement. In other words, there is a job in management for nearly every interest and talent. The jobs pay well and the highest-level jobs are equal to any in our economy.

IMPORTANT POINTS IN THE CHAPTER

1. As a society progresses economically, specialization of work occurs, resulting in surpluses. Marketing becomes indispensable, since these surpluses must be exchanged for the necessities that are the surpluses of other workers.

2. There are many ways in which the word *market* is used. One of these is: a market is an area in which the aggregate of forces or conditions result in decisions that satisfy demand by the transfer of goods and services.

3. *Marketing* may be defined as: the performance of business activities that direct the flow of goods and services from the producer to the consumer or user.

4. The marketing division is directly responsible for such activities as selling, advertising, transportation, and promotion and indirectly involved in production and accounting.

5. The two basic elements of a marketing system are the surplus of a good or service in one sector of the economy (the producing sector) and a demand for such good or service in another sector of the economy (the consuming sector).

6. The Industrial Revolution increased the importance of marketing because a surplus of manufactured goods was produced at urban centers, whereas the urban population required food and other farm products that were produced outside the cities.

7. When the demand for goods exceeds the supply, the emphasis of a nation's business is on production. After World War I, mass production resulted in a situation in which the supply of goods exceeded the demand. Marketing then came into its own, since it is responsible for the distribution of excess goods.

8. A business enterprise must perform four functions: form (production), place (transportation to the customer), time (getting goods to the consumer when he demands them), and ownership (transfer of title). The marketing division is fully responsible for place, time, and ownership, and must direct form.

9. Some reasons why marketing is important to our economy are: effect on price, effect on number of people employed, effect on the standard of living, and importance to the individual firm.

10. The evolution of business from the production stage, the sales stage, and the market-planning stage to the market-control stage has coincided with the increased importance that is attached to the marketing manager.

11. The four areas that must be blended together to achieve marketing success are called the marketing mix. The marketing mix consists of product, place, promotion, and price.

REVIEW QUESTIONS

1. Explain the relationship of specialization and marketing.
2. Indicate four ways in which the term *market* is used. Give examples of each.
3. Give the American Marketing Association's definition of *marketing*.
4. Which business activities are the full responsibility of the marketing division? Which business activities are directed rather than fully controlled by marketing?
5. The two basic elements of marketing importance are surplus and demand. Discuss these in terms of the growth in importance of marketing in the post–World War I period.
6. How do marketers use the word *time*? Explain their responsibility in the area of time.
7. What is meant by *passing title*? What is the marketer's responsibility in this area?
8. Discuss the effect of marketing on our standard of living.
9. How important is marketing in our society with regard to the number of people employed in marketing? What are the future trends in regard to marketing employment?
10. Explain the market-planning stage of marketing development at Pillsbury. Relate it to the production stage and the sales stage at that company.
11. Discuss the market-control stage of marketing development at Pillsbury. How has the relative importance of the marketing division changed during the evolution from the production, sales, market-planning and market-control stages?
12. What are the four elements of the marketing mix?
13. Explain the importance of promotion to marketing. Indicate methods of promotion.
14. Which is the most important element of the marketing mix?
15. Why is the marketing mix of a successful product kept under careful study?
16. Discuss the compensation of marketers at the first level of employment and at later levels.

CASE PROBLEMS

Case Problem 1

Techtronics, Inc. is a medium-sized electronics manufacturer whose total production is an electronic component shipped directly to the NASA space agency. The firm was extremely successful throughout the early 1960s, but as of 1971 it became apparent that federal budget cutbacks would present serious problems in the future.

In view of this ominous threat, the company, during the late 1960s and early 1970s, designed consumer products, in the hope of offsetting lost government business. Although these consumer products were well-designed and competitive, they did poorly on the market and the company was forced to abandon them.

The company's top management consists of five extremely bright, capable engineers. They are fine research men and their production-planning capabilities are excellent. This, teamed with up-to-date equipment, insures a high level of product research and production.

At present, the research department has developed a device that can easily be attached to an automobile radio in order to give it FM as well as AM capability. Competitively, the product is inexpensive, of excellent quality, and suited to yield a high profit.

Questions

1. What do you think should be done to make the firm more marketing-oriented?
2. What organizational changes would you recommend to put the firm in a better position to sell on the consumer market?

Case Problem 2

Tropicania is an emerging African nation that achieved its independence ten years ago. At great personal sacrifice and with the help of foreign aid, the country has since its formation built many schools and hospitals and supplied a minimal standard of living to its citizens. Although this has been a great stride forward, the country's standard of living is still very low.

The government, having raised the conditions to minimal standards, is now ready for an economic step forward. The goal is an improved standard of living for its citizens. Foreign aid is available for use in any way the government wishes.

The economy of Tropicania is chiefly agricultural. Typically, the farms are family-owned and the crops grown are those necessary to family survival. When possible, the individual farms grow a little cotton that they are able to sell for currency, with which they buy simple manufactured products and tools. The soil and climate are excellent for the growth of a long-staple variety of cotton that is avidly sought after by wealthier nations for the manufacture of high-cost clothing.

The problem faced by the government is to decide the form that foreign aid should take to raise the country's living standards. For example, the aid could be in the form of manufactured products used by the people, machine tools for manufacturing a variety of high-demand products, and so on.

Question

1. Develop a program that would have the most beneficial, long-run effect on Tropicania's economy.

BIBLIOGRAPHY

Buskirk, Richard H., *Principles of Marketing*. New York: McGraw-Hill Book Company, 1967.

Drucker, Peter F., "Marketing and Economic Development," *Journal of Marketing,* January, 1958.

Eldridge, Clarence E., "Management of the Marketing Function," *Printers' Ink,* January 27, 1967.

Endicott, Frank S., "Trends in Employment of College and University Graduates in Business and Industry." Unpublished Master's thesis, Northwestern University, 1967.

Frey, A. W., "The Effective Marketing Mix." Unpublished Master's thesis, Dartmouth College, Amos Tuck School, 1956.

Hise, Richard T., "Have Manufacturing Firms Adopted the Marketing Concept?" *Journal of Marketing,* July, 1968.

Lalonde, Bernard J., and Edward J. Morrison, "Marketing Management Concepts Yesterday and Today," *Journal of Marketing,* January, 1967.

Louth, John D., "The Changing Face of Marketing," *Dun's Review,* April, 1966.

McCarthy, E. J., *Basic Marketing, A Managerial Approach.* Homewood, Ill.: Richard D. Irwin, Inc., 1968.

Robbins, George W., "Notions about the Origins of Trading," *Journal of Marketing,* January, 1947.

Shaw, Arch W., "Some Problems in Market Distribution," *Harvard Business Review,* July–August, 1962.

Stanton, William J., *Fundamentals of Marketing.* New York: McGraw-Hill Book Company, 1967.

Viebranz, Alfred C., "Marketing's Role in Company Growth," *Business Topics,* Winter, 1967.

Wakefield, John E., "Make Your Company Marketing Conscious," *Business Management,* October, 1965.

THE CONSUMER MARKET

2

INTRODUCTION

The principal object of an economic system and of the marketing institutions that make up that system is the satisfaction of consumer demand. From a marketer's viewpoint, in a capitalistic society, the successful satisfaction of consumer demand requires that the distribution of his product result in a profit. A market is made up of many institutions competing for the opportunity of satisfying consumer demand at a profit. It is obvious that an important factor of marketing success is the knowledge of consumer demand. This market knowledge can be broken down into two broad areas: the habits and motivations of the consumer, and the size of the population and purchasing power that is available.

CONSUMER MOTIVATIONS

Granted that the hard demographic factors of the market (size of the population and available purchasing power) can be determined, the marketer is faced with the need to predict which of many competing products the consumer will buy. That is, if a person has four hundred dollars that he wants to spend for a color television set, how can we determine which of the many competing products he will select? To answer this question, one must know a great deal about the psychological makeup of the consumer. The following are some of the motivations for purchasing. These may be divided into emotional and rational motives.

Rational Motives

Rational motives are those that result from a carefully studied group of factors in which the long-run use of the article is weighed against the cost of the purchase. The information that is usually considered before such purchases are made includes:

1. The cost of the purchase.

2. The cost of operation.

3. The frequency of breakdown and the dependability and cost of repair service.

21

4. The useful life of the article.

5. The effectiveness of the article with regard to the purpose for which it was bought.

The use of the term *rational motive* for purchasers who consider the above list before making purchases does not mean that a person using such a list buys intelligently. Frequently people purchase items they do not need or cannot afford after a most careful study of the available choices.

Producers should understand the rational buying motivations of consumers because the marketing of goods that are aimed at such consumers must follow the rational approach with reasonable consistency. That is, advertising, sales promotion, and product development must be geared to appeal to the rational buyer. Of course, this portion of the market is not available to all producers. Fashion merchandise, for example, will have very little appeal for rational shoppers, since such goods are not designed for long-range durability or use. It would be foolish for the manufacturer of a midi skirt to construct a garment that will give ten years of serviceable wear. The customer, realizing that the skirt has a relatively short fashion life, would be unwilling to pay an additional premium for durability beyond its period of popularity.

Emotional Motives

Any listing of the emotional factors that may go into a buying decision is difficult, since the definitions tend to run together and the list would be enormous and highly technical. However, the following are some of the more common nonrational reasons upon which purchasing decisions are based.

APPEAL TO THE SENSES.   The five senses—touch, taste, sight, smell, and hearing—are important factors in the selling of many varieties of goods. Most people are willing to make purchases to satisfy these senses. For example, a cashmere sweater offers no better protection against cold than one made of sheep's wool but it feels better to the touch. Food odors attract people to certain products and the sight appeal of fashion merchandise is critical in selling. The avoidance of displeasure might also be listed under this category. Typical of such goods are deodorants, air conditioners, and a host of nonprescriptive drugs.

COURTSHIP.   The drive to mate and have children (to marry, in our society) is very strong. Many people, particularly young girls, are willing to make purchases that will enhance their prospects at courtship. Clothing and cosmetics appeal to this emotion. Also under this section come homemaking products for young marrieds such as furniture and appliances and merchandise for children.

PROTECTION.   The emotional drive for self-preservation and the protection of family and friends often leads to such purchases as vitamin pills, insurance, and safety devices. Producers of such goods and services usually appeal to the fears of the consumer and indicate the manner in which their product will diminish them.

PRESTIGE AND STATUS.   Some products become symbols of status and success. These items give an aura of prestige, leadership, and high social position to their users and although they may be little more functional than competing products, they are able to command higher prices because of their identification with success. Expensive homes, art objects, and *haute couture* clothing fall into this category.

PERSONAL SATISFACTION.   A person's self-pride, rather than the attitude of others, may be used as a selling tool. Such characteristics as personal and home cleanliness and neatness can be appealed to by products such as soaps, cosmetics, waxes, and the like. It is frequently difficult for advertisers to choose the most important of several motives—for example, should a dish washing detergent appeal to youthful hands or to clean dishes?

As has been indicated, an understanding of the motives of buyers, rational (aroused by appeals to reason) and emotional (aroused by appeals to appetites) is necessary to successful marketing. Generally, the promotion of a product takes into account both the rational and emotional motivations of prospective customers. Cadillac, for example, emphasizes both quality (rational) and status (emotional) in its advertisements.

CONSUMER HABITS

In addition to an understanding of the buying motives of consumers, it is necessary to know their habits. If goods are to be successfully marketed, knowledge of when, where, and how goods are purchased is required. To satisfy the demand of a man for a new overcoat, the supplier must know when he will probably buy it (time of year), where he will probably buy it (department store or specialty store), and how he will probably buy it (one at a time?).

When

The time habit for much consumer spending is seasonal. For example, consumer spending for clothing has yearly peaks in the spring and fall. Automobiles are generally purchased in the fall and most food buying takes place toward the end of the week.

Where

Consumers generally have a preconceived notion of where certain products can be purchased. It must be understood that this is not a static situation. For example, discount stores overcame the preconception of buying exclusively from department stores. Once the source of such supply has been satisfactorily established, it is not likely to be changed, for two principal reasons: the source of supply has given previous satisfaction and the fear exists that a new source may result in dissatisfaction.

How

The product quantity a consumer buys is generally based upon convenience (buying cigarettes by the carton rather than shopping daily) or economy (large economy size).

Current Trends in Buying Habits

Although individual habits, once established, are difficult to change, the group habits of the consuming public are in a constant state of flux. The following is a partial list of some of the observable trends in consumer buying habits.

SHOPPING HOURS.   The trend has been toward later shopping hours in the evening and open stores on Sunday. This may be due to the fact that men are more involved in the buying decision and the increased number of working women who are unable to shop during the day. The same factors seem to be resulting in later store openings. This is particularly true of downtown stores that depend, in part, upon commuters as customers.

QUANTITIES.   Modern shoppers are buying in larger quantities. For one thing, they have more money. The shopper who could only afford one shirt during the depression is now able to buy three at a time. Quantity buying is a convenience, since it reduces the required number of shopping trips. There are also frequently savings for purchasers who buy in large quantity. Many producers package their goods to take advantage of this trend.

SELF-SERVICE AND VENDING MACHINES.   Although initiated in the supermarket, self-service retailing has spread to many other areas. It appears that certain types of goods are more easily sold without a salesman than with one. Self-service adds greatly to customer convenience by permitting purchasers to fill their needs without having to wait for the attention of a salesperson. Since self-service reduces selling costs, it is encouraged by retailers and will undoubtedly continue to grow in importance.

CHANGE IN PURCHASERS.   Until recently, women accounted for the major part of all purchasing. At present, possibly on account of the shortened workweek, men frequently take part in buying decisions. They accompany their wives more and more on shopping trips. As a result, advertising for such household goods as foodstuffs and detergents, which was previously aimed exclusively at the homemaker, is now shifting to attract the male buyer as well.

CONVENIENCE OF USE.   The rapid dominance of such new products as instant coffee, wash-and-wear fabrics, and cake mixes indicates that American shoppers are anxious to buy merchandise that will increase their leisure time. In only a few years, wash-and-wear materials requiring little or no ironing have taken over the haberdashery industry.

LOCATION OF BUYING.   Since World War II, there have been some very significant changes in the places where people buy. As the customers of the downtown department stores moved to the suburbs, the institutions followed by means of branch stores. As a result, suburban shoppers are spared the inconvenience of commuting to downtown centers for their purchases. This has led to an enormous growth in suburban shopping at the expense of the downtown shopping districts.

The type of store in which shopping is done has changed as well as is testified by the emergence of the discount store. Another example is the fact that many drugstore items are now sold in supermarkets rather than in drugstores. To offset this condition, most drugstores now carry a wide variety of nondrug items.

CREDIT.   The use of credit purchasing is another customer convenience that has grown in recent years and will probably continue to expand. Credit buying affords the purchaser the opportunity to have the use of desired goods before he has saved up the money for it. To another class of purchaser, credit buying permits purchases to be paid by check once a month, so that they do not require the frequent use of cash.

MARKET UTILIZATION OF CONSUMER MOTIVATIONS AND HABITS

The goal of a profit-seeking marketing institution is customer satisfaction. This can only be achieved by tailoring the product, its price, and its promotion to the clearly understood motivations and habits of the consumer.

The Product

The product must serve the function for which the customer was motivated to buy it. A style product, which a customer buys to be up-to-date, must actually be in the latest fashion and need not have the durability of a product designed for practical use. The addition of durability to a style product or style to a functional product would entail unnecessary costs without increasing the appeal of the merchandise.

This is not as simple as it sounds, since many products straddle the fence (a fashionable refrigerator) and other goods are treated differently by different manufacturers (foreign cars that never change style vs. style-conscious domestic production). The point is that the manufacturer must clearly define the motivation of the customer to whom he will appeal and design his product accordingly. Thus, Volkswagen, appealing to a rational market, will design a durable, inexpensive product with no emphasis on design. General Motors, on the other hand, hoping to attract buyers that are emotionally motivated, will produce a car that emphasizes style, comfort and prestige. When you see a Volkswagen and a Cadillac in the same garage, it clearly shows that a person may buy both for emotional and rational reasons.

The Price

The price of an article can have a considerable effect on the appeal to customer motives and habits. Customers who buy exclusive goods for reasons of image or prestige do so with the understanding that, in part, the goods owe their high status to the fact that the high price limits salability to people in the top socioeconomic level. The Cadillac is probably America's most prestigious automobile. Its ownership is the mark of success and high social position. There could be no quicker way of losing this image than a drop in price that would make the car available to a much broader class of purchasers.

Price is an important means of appealing to both rational and emotional motives. Often high prices indicate quality to a buyer, whereas low prices, particularly odd ones ($2.99), are an indication of a bargain.

Promotion

The promotion of goods is the most obvious area to benefit from an understanding of customer habits and motivations. The producer of toothpaste whose target is the teen-age market must emphasize the cosmetic effect of his brand rather than the decay-inhibiting qualities that would appeal to a parent. Similarly, a car that is to be sold as a success symbol should not be promoted as a low-priced, economical automobile.

A product must be designed for a specific target, by designing it to meet the motivational needs of that target. It must be priced consistently with its goal and the sales promotion and advertising must be aimed at the exact motives of the individuals that make up the target.

Time and Place

Having the goods available at the right time and at the right place is a question of understanding the customer's habits rather than his motivations. If customers habitually shop for clothing just before Easter, production and distribution must be planned so that the goods will be available for them at that time. If the customer is accustomed to buy the product at a department store, the channel of distribution that is set up must insure his finding it there. A major challenge for marketers is to alter customers' habits and motivations to suit the advantage of their businesses.

THE SIZE OF THE MARKET—POPULATION

After deciding upon a target market the next step in setting a marketing plan is the determination of the size, location, and composition of the prospective market. This is necessary because estimates of sales are a vital factor in the budgeting, production, and distribution of the product.

The size of the population is one of several factors that are used to help determine the extent of the market. Others are personal incomes and prices. Since most products are intended to have a relatively long life, the statistics of the size of the market are generally studied over a long period of time so that trends may be determined. Table 2–1 shows the population of the United States between 1930 and 1980.

TABLE 2–1
POPULATION IN THE UNITED STATES, 1900–1980
(1980 estimated)

Year	Millions of Persons
1930	123
1940	132
1950	151
1960	179
1970	211
1980	226

Source: Department of Commerce, *Statistical Abstract of the United States,* 1970, pp. 8–9.

The market for many products is dependent upon the number of people in the country. Consequently, population growth as indicated in Table 2–1 is important. It should be noted that forecasts of the rate of national population growth have been scale downward in recent years, but the annual population growth is still expected to be significant.

Market Segmentation

The target of many products is a particular segment rather than the total population. For producers of these products the population statistics must be broken down into relatively small, homogeneous groupings. For example, businessmen interested in marketing their products in a specific region would be interested in Table 2–2, which indicates the population by regions. Another example is a manufacturer of juvenile furniture who is interested in recent birth information.

Population Shifts

A study of the U.S. population during the period covered by Table 2–2 shows that percentagewise there has been a considerable shift in favor of the Mountain and Pacific areas, but that the major population centers are still to be found in the Middle Atlantic and east–north central area. Consequently, a producer whose target market is a densely populated area should concentrate his distribution in those areas. Products that depend upon population expansion will do well to aim at the Mountain and Pacific areas.

TABLE 2–2

POPULATION OF THE UNITED STATES BY REGIONS,
1930–1969 (millions)

Region	1930	1940	1950	1965	1969
New England	8	8	9	11	12
Middle Atlantic	26	28	30	36	37
East–north central	25	27	30	38	40
West–north central	13	14	14	16	16
South Atlantic	16	18	21	29	30
East–south central	10	11	11	13	13
West–south central	12	13	15	19	19
Mountain	4	4	5	8	8
Pacific	9	10	15	24	26

Source: Department of Commerce, *Statistical Abstract of the United States*, 1970, p. 12.

FARM TO URBAN. Producers of merchandise designed for farm consumers have been aware of a steady decrease in farm population. Comparative statistics since 1920 indicate a decided trend away from the farms. This, in part, is the result of technological improvements in farm machinery that make possible increased agricultural production with fewer workers. It is likely that the large corporate farms, completely mechanized, will result in a continuation of this trend. Table 2–3 illustrates the movement of population away from the farms.

Research in present-day farm population indicates that there is also a decreasing difference between farm and nonfarm consumers. Present-day farmers are well-educated, style-conscious buyers. This is of considerable interest to marketers, since the demands of the rural customers are now pretty much the same as those of their urban cousins.

URBAN TO SUBURBAN. The growing shift of the more affluent city dwellers to suburban communities has required a considerable adjustment

TABLE 2–3

FARM POPULATION IN THE UNITED STATES, 1920–1969

Year	Total (in thousands)
1920	31,974
1930	30,529
1940	30,547
1950	23,048
1960	15,635
1969	10,307

Source: Department of Commerce, *Statistical Abstract of the United States,* 1970, p. 582.

on the part of business. The first step taken was to locate retail branches within easy reach of their suburban customers. The next phase was the movement of light industry and administrative offices to suburban locations. On the industrial market this has led to a reshuffling of sales territories and transportation methods. The suburbs, rather than a place for city workers to sleep, are fast becoming a place for suburban workers to live, shop, and spend their leisure time.

Age

It is very useful for business to know the trend in the age distribution of the population. For example, the great increase in births during the 1940s resulted in a boom for the toy industry in the 1950s.

Table 2–4 indicates the probable trends in age segmentation until the year 1975. It is expected that the largest increase will be in the fourteen to

TABLE 2–4

POPULATION AGE DISTRIBUTION TO 1975

Age	Percentage	Trend
Under 14	27	Slightly declining
14–19	11	Increasing
20–24	7	Increasing
25–44	25	Declining
45–64	20	Level
Over 65	10	Slightly Increasing

Source: Bureau of the Census, *Current Population Reports.*

nineteen and twenty to twenty-four age groups. Based on this information, much present-day sales promotion is aimed at the teen-age and young-adult market. On the other hand, the percentage of the population in the twenty-five to forty-four group is expected to decline. Further breakdowns of the age of the population are available from Bureau of Census reports. Such a population analysis of age by sex might be useful to marketers of razor blades, menswear, and sporting equipment in the planning of future expansion.

THE SIZE OF THE MARKET—INCOME

A market requires more than just people. They must have money to spend as well. An analysis of income, its distribution, and the way it is spent is essential to determine the trends in purchasing power that a marketer must know to understand his market.

Income is the result of producing and selling goods in the market place. The gross national product (the total market value of goods and services produced in a year) has been growing in the United States at an annual average of 3 percent. At this rate the GNP doubles every twenty years, and indications are that it will continue to do so until the year 2000 at least. Although this information is of overall interest, individual producers need more specific information. For example, the manufacturer of a high-cost prestige product would be interested to know the percentage of the population that could afford his merchandise. Table 2–5 shows the money income by families at various income levels.

Two important trends can be determined by analyzing Table 2–5. First, the median income per family has increased steadily and significantly during the years pictured. The amounts indicated in the table have been adjusted to remove the effect of inflation. Consequently, true income has gone from a median of $5,377 in 1955 to a median of $7,436 in 1966. This represents an increase in family income of approximately 40 percent.

The second important trend shown in Table 2–5 is the shift of the population in the direction of the higher income levels. In 1955, only 11.7 percent of the population earned in excess of ten thousand dollars. This percentage grew to 29.6 by 1966. At the other end of the scale, the number of families earning less than three thousand dollars fell from 22.8 percent in 1955 to 14.3 percent in 1966.

Table 2–5 indicates that an enormous increase in spending power has been available to the marketplace during the years mentioned. Obviously the next question is, how much of a family's total income has to be spent for necessities and how much is available for other goods. Basic spending refers to money disbursed for necessities. Discretionary expenditures are those that are available to a family after the basic needs have been satisfied. Until a certain income level is reached, a family has no control over its expenditures; it is needed to buy food, shelter, clothing, and other necessities. As the family's level of income rises and these basic needs are met, the family may spend the excess earnings at its discretion. One of the important marketing results of the shift in family earnings from the lowest to the highest

TABLE 2–5

PERCENTAGE DISTRIBUTION OF U.S. FAMILIES
BY INCOME RANGE, 1950–1969

Percentage of Families with Income
(in constant 1969 dollars)

Year	Under $3,000	$3,000–$4,999	$5,000–$6,999	$7,000–$9,999	$10,000–$14,999	$15,000 & Over	Median Income in Constant 1969 Dollars
1950	24.4%	24.8%	23.1%	16.6%	— 11.3% —		$5,069
1957	17.9	16.3	21.5	25.0	14.1	5.2	6,456
1958	18.1	16.5	21.3	24.7	13.8	5.6	6,441
1959	16.8	15.6	19.4	24.8	16.2	7.1	6,808
1960	16.8	15.0	18.5	24.5	17.3	7.9	6,962
1961	16.9	14.9	17.9	23.8	17.6	8.8	7,034
1962	15.7	14.7	17.6	23.8	19.0	9.3	7,228
1963	14.8	14.1	16.8	23.7	20.3	10.1	7,487
1964	13.8	14.1	15.7	23.4	21.9	11.0	7,558
1965	13.0	13.3	14.9	24.0	22.6	12.3	8,082
1966	11.9	11.9	14.1	23.9	24.9	13.5	8,476
1967	10.9	11.5	13.7	23.1	24.8	15.9	8,764
1968	9.6	11.5	13.2	22.3	26.4	17.2	9,102
1969	9.3	10.7	12.3	21.7	26.7	19.2	9,433

Source: Bureau of the Census, *Current Population Reports*, Series P-60 (Washington: GPO), No. 75, December 14, 1970, Table 8.

levels is an increase in the purchasing power for discretionary spending. The rapid growth of the leisure industries is evidence of an increase in discretionary funds available in the market.

FACTORS AFFECTING CONSUMER SPENDING

A further sophistication in understanding the way people spend requires a breakdown of family earnings into various categories of spending.

Engels's Laws

Ernst Engels was a German statistician who studied the budgets of wage earners in the middle 1800s. From the spending patterns of these workingmen's families he published, in 1857, a group of generalizations concerning the manner in which families spend their income. These statements, called "Engels's Laws," are remarkably accurate even today. The following are Engels's four statements describing family spending patterns:

1. The percentage of income spent on food decreases as family income increases.

2. The percentage of income spent for household expenditures such as rent stays about the same as family income increases.

3. The percentage of income spent for clothing remains about the same as family income increases.

4. The percentage of income spent on other items (recreation, education, medical care, savings, and so on) increases as family income increases.

Although Engels's laws are still sufficiently accurate to be used as generalizations by marketers, present-day information requires that certain modification should be made.

Food

Unquestionably as incomes increase people eat better. However, although they actually spend more for food, this expense diminishes in proportion to total earnings. But the decrease in food spending is less dramatic than Engels expected. Movement of the population from rural to urban and suburban areas, smaller family units, prepackaging, freezing, precooking and eating out are no doubt responsible for higher food expenses.

Housing

The percentage of income spent on housing is another area in which Engels is still correct. That is, although the amount spent for housing goes up as the family's income increases, the proportional share of total income allocated to housing diminishes.

Clothing

According to Engels, the percentage of income spent for clothing remains about the same as total family income increases. This is close, but not quite accurate in our present-day economy. In fact, as the total income goes up, the proportion spent for clothing gets slightly higher as well. This may be due in part to expenditures for special-use clothing (sneakers, ski pants), which were unheard of in Engels's day. Apparently, the increased leisure time today, particularly for the more affluent, results in proportionately more expense for clothing.

Other Items

Expenditures for such other items as education and savings increase with increased earnings, as Engels suggested. Since he could not have predicted hospitalization, Medicare, and group-insurance programs, he can be excused for not realizing that expenditures for health and insurance decrease proportionately as incomes rise.

It is important for marketers to know that the trend toward higher incomes of the American families will increase the amount of discretionary spending money available in the marketplace. This will lead to an expansion of the sales of such luxury products as expensive food, clothing, travel, and amusements.

THE EFFECT OF FASHION ON THE CONSUMER MARKET

As the nation's discretionary income rises, the marketplace becomes the scene of fierce competition, with many producers of similar products trying to catch the buyer's eye. One means of attracting customers is by fashion. Style is "a characteristic or distinctive method of presentation." Fashion is "a style that is popular at a given time." Thus, a split-level house is a style of housing. Some years ago split-level housing was very much in demand. It was the fashion.

FASHION AND THE CONSUMER

Today's market is enormously fashion-minded. Years ago, fashion was confined to certain merchandise and a small group of customers. During the last few decades, the ability to copy costly fashion goods on a mass-production basis has made fashion merchandise available to nearly all of the population. People become aware of fashion through advertising and are able to purchase fashion goods with ever higher annual income during their constantly increasing leisure hours.

Fashion has gone far beyond the clothing and automobile industries. Such diverse merchandise as furnaces, shotguns, appliances, and cameras depend upon fashion for sales volume.

The advent of fashion as a requirement for selling has increased producing and marketing risks considerably. For one thing, the costs of advertising and promoting are extremely high. This is particularly true when one considers that such expenditures are frequently made on unproven fashions that are as likely as not to prove poor sellers. The uncertainty of fashion adds greatly to its risk. The point is that one can never be certain of customer acceptance, and the large sums of money invested in producing and promoting a fashion may be wasted. The automobile industry invests one billion dollars each year in retooling (mostly for fashion changes) and a good deal of the retooling is to effect changes that are not acceptable to the public.

Retailers, manufacturers, and middlemen all find that the growing importance of fashion has increased the risk of doing business. The problem is not only the high cost of promotion, but the necessity of guessing the *right* fashions as well. Consider the ladies' clothing industry. As the time of this writing, miniskirts have been declared passé. Mid-calf lengths, which are considered the *in* style by fashion leaders, are simply not selling. Now fashions must be selected for the spring line. Should they make minis, midis, or both? An error in this decision would be enormously costly, since wrong styles have almost no value. Problems such as this may force many marginal producers into bankruptcy.

The Fashion Cycle

Fashion, like all newly innovated products, is cyclical in nature. That is to say, new fashions follow a definite pattern of stages. The cyclical life of new products includes its innovation by the designer, its acceptance by the customer, its peak of customer popularity, and its rapid decline. A more extensive discussion of the life cycle of new products will be found later in the text, but it must be emphasized here that although cycles vary in length from a single season to many years, there will eventually be a period of decline. The maintenance of sales volume, therefore, requires that new fashions always be in varying stages of development to replace those in decline.

Reducing Fashion Risks

It is impossible to take all of the risks out of fashion but they can be minimized.

1. Although it is impossible to force public acceptance of a style, the risk can be split among many fashions, and intensive promotion of any single unit can be delayed until the public has had an opportunity to accept or reject it.

2. As median family income increases nationally, the speed of the fashion cycles can be expected to rise and fashion life to get shorter.

3. As fashion life decreases and the importance of fashion increases, the cost of goods and the risk of doing business will get higher.

IMPORTANT POINTS IN THE CHAPTER

1. Producers seek to improve their competitive position by studying the motivations, habits, and purchasing power of the market.

2. Rational purchasers make purchasing decisions by weighing the long-run use of the article against the cost of the purchase. Emotional purchasers are motivated by appeal to the senses, courtship, protection, prestige, status, and personal satisfaction.

3. To be successful in the market, producers must understand when, where, and how goods will be bought. This requires constant study, since the habits of the consuming public are always in a state of flux.

4. The knowledge of consumer motivations and habits enables the producer to pick out a target market. Once this is done, the product, price, promotion, timing, and place must be fitted to the target.

5. Understanding the consumer market consists of more than the knowledge of habits and motivations of the consumer. Producers must also know the population and purchasing power that is available. Population and income statistics are customarily broken down into the smaller groupings that make up the producer's target. This is called market segmentation.

6. Some of the population shifts that are taking place include an increase in the size of the West-Coast market, migration from farms to urban areas, and movement from urban to suburban locations.

7. Important trends in family income are an increase of the median income and a general shift to higher income levels.

8. Family spending patterns were described by Engels in 1857. With slight modification they are still valid. They describe the effect of an increase in income on expenditures for food, clothing, shelter, and so on.

9. Producers use fashion as a means of competing for a share of the market. Improvements in communications and enlarged discretionary spending have increased the importance of fashion in recent years.

10. More dependence on fashion as a means of selling has augmented both the cost and risk of doing business.

REVIEW QUESTIONS

1. Why is the nature of the market of importance to marketers?
2. Differentiate between rational and emotional motivation. Give an example of each.
3. Is it important that a producer understand the motives of a rational purchaser? Why? Give an example.
4. *Protection* is defined in the text as an emotional motive. Explain it and give examples of goods designed to satisfy this motivation.
5. Is it true that rational buyers always buy intelligently?
6. Explain the difference between habits and motivations.
7. What do you think will be the future store hours of a department store?
8. Discuss the effect of the increase in male shopping. Why are men shopping more?
9. Sales of "convenience" goods have multiplied. Define, explain, and give examples.
10. Explain the importance of consumer motivation to the field of sales promotion.

11. What are the factors that determine the extent of the market?

12. Define and give examples of *market segmentation*.

13. Why is it important for a marketer to understand the shifts in the population's age?

14. Discuss the most important two trends in the income structure of the population.

15. Define *discretionary income*. Why is the rise in discretionary income of significance?

16. What are "Engels's Laws"?

17. Discuss Engels's laws of housing and miscellaneous expenditures as they apply to today's economy.

18. Explain the statement "fashion cannot be forced."

19. What is the effect of improved communications on fashion? On the life cycle of fashion?

20. How may fashion risks be minimized?

CASE PROBLEMS

Case Problem 1

The Apex Construction Company is the builder of a highly successful condominium in Dallas, Texas. (A condominium is an apartment house in which the individuals own their own apartments and share in the ownership and maintenance of such common facilities as the corridors, gardens, roofs, and heating equipment.) The building was designed to accommodate retired persons. In addition to building and selling the units, Apex operates the building on a long-term contract for the apartment owners. The operation is geared to the needs of the well-to-do elderly. It provides for optional linen service, maid service, protection, and other services that are demanded by the residents. This, plus the apartment design (small, convenient to maintain, and terraced), has resulted in the rapid, profitable sale of the units and a long-term lucrative operating contract.

The success of the Dallas operation has provided Apex's management with the financial means and know-how to expand. They are searching for a new site and have decided to locate in a warm-weather area that is attractive to retired couples. At present there are two locations of interest to them. One is in Saint Petersburg, Florida, the other in the vicinity of New Orleans, Louisiana.

Questions

1. In comparing the two locations, indicate the information concerning population and income you would require.

2. Explain the reason for your selection.

Case Problem 2

Technico Products, a large manufacturer of electronic products, is engaged in a search for new consumer products. Until now, the company has been successful in manufacturing for the Defense Department, either as a prime or subcontractor. In the past few years reductions in the Defense Department's budgets have resulted in the sudden cancellation of several important contracts. Realizing that more cancellations might occur in the future, Technico's management has been searching for a consumer product to take over the slack.

The company's research and development division has come up with a simplified automatic garage-door opener. The device has proven satisfactory in all the tests to which it was put and it will undoubtedly be marketable, since its cost estimates indicate that it can be offered at a competitive price.

Traditionally, automatic garage-door openers are sold at retail on an installation basis. Technico's model is so simple that it can easily be sold as a do-it-yourself item, at a considerable saving to the consumer.

Questions

1. Discuss the motivational aspects of the type of consumer Technico should aim at.
2. Having decided on the motivations of the target market, discuss their effect on the product's development, price, promotion, and channels of distribution.

BIBLIOGRAPHY

Bookstin, Daniel J., "Welcome to the Consumption Community," *Fortune,* September, 1967.

Engel, James F., David T. Kollat, and Roger O. Blackwell, *Consumer Behavior.* New York: Holt, Rinehart & Winston, Inc., 1968.

Hopkinson, Tom H., "New Battleground, Consumer Interest," *Harvard Business Review,* September–October, 1965.

Kotler, Philip, "Behavioral Models for Analyzing Buyers," *Journal of Marketing,* October, 1965.

Lazer, William, and Eugene J. Kelley, "Interdisciplinary Horizons in Marketing," *Journal of Marketing,* October, 1960.

Linden, Fabian, ed., *Expenditure Patterns of the American Family.* New York: National Industrial Conference Board, 1965.

Loeb, Benjamin S., "The Use of Engels's Laws as a Basis for Predicting Consumer Expenditures," *Journal of Marketing,* July, 1955.

McNeal, James V., *Dimensions of Consumer Behavior.* New York: Appleton-Century-Crofts, 1965.

Newman, Joseph W., *On Knowing the Consumer.* New York: John Wiley & Sons, Inc., 1966.

Nicosia, Francesco M., *Consumer Decision Processes.* Englewood Cliffs, N.J.: Prentice-Hall, Inc., 1966.

Reynolds, W. H., and James H. Myers, "Marketing and the American Family," *Business Topics,* Spring, 1966.

"Survey Shows How American Women Buy," *Printers' Ink,* October 2, 1959.

Tucker, W. T., and John J. Painter, "Personality and Product Use," *Journal of Applied Psychology,* October, 1961.

Udell, John G., "A New Approach to Consumer Motivation," *Journal of Retailing,* Winter, 1964–65.

CONSUMER GOODS AND INDUSTRIAL GOODS

3

INTRODUCTION

As we have previously discussed, the marketing manager's responsibility can be summed up as the selection of the proper marketing mix and the constant adjustment of that mix to changing market patterns. Since different products require different marketing mixes, marketing strategy must begin with the proper classification of the product. That is, although dresses and hosiery are both women's clothing, they require a different marketing mix to be successfully distributed. As is frequently the case with general classification systems, many products are difficult to place into specific groups. They either fit into more than one of the arbitrarily established categories, or in none of them. However, if the items fit—and mostly they do—the marketer has the advantage of keying his strategy to the preferred marketing mix for his type of goods.

CONSUMER GOODS AND INDUSTRIAL GOODS

Products are classified as either consumer goods or industrial goods. Consumer goods and services are produced for the personal use of the ultimate consumer. Industrial goods and services are produced for industrial purposes; they will be used to produce other goods and services or to facilitate the operation of a business. Many products, such as lighting fixtures, stationery, typewriters, and electrical services can be classified as both industrial and consumer goods. The proper classification should not be based on the type of goods, but on the type of purchaser (consumer or industrial), since the marketing strategy must be entirely different for each type.

CONSUMER GOODS

Many classifications are possible but the most common method of differentiating among goods is to sort them focused on the habits and motivations of the buyers, the starting point of any good marketing strategy.

There are five categories of goods based on consumer buying habits.

Each category requires a separate marketing strategy. When a marketer relates his product to one of these classifications, he can make use of proved selling methods for that type of goods. The categories are:

Convenience goods
Shopping goods
Specialty goods
Impulse goods
Emergency goods

We shall discuss the marketing strategy that is best suited to each of these classifications.

Convenience Goods

Convenience goods are bought with a minimum of shopping effort. Typical examples are cigarettes, candy, chewing gum, newspapers, magazines, and most grocery products. Some of the characteristics of convenience goods are:

1. They are nondurable—they are quickly used up and frequently purchased.

2. They are often bought by brands.

3. They are inexpensive.

4. They are bought according to habit and the buying decision is made quickly and easily. In buying cigarettes and gasoline, for example, the consumer knows his preference and habitually buys the same brand at the same store without price and quality comparison with competing brands.

MARKET STRATEGY. The market strategy for convenience goods is characterized by an emphasis on *convenience,* affecting the marketing mix in the following manner:

Place. Since shopping convenience is of utmost importance, place is a vital factor. Customers will not go out of their way to purchase convenience goods. Frequently, purchase is not even planned. Consequently, to be successfully marketed, convenience goods must be placed in as many outlets as possible. Customers will not search for these goods and they must be placed in front of them wherever possible. For this reason there is constant competition among supermarket suppliers for the more noticeable eye-level shelves. Convenience goods require minimum shopping effort and maximum exposure. Their distribution requires a large sales force and many producers turn to middlemen to perform the place function. This is economically sound because the middlemen can place the lines of many manufacturers at once, thereby reducing the place cost for each line.

Price. Although brand identification is important in the marketing of convenience goods, most consumers believe that competing goods are similar in quality. As a result, most convenience goods are very competitively priced and an increase in the price of one producer's merchandise might encourage the customer to switch to another brand. Thus, an increase of a few cents a gallon of gasoline often results in a change of brands. On the other hand, many customers are willing to pay a premium price for an increase in shopping convenience. Home deliveries of newspapers, milk, and bakery products are examples of this.

Promotion. Convenience goods require mass selling to be successful; therefore, they need large promotional budgets. The industrial giants who produce most of these goods are among the largest advertisers in the nation. Their promotion is aimed at brand identification.

It is common practice among distributors of convenience goods to invest heavily in in-store and point-of-purchase displays. Liquor dealers go so far as to dress the windows of stores at no charge to insure the preferential display of their products.

Shopping Goods

Shopping goods are purchased only after making comparisons as to the suitability, price, quality, and style of the item. Before purchasing such goods, the shopper usually visits several stores. Typical shopping goods are furniture, automobiles, coats, and appliances. Some of the characteristics of shopping goods are:

1. They are relatively durable and long lasting.
2. They are generally high-priced items.
3. They do not stress brand identification.
4. They require much shopping time and a difficult buying decision.

Shopping goods come in two categories.

HOMOGENEOUS GOODS. These are the goods that the consumer considers to be of equal suitability, quality, and styling. Comparison with competing merchandise is limited to price. Some examples of homogeneous goods are automobiles and household appliances.

HETEROGENEOUS GOODS. These are the goods that the consumer compares for suitability, quality, and styling with price relatively unimportant, but not totally ignored. Some examples of heterogeneous goods are furniture and famous-brand clothing.

The shopper frequently does not know all the characteristics of the goods he will buy—as he does when buying convenience goods—and part of the shopping effort is spent learning about the product. An automobile purchaser, for example, learns about the features of a particular model from the salesman. This extra time spent in shopping is relatively unimportant because the purchase of shopping goods is generally planned and there is no rush to get the product.

MARKET STRATEGY. As in all market planning, the strategy used in distributing shopping goods is based on the target customer's habits and motivations.

Place. For shopping goods the customer is willing to visit more than one store. As a result, shopping goods do not require a maximum number of outlets. Producers place their merchandise in relatively few stores, generally near others, and in similar types of shops so that it is convenient for customers to make comparisons. In addition, retailers carrying shopping goods do not want competition from the same manufacturer's goods at a nearby store and frequently are granted territorial exclusivity. A woman interested in a coat will go to a location that has several stores at which she can make comparisons. Any store located by itself is likely not to be visited. As far as place is concerned, both heterogeneous and homogeneous goods are given the same treatment. Because the number of retail outlets is comparatively small, many producers of shopping goods maintain their own sales staffs and do not use middlemen for the distribution of their products.

Price. As regards price, there is a sharp differentiation between homogeneous and heterogeneous shopping goods. Shoppers for homogeneous goods are chiefly interested in price and any variation in selling price has an immediate and drastic effect on sales volume and profits. Consequently homogeneous goods are highly competitive in price and yield relatively small profits.

Price is a secondary factor in the sale of heterogeneous shopping goods. Furniture, clothing, and jewelry are bought for reasons of style and quality, resulting in higher markups and better profitability. Heterogeneous shopping goods have in general a highly individual styling. This makes comparisons difficult. Selections depend more on suitability and taste than on price differences.

Promotion. The advertising of both homogeneous and heterogeneous shopping goods is usually the responsibility of the retailer, although many producers encourage the promotion of their products by means of advertising allowances or outright cash grants.

Large manufacturers of nationally distributed products indulge in institutional advertising. This is a means of drawing the public's attention to the brand name. Unlike retail advertising, which is usually promotion- or product-oriented, institutional advertising is concerned with a company's overall image in style and quality rather than with the features of specific items in its line.

Although the retail advertising of homogeneous shopping goods attempts to point out the important features of the product, the main advertising thrust is in the area of price. Advertisers of heterogeneous shopping goods, on the other hand, are more interested in informing the public of the quality and styling of their merchandise.

Specialty Goods

Specialty goods are those products for which consumers are willing to make a special purchasing effort. Substitutes will not be made because of a brand name or some characteristic that the customer insists upon. Typical are gourmet foods, hi-fi components, stamps for collectors, or prestige-brand men's suits. Shoppers for these goods are willing to travel to far-out locations at which they can buy them. They do not make comparisons before purchasing and are relatively disinterested in price. Specialty goods are found in low as well as high price ranges and are mostly sold either in a high-image retail store or under a thoroughly accepted brand name (Corning ware, Hickey-Freeman men's suits, and Rolls Royce automobiles).

MARKET STRATEGY. Every producer would like his product to be classified under the specialty-goods label. Such merchandise is the most sought after and yields the highest profits. Once this level is attained, the marketing mix chosen must be carefully planned.

Place. Characteristic of specialty goods is the customer's insistence on the particular product. With regard to place, the insistence brings about a willingness to travel a considerable distance to make his purchase. As a result, specialty goods are generally restricted to single outlets in each geographical area. Since the outlets are few in number, distribution brings minor problems and is inexpensive. Middlemen are rarely found in the distributive channels of specialty goods. This permits a very close, cooperative relationship between the manufacturer and the retailer, which works to the benefit of both parties.

Price. Here again, the customer's insistence on the product sets the stage for the market strategy. Producers of specialty goods are able to capitalize on the customer's degree of motivation for the product by charging a relatively high price for it. This should not be understood to mean that producers of specialty goods set extravagant prices. Remember, every producer tries to get his product into the specialty-goods category. Unusually high prices form one of the surest ways to lose that advantage. However, the markup on specialty goods is usually higher than normal.

Promotion. Much of the advertising of specialty goods is done by retailers (frequently with producer cooperation). Such mass media as newspapers and billboards are used. The advertisements generally serve to remind the public where a product can be bought; they do not contain any specific information. The buying public is capricious. Once a product has achieved the specialty-goods status, a high advertising budget is required to keep it there.

Impulse Goods

Many authors consider impulse goods to be a specific type of convenience goods. By definition, impulse goods are those bought without planning. A woman goes to a supermarket with a shopping list. If she buys a box of strawberries that was not on her list, that purchase is impulsive. Impulse goods are relatively low-priced products, such as drugs, toys, food, inexpensive clothing, and cosmetics.

MARKET STRATEGY. The market strategy for impulse goods is the same as that for convenience goods in general.

Place. Impulse goods do not compete with other similar products. Instead, they are in competition with other goods that could take a part of the consumer's dollar. A child with a quarter to spend can buy either candy or ice cream. His selection frequently depends upon the product that is most prominently displayed. Impulse goods must be widely placed in heavy traffic areas. They should be displayed on the most obvious shelves. The checkout counter in most supermarkets is a prime location for these items.

Price. As is the case with most other convenience goods, impulse goods are highly competitive and sensitive to price differences. One reason is that substitutions are easily made. The shopper who sees a candy bar will not buy it if it is overpriced, since a cheaper one is available a few steps away.

Promotion. Impulse goods require massive advertising in the largest media. Such advertising is the responsibility of the producer, who must impress not only the consumer but also the retailer, to insure his willingness to give the product prime display space.

Since the location in the store is vital to the success of impulse products, manufacturers devote high budgets to point-of-purchase and in-store displays.

Emergency Goods

Emergency goods must be purchased immediately to fill an urgent need. They may be convenience goods—for example, a mother discovers that she is out of milk after the stores are closed—or shopping goods—for example, a sudden need for an ambulance.

MARKET STRATEGY. Most of the goods sold under emergency conditions are convenience goods. Market strategy for emergency goods is chiefly concerned with getting them to the places where the customer expects them.

Place. A customer, needing goods in an emergency, has an idea of where they can be found. A woman with unexpected Sunday company knows where to find an open store. The producer whose goods are carried by that store will make the sale.

Many retailers stock emergency goods in anticipation of their customers' needs. The neighborhood gas station sells very few snow tires—until it snows. Small downtown stores suddenly come up with umbrellas and rubbers in a rainstorm.

Price. In return for the convenience of getting the goods in an emergency, the customer is willing to pay a higher than normal price. The neighborhood grocer can only compete with the supermarket giants by taking the role of an emergency store and remaining open seven days a week and far into the night. In return for this service, his customers are willing to pay a premium for their foodstuffs.

Promotion. A manufacturer promoting his convenience goods is promoting his emergency goods at the same time, since they constitute the identical merchandise sold under a different condition.

For the most part, emergency goods are sold in neighborhood stores and the necessary promotion requires nothing more than informing the neighborhood customers of the store's location and working hours. This may be done by handbills, limited direct mailings, local newspaper advertising, or signs in the window.

Difficulty in Classification

Most marketing managers find it very difficult to classify their goods according to the categories discussed above. A motel is a good example of this. A tired salesman might take the first motel he comes to (a convenience good), another motorist may keep driving until he finds the best value (a shopping good). Yet another driver may reserve a room in advance in the particular spot he considers best (a specialty good). It is not at all unusual to find the same product classified in different ways, both by different shoppers and at different times. This does not mean that a marketing strategy based on product classification is worthless. An alert marketer can classify his product in two or more categories and employ a separate marketing strategy and distribution channels for each category, with the most important category getting the major effort.

Since the marketing mix (market strategy) is based upon product classification, the system described above for classifying goods is important. However, there is an unquestionable need for more research in this area.

INDUSTRIAL GOODS

In many cases the same goods may be classified as industrial or consumer goods, but it is important that they be classified and distributed separately, since the market strategies required in the distribution of the two types are completely different.

Most of the discussion of consumer goods was familiar to the reader. The products' names were commonplace, the places in which such products were to be found were widely known, and the examples of the promotion of the goods were always in the public eye. The industrial market, on the other hand, involves astronomical annual sales, employs millions of people, and is widely dispersed throughout the country, but is relatively unknown to the consuming public. Industrial goods rarely make the newspapers, are not promoted in the consumer media, and are not labeled with familiar brands. An understanding of such goods and their marketing-mix requirements are vital to the marketing student.

CLASSIFICATION OF INDUSTRIAL GOODS

Industrial goods may be divided into the following categories:

Raw materials
Fabricating materials and parts
Installations
Accessory equipment
Supplies
Services

Raw Materials

Raw materials are industrial goods that will be used in the production of other goods. Such goods may be sold in their natural state or processed to the extent necessary to insure safety or economy of shipping or handling. An ore from which some of the unusuable elements have been removed (to save shipping costs) is an example of the minor processing that is done on raw materials. Raw materials are generally divided into two categories:

1. Products found in their natural state, such as ores, oil, and lumber.

2. Livestock and agricultural products such as grains, fruits, vegetables, tobacco, and cotton.

MARKETING STRATEGY. The two categories of raw materials pose completely different marketing problems.

Natural State. Raw materials in their natural state are characterized by limited supplies, small numbers of large producers, and importance of transportation costs to high-bulk, products with a low cost per unit. Since extractive industries must be located where the product is found, the cost of transportation is often a major part of the overall cost of the product.

These characteristics require that physical handling be minimized and that the channels of distribution be short, with rarely more than one middleman involved. Brand identification is relatively unimportant to industrial users, who are more concerned with low prices and certainty of supply. Advertising and sales promotion are minimal and sales are frequently made by a contract for a total year's needs.

Vertical integration (the ownership of the raw-material source by the manufacturer) is common with natural-state raw materials. For example, U.S. Steel owns its iron mines and the Weyerhauser Lumber Company its forests. Similarly, many petroleum, copper, and aluminum companies own their raw-material sources.

Agricultural Products. These are sold on the industrial market to such businesses as restaurants, canners, and packers. Although they fit the definition of raw materials, they require another marketing strategy. Agricultural products are perishable seasonal goods that are grown some distance from the market. They must be graded and standardized. Agricultural products are generally produced by many small farmers. All of this means that the goods need a great deal of handling, which can only be done through long channels of distribution. Many middlemen are necessary to deliver the goods from the farmer to the industrial user. Their functions include gathering large lots from small producers, standardization and grading, storing, refrigerating, transporting, and selling. Typical of most industrial products, very little attention is paid to the promotion or branding of agricultural goods that are destined for industry.

Fabricating Materials and Parts

Many manufacturers, particularly when technical, highly complicated products are involved, purchase rather than construct some of the component parts of their product. These parts become a part of the product, either in the same state in which they are received, or after further refinement. Generally such fabricating materials and parts are custom-made according to the specifications of the buyer.

The automobile industry is a prime example of the industrial market for fabricating materials and supplies. The major producers are essentially assembly plants that put together such parts as bodies, tires, carburetors, batteries, and so on that have been purchased (frequently from affiliated companies) rather than internally produced.

The individual fabricated part that is included in the product may lose its identity (as in the case of carburetors) or maintain it (as in the case of batteries).

MARKETING STRATEGY. Producers of fabricating materials and parts are usually located near their important customers. The sale of such goods is usually by contract, according to buyer's specifications, and for a long period of time. As a result, marketing is minimal and frequently handled by an executive. The channel of distribution for such goods is generally short.

Where branding is important in the production of fabricated parts (batteries, fabrics, spark plugs), promotion becomes a significant factor.

Installations

Installations are the major machinery and equipment of an industrial producer. Examples of installations are blast furnaces, factory buildings, and locomotives. Such goods are used in the production of the company's product and they are so large that they affect the scope of manufacturing operations. Thus, the purchase of twenty adding machines for the office of a large railroad would not be an installation, but the purchase of twenty locomotives would be so classified.

MARKETING STRATEGY. The marketing strategy for the sale of installations is dictated by the size of the individual purchase. These are so large and important that middlemen are rarely used and the channel of distribution is short, usually running from the producer directly to the industrial user. Installations are usually sold on a custom-made basis according to very exact specifications. Negotiations frequently take months or even years. The selling of installations is generally done on a personal basis with a minimum of advertising and sales promotion. The marketing of such products should only be entrusted to high-caliber, knowledgeable men. Engineers, trained in selling, are usually found in this position. The marketing of installations is characterized by the high degree of servicing required after the delivery of the product.

Accessory Equipment

Accessory equipment is used to facilitate rather than to perform the basic operations of a manufacturing plant. Typical items are small motors, forklifts, office furniture, and time clocks. Sales of accessory equipment amount to less money than sales of installations. Accessories are rarely made to order; they are standardized and kept in stock by their manufacturers.

MARKETING STRATEGY.   Generally accessory goods are relatively low-priced. Their distribution requires fairly long channels of communications, including retail outlets for such products as typewriters. As is the case with all low-value items, the wide coverage that wholesalers offer is necessary for successful distribution over extensive geographical areas. Advertising and other sales-promoting strategies are commonly used in marketing accessory goods. This is particularly effective with items that may be purchased by both consumer and industrial users, such as batteries and powered hand tools.

The more expensive the accessory product, the shorter the channel of distribution. The reason for this is that the higher-priced articles have a smaller market and that their sales are large enough to make it worthwhile for a manufacturer to send a salesman to a prospective customer. The Hyster Company, for example—a manufacturer of forklift trucks—distributes directly to its customers.

Supplies

Supplies are materials used in the operation of a business that do not become a part of the finished product. Some examples of supplies are lubricating oil, stationery, shipping-room supplies, coal, floor wax, and washroom supplies. Supplies are the convenience products of the industrial market. They are of low value and frequently bought in small quantities.

MARKETING STRATEGY.   Those industrial supplies that are an important part of the cost of manufacture, such as coal and oil, require special treatment in their distribution. The channel of distribution for these goods is short, and the goods are frequently negotiated in large contract lots by top executives.

Low-cost industrial supplies, like consumer convenience goods, require extensive channels of distribution to provide the broad coverage necessary for success. Wholesalers, by carrying the lines of many manufacturers, are able to call on many users and sell large enough quantities of the goods of various manufacturers to make the call profitable. The standardization of most low-end industrial supplies is so great that there is little to choose among the goods of various manufacturers. This results in heavy competition, with price, availability, and speed of delivery among the most important factors. Brand identification of industrial supplies is rare.

Services

Even the largest manufacturers are unable to fulfill all their needs internally. When problems arise, they turn to highly specialized service companies for help. These may be trained engineering or management consultants, data-processing specialists, or such low-level service specialists as window cleaners, painters, or maintenance servicemen. Other service organizations include in-service lunches and piped-in music.

Generally, outside service companies are used when the cost of self-servicing is higher than the cost of buying the service because of special equipment or infrequency of use.

MARKETING STRATEGY. The most important factors in the success of a service company are speed and satisfaction. To accomplish this, it must be located near its customers, maintain an adequate stock of parts and supplies, and have enough skilled servicemen. Because of the infrequency of use, manufacturers are willing to pay a premium for fast, effective service.

Services are rarely sold through middlemen. The normal distribution channel is from the service company directly to the user. Services of high-level companies such as advertising agencies or management consultants are generally negotiated *in extenso* by important executives of both companies. Compared to personal selling, advertising and sales promotion are unimportant in the selling of services.

IMPORTANT POINTS IN THE CHAPTER

1. Past experience has shown that certain market mixes are best for specific categories of goods. By classifying goods according to these categories, a producer can benefit from this experience.

2. Consumer goods are produced for the ultimate consumer. Industrial goods are produced for the industrial market, where they will be used to produce other goods. The classification of goods must be based on the type of purchaser, not on the type of goods.

3. Consumer goods are categorized according to the buying habits of the consumers. They consist of convenience goods, shopping goods, specialty goods, impulse goods, and emergency goods. (The last two are special cases of convenience goods.)

4. Convenience goods are those a shopper buys with a minimum of shopping effort. They are frequently bought—by habit and brand name—and inexpensive. They must be widely distributed, heavily promoted, and competitively priced.

5. Shopping goods are purchased after comparisons of price, suitability, style, and quality. Characteristically they are long-lasting, high-priced, and brand-identified. Shopping goods do not require wide distribution but must be well styled, competitively priced, and well promoted (generally by the retailer). Price is the most

important factor in the marketing of homogeneous, and product in the marketing of heterogeneous goods.

6. Specialty goods are products for the purchase of which customers are willing to make a special effort. These are high-priced, fine-quality products sold at prestigious dealers, and customers will not accept substitutes. Specialty goods are distributed through short distribution channels. The principal elements of the marketing mix are product and promotion.

7. Impulse goods are bought without prior planning. They are inexpensive and, like other convenience goods, they must be widely displayed, heavily promoted, and competitively priced.

8. Emergency goods must be purchased immediately to fill an urgent need. Place is the vital factor in the distribution of emergency goods. Price is relatively unimportant and promotion is usually limited to place information.

9. Raw materials are goods that will be used in the production of other goods. Natural-state raw materials require little handling and are sold in large quantities through short distribution channels. Agricultural products, which are subjected to a great deal of handling, require long channels of distribution.

10. Fabricating materials and parts are goods, processed to some extent, that become an actual part of the finished product. Such goods are produced to the customer's specifications and marketed through short channels of distribution.

11. Installations are major items of equipment that affect the scope of a manufacturer's operations. They are produced to the customer's specifications and marketed through short channels of distribution.

12. Accessory equipment is used to facilitate rather than to perform the basic operations of a manufacturing plant. Since accessories are often low-value, standardized items, they generally require wide placement, promotion, and fairly long channels of distribution.

13. Supplies are materials used in the operation of a business that do not become part of the finished product. They are generally low-value products that must be widely distributed (through extensive channels) and are very sensitive to price changes.

14. When the cost of providing internal services is high, institutions turn to private servicing companies. Middlemen are rarely used to sell services. Speed and customer satisfaction are the important factors for the successful marketing of services.

REVIEW QUESTIONS

1. Discuss the advantages of product classification to the producer.
2. Define *consumer goods*. Can the same goods be both consumer and industrial goods? How do you differentiate?
3. What are convenience goods? Give examples and characteristics.
4. Discuss in detail the importance of place in the marketing of convenience goods.
5. Explain the meaning of *homogeneous shopping goods*. Give examples. How are they marketed?
6. Differentiate between the placing of shopping and convenience goods. Why is there a difference?
7. How are shopping goods promoted? Who is responsible for the promotion of shopping goods?
8. What are specialty goods? What are their characteristics? Give examples.
9. Does overcharging for specialty goods involve dangers? Discuss the pricing of such goods.
10. Discuss the importance of place in the market strategy for impulse goods.
11. Is promotion important in the sale of impulse goods? Why?
12. Define *emergency goods*. Give examples. Compare them with other convenience goods.
13. How should emergency goods be placed? Why? Give examples.
14. Define *industrial goods*. Give examples. Why is the industrial market practically unknown to most people?
15. Discuss the market strategy for the distribution of agricultural products. Why are the channels of distribution different from those of other raw materials?
16. In which way are fabricating materials and parts usually marketed?
17. Define *installations* as industrial goods. Give examples. Differentiate between installations and fabricating materials.
18. Define *accessory equipment*. Give examples.
19. Discuss pricing, placing, and promoting industrial supplies.
20. What are industrial services? Give examples.

CASE PROBLEMS

Case Problem 1

The Home-Easy Tool Company is the largest producer of electrical hand tools for the consumer market in the United States. The firm has been in operation for over 100 years. Their brand is very well known and belongs as a consumer product in the specialty-goods category. This classification has been well earned, since the product line is of uniformly high quality, durable, well promoted, and conveniently serviced.

Since World War II the movement of the middle class from inner-city apartments to individually owned homes has resulted in a dramatic spurt of profitable growth for Home-Easy. At present, they are in an excellent financial position.

Management at Home-Easy is interested in expansion to the industrial market. A survey of their potential competitors on the industrial scene has indicated that production facilities, financing, experience, and engineering know-how at Home-Easy are second to none. In addition, several of their most successful consumer products, with minor modification, would fit the industrial market perfectly.

You have been called in as a marketing consultant. Your job is to prepare a marketing strategy with which the company may successfully enter the industrial field. Your report should include the following areas:

1. How would you classify the product?
2. Place
3. Price
4. Promotion
5. Suggest areas that might warrant further research.

Case Problem 2

In 1965, Tom Hanson, a chemical engineer, developed an excellent new product for homeowners. The item consisted of a simple device powered by water pressure which, when used with the inexpensive chemicals provided, did an excellent job on cleaning out stuffed drains. The cost of producing the device and chemicals was so low that it could be retailed for $2.75. Considering the rising costs of plumbing services, the product seemed certain to be successful.

Tom patented his invention, built several thousand in his garage, and personally placed them in several neighboring hardware stores. After a brief breaking-in period, the product showed sufficient potential for Tom to quit his job and invest his savings in a small plant for the production of the new product.

At the beginning of 1966 Tom was in business. He hired salesmen and began production.

By 1971 Tom had a moderately successful small business. This was disappointing to him, since his was by far the best and cheapest product of its kind on the market. The most serious problem seems to be his inability to keep salesmen. They rarely stay longer than a few months and much of Tom's efforts are spent in recruitment. Tom feels that he can solve the problem by hiring a professional sales manager who will be expert at the recruitment, training, and directing of sales people.

Questions

1. What do you think of Tom's solution?
2. Do you agree that the trouble lies in the sales area?
3. What would you suggest?

BIBLIOGRAPHY

Alexander, R. S., "Goods for the Market: Industrial Goods," in C. F. Phillips, ed., *Marketing by Manufacturers*. Homewood, Ill.: Richard D. Irwin, Inc., 1950.

Bucklin, Louis P., "Retail Strategy and the Classification of Consumer Goods," *Journal of Marketing*, January, 1963.

Duncan, Delbert J., "Some Basic Determinants of Behavior in Industrial Purchasing," *Pacific Purchaser,* May–August, 1965.

"Fundamental Differences between Industrial and Consumer Marketing," *Journal of Marketing,* October, 1954.

Groenveld, Leonard, "A New Theory of Consumer Buying Interest," *Journal of Marketing,* July, 1964.

"How Buyers Buy in Construction Field," *Industrial Marketing,* August, 1962.

Istvan, Donald F., "Capital-Expenditure Decisions: How They Are Made in Labor Corporations," *Indiana Business Report No. 33.* Bloomington, Ind.: Indiana University Press, 1961.

Klenenhager, Arno K., "Shopping, Specialty, or Convenience Goods," *Journal of Retailing,* Winter, 1966–67.

Kollat, David T., and Ronald P. Willett, "Customer Impulse Purchasing Behavior," *Journal of Marketing Research,* February, 1967.

McCarthy, E. J., *Basic Marketing—A Managerial Approach.* Homewood, Ill.: Richard D. Irwin, Inc., 1968.

Rich, Stuart U., "Shopping Behavior of Department Store Customer." Unpublished thesis, Harvard University, 1963.

Twedt, Dik W., "What is a 'Convenient Food'," *Journal of Marketing,* January, 1967.

Wittreich, Warren J., "How to Buy/Sell Professional Services," *Harvard Business Review,* March–April, 1966.

CONSUMERISM

4

INTRODUCTION

The complaints of the consuming public have been heard and echoed for many years but in the past, marketers have generally turned deaf ears to them. The consumer has been constantly plagued by disagreement between actual and published weights, poor performance of appliances, late delivery dates without any customer recourse, false claims concerning material content, and advertisements of special sales when the merchandise was "already sold."

Until recently neither the government nor private industry has provided legislation or the self-regulation necessary to heal the woes of the complaining public. Today consumerism and ecology are the two glamorous words discussed by industry and the government alike.

Consumerism, the protection of the interests of consumers, is a subject with the broadest implications for marketers. The education of the consumer does not rest solely with any one specific institution but seems to be the joint responsibility of both government and industry. President Nixon, in a message to Congress dated October 30, 1969, has, perhaps, set the tone for consumerism. In it he made recommendations for a "Buyer's Bill of Rights." The president was careful to point out that his conception of consumerism in America "does not mean that caveat emptor—let the buyer beware, has been replaced by caveat venditor—let the seller beware." It was his feeling that these buyer's rights should include:

1. The right to make an intelligent choice among products and services.

2. The right to accurate information on which to make free choice.

3. The right to register dissatisfaction and have his complaint heard.

Through imposed regulation, all levels of government are seeking to educate and protect the consumer. Through self-regulation, many of our industries are spending sums equal to that of the government, trying to achieve these same ends.

In this chapter we shall explore the involvement of both government and business in consumerism and the services of agencies and individuals concerned with consumer protection.

GOVERNMENTAL PARTICIPATION

Although the participation of federal, state, and local governmental agencies in programs designed for consumer protection is not new, its impact is being felt by marketers more than ever before. There is hardly an agency at any level of government that is not in some way involved in the protection of the consumer.

FEDERAL GOVERNMENT

A study of the federal government's involvement in consumerism shows that the Office of Consumer Affairs presently plays a leading role in the crusade for consumer justice. Other agencies such as the Federal Trade Commission, the Food and Drug Administration, and the Department of Agriculture continue to make meaningful contributions to the consumer, as they did in the past.

The Office of Consumer Affairs

This office and its director, the president's special assistant for consumer affairs, have the central responsibility for coordinating all federal activities in the consumer-protection field. The department advises the president on consumer matters and alerts other governmental officials of the potential impact of their decisions on consumer interests. The office receives complaints from individual consumers and refers them to the appropriate agencies or industries concerned. Some of the specific roles that the Office of Consumer Affairs plays are testifying at congressional hearings concerned with consumerism, educating the public in consumer skills, exchanging information with industry, and assisting state and local consumer-protection programs. It is important to understand that this department does not in any manner replace such agencies as the Federal Trade Commission and the Food and Drug Administration, nor does it undermine their responsibilities. It is equally important to note that the Office of Consumer Affairs does not intentionally usurp the powers of similar departments at the state and local levels. The department, on the federal level, operates on the assumption that a smoothly functioning relationship between the federal, state, and local consumer-protecting agencies is essential in order to properly serve the needs of the consumer.

At the Fifty-fourth National Conference on Weights and Measures in 1969, Virginia H. Knauer, special assistant to the president for consumer affairs, addressed the large group of officials from various states, countries, and cities, and representatives from U.S. government and consumer organizations. Near the conclusion of her speech, in which she discussed the responsibility of government role in consumer protection, she made a statement that sums up her office's potential involvement with consumerism.

Much remains to be done for the consumers. Your responsibilities will increase as well as mine in the days ahead as consumers demand more laws and regulations in their never ending battle to protect themselves in the marketplace and to exercise their four consumer rights—the right to be safe, the right to choose, the right to be fully informed, and the right to be heard.

The Federal Trade Commission

Along with other regulatory agencies, the Federal Trade Commission was organized to prevent unfair business practices. The FTC is specifically charged with the investigation of unfair methods of competition and unfair practices in commerce. Since its establishment in 1914, the FTC, acting as an independent body, has played a leading role in the fight against these unfair practices.

At the American Association of Advertising Agencies' annual meeting in 1970, Commissioner Mary Gardiner Jones, of the FTC, in a talk entitled "The Commission's Consumer-Protection Role" emphasized the commission's three overall objectives to eliminate unfair and deceptive practices from the marketplace.

> First, the commission must see its role as one which is primarily designed to translate the consumer's expectations about the marketplace into enforceable business obligations. Second, the commission must devise its programs with a view to redressing the imbalances of power which exist between the consumer and his seller. These imbalances reflect themselves in the lack of availability of hard data about the products being offered. They also reflect themselves in the inability of consumers either to protect themselves from frauds or deceptions or to obtain redress if their interests have been damaged when a violation of law takes place. Third, the commission must use its powers so as to supplement or complement the workings of the competitive system where it fails in fact to bring business practices into line with the needs of consumers or to eliminate practices which are false or unfair to consumers or competitors.

Advertising has been and continues to be a major area of concern for the FTC. Many citizens' groups have been formed to voice specific complaints about advertising. In response to these complaints and in line with its statutory responsibilities, the FTC is involved in areas such as:

1. Advertising monitoring—a program in which storyboards, photos, and scripts of commercials of the major networks are carefully examined.

2. Screening the audio tapes of commercials.

3. Investigating the use of testimonials.

The Food and Drug Administration

The responsibilities of Food and Drug Administration cover not only food and drugs but also cosmetics and therapeutic devices. The FDA is part of the Department of Health, Education, and Welfare. Compliance with its established regulations is enforced through the administration's regular inspection program.

In addition to the general areas of concern, such as the proper labeling of foods containing preservatives and artificial coloring and the warning on the labels of drugs that they are habit forming, the FDA is expanding its duties. In the message to congress of October 30, 1969 the following task was assigned to the FDA:

1. That a full review be made of food additives.

2. That a system be devised for the rapid identification of drugs in time of personal emergency.

3. That certain minimum standards be established for devices such as contact lenses, hearing aids, and artificial valves that are implanted in the body.

The Department of Agriculture

The consumer receives protection in the selection of agricultural products through inspection work carried out by the Department of Agriculture. The department establishes certain standards for these products and a grading system for canned goods. Inspection of agricultural and of meat and poultry products takes place at regular intervals. In addition to the inspection at canneries and packing plants, the department, at the request of manufacturers, inspects their goods to be marketed and issues certificates for these goods.

Major Consumer Laws

The government continuously introduces legislation that either directly or indirectly affects the consumer. The Sherman Antitrust Act of 1890, the Clayton Act, 1914, and the Federal Trade Commission Act of 1914 were forerunners of the major consumer laws of recent years. The following is a listing of those laws enacted since 1964, with a brief synopsis of their major provisions:

Federal Insecticide, Fungicide, and Rodenticide Act Amendment, May 12, 1964	Closed consumer-protection loopholes that permitted pesticides to be sold before they were federally passed as safe. It required federal registration numbers on the labels.
Truth-in-Securities Act (Securities Act Amendment), August 20, 1964	Provided greater protection to investors by extending disclosure requirements to over-the-counter securities and by requiring improved qualification and disciplinary procedures for registered brokers and dealers.
Drug-Abuse Control Amendments, July 15, 1965	Protected public health and safety by preventing both misuse and illicit traffic of potentially dangerous drugs, especially sedatives and stimulants.

Fair Packaging and
Labeling Act,
November 3, 1966

Protected consumers by preventing unfair and deceptive methods of packaging and labeling. Made value comparisons easier by requiring manufacturers to clearly label each product as to manufacturer's name, ingredients, and weight.

Child Protection Act,
November 3, 1966

Protected children by banning sale of hazardous toys and other articles intended for children. Protected all consumers by banning sale of general household articles so hazardous as to be dangerous regardless of labeling.

Traffic Safety Act
(Highway Safety Act),
September 9, 1966

Increased public highway safety by creating a federal–state partnership for coordinated and accelerated national highway-safety programs.

Traffic Safety Act
(National Traffic and Motor
Vehicle Safety Act),
September 9, 1966

Protected drivers by providing a coordinated national safety program and establishment of national safety standards for motor vehicles.

Bank Supervisory Act
(Financial Institutions
Supervisory Act),
October 16, 1966

Protected investors by strengthening the ability of federal supervisory agencies to safeguard soundness of the nation's financial system and by increased insurance coverage for depositors and savers.

National Commission on
Product Safety Act,
November 20, 1967

Protected consumers by establishment of the National Commission on Product Safety to point out dangerous products, determine effectiveness of regulatory laws, and recommend additional protective measures if necessary.

Clinical Laboratories
Improvement Act (enacted as
Title 3 of Partnership for
Health Amendments of 1967),
December 5, 1967

Protected public health by elimination of substandard clinical laboratories. Required clinical laboratories in interstate commerce to be federally licensed and to comply with federal minimum standards.

Flammable Fabrics Act
Amendment,
December 14, 1967

Protected consumers from flammable clothing and household products by broadening the federal authority to set safety standards as well as the range of fabrics and articles covered.

Wholesome Meat Act,
December 15, 1967

Protected consumers from impure and unwholesome meat by offering states federal assistance in establishing interstate inspection system, but providing that federal inspection will be made if after two years no state inspection system as good as the federal system has been established; by giving the federal government power to inspect state plants; and by raising quality standards for all imported meats.

Fire Research and Safety Act, March 1, 1968	Protected public health by developing improved information about the number and causes of fires and their costs in terms of property, lives, and injuries; initiation of a fire-safety research and education program; and pilot projects to improve and upgrade efficiency of firefighters.
Automobile Insurance Study Resolution, May 22, 1968	Safeguarded consumers from inequalities and inadequacies of automobile insurance by authorizing a comprehensive study of the existing compensation system, including recommendations for improvement.
Truth-in-Lending Act (Consumer Credit Protection Act), May 29, 1968	Safeguarded consumers by requiring full disclosure of terms and conditions of finance charges in credit transactions; by restricting garnishment of wages; and by creating the National Commission on Consumer Finance to study and make recommendations on the need for further regulation of the consumer finance industry.
Securities Market Review Act (Securities Exchange Act Amendment), July 29, 1968	Protected investors by authorizing an investigation of the effect on the securities market of the operation of institutional investors.
Interstate Land Sales Full Disclosure Act (incorporated as Title 14 of the Housing and Urban Development Act of 1968), August 1, 1968	Protected consumers with greater safeguards against shrewd and unscrupulous practices in interstate land sales by requiring sellers to provide potential buyers fully, simply, and clearly all material facts needed for an informed choice.
Natural Gas Pipeline Safety Act, August 12, 1968	Protected the public by creating enforceable safety procedures regulating the pipeline transportation of flammable, toxic, and corrosive gases.
Wholesome Poultry Products Act, August 18, 1968	Protected consumers from impure and unwholesome poultry and poultry products, just as the Wholesome Meat Act increased protection from impure meat.
Radiation Control for Health and Safety Act, October 18, 1968	Protected consumers from dangerous radiation emissions from electronic products by providing mandatory control standards and recall of faulty products. It also provided for research on biological effects of radiation, advisory standards for accrediting schools for medical X-ray technicians, and development of model state laws for licensing technicians.
Amend National Commission on Product Safety Act, August 4, 1969	A bill to amend the National Commission on Product Safety Act in order to extend the life of the commission for completion of its assigned tasks.

Child Protection and Toy Safety Act of 1969, November 6, 1969	To protect children from toys and other articles intended for children that are hazardous because of electrical, mechanical, or thermal reasons.
Council on Environmental Quality Act, January 1, 1970	To authorize the secretary of the interior to conduct investigations, studies, surveys, and research relating to the nation's ecological systems, natural resources, and environmental quality and to establish a Council on Environmental Quality.
Amend Federal Credit Union Act, March 30, 1970	To amend the Federal Credit Union Act so as to provide for an independent federal agency for the supervision of federally chartered credit unions.
Public Health Smoking Cigarette Act of 1969, April 1, 1970	To extend public health protection with respect to cigarette smoking.
Amend National Traffic and Motor Vehicle Safety Act of 1966, May 22, 1970	To amend the National Traffic and Motor Vehicle Safety Act of 1966 to authorize appropriations for fiscal years 1970 and 1971.
An Act to Prohibit the Business of Debt Adjusting in the District of Columbia, May 22, 1970	To prohibit the business of debt adjusting in the District of Columbia except as an incident to the lawful practice of law or as an activity engaged in by a nonprofit corporation or association.

STATE AND LOCAL GOVERNMENT

The degree of involvement in consumer protection at the lower levels of government varies from state to state, county to county, and city to city. Although just about every city, county, and state government concerns itself with consumer problems, the amount of participation and mechanics involved in aiding the consumer differs considerably. At the time of this writing, Virginia Knauer is involved with the National Association of Attorneys General to codify all state consumer-protection laws and to encourage the formation of a Bureau of Consumer Protection in all fifty states and territories. There are presently thirty-three such bureaus, many operating under budgetary handicaps, which virtually makes their operations less effective. One of the most successful consumer-protection bureaus is located in Pennsylvania. The federal government, through its Special Assistant on Consumer Affairs, suggested that the formation of these state bureaus be organized in a fashion similar to that of Pennsylvania. New York State, at this time, does not specifically have a consumer-affairs office but deals with consumer protection through its attorney general's office. In the large cities of New York State, such as New York City, Albany, and Buffalo, the attorney general's office has a Consumer Frauds Bureau. Under the direction of Attorney General Louis J. Lefkowitz, the bureau was established in 1957. The primary purpose of the bureau's establishment was to "drive the cheat out of business and to recover monies for the victimized consumer." Unlike the consumer departments of the federal government and of many states and municipal governments, which concern themselves with consumer education and measures to prevent unfair practices, New York State's bureau is more concerned with following up complaints. Most of the complaints handled by the bureau deal with bait advertising, business opportunity frauds, phony training schools, home improvement frauds, and misrepresentation. Some information is provided by New York State for the enlightenment of the consumer in a brochure, "Your ABC's of Careful Buying," a ten-point buying guide for consumers.

Specific Example of a Large Municipal Department of Consumer Affairs

New York City has one of the most extensive and vital municipal departments of consumer affairs. It was created by the New York City Council in 1968 and it was the first municipal agency in the United States mandated to develop a comprehensive program for consumer protection and education.

To facilitate the enforcement of its responsibilities, the New York City department has authorization to conduct investigations, hold public and private hearings, and issue subpoenas. The department has both the staff and the powers of two former city agencies, the Department of Markets and the Department of Licenses. The Department of Markets is now the Markets Division of Consumer Affairs and deals primarily in weights and measures. This department is charged with the responsibility for the administration of a number of both state and city laws that relate to accuracy of weights and measures, quality of food and other commodities that are sold by weights and measures, and posting of price information about such commodities. The Department of Licenses, now known as the License Division of the Department of Consumer Affairs, has the responsibility for the regulation of more than one hundred licensed industries and trades. Their licensing jurisdiction includes such trades as secondhand automobile dealers and home-improvement contractors, two industries that have regularly plagued the consumer.

When Commissioner Bess Myerson took office in 1969, the Consumer Protection Act was proposed and passed by the city council. Upon signing by Mayor John V. Lindsay, the department was given those powers necessary to carry out its full assignment. Briefly, this act outlawed all "deceptive" and "unconscionable" trade practices, empowered the department to promulgate regulations defining such practices, and to go to court seeking a range of remedies for violations.

In the area of consumer complaints, if a complaint relates to any law or regulation under the department's jurisdiction, a field investigation is instituted. If a violation is uncovered, the department can litigate. Where complaints do not relate to the department's laws and regulations, strong efforts are made to adjust the complaints through visits to the company about which the complaints have been filed.

Aside from actual protection, in an effort to make the consumer more knowledgeable, the New York City Department of Consumer Affairs conducts many educative programs, provides speakers for public groups, utilizes the media to caution the public about possible misrepresentation, and publishes a variety of literature dealing with topics of interest for the consumer. One such pamphlet entitled, "Wise Up! Know Your Department of Consumer Affairs" covers such topics as the many consumer-protection laws, specifically the new Truth-in-Lending Law and caution about credit purchases. Another brochure, "Act on Fact," is a guide to wise buying.

In order to make certain that the public can avail itself of the various functions of the department, Consumer Affairs maintains a "Consumobile," which is a van equipped with consumer-education exhibits, films, and recorders that are used to tape consumer complaints.

Finally, the department recommends for consumers several points that will help in the saving of money. These points are:

1. See that the store has a scale that can be easily read and bears the official seal of approval of the Department of Consumer Affairs.
2. Get the price per pound before you buy.
3. See that the scale pointer is at zero before the merchandise is weighed and that it is at rest before a weight or price is granted.
4. Figure the total price yourself; question any higher amount.
5. Ask to have every obstruction removed to give you a clear view of the scale or the cash register.
6. Check purchases against itemized register tape and re-add the total on the tape.
7. You are entitled to net weight of your purchase, not including boxes, cartons, bags, or wrapping paper.
8. Buy fresh fruits and vegetables *in season;* they taste better and are much lower in price.
9. If in doubt, check weights of prepackaged items on the customers' scale, or ask that they be weighed in your presence.
10. Don't be fooled by the size of the container or box; look for the weight or content *statement.*
11. Wherever possible, buy in person. If you must order by phone, insist on itemized bills accompanying your order.
12. Be wary of sensational claims and ridiculous reductions in price.
13. If a reputable store has a *special sale,* stock up, especially on staples and canned goods.
14. Make sure that *sale* items are charged out at the advertised prices.

15. If an advertisement interests you, bring the ad with you and ask to examine the merchandise.

16. Ask salesperson to put on the bill or invoice any claims made, such as *all silk* and *handmade.*

17. If you have your meat ground to order, see that the grinding takes place in front of you.

18. All merchandise on display in the store must have its price clearly marked on a tag, sign, or poster.

INDUSTRY PARTICIPATION

With the amount of attention being paid to consumer protection by the various levels of government, it becomes quite obvious that the business world has, for many years, caused customer unhappiness and dissatisfaction. Ralph Nader, the crusader for the consumerism movement, has spent years in the investigation of companies and has uncovered many product deficiencies that proved to be hazardous to the consumer. Aside from his probes into industry, Nader has continuously blasted the government. In a recent attack on the Federal Trade Commission, based upon a three-month investigation, he accused the commission of neglecting one of its major responsibilities, that of the investigation of deceptive practices. Perhaps the strongest single action that has prompted industry to impose self-regulation was Nader's investigation of the automotive field (the Corvair). Whatever the reasons were for the initiation of consumer programs, industry is now spending millions of dollars for the protection and education of the consuming public.

Independent Consulting Firms

Probably the first national consulting firm specializing in consumer affairs is Kay Valory Consultants. Kay Valory is the former Consumer Assistant to Governor Reagan of California. After three and a half years and ten thousand letters of consumer complaints as Consumer Counsel, Mrs. Valory has organized her own firm for the purpose of what she describes as "preventive consumerism." She charges that the expense of government regulation through the many consumer affairs departments is costing the taxpayer many millions of dollars. "The Dear Abby of Consumerism" as she was known in California, Mrs. Valory feels that much of the cost to the taxpayers could be avoided if industry became self-regulatory.

Among her clients are a hearing-aid manufacturer and a chain of supermarkets. With offices to be set up in such states as New York, California, and Illinois, businessmen in those areas can avail themselves of consumer-affairs counseling for a minimum fee of fifty dollars per hour. The firm's services include the conducting of surveys in order to measure consumer reaction to products, the development of practical policy changes, and the creation of complete programs to improve the business–consumer relationship.

The ever growing list of businesses that have established departments specifically organized for the benefit of the consumer is probably an effort to reverse the present adverse public opinion of marketers. Every day more and more companies are jumping on the consumer-programs bandwagon. As is true in the governmental, state, and municipal programs, those organized by businesses vary considerably.

Individual Businesses

The General Motors Corporation established a Public-Policy Committee for internal advice on matters that affect the general public. General Motors, which is the world's largest corporation, has been a major target of leaders of both environmental and consumer movements. The committee is composed of five members of the twenty-three member Board of Directors of General Motors; four are not officers in the company and one is a former vice-chairman of the corporation. The committee's task is to give advice to the board of directors on how to handle problems such as safety and pollution. Although the establishment of such a committee is considered a step toward self-regulation, the organization and composition of the committee is "genuinely preposterous," according to Ralph Nader. Nader in an interview said, "The fact that they couldn't go outside of the company for the men is an indication of General Motor's insecurity. It's so ridiculous that it will backfire." Although not quite as critical as Nader, Philip Moore, Executive Secretary of Campaign G.M., an organized group of critics of General Motors, said, "While we wish the committee well and will do everything in our power to assist its efforts, we are dismayed to observe that it suffers from the same parochialism as the board itself." Obviously, General Motors action concerning consumer protection is looked upon with considerable skepticism.

At a conference in June, 1970, sponsored by Advanced Management Research International, Inc. dealing with "Consumerism, and its Dramatic Impact on Corporate Profits," many consumer experts from government, business, and consumer-interest groups evaluated the consumer information gap. Representing the Maytag Company, probably best known for its washing machine, was the concern's marketing vice-president, Mr. Claire G. Ely. In his speech Mr. Ely emphasized the reason that Maytag has been successful since 1893 while many competitors, over the years, fell by the wayside. Serving the consumer seems to be Maytag's key to success. The company makes available to dealers, without cost, an information tag to hang on every product. The information covered includes the company's name, address, and telephone number so that when problems arise customers can directly contact the organization. In order to make certain that the consumer is completely satisfied with servicing and repairs, the company sends out field service supervisors to meet and help train servicemen. In this way it can be sure that the customer will be satisfied. Examination of Maytag's warranty showed need for change. The small print was eliminated and the warranty was restated in language that was designed to be easily understood. Finally Mr. Ely concluded by discussing the handling of complaints. It is company policy that all correspondence is answered immediately and individually, without the use of form letters. Complaints are always followed up.

Maytag's Information Center has produced a pamphlet on its consumer programs. It fully covers the areas of consumer concern, such as warranty, service training, parts availability, operating instructions, and safety control. The company presents consumer-education programs (549 in 1969 to a total audience of 104,453) to many types of consumer groups. Also made available is such free consumer-education literature as a stain-removal chart.

Maytag people think of themselves as a customer-oriented company. They do not consider themselves good Samaritans or do-gooders but good businessmen.

Many retailers provide consumer protection through their standards bureaus and testing bureaus, such as R. H. Macy & Co., Inc. and Sears, Roebuck and Co. Before goods are offered for sale they undergo specific tests that separate the inferior from the desirable products. In this way the consumer is almost certain to be assured of product satisfaction.

Study of many businesses showed a definite trend toward consumerism as conceived by Maytag. Some business firms are not likely to confess their sudden expansion into consumer programs, but it is evident from their actions that, in order to survive, the consumer-is-king philosophy must be carefully followed.

Business Conferences

An indication that business is deeply concerned with the consumerism movement is evidenced by the great number of sessions concerning consumerism at business-sponsored conventions.

At the annual American Marketing Association Conference in Kansas City in 1970, Mr. Lee S. McDonald, manager of consumer market planning for Goodyear Tire & Rubber Co. spoke about consumerism and its implications for marketers. It was his feeling that without the initiative of business itself in the area of consumer enlightenment the result will be "increasing government intervention, growing consumer frustration, increasingly unpredictable consumer behavior, and increasing rejection of new product programs."

A look at the list of companies that attended the Advanced Management Research Conference on Consumerism in New York City in June,

1970 is probably the best indication that business is ready to accept its responsibilities concerning the consumer. Such topics as consumer instruction, consumer credit, product information, views from government and business, consumer service, and packaging and labeling were examined.

The Better Business Bureaus

As part of the Association of Better Business Bureaus there are Better Business Bureaus located throughout the United States. The objective of the bureaus is the promotion of ethical business practices.

All of the bureaus are nonprofit service corporations, maintained by business firms to elevate the standards of business conduct, fight frauds, and assist the public to achieve maximum satisfaction from its relations with business. They do not endorse or recommend any security, product, service, or concern, and no concern is permitted to indicate otherwise in its advertising or selling.

Basically, the local offices handle complaints that have been brought about by unfair practices of local businesses. For example, a complaint involving a company located in upper Manhattan may be brought to the attention of the Better Business Bureau of metropolitan New York. If the customer's dissatisfaction is with a company located more specifically in the Harlem area, the complaint would be handled by the Harlem branch of the bureau. In small cities one central office handles all the complaints; in larger metropolitan areas, branch bureaus are established due to the enormous number of complaints.

The Association has an Office for Consumer Affairs in Washington, D.C. to deal with complaints against national companies and to permit information to filter from the government to the local bureaus.

Aside from the handling of complaints, the bureaus operate in a fashion that will stop the consumer from being cheated. Advertisements are carefully scrutinized by bureau personnel in an attempt to uncover false or misleading contents. When the bureau comes across advertising that appears to be deceptive, it makes an investigation. If the advertisement is not truthful, for example the merchandise at the advertised price does not fulfill the vendor's claims, the bureau approaches the seller. Where a merchant refuses to rectify the situation, the bureau might inform the media in which the questionable advertisement has taken place to prevent further promotion (most newspapers, magazines, TV stations, and so on will not permit unfair advertising) or, if a law or regulation has been violated, the bureau will notify the appropriate government department, such as the attorney general's office. The bureau does not have the legal power to prosecute, but, as an investigative agency, it has been responsible for the bringing of legal suits against offenders.

Most of the bureaus make available to consumers brochures designed for their education with regard to purchases. For example, the Education and Research Foundation of the Better Business Bureaus of Metropolitan New York, Inc., has developed a "Wise-Buying Guide Series." These bulletins deal with various consumer products. To name one, "The Careful Way to Buy a Car" outlines such areas as used cars, ability to afford the price, contracts, guarantees, and sales tricks to be wary of.

Trade Associations

Industries organize associations to upgrade and improve their operations and standards. Although the goal of the trade associations is the overall improvement of their industry, the consumer often is the beneficiary of their efforts. For example, most trade associations—such as the National Retail Merchants' Association—frown upon unfair and unethical advertising practices. Self-regulation of advertising has been the aim of many associations. The cigarette manufacturer, having established an advertising code for his industry, enforces substantial fines for its violation. Besides advertising, trade associations are involved in other areas that help the consumer. The following is a list of accomplishments or areas of concern of specific trade associations in connection with package sizes that often confuse the customer:

1. The Soap and Detergent Association is studying sizes for liquid detergents and liquid household cleaners.

2. The Toilet Goods Association is planning a reduction in toothpaste tube sizes.

3. The National Coffee Manufacturers' Association plans the elimination of odd-ounce sizes between two and sixteen ounces.

Although trade associations cannot force businesses within their industries to heed their recommendations, they continue to make meaningful changes that ultimately benefit the consumer.

PRIVATE PARTICIPATION

Ralph Nader, Self-appointed Consumer Guardian

Sometimes called the United States' toughest customer, Ralph Nader has become the self-appointed and unsalaried guardian of the interests of over two hundred million consumers. Champion of numerous causes, Nader has stirred enough trouble to warrant industry to reappraise its responsibilities. In his book *Unsafe at Any Speed* Nader condemned General Motors' Corvair. Eventually, and perhaps because of the adverse publicity for the Corvair, General Motors halted production on that automobile.

Nader has influenced the passage of the following federal laws:

1. The National Traffic and Motor Vehicle Safety Act of 1966.

2. The Wholesome Meat Act of 1967.

3. The Natural Gas Pipeline Act of 1968.

4. The Radiation Control for Health and Safety Act of 1968.

5. The Wholesome Poultry Products Act of 1968.

6. The Federal Coal Mine Health and Safety Act of 1969.

Other areas of consumer concern that he brought to the attention of the public were the dangers of monosodium glutamate, cyclamates, and DDT. Color televisions, sometimes dangerous because of leaking radiation, were recalled because of the result of one of his investigations.

Besides his attacks on business, Nader has also leveled attacks on government agencies. He has probed the Federal Trade Commission, the National Air-Pollution Control Administration, and the Federal Railroad Administration, among others.

In order to expand his investigations, Nader employs the services of students. Collectively the group has become known as "Nader's Raiders."

Perhaps the magnitude of his reputation as the consumer's guardian can best be realized through the thousands of pieces of mail that reach him, simply labeled: Ralph Nader, Washington, D.C.

Although the government (federal, state, municipal) and industry are deeply involved in consumerism, most of those involved confess (either publicly or privately) that Ralph Nader began the entire movement.

Testing Organizations

A number of organizations were established to bring to the consumer product information that will enable him to make more knowledgeable purchases. The best known is the Consumers Union. Through its monthly publication of *Consumer Reports* potential customers are able to equip themselves with sufficient knowledge of various products. For example, the prospective automobile purchaser need only examine the issue on automobiles (they are evaluated each year) to gain enough product information. At the end of each year Consumers Union publishes an annual volume that covers all products tested throughout the year.

In their own words, "the purposes of Consumers Union are to provide consumers with information and counsel on consumer goods and services, to give information on all matters relating to the expenditure of the family income, and to initiate and to cooperate with individual and group efforts seeking to create and maintain decent living standards."

Consumers Union, established in 1936, is a nonprofit organization. It derives its income solely from the sale of its publications.

Unlike the magazine institutes, such as Good Housekeeping and Parents' Magazine, which test products and assign *seals* to satisfactory products, Consumers Union *rates* goods. For example, goods are rated from excellent to poor. By reading the ratings, consumers are able to compare products and are made aware of those that are poor in quality. Often consumers save money by purchasing a lesser-known product, with higher quality and lower cost than the better-known brand.

OUTLOOK FOR CONSUMERISM

The enormous sums being invested by both government and industry seem to indicate that the day of the consumer is here. It is obvious that if industry shirks its responsibility to the consumer, government is able to step up its involvement. Such private organizations as Consumers Union are not ready to believe that industry will sufficiently self-regulate. Ira J. Furman, Director of Communications for Consumers Union recently expressed the opinion, "Self-regulation has never worked and there is no reason to believe it ever will." If this statement has meaning, consumerism is bound to hear more from "Nader-type consumer advocates" and all the levels of government.

IMPORTANT POINTS IN THE CHAPTER

1. In his recommendation for a buyer's Bill of Rights President Nixon has set the tone of the federal government's involvement in consumer protection.

2. Participation of the federal government in consumerism is through such agencies as the Office of Consumer Affairs, the Federal Trade Commission, the Food and Drug Administration, and the Department of Agriculture.

3. The federal government has passed numerous consumer laws since 1964. Those of great significance are the Fair Packaging and Labeling Act, Flammable Fabrics Act Amendment, Consumer Credit Protection Act (Truth-in-Lending), and the Child Protection and Toy Safety Act.

4. Consumer affairs departments exist in most states, but their operations are hampered by budgetary problems.

5. New York City has one of the most complete municipal departments of consumer affairs. Besides the investigation of consumer complaints, it also has programs designed for the education of the consumer.

6. Industry is somewhat involved in self-regulation. Maytag, for example, has extensive consumer programs.

7. Kay Valory Consultants, headed by California's former consumer

affairs assistant, is the first consulting organization for consumer affairs. It was organized for the purpose of "preventive consumerism."

8. Many large associations, such as the American Marketing Association, are concentrating their conference agendas on the topic of consumerism.

9. The Better Business Bureaus handle customer complaints and try to correct false advertising claims.

10. Ralph Nader, the foremost name in consumerism, is involved in righting the wrongs of both business and government in their relationships with consumers. He is credited by many to be the individual responsible for the entire consumer-protection movement.

REVIEW QUESTIONS

1. Define the terms *consumerism, caveat emptor,* and *caveat venditor.*
2. Outline the major points of President Nixon's buyer's Bill of Rights.
3. What are the purposes of the federal government's Office of Consumer Affairs?
4. As outlined by Virginia Knauer, what are the "four consumer rights"?
5. How does the Federal Trade Commission involve itself in the protection of the consumer?
6. Describe the program that the Federal Trade Commission has designed to combat advertising complaints.
7. Briefly discuss the role of the Food and Drug Administration in connection with consumerism.
8. Which federal governmental agency concerns itself with standards and grades of products?
9. Cite the most important provisions of the Fair Packaging and Labeling Act of 1966.
10. Discuss the relationship of the federal government's Department of Consumer Affairs with those established by the states.
11. Through what department does New York State offer protection to the consumer?
12. New York City's Department of Consumer Affairs is staffed by the personnel of two former departments. Name them.
13. What did the Consumer Protection Act outlaw in New York City?
14. Aside from protection, what does New York City's Consumer Affairs Department offer consumers?
15. What is the "Consumobile"?
16. Name the first private consulting organization specializing in consumer affairs. Whom does it represent?

17. Why has General Motor's Public Policy Committee been critized by such people as Ralph Nader?

18. Describe the outstanding features of Maytag's consumer-education programs.

19. Discuss the role of the Better Business Bureaus and trade associations in connection with consumerism.

20. Ralph Nader is considered to be the consumer's guardian. Briefly discuss some of the areas of his involvement for consumer protection.

CASE PROBLEMS

Case Problem 1

For the past year much criticism has been levied against the olive industry. The companies that produce and distribute olives bottle their products and assign such descriptive terms as *super, colossal, giant,* and *large* to describe the size of their products. Housewives, unable to determine the actual olive size because of the confusing labels, have been continuously plagued by the problem.

Since the descriptive terms used are not in violation of any law, the olive companies have continued to follow their labeling practice. Moreover, many distributors package their olives in cans, which prevents inspection of size.

With the problem ever increasing, *Action,* a consumer-protection association, served notice on the olive industry. They insisted upon labeling reform, self-imposed by the industry, or formal complaints would be made to the appropriate governmental agencies, such as the Department of Consumer Affairs and the Department of Agriculture.

At a meeting of the major olive companies, the problem was discussed. Although a number of suggestions were made, two positions seemed to be dominant. One was to self-regulate and change the present labeling practice, the second was to continue with the current system, since the practice is not violating any laws.

Questions

1. From a marketer's standpoint, which position should be followed?

2. Why?

Case Problem 2

The city of Oceanview has a population of 2 million and is located in a large eastern state. Oceanview's major industries are retailing and light manufacturing, with most of the manufacturers' goods being limited to distribution within the city. Over the years, business in Oceanview has had its share of complaints. Both retailers and manufacturers had to remedy poor situations.

In order to aid the consumer, a Better Business Bureau was established in Oceanview. Besides handling complaints, the bureau sought out businesses that practiced deceptive advertising and other unfair practices. In spite of this, the complaints continue to mount and the consuming public has become extremely upset. At the present time there is a citizens' movement under way for the establishment of a Consumer Affairs Department. Some of the arguments that have been made are:

1. Creation of such a department would call for higher taxes.

2. The federal government has a Consumer Affairs Department. Why can they not handle our problems?

3. If the Better Business Bureau has been unsuccessful, the new department would not fare much better. What more could they do?

4. It is industry's responsibility to self-regulate; why should the government bother?

Questions

1. With which side do you agree? Defend your position in terms of the arguments posed.

2. Are there any additional arguments for either side? Discuss.

BIBLIOGRAPHY

"Actions by the Subcommittee on Consumer Affairs re H.R. 11601, The Consumer Credit Protection Act," *Congressional Record,* October 4, 1967.

"Anticonsumerism Is Lost Battle, AMA Told," *Marketing Insights,* April 13, 1970.

"Can Betty Furness Help the Consumers?" *Consumer Reports,* Vol. 32, May, 1967, 256–58.

Caplovitz, David, *Poor Pay More.* New York: The Free Press, 1963.

Directory of Government Agencies Safeguading Consumer and Environment. Alexandria, Va.: Serina Press, 1968.

Gentry, Curt, *The Vulnerable Americans.* Garden City, N.Y.: Doubleday & Company, Inc., 1966.

Hafnor, William Lincoln, "An Analysis of Research in the Negro Retail Food Market." Unpublished Master's thesis, Vanderbilt University, 1965.

Magnuson, Warren G., and Jean Carper, *The Dark Side of the Marketplace.* Englewood Cliffs, N.J.: Prentice-Hall, Inc., 1968.

Schlink, F. J., and M. C. Phillips, *Don't You Believe It.* New York: Pyramid Publications, 1966.

Smith, Ralph Lee, *Bargain Hucksters.* New York: Thomas Y. Crowell Company, 1962.

Sturdivant, Wilhelm, and Fred D. Sturdivant, "Poverty, Minorities, and Consumer Exploitations," *Southwestern Social Science Quarterly,* Vol. 49, No. 3, December, 1968.

Toyer, Aurelia, *Get Your Money's Worth.* New York: Holt, Rinehart & Winston, Inc., 1965.

Trump, Fred, *Buyer Beware.* New York: Abingdon Press, 1965.

Wharton, Don, "Five Common Frauds, and How to Avoid Them," *Reader's Digest.*

THE INDUSTRIAL MARKET

5

INTRODUCTION

In Chapter 3 goods were divided into two main categories: consumer goods and industrial goods. The classification was based upon the purpose for which the goods are intended. Those goods destined to be used in the production of other goods, or the operation of a business, were labeled industrial goods. In this chapter, the marketing of such goods will be discussed.

Considering that annual sales in the industrial market amount to hundreds of billions of dollars, and that the market's growth has been large and constant, it is strange to find that the marketing of industrial goods has been somewhat neglected. There are many reasons. For example, the engineering functions of the producers of industrial goods are usually considered more important than the marketing functions. This results in an overshadowing of the marketing functions, with many marketing decisions being made or at least being shared in by nonmarketing experts. Another possible reason for the neglect of industrial marketing is that those who research, write, and teach marketing are not trained in the highly technical problems of the industrial-marketing field and tend to steer clear of it. Considering the importance of this vast market, it is obvious that much study must be devoted to bringing the industrial market up to the level of the importance of consumer marketing.

EXTENT OF THE INDUSTRIAL MARKET

The market for industrial goods is very broad. It includes a wide assortment of goods that must be distributed to many different types of users for varied purposes. Full understanding of the industrial market requires knowledge of its characteristics as well as the buying habits and motivations of the individual industries that form it.

The enormous size and significance of the industrial market can be deduced from the fact that all the following industry groups are involved:

Extractive industries—lumbering, mining, and fishing
Agriculture
Construction contractors
Manufacturers

Commercial buyers—wholesale, retail, and service trades

Institutions—schools, colleges, and hotels

Government—federal, state, and local

Transportation, communication, and public utilities

CHARACTERISTICS OF THE INDUSTRIAL MARKET

The industrial market is characterized by certain features that are uniquely different from those involved in the distribution of consumer goods. These include the following.

Derived Demand

Since industrial goods are used to produce consumer goods, the demand for industrial goods is derived from (that is, dependent on) the demand for the consumer goods they are destined to produce. Thus, the demand for such industrial goods as steel is dependent on the sale of such consumer goods as automobiles and refrigerators. Similarly, the demand for tanned leather is derived from the consumer demand for leather goods like baseball gloves and shoes.

The demand for industrial goods such as installations—the long-lived, expensive, major machinery and equipment of an industrial user—is also derived from consumer demand, but of a long-run nature. Only when consumer demand is expected to increase dramatically in the future, industry makes huge expenditures for capital improvements, such as new factories or major producing equipment. Public utilities, for example, must estimate *future* population shifts so that the necessary pipelines, cables, and other equipment will be available when required.

The marketing implications of the derived demand for industrial goods are important, particularly in the area of promotion. Because the demand for industrial goods is ultimately in the hands of the consumer, many producers of goods for the industrial market do not promote their goods to their customers. Instead, they pitch their message to their customer's customers, the consumers. Thus, we find Du Pont de Nemours, with no direct consumer sales involved, advertising the characteristics of Dacron in the consumer media.

Inelastic Demand

The demand for a product is inelastic when an increase or decrease in the price does not significantly affect the demand for the goods. When a price increase lowers the demand for the commodity, or a price decrease results in an expanded demand, the demand may be referred to as elastic. That is, the demand varies as the price fluctuates.

The demand for industrial goods is derived from the consumer demand for the finished product. Consequently, the demand for the component parts of the consumer goods is based upon consumer demand, not upon the price charged to the producer for the industrial goods. The demand, therefore, for the industrial goods is said to be inelastic. It does not vary with price changes. When the demand for a manufacturer's product is high, he will not let a price increase reduce his purchases. Similarly, if the consumer demand for his product is low, he will not buy more industrial goods, no matter how much the price declines.

Industrial goods are inelastic in many cases because the cost of the individual product is not significant in the total cost of the item. A change in the cost of zippers to a dress manufacturer will have no effect on the amount of zippers he buys and very little effect on the profitability of the garment he manufactures.

Although the total demand for industrial goods should be considered inelastic, the individual firm marketing such goods may be faced with a very elastic demand situation. The dress manufacturer mentioned above has a specific, inelastic demand for the number of zippers equal to the orders for dresses he sells. However, he may take another supplier for zippers when the price for zippers changes. Price competition is not very common among suppliers of industrial goods, since any lowering of prices is usually quickly met by the competition to the disadvantage of all. Only through monopolistic conditions or outstanding reputation can producers of industrial goods consistently get higher prices than their competitors for a seemingly similar product. IBM's electric typewriters and Weyerhauser's plywood are examples of that situation.

Fluctuating Demand

There is a wide fluctuation in the demand for many types of industrial goods. This is particularly true of the demand for basic installations and accessory equipment, for which the demand varies with general business conditions. During times of business prosperity, producers are generally optimistic about future sales possibilities and invest heavily in expanded production facilities and improved manufacturing equipment. This results in heavy orders of installations and accessory equipment. During periods of business slowdown, manufacturers find their facilities more than adequate to meet the demand of reduced sales, and orders for installations and accessory equipment dwindle. Not only does equipment that is used at less than capacity outlive its expected usefulness, but the general air of pessimism results in the continued use of equipment that should be replaced. This overuse has the effect of building up the demand for new basic equipment when the business cycle turns upward. The result is a widely fluctuating demand for major capital expenditures.

Fluctuation in demand has broad implications for marketers of *heavy* business goods. For one thing, sales forces cannot be increased or decreased with the rapidity required by the business cycle. Producers, then, have the choice of using middlemen or carrying an excessive sales department during periods of low sales activity. Another problem marketers must face, during conditions of fluctuating demand, is price instability. Producers, faced with periods of declining business activity, cut their selling prices substantially in an effort to keep their production lines in operation. Management of an individual firm must decide whether or not to follow suit in the face of such keen price competition. Promotion is another problem. In times of falling sales, should the promotion budget be increased or decreased?

Expert Buyers

Industrial buyers are generally much more knowledgeable regarding the products they purchase than consumers are. In fact, most large companies maintain purchasing departments that are staffed by well-informed, competent people who are responsible for purchasing. These people may be called upon to justify their choices; they are keenly aware of the importance of their decisions. Only by matching the needs of their firm with the quality, price, and service being offered by their suppliers can they be certain of fulfilling their jobs effectively.

The satisfaction of these well-trained buyers requires a particularly knowledgeable salesman. He must have the following characteristics:

1. The ability to present the product intelligently.

2. The capability of furnishing prices and delivery dates on request. This is more difficult than it seems, since many industrial goods are sold on a designed-to-order basis.

3. The knowledge necessary to provide up-to-date information on new research, improvements in methods, and uses in the field.

4. The willingness to give prompt attention to errors in shipment, credits, and other areas of disagreement.

Since orders for industrial goods are generally large and lucrative, suppliers of such goods can afford to hire and train highly skilled men for selling jobs. This is necessary because the qualifications, for sales jobs in the industrial market, are stringent.

Few Buyers

Another peculiarity of the industrial market is the relatively small number of buyers involved. Consider, for example, the small number of producers of automobiles, locomotives, or major household appliances. In the area of basic installations, this is even more pronounced. If Consolidated Edison Company requires a new generator to expand its electrical generating capacity, it can only turn to a handful of producers who are capable of manufacturing such equipment.

An example of the numbers of buyers available to producers of accessory equipment and fabricated parts is found in the fact that General Electric Company produces electric motors for more than two hundred thousand customers, but over 90 percent of its electric motor business is done with its five thousand major customers.

As for operating supplies, it has been estimated that 20 percent of the total market can be reached by calling on slightly more than five hundred of the largest users.

This results in violent competition, encouraged, in part, by the industrial buyers who want to have multiple sources of supply and often seek out new suppliers. Moreover, the many small producers for the industrial market are usually equipped to produce a variety of parts in accordance with customer specifications.

Geographic Concentration

Not only are industrial buyers few in number, they are also highly concentrated geographically. By far the most important manufacturing areas in the United States are clustered in the northeast and Great Lakes regions. There seems to be a trend toward an increase in the manufacturing importance of the South and Far West, but as yet, these changes have had very little effect on the Northeast's manufacturing concentration.

Some types of industrial users have their locations dictated by the source of raw materials; for example, the lumber industry in the Northwest and copper mining in Arizona, Montana, and Utah. Other locations are selected as a compromise so that they offer easy access to both raw materials and large markets. For this reason, there is a high concentration of the steel and automobile industries in the Great Lakes region. When highly trained scientific personnel is a prime business requirement, firms locate at such centers of specialized talent as Long Island, Boston, and the major California cities.

It would seem, then, that business locations are not arbitrarily selected but dictated by a variety of sound business reasons. It is unlikely, therefore, that industrial concentrations will be altered without a change in the economic geography of the country, such as a major population shift or new sources of raw materials.

To the industrial suppliers these concentrations are a blessing, since they reduce distribution expenses. By locating near their geographically clustered market both transportation costs and the expense of maintaining a sales force can be minimized. In turn, the suppliers of the industrial suppliers of the major manufacturers locate in these highly concentrated areas as well. All of this, of course, adds to the density of the manufacturing area.

Quality and Standardization

As the rate of technological advance increases, the importance of high-quality, standardized raw material becomes emphasized. As producers become more scientifically oriented, automatic machinery and highly trained personnel become relatively more important than raw materials. Thus, a highly sophisticated piece of equipment that has been designed to handle a specific type of material in a specific manner is too important in terms of time and money to be forced to remain idle because of poor quality material, or goods that do not meet specifications. In much the same way, any halt in the production line results in the unproductivity of high-priced labor. Production delays are inevitable, but they should never be caused by low-quality materials or goods that do not conform to specified standards.

In some industries, suppliers are able to guarantee quality and standardization with a high degree of certainty. This is not always the case with raw materials. Agricultural products offer a good example. The sugar quantity of grapes is important to wineries. Unfortunately, this cannot be accurately predicted in advance, varying as it does from season to season, farm to farm, and even vine to vine. As a result, wine makers, like many other users of raw materials, must be prepared to make adjustments from the expected quality standard.

On the whole, industrial suppliers, even of raw materials (by testing and sorting) have been able to set realistic standards of quality and conform to them. In industries relying on raw materials, however, quality standards are a source of frequent irritation between the industrial producer and his suppliers.

Reliability of Supply

Just as quality and standardization are important to the industrial market, so too is an uninterrupted supply of goods. Anyone who has anxiously awaited the completion of a building to move his home or office to, and who has seen production come to a complete halt because of a minor unavailable part, understands the problem. Among those industrial producers to whom equipment and labor are expensive and important, the firm supplying the necessary industrial goods is chosen as much for its ability to deliver the goods on time as for any other characteristic.

Often the failure of the source of supply is not the fault of the supplier. Droughts, floods, freezing temperatures, and even strikes may frequently be put into the no-fault category. However, industrial users are frequently willing to pay a premium to large, well-financed suppliers rather than accept similar goods at a reduced price from a weaker competitor. The reasons for this are that enormous losses may be incurred from a forced shutdown because of a failure of the raw-material supply. A minor delay of a few hours causes labor and overhead losses. A cessation that causes a complete production shutdown may lead to cancellation of orders, perhaps permanent loss of customers, and possible loss of a skilled labor force. The dependability of supply is the chief reason for industrial purchasers to refuse to limit their purchases to a single supplier and to be always on the lookout for new sources. Many large users expand vertically (own their raw-material sources) to offset the possibility of shutdowns because of lack of supplies.

INDUSTRIAL BUYING HABITS

To effectively understand the marketing of industrial goods, one must study the habits of industrial buyers. As is the case with all phases of the industrial market, industrial buying habits are different from those of the consumer and relatively unknown to nonmarketers.

Direct Buying

Most consumer goods are not purchased directly from the producer. Instead, they are bought through middlemen, such as wholesalers and retailers, who purchase in large quantities from the producers and sell in smaller quantities to their customers. Although middlemen are important on the industrial scene, they are far less significant than on the consumer market. Both the buyer and the seller of industrial goods benefit from this fact. From the seller's point of view, the concentration of industrial users makes for a small geographic area, easily covered by his salesmen, and the size of the individual industrial order is large enough to warrant a sales force, even to a producer with a limited product line. By cutting out the middleman, the producer is able to use the middleman's profits to increase his own profits and to reduce his selling price. However, the manufacturer must be certain that he can perform as efficiently as the middleman. Direct buying benefits the industrial customer by insuring a close contact with his supplier, on whom he depends for technical information and service.

Large Orders

Basically, the reason for the fact that suppliers of industrial goods are able to sell directly to their customers is that, unlike the consumer-customer who might spend thirty dollars on a buying trip, the industrial purchaser may in one order contract for a full year's supply of goods at a cost of thousands of dollars. Consequently, a salesman making relatively few stops a day can earn a considerable amount of commissions. Because of the size of the individual orders, industrial suppliers cannot afford to lose a sale. Consequently, most suppliers pay well to get capable salesmen, are careful to price competitively, and attempt to be extremely exact in their quality control and delivery dates. To do otherwise would jeopardize a profitable customer who would be difficult to replace in the small industrial market.

Infrequent Purchases

Since orders are usually large, they are also infrequently made. This is particularly true in the case of major installations and accessory equipment designed to last for many years. Although less dramatic, purchases of industrial supplies are not very often made as well because the orders, when given, are large.

The infrequency of purchasing poses a problem to many industrial suppliers, particularly those selling major installations and accessory equipment, of not knowing when the customer is in the "buying mood." This may be somewhat offset by advertising in trade periodicals and maintaining contact through occasional salesman's visits.

Multiple Influence on Purchases

Despite the fact that industrial goods are frequently bought by a purchasing department consisting of specialists, it is unusual for one person, acting alone, to make the purchasing decision. Although the purchase order will certainly be handled by the purchasing agent, he must depend on the people who actually use the equipment or material for advice as to specifications. Commonly, the decision on what to buy is the responsibility of a group of executives that may include production, marketing, and cost-accounting representatives, as well as the purchasing agent.

As far as the marketing of industrial goods is concerned, the salesman who limits his appeal to the purchasing agent alone is likely to miss out. Salesmen of industrial goods must get their product message across to every person who is involved in the purchasing decision. To do this they must fully understand the customer's manufacturing processes and problems, so that they may alter their pitch to fit every interested person.

Extended Negotiations

Since the size of the typical industrial order is very large and the number of people involved in the purchasing decision is considerable, it follows that the period of negotiation preceding a sale, particularly of major installations, is extended. Another reason for the length of negotiations is that many industrial purchases are made according to exact specifications that require many meetings before a perfect understanding between buyer and seller can be reached. Major installations are frequently purchased through competitive bidding. Where contracts are awarded through competitive bidding, negotiations are lengthened to provide time for the bidders to study the problem and prepare their bids.

Reciprocity

Many industrial firms maintain a policy of reciprocity in their purchasing procedures. That is, where possible, they buy only from firms who buy from them. Reciprocity has long been the rule in such basic industries as oil, steel, rubber, chemicals, and machinery. In today's industrial market, reciprocity has become very widespread. Some firms carefully analyze all of their purchases in an attempt to find potential customers who can be pressured into buying their products under the threat of purchase cancellations. Recent times have seen an increase in the use of reciprocity. This is no doubt due to a tightening of the nation's economic conditions, causing producers to search for ways to offset sagging sales volumes. Moreover, the increase in foreign imports is forcing the domestic manufacturers to compete more strongly. Finally, many producers are diversifying their product lines by adding broad lines of new products. Reciprocity both increases the probability that their suppliers can use some of their broad line of product offerings and helps get a new product off the ground.

Generally, purchasing agents oppose reciprocity. They prefer to buy the goods that are best suited to their needs rather than to have to purchase from the suppliers to whom the company sells. However, the pressure placed upon them by the sales department is so great that reciprocity is forced on them. This last argument is somewhat less important than it used to be because in today's market most products are of such a highly standardized quality that an item made by one supplier, who refuses a reciprocal agreement, can be easily produced by another who will accept such an agreement. In the long run reciprocity probably leads to paying higher prices, since the buyer is not shopping for goods in a competitive market.

The small company suffers most from reciprocity. Unable to fight off the demands of its giant customers, it may lose control of its own destiny. Morale losses may result in both the selling force of the small company and the buying department of its customer.

Catalogs

Producers of operating supplies, fabricated parts, repair parts, and many other standardized, low-cost products rely heavily on catalogs to sell their merchandise. There are two types of catalog selling: common catalogs in which the offerings of many companies are listed, and individualized catalogs that are issued by the producer.

An individual catalog can consist of a few pages of products that have been carefully selected from the line, or of an expensive book running to hundreds of pages. The Graham Field Surgical Company, a wholesaler and producer of medical supplies, distributes ten thousand catalogs of three hundred pages each to its customers. The company pays seven dollars for each of the catalogs and delivers them free of charge. The cost is increased by the subsequent mailings of supplementary sheets that are required by constant changes in the line. Finally, a brand new catalog is issued every three years to incorporate the product changes and bring the publication up-to-date. The high catalog cost is necessary, since practically all sales are made by catalog. Salesmen make infrequent visits to customers for the purpose of pushing new items and reminding customers of the firm's existence.

Common catalogs, sometimes referred to as trade directories, are produced by publishing companies. Space in common catalogs is sold to individual suppliers in much the same fashion as advertising space is sold. The information presented in common catalogs is generally limited to the requirements of a particular industry. Examples of such catalogs are the Reinhold Publishing Company's Chemical Engineering and Chemical Materials catalogs.

To point up the importance of catalog use in industrial selling, a study of the purchases of about fourteen hundred products disclosed that 470 of them were made directly by catalog and another 360 of the purchases resulted from leads found in catalogs.

LEASING

There is nothing new in the idea of leasing equipment rather than buying it. Traditionally, shoe-manufacturing machinery (United Shoe Machinery Company), data-processing equipment (IBM), packaging equipment (American Can Company), heavy-construction equipment, and textile equipment have been distributed in this manner. Similarly, locomotives and freight cars have for years been purchased by insurance companies and leased to the railroads. Until recently, however, leasing has been limited to heavy equipment requiring an extensive capital outlay. During the past ten years the idea of leasing has been extended to less-expensive equipment, such as automobiles and trucks. Several major companies have recently come into being whose function it is to buy equipment from manufacturers and lease it to users. Examples of these include the U.S. Leasing Corporation and the National Equipment Leasing Corporation. In addition, such credit companies as the Commercial Credit Corporation and many commercial banks are getting into the act. Current trends seem to indicate a continued expansion of leasing arrangements.

Leasing Advantages—Lessor

Some of the reasons for which equipment producers encourage leasing are:

1. Leasing requires a much smaller capital outlay and thus increases the number of potential customers. Many firms who could not afford to purchase equipment outright are quite capable of living up to the terms of a lease.

2. The total income from a piece of equipment distributed under a leasing arrangement is greater than that received from an outright sale.

3. The continual producer–customer contact results in a close relationship that may affect the purchase of future equipment, operating supplies for the equipment, and service contracts.

4. Leasing, which generally includes service contracts, insures the producer that his equipment will be used to its best advantage. This promotes the possibility of future sales to the customer and goodwill beyond the customer. Many pieces of equipment that are sold outright perform poorly due to inefficient servicing by outsiders. This frequently is damaging to the goodwill of the manufacturer.

5. In the rare instances in which a patent may give the manufacturer a monopoly, leasing brings in far greater profits than could possibly be obtained in an outright sale. Pitney-Bowes postage meters are an example of such a situation.

6. Leasing offers an excellent method of distributing a new, untried product. A prospective customer, unwilling to risk the cost of an outright purchase, might be willing to enter a leasing agreement that may be canceled after a few months if the equipment proves unsatisfactory.

Leasing Advantages—Lessee

The following are the advantages of leasing to the lessee:

1. The smaller financial investment required by a leasing arrangement permits the use of capital for other purposes.

2. There are income-tax savings involved with rentals, since the rent payments (a deductible expense) are usually higher than the depreciation deduction that would be taken on the same equipment if it were owned outright.

3. There is no hesitation in trading-in obsolete equipment when it is rented. Fully owned equipment, particularly when business is slow, is not so quickly replaced.

4. It is to the owner's advantage, since he owns the equipment, to keep it in perfect condition. This guarantees effective servicing.

5. By leasing, a firm can test new equipment with a substantially reduced risk.

6. Where the need for equipment is sporadic, it can be rented only when needed, or paid for only when used.

Leasing Problems

Although many firms reap substantial benefits from leasing rather than purchasing, there are problems involved as well. From the point of view of the lessor, leasing requires an enormous amount of capital, since all of the machines being used by customers belong to him. Secondly, all of the risks of obsolescence, instead of being spread out among many users, fall on the shoulders of the producer of the equipment. The result of these problems are higher machinery costs, which are ultimately passed on to the consumer as higher prices.

PROMOTING INDUSTRIAL GOODS

The promotion of industrial goods differs from that of consumer goods in that there are far fewer, but better-informed potential customers. Industrial buyers are very much interested in quality, price, and the dependability of supply. The advertising aimed at them is usually rational as opposed to emotional. That is, they are more interested in performance than in pretty patterns.

Since the market is small, mass selling is ruled out in favor of direct mail. When media are used, they are generally the trade journals, where technically oriented copy is displayed. Unlike consumer advertising, industrial promotion is not carried on in expectation of a sale, but rather of a lead to be followed up by a salesman.

Prominently featured in many industrial promotions are the research-and-development capabilities of the supplier, his excellent service facilities, and the technical help furnished to his customers.

Trade Shows

Periodically, many industries hold trade shows. They meet once or more a year (frequently in a different city each year) and show their lines. Trade shows offer the manufacturer the opportunity to make contacts with wholesalers and retailers. In addition to showing their wares, trade shows give producers the opportunity to learn of new developments in the industry, introduce new sales personnel, fill personnel needs, and demonstrate new equipment.

In recent years, trade shows have been located in resort cities, where they have become a social as well as a business event. It is likely that trade shows are as important for cementing personal relationships between buyers and sellers as for making actual sales.

IMPORTANT POINTS IN THE CHAPTER

1. The demand for industrial goods is dependent on the demand for the consumer products for which they will be used. Consequently, price has little effect on the demand for industrial goods. This is only true of total demand for a particular industrial product. The price charged by an individual producer for his product will affect

its demand. The demand for industrial goods fluctuates widely with general business conditions.

2. Industrial goods are purchased by expert buyers in a geographically concentrated area. They are much fewer in number than consumer buyers and insist upon quality, standardization, and reliability of supply.

3. Industrial goods are usually bought in infrequent, large lots, directly from the producer. Because of the complexity of the orders, many people are involved in the buying decision and negotiations tend to be extensive.

4. Reciprocity—pressuring suppliers to buy the purchaser's product— is increasing as industrial competition becomes more severe.

5. Producers of operating supplies, fabricated parts, repair parts, and other standardized low-cost products use catalogs to sell their products. The use of catalogs minimizes the need for salesmen.

6. There is a growing trend toward lease of equipment instead of outright purchase. This increases the potential market of equipment producers and reduces the cash outlay of the equipment user.

7. The most important factor in the distribution of industrial goods is personal selling. In addition to the characteristics required by any salesman, the industrial salesman must be technically trained in the area of his product as well as in the problems of his customers. Frequently engineering and scientific skills are required.

8. The promotion of industrial goods is generally limited to rational appeals for leads through direct mail or trade journals. Trade shows offer the industrial producer an opportunity to show his line, stay up-to-date, and socialize with his customers.

REVIEW QUESTIONS

1. Discuss the industrial market in terms of types of goods handled, types of customers, and size.

2. What is derived demand? Differentiate between the derived demand for office supplies and for major installations.

3. Explain the effect of consumer demand on the industrial market in relation to the promotion of industrial goods.

4. A manufacturer of small electric motors for the industrial market must take into account the inelasticity of the demand for his product. How does this affect the total industry? The individual producer?

5. Discuss the fluctuating demand for industrial products. What effect does it have on the marketing of major installations?

6. What characteristics are required for a salesman of industrial products?

7. How can a producer selling his products on the industrial market afford to employ high-priced salesmen for his limited line of products?

8. Explain the reasons for the geographic concentration of the industrial market. How does this affect the distribution of industrial goods?

9. Why are industrial producers willing to pay a premium for high-quality, standardized products?

10. Discuss the standardization problems facing users of raw material. How may these problems be offset?

11. Some producers for the industrial market are able to get higher prices for their products than their competitors despite a similarity of quality. Discuss.

12. Habitually, industrial buyers purchase directly from their suppliers. Why? What are the advantages to the buyer? The seller?

13. Explain the effect of buying in large orders on the marketing of industrial goods. How does this affect the frequency of purchases?

14. What is meant by multiple influence on industrial purchases? What problems does this create in the selling of industrial goods?

15. Define *reciprocity*. What are its advantages and disadvantages to a large firm? A small firm?

16. How are catalogs used on the industrial market? Describe a common catalog and an individualized catalog.

17. Explain the leasing of industrial goods. Give examples. What are the advantages and disadvantages of leasing to the producer of the equipment?

18. Discuss the advantages and disadvantages of leasing to the firm renting the equipment.

19. How are industrial goods promoted?

20. What is a trade show? What are its purposes?

CASE PROBLEMS

Case Problem 1

The Fit-Rite Shoe Manufacturing Corporation has been a manufacturer of high-styled, popular-priced ladies' shoes for the past eight years. During that time, thanks to the superb style selection of the owners, the company has been extremely successful.

Each year's profits after taxes have been reinvested in the business. As a result, Fit-Rite's sales and profits have soared. At the present time the company is an industry leader with a well-earned reputation for style and value.

The extremely rapid growth of the company has required enormous demands on the company's working capital. All profits had to be immediately reinvested in expanded inventories and manufacturing facilities. At times the shortage of cash has been chronic and Fit-Rite has been forced to mortgage its assets and borrow heavily from banks.

At the moment the company's salesmen are bringing in sales far in excess of its production capacity. Undoubtedly further expansion is warranted, but the capital required for such growth is simply not available.

The board of directors of Fit-Rite has been studying a proposal by the American Shoe Machine Manufacturing Corporation to lease the equipment required for the proposed expansion.

Questions

1. What information would be needed to make the leasing decision?
2. What are the advantages and disadvantages of leasing?
3. Should Fit-Rite expand by leasing?

Case Problem 2

The Do-All Supply Company is a producer of plastic containers for the industrial market. Its operation consists of buying plastic in powdered form, adding dyes and certain chemicals, and molding containers to the specifications of its industrial customers. It is located in an industrial area and all of its customers are within a two hundred mile radius of the plant.

Do-All is a family-owned company whose executives consist of a father and two sons. The business is small but very lucrative. Sales are handled by the father, with very little effort, since all customers have been with the firm for many years and a close social relationship exists between the firm and its clients. Orders are usually large, long-term commitments which, thanks to Do-All's reputation for quality, fair prices, service, and dependability, require little negotiation.

Recently, Do-All's largest customer (25 percent of gross sales) was bought out by a large chemical company. The new management has informed Do-All that if its present contracts are renewed, it should buy its raw materials from the new owners. Although the prices charged by the new chemical company are slightly higher than the amount Do-All is presently paying, the profits would still be considerable. In addition, the new company has indicated that if Do-All co-operates, it might also be given business from other units controlled by the new owners.

Questions

1. Discuss the advantages and disadvantages of the new deal.
2. What would you advise?

BIBLIOGRAPHY

Alexander, R. S., J. S. Cross, and R. M. Cunningham, *Industrial Marketing.* Homewood, Ill.: Richard D. Irwin, Inc., 1961.

Bursk, Edward C., "A Rationale for Marketing Growth," *Industrial Marketing,* June, 1966.

Corey, E. R., *Industrial Marketing: Cases and Concepts.* Englewood Cliffs, N.J.: Prentice-Hall, Inc., 1962.

Day, Cameron, "Service: "The 'Something Extra' in Industrial Selling," *Sales Management,* May 15, 1964.

Duncan, Delbert J., "Some Basic Determinants of Behavior in Industrial Purchasing," *Pacific Purchaser,* May–August, 1965.

Hamel, Henry C., and G. Clark Thompson, "Another Look at Leasing," *Business Management Record,* November, 1963.

Industrial Marketing Committee Review Board, "Fundamental Differences between Industrial and Consumer Marketing," *Journal of Marketing,* October, 1954.

Murray, Thomas J., "Systems Selling: Industrial Marketing's New Tool," *Dun's Review,* October, 1964.

Phillips, Charles F., ed., Marketing by Manufacturers. Homewood, Ill.: Richard D. Irwin, Inc., 1946.

"Reciprocity: Dangerous Selling Tool Winning New Users," *Sales Management,* May 20, 1960.

Schon, Donald A., "The New Regionalism," *Harvard Business Review,* January–February, 1966.

Webster, Frederick E., "The Industrial Salesman as a Source of Market Information," *Business Horizons,* Spring, 1965.

CHANNELS OF DISTRIBUTION

6

TYPICAL CHANNELS

Convenience Goods and Staples

Impulse Goods

Emergency Goods

Shopping Goods

Industrial Equipment

Agricultural Products

Raw Materials

Maintenance Supplies

MANAGING THE CHANNEL

Gravity

Pull

Push

Channel Cooperation
CONSUMER GOODS
INDUSTRIAL GOODS

The Channel Captain

Frequent Channel Evaluation

IMPORTANT POINTS IN THE CHAPTER

REVIEW QUESTIONS

CASE PROBLEMS

BIBLIOGRAPHY

INTRODUCTION

A channel of distribution is a route over which goods move from the producer to the user. In a simple society producer and consumer are in close proximity to each other. As the society becomes more complex, moving goods from producers to widely dispersed users becomes complicated and channels must be set up to insure an economic flow of produced goods from the manufacturer to his market.

ECONOMIC IMPORTANCE OF MARKETING CHANNELS

Market channels play a far more important role than the mere transporting of goods from producers to users. The economic functions of the various institutions that make up a channel are cost reduction, financing, cooperation in setting prices, communications' link between buyer and user, promotional assistance, and reduction of the number of transactions.

Cost Reductions

Setting up an efficient, working channel has the effect of reducing costs by establishing automatic systems for supplying goods to customers. For example, a greeting-card manufacturer whose channel of distribution includes R. H. Macy & Co., Inc. is not required to send salesmen to the store after the channel has been established. When Macy's greeting-card stock is low in a particular number, an automatic reorder is placed via a punched-card system. The salesman's calls are in this way restricted to showing new cards that have been added to the line.

Cost reduction also results from established channels through specialization. Essentially, the effect of the marketing channel is that the total producing, distributing effort is broken down into separate functions. Individual channel members who deal in one specific phase of distribution are able to devote all their energies to their own area of responsibility, thereby increasing their efficiency. In general an agent-middleman who is chiefly responsible for selling can set up a better sales force than an institution that has many other functions besides selling.

Financing

Channel members play an important role in helping to finance the entire product-distribution effort. Most successful businesses need financial help in order to expand or pay a return to their investors. They are required to tie up large sums of money in inventories and accounts receivable (money due from customers). By setting up channels, the producer can share the burden of this capital requirement with the various channel members. In the ladies' shoe business, for example, a large inventory must be carried from which customer's orders may be quickly filled. The manufacturer who sells to a wholesaler who in turn sells to retailers, shares the financial burden (and risk) of carrying the necessary inventory with the other channel members. Of course, he shares the profits from the total operation with them as well.

In some cases, wholesalers buy a manufacturer's total production and pay promptly. The wholesaler then resells the merchandise, giving long-term credit. In such instances, the wholesaler is helping to finance the producer by taking over the financial burden of extending long-term credit to customers.

Cooperation in Setting Prices

Channel members in a distributive system have an important effect on user prices. The selling price of a product is usually cooperatively determined by the various channel members, who are in much closer contact with the customers and more familiar with the competition than the producer. In addition, the final price must be set at a level at which it will provide each channel member with a fair share of the total profit. In a channel distributive system, the difference between the selling price and the cost of a product is split up among the various channel members.

Communications Link

As a producer grows in size, contact with the final user of his product diminishes. The other members of the channel, particularly those that come in contact with the user, act as an intelligence network for feeding information on style changes, prices, and competitor actions back to the producer. Without this feedback, many producers would lose their competitive position in the market.

Promotional Assistance

Since the retailer is the channel member who is in direct contact with customers, he is generally the most effective advertiser and promoter of goods. Normally, other channel members advertise to achieve product or brand familiarity, but the retailer's advertising display and promotional activities are concerned with the actual sale. Producers are aware of this and see to it that the share of channel profits going to the retailer is adequate to cover promotional costs. In addition, many producers give advertising allowances and outright cash to encourage retailers to advertise their products. In the clothing industry, the cost of the expensive catalogs that department stores send to their customers before the holiday season is often paid for by the producers whose merchandise appears in the brochure.

Reduction of the Number of Transactions

If there were no channels of distribution and every producer sold directly to retailers, the number of transactions would be many times greater than it is at present. This would enormously increase the costs of record keeping and transportation, and ultimately the cost of goods to the consumer. The insertion of the middleman into the channel greatly simplifies ordering. This wholesaler may carry the lines of many manufacturers from whom he receives goods in large lots. The middleman's subsequent sale to the retailer will include the offerings of several producers. The retailer then receives the goods from all these sources in a single order and shipment, rather than individually ordering and receiving from each manufacturer.

CONSUMER CHANNELS

There are many choices of channels. A marketer can select the one that is best suited to the characteristics of his product and his other requirements. The most widely used six channels for distribution of goods to the retail consumer are:

Producer ───────────────────────────────────► consumer
Producer ─────────────────► producer-owned retailer ───────────► consumer
Producer ─────────────────► franchised retailer ───────────► consumer
Producer ─────────────────► independent retailer ───────────► consumer
Producer ───────────► wholesaler ───────────► retailer ───────────► consumer
Producer ───────────► agent-middleman ───────────► retailer ───────► consumer

Producer to Consumer

Producers of goods may reach the retail consumer directly by two methods of selling: door-to-door salespersons (Avon Products, Fuller Brush) and direct mail (many small manufacturers). Direct selling to the consumer has these advantages for the manufacturer:

1. Ability to control selling, since the sales force is directly under the producer's supervision.

2. Close relationship to the consumer makes the manufacturer constantly aware of style changes and other consumer needs.

3. Profits do not go to middlemen.

4. Goods get to the consumer more quickly because they do not have to travel through middlemen.

5. Certainty that the sales force is properly trained if technical knowledge is required to sell the product.

Despite these apparent advantages, it is probable that less than 3 percent of total consumer sales are made in this manner. Some of the reasons for this are:

1. The effort and expense of training, maintaining, and supervising a large sales staff.

2. The difficulty of providing and maintaining inventories of goods at many locations to assure prompt delivery to customers.

3. The enormous cost of financing and high risk involved in carrying multiple inventories and customer credit that would otherwise be shared by channel members.

Producer to Producer-Owned Retailer to Consumer

Manufacturers such as Singer Sewing Machines, Castro Convertibles, and Thom McAn Shoes maintain their own retail outlets for reasons similar to those indicated above.

Producer to Franchised Retailer to Consumer

Moving goods to the consumer through franchised dealerships is an old idea that has grown in importance since World War II. Because of the great variety of franchising agreements it is difficult to define a franchise. It is estimated that there are between fifteen hundred and two thousand companies offering franchising deals, and each company's contract is different. The broadest definition is given by the Small Business Administration:

> A franchise contract is a legal agreement to conduct a given business in accordance with prescribed operating methods, financing systems, territorial domains, and commission fees. It holds out the offer of individual ownership while following proven management practices. The holder is given the benefit of the franchiser's experience and help in choice of location, financing, marketing, record keeping, and promotional techniques. The business starts out with an established product or service reputation. It is organized and operated with the advantage of "name" and standardization.

This definition contains a large amount of information. However, all franchising agreements do not include every item mentioned. For example, many franchisers make their profit by selling the product to the franchisee, others profit by charging a commission on all franchisee sales.

The parent company benefits from a franchise operation as a means of distributing goods in many important aspects.

1. The franchisee, by supplying a large amount of the capital needed for building new units, permits rapid expansion without decreasing the ownership of the company (as would be the case if capital were to be raised by the sale of stock).

2. A serious problem faced by expanding companies is finding management with the proper ambition. In franchising, each unit manager is in business for himself with his own capital to protect and future to insure; thus, he is vitally interested in success and anxious to operate efficiently and profitably to protect his cash investment.

3. Overhead is reduced, since managers need not be hired, and franchisees do not require the close supervision that is necessary in units operated by disinterested managers.

4. The chance of success of an outlet owned by a local person is greater than one owned by a distant, impersonal corporation. The community is more likely to accept a product sold to them by one of their own.

An example of the economic advantage available to the franchiser is the fact that in the first three years in which Kentucky Fried Chicken published their quarterly earnings, every quarter showed an increase of 80 to 100 percent over the same period of the preceding year.

Producer to Independent Retailer to Consumer

Although there are disadvantages involved in a distributive system that runs directly from a manufacturer to an independent retailer, this method is widely used for certain types of products. Among the goods that are frequently sold in this way are:

1. Fashion merchandise, for which the time lost in distributing through middlemen is an important factor.

2. High-value goods whose markup offsets the additional distributing costs to the manufacturer.

3. Goods sold in large-quantity individual orders, which minimizes transportation costs.

4. Products requiring installation.

Producer to Wholesaler to Retailer to Consumer

The most common method of distribution is one in which the producer sells to the wholesaler who, in turn, sells to the retailer who sells to the consumer. In this channel system, the wholesaler is granted a part of the total profit, in return for which he buys, stores, sells, delivers, and extends credit. It is not unusual for a producer who sells through wholesalers to reserve the right to sell directly to certain classes of retailers.

Producer to Agent-Middleman to Retailer to Consumer

The function of an agent-middleman is to buy or sell merchandise for clients. Agricultural products are examples of goods that are bought and sold by agent-middlemen. The buying or selling may be for wholesale or retail clients.

It should be understood that the channels of distribution available to producers are not limited to those listed above. For example, a bushel of apples grown in the state of Washington goes through seven channel members before reaching a New York consumer:

Grower→cooperative→broker→auctioneer→wholesaler→retailer→ consumer.

INDUSTRIAL CHANNELS

The channels of distribution used for goods sold to industrial users are generally much shorter than the channels required to get merchandise to consumers. Most industrial products follow one of the following four routes:

Manufacturer————————————————————————→industrial user
Manufacturer————————→ industrial distributor ————————→industrial user
Manufacturer————————→ selling agent ————————→industrial user
Manufacturer————————→selling agent→industrial distributor ————————→industrial user

Manufacturer to Industrial User

The greatest dollar volume of industrial goods is channeled directly from the manufacturer or producer to the industrial user. This is particularly true for products requiring large capital expenditures such as generators, heating plants, and major construction.

Producer to Industrial Distributor to Industrial User

Operating supplies and accessory equipment are generally channeled through an industrial distributor before arriving at the industrial users place. These are relatively small, inexpensive products, such as small electric motors, building materials, air conditioning equipment, and maintenance supplies.

Producer to Selling Agent to Industrial User

Producers that do not maintain their own marketing departments frequently turn this function over to a selling agent. Industrial goods, piece goods, and other textiles and groceries are often marketed in this manner.

Producer to Selling Agent to Industrial Distributor to Industrial User

This channel also is used by producers who do not maintain their own marketing departments. The inclusion of an industrial distributor is necessary when a wide dispersion of inventory is required to insure rapid supplies to users. Industrial distributors are then needed to store the product and service many small-order customers.

Industrial channels are simpler than consumer channels for the following reasons:

1. Since the selling of industrial goods frequently requires technical know-how on the part of the salesman, the manufacturer must have adequate control over the sales force. The shorter the channel length, the more effective the manufacturer's control over selling.

2. Orders for industrial goods are generally large. This reduces shipping costs, clerical order handling, and the number of salesmen required. Because these are among the most important functions of a middleman, he can be eliminated.

3. Much industrial selling is specially designed to fit the requirements of a specific customer. This reduces the capital invested in finished goods. Inventories and middlemen are not needed for assistance in this function.

4. The industrial market is usually clustered into a small geographic area, which permits the producer to service his customers with a relatively small sales force. As a result industrial channels are generally shorter.

HOW TO SELECT A CHANNEL

There are a number of factors that must be considered when a channel of distribution is to be selected. Many choices are available, so that a careful study is required before a decision can be reached that will fit the problems of the specific institution to the best channel of distribution. Some of the guidelines are:

1. Study the channels that are available, particularly those used by competitors.

2. Determine the channel that will best match the characteristics of the product to be marketed.

3. Estimate the probable demand for the product.

4. Consider the available financial resources.

5. Approximate the costs, sales, and profits for each available channel.

6. Determine the size of the product line and the amount of a typical order.

Study of Available Channels

It is rare to find a product so new that no similar product is being distributed. Before making a distribution decision, the channels of distribution being used by similar products should be studied. The distribution procedures used by competitors require careful analysis to determine their adequacy, profitability, cost, and effectiveness.

The present trend toward broadening retail offerings has complicated channel selection. There are no longer clear indications of product channel requirements. Twenty years ago, a drug manufacturer distributed through channels whose salesmen called on drugstores. At present, drug items are sold in supermarkets, variety stores, department stores, and door-to-door. Since each system requires a somewhat different channel, it is commonplace to move the same item through several different distributional channels.

Characteristics of the Product

Goods may be broadly classified into two areas; wholesale and retail. Within each classification further breakdowns may be made into more specific categories. In the determination of the type of channel to be used the distributional requirements of the specific item to be sold are perhaps most significant. The characteristics of each product are unique and the manner in which it is distributed should be based on its necessities. For example, perishables must get to the consumer quickly. The same is true of fashion merchandise. Heavy equipment, whose installation requires a technology that only the manufacturer can provide, must be sold directly. Seasonal goods, which require large investments in inventory, may need middlemen to help with the financial burden.

Although the nature of the goods dictates their channel treatment, other considerations must also be taken into account. The financing of large inventories can be done through wholesalers, but this is not mandatory for a manufacturer with ample funds. Again, it is not impossible for the producer of heavy equipment to find a distributor-middleman whose staff has the know-how to handle the installation problems, or perhaps the middleman can sell the equipment and the responsibility for installation can remain with the manufacturer.

Estimate of Probable Demand

Since the function of the channel is to get the goods to the customer, the channel must be based upon the customer, his habits, and his convenience. A product that is retailed only in hardware stores *must* be sold in hardware stores and if the manufacturer is unable to economically sell to such stores, he must set up a channel that will include wholesalers who distribute to hardware retailers. On the wholesale scene, manufacturers who habitually buy manufacturing supplies, along with other merchandise, from supply houses, are unlikely to change their procedures to buy a particular type of supplies directly from the producer.

The geographical location of the market is important. The producer of a product that is to be distributed nationally must weigh the decision to market through wholesalers or to set up and maintain a nationwide network of distribution centers.

Financial Resources

The system of distribution used by many firms is dictated by their financial resources. Small firms, of limited financial strength, are often forced to select channels by cost rather than by effectiveness. Frequently, weak producers select channels for the financial help they get in carrying inventories and extending credit. It is not unusual for a financially strong wholesaler to lend money to a manufacturer to insure the continuation of high production.

Approximation of Costs, Sales, and Profits

In a highly competitive market, the price the final user of the product will pay depends more on the market than on the wishes of the producer. The channel profit, the difference between the producer's cost to manufacture and the selling price paid by the user, is available for distributing the product and return on investment for the producer and the various institutions that make up the distributive channel. Various channel members demand various shares of this profit. Consequently, the makeup of the channel depends in large part on the approximate amount of profits available in the product. For example, if the difference between the cost to produce the item and the selling price to the user is 40 percent, the channel selected must be one whose members are willing to perform their functions for a share of the 40 percent. Each channel member is paid according to the function he performs. A food broker, whose responsibility is limited to selling, is paid 2 to 5 percent of sales. General-line grocery wholesalers who store goods, give credit, deliver, and sell, operate on approximately 10 percent of sales. Which channel the product can afford can be determined by approximating the cost, selling price, and profitability of the item.

Size of the Line and Amount of a Typical Order

As a rule, middlemen can be eliminated when a salesman can make a living carrying the product. A salesman can make a limited number of calls per day. If the typical order is too small to pay for his salary, middlemen, whose sales force carries many products, must be used. Orders increase in size as the size of the line and the selling price per unit increase. Manufacturers of extensive lines of merchandise or high-priced merchandise are more likely to have their own sales force than single-product, low-priced producers.

INTENSITY OF DISTRIBUTION

After the channels of distribution have been determined, a manufacturer must decide upon the number of members he should install at each level of distribution. This can be thought of as the degree of intensity with which he wants his product to be marketed. Although there are many degrees in between, this topic can best be discussed in terms of intensive (mass) distribution, selective distribution, and exclusive distribution.

Intensive Distribution

Highly competitive convenience goods—for which customers will not go out of their way to buy and for which substitutes are readily available—require maximum exposure and mass distribution. Goods such as cigarettes, candy, and toothpaste should be placed in every available outlet. Since the extent of distribution is vast, merchant wholesalers are an absolute necessity.

Selective Distribution

Selective distribution is the practice of distributing through a carefully selected channel in each geographical area. By carefully choosing the institutions through which the goods reach the consumer, many advantages may be effected:

1. The placing of goods in certain high-reputation stores can increase sales. A manufacturer whose goods are handled by the R. H. Macy chain of department stores stands a good chance that his merchandise will get excellent market exposure. (It should be noted that Macy's does not sucessfully promote every one of the lines it carries.)

2. Selectivity can reduce credit risks by limiting sales to those stores that are financially secure.

3. By limiting the accounts to be sold, marketing costs are reduced. Since the shipments are larger and fewer, transportation costs drop. In

addition, fewer customers mean fewer salesmen. Selling only to retail leaders who advertise extensively reduces the producer's advertising costs.

4. Most firms that distribute their products on a selective basis feel that the small loss in gross sales resulting from this system is more than offset by a considerable increase in profits.

The chief disadvantage of selective distribution is the difficulty most firms have in getting the desired high-volume, prestigious retailers to handle their lines. Obviously, every household-appliance manufacturer would like Nieman-Marcus of Dallas to handle his products, but not every line can be accommodated by them.

Another problem faced by producers who distribute exclusively through major retailing outlets is loss of control. The producers who sell to R. H. Macy & Co., Inc. must be prepared to extend maximum service, give prompt delivery, make large advertising allowances, adopt a liberal returned-merchandise policy, and perform all the special services demanded by a powerful channel member.

Exclusive Distribution

Exclusive distributorships are granted by some manufacturers to wholesalers and retailers. It is a guarantee by the wholesaler that he will not sell his product to any competitor in the area. In return, it is common for the distributor to agree not to handle any competitive lines. Exclusive distribution has the effect of including the dealer as part of the producer's organization. Generally, exclusive distribution either on the wholesale or retail level is awarded to the channel member in compensation for some specific service he performs. For example, an automobile agency requires a large capital investment. It is doubtful that anyone would make such an outlay without exclusive distributional rights. Other exclusive distributions are given in return for large advertising guarantees or the right to be carried by a high-volume distributor.

Examples of exclusive distribution may be found among marketers of such products as farm equipment, women's apparel (L'Aiglon), and television manufacturers (Magnavox).

The following are some of the advantages to the dealer who is granted an exclusive distributorship:

1. The product is only carried in his area by his store, so all benefits of promotion and advertising accrue to him.

2. The service and repair-parts inventory is set up exclusively for one product line. As a result, the service department is efficient, which adds to his good will.

3. The absence of competitors carrying the line minimizes competition and price cutting.

4. The importance of his business to the producer is so great that he may expect maximum cooperation.

5. The total inventory is reduced, since only one line is carried.

The disadvantages of being granted an exclusive dealership are: loss of business in competing products and losing the line, after heavy investment, if the sales volume does not satisfy the granter of the exclusive distributorship.

The granter of the distributorship has the advantage of placing his product in the hands of a dealer who does not handle any competitive goods. The result is more aggressive selling, better customer service, and retail-price maintenance. Moreover, since the number of accounts that must be serviced is reduced, marketing and clerical costs are also smaller.

Obviously not all goods can be marketed through exclusive distributorships. Some merchandise is not important enough to be granted exclusive rights. Convenience goods, for example, need maximum exposure. Generally, at the retail level, specialty merchandise, men's clothing, and products such as automobiles that require special services or large investments are marketed exclusively. Industrial goods that are sold under exclusive dealerships are those that require installation and service, such as farm equipment, turbines, and furnaces.

TYPICAL CHANNELS

Although the producer has many variations of channels available to him, the specific channel used is generally determined by the type of goods being marketed. The following is a broad classification of merchandise and the typical channels through which such goods are marketed.

Convenience Goods and Staples

Since convenience goods, particularly staples, require intensive distribution over a widely dispersed market, middlemen are always found in the channels that distribute such goods. The goods are generally uncomplicated and require no installation or service. Intensive promotion of such goods is usually taken up by the producer. Various middlemen store, break bulk, and sell to retailers who, in turn, sell to consumers with little more sales effort than shelf arrangement and display.

Impulse Goods

Impulse goods are those products that are bought on the spur of the moment, without previous planning. A soft drink or an ice-cream cone are typical of such merchandise. Impulse goods must be prominently displayed and promoted to be sold. They require aggressive middlemen and retailing activity. Frequently middlemen can not be found to push the article to the producer's satisfaction, so he will use his own salesmen to sell direct to retailers.

Emergency Goods

Emergency goods, since they must be available at all times, require wide distribution and availability. The channels of such goods must include all-night service stations, vending machines, and other outlets that are open on late hours and holidays.

Shopping Goods

Items such as high-grade clothing, furniture, and appliances, which are subject to price and style comparisons by shoppers, are called shopping goods. Like for all goods that require aggressive selling and promotion, the channel must be designed to keep the producer as close as possible to the retailer. At best, shopping goods should be channeled directly from the producer to the retailer. This close contact results in better retail promotion, feedback on styling, and technical information to the retail sales force.

Industrial Equipment

Industrial equipment is usually channeled directly from the producer to the user. The sales are few and large and the technical training required for selling, installation, and service requires the salesman to be controlled directly by the producer.

Agricultural Products

Agricultural products require many middlemen. The harvests of many small farmers must be collected, sorted, and in some cases processed before they can be sold at retail. This requires the efforts of many brokers and agent-middlemen.

Raw Materials

Raw materials generally have few producers and users; both are large and well financed. Consequently, there is no necessity for middlemen in the marketing channels of these goods. They are usually marketed directly from the producer to the user.

Maintenance Supplies

Essentially, maintenance supplies are industrial convenience goods. There are many widely dispersed customers who buy in relatively small quantities and rarely require technical help. It is an area in which such middlemen as office-supply stores and mill-supply houses are very active.

MANAGING THE CHANNEL

The success or failure of a marketing channel depends not only on the choice of channels and the effectiveness of the channel members but on certain channel policies as well.

Gravity

Gravity is a policy of putting goods into the channel and then letting nature take its course. It is based on the theory that there is an economic need for the goods, and after the product is placed in the channel, it will find its way to the consumer. This policy is typically used by the small producer. The farmer sells his wheat to a wheat elevator and forgets it. The small manufacturer sells to a jobber and drops out of the picture.

Pull

A better operation may result when pull is added to gravity. Pull is a policy in which the product is pulled through the channel by applying suction at the consumer end. Branding, consumer advertising, and premiums are examples of pull. The successful use of consumer advertising can result in a demand for a product that will make retailers and wholesalers extremely anxious to handle the product. This may increase the channel opportunities open to the producer and improve his control over the channel members.

Push

Push is a policy of improving channel operation by putting pressure on the channel members to sell more effectively. Unlike pull, which appeals to the ultimate consumer, push is directed at channel members. Push may be applied through cooperative advertising, missionary men to aid the distributor's sales force, manufacturer's representatives, called detail men, sales promotional materials, and window trimming. In the pharmaceutical field detail men visit doctors and hospitals, distributing samples and literature to influence prescription writing, even though the product will be sold through wholesalers.

Channel Cooperation

The effectiveness of any channel of distribution can be improved by the amount of cooperation the producer gives his channel members.

CONSUMER GOODS. The following are instances typical of the manufacturer's cooperation with channel members:

1. Johnson & Johnson maintains a sales training program for drugstore sales personnel.

2. Chrysler Airtemp runs an annual workshop on distributor operations.

3. The Maytag Company has a program designed to aid customers in reconditioning and selling trade-ins.

4. General Electric conducts a school for repairmen.

5. Rexall Drug gives their retail outlets help in store design, fixture planning, merchandising, and financing.

INDUSTRIAL GOODS. Manufacturer's assistance to channel members in the marketing of industrial goods is generally limited to advertising and training programs such as service, installation, and sales.

The Channel Captain

It should not be assumed that the channel captain of every distribution line is the manufacturer. The strongest institution in the channel generally assumes all interchannel responsibilities. When Sears selects a factory to manufacture a line of appliances to be sold under the Kenmore brand name, that manufacturer has no responsibility other than production.

Frequent Channel Evaluation

The changing business environment requires frequent channel evaluation. Not only must the individual channel members be checked in terms of costs and sales quotas but the total system must be studied as well. New types of wholesale and retail establishments and the services performed by old ones are always changing. It is not uncommon for marketers to work diligently to set up an excellent channel and stay with it long after it has become obsolete.

IMPORTANT POINTS IN THE CHAPTER

1. A channel of distribution is a system through which goods move from the producer to the user. The channel serves an economic need, since it reduces marketing costs, helps to finance the marketing system, and acts as a communications link between the producer and the user.

2. There is a wide variety of channels available; the type selected depends, in large part, on the characteristics of the goods and the financial strength of the producer.

3. Generally, the more expensive, technical, and highly styled the goods, the shorter the channel. The reason for this is that such goods require the producer to be in close contact with the user. Industrial goods usually have shorter channels than consumer goods.

4. The choice of a specific channel must be based upon distinctive qualities of the merchandise, estimates of the probable demand, channels that are available, approximation of sales, costs, and profits, number of items in the line, size of a typical order, and financial resources.

5. The intensity of distribution (the number of channel members at each level of distribution) can be intensive, selective, or exclusive.

6. The producer can influence the flow of goods through a channel by a policy of gravity (put the goods into the channel and let nature take its course), pull (promote the goods to the final consumer and have his demand act as suction to pull the goods through the channel), and push (apply pressure to the channel members to improve their selling and promotion efforts).

7. The changing enconomic scene requires frequent review of channel operations.

REVIEW QUESTIONS

1. Define *channels of distribution* and explain the reasons for their existence.

2. Explain the part channels of distribution play in the financing of a marketing system.

3. Discuss channels of distribution as a communications link between the producer and the user of his merchandise.

4. Producers who sell directly to consumers use one of three methods. Discuss and give examples of each method.

5. Define *franchising* and give examples of franchisees.

6. What are the disadvantages of direct producer-to-consumer selling?

7. Discuss the type of goods that generally go directly from the producer to the independent retailer.

8. Explain the function of an agent-middleman in the buying and selling of agricultural products.

9. Why is an estimate of the demand for a product important to the selection of the channel that is to distribute it?

10. Discuss the importance of the size of the product line to channel decisions.

11. What effect does a company's financial condition have on its choice of channels?

12. Explain the effect on distributive channels of such changes as the sale of drugs in supermarkets.

13. Why is the approximation of a product's profit an important consideration in channel selection?

14. Define, discuss, and give examples of *exclusive distribution*.

15. What are the advantages and disadvantages to the dealer of selective distribution?

16. What are the advantages and disadvantages to the retailer of exclusive distribution?

17. What channels of distribution would you expect to find for distributing raw materials? Agricultural products? Why?

18. Define the policy of *gravity* as the term is used in marketing.

19. Give examples of the type of cooperation one might expect to find between a producer and other channel members.

20. Why should channels of distribution be constantly evaluated?

CASE PROBLEMS

Case Problem 1

The Cure-All Manufacturing Company manufactures a line of non-prescription medications, such as aspirins and cold remedies. The company has been in business for many years with great success and the brand name is important in the industry. The product is channeled through wholesale and retail druggists.

Because the brand is well known, most supermarkets carry the product. To obtain the product line, supermarket buyers are forced to go to wholesale druggists, since their normal suppliers, the food wholesalers, do not carry Cure-All products. This is an inconvenience to the supermarkets; they could cut down on their transportation, handling, and clerical costs if they were able to order the line with their regular merchandise from their regular suppliers.

Women seem to prefer buying the products at supermarkets because they are there often. Drugstore purchases frequently require an extra trip.

It is apparent that the line should be distributed through food wholesalers. This would probably increase sales, since many small grocers who do not carry the product now would take then in the line.

Questions

1. What channels of distribution should be set up to reach the food trade?

2. It has been suggested that the most promising one hundred food wholesalers out of the two thousand available in the directory should be chosen and given exclusive territories in which to sell the line. What is your opinion?

Case Problem 2

The Wing Ski Corporation is a manufacturer of metal skis. When the item was first produced, it was exclusively distributed through the major ski shop in every geographical area. This worked out very well, since metal skis were a new idea requiring the promotional help that only the leading retailers could supply. Both Wing Ski and its exclusive retailers prospered.

As the sport increased in popularity, many new ski shops opened. They needed a metal-ski line and turned to Wing, the leader in the field. Wing remained loyal to its dealers who had helped build its success and refused to sell to the new retailers. This gave Glide-Ease, a competitor in metal skis, the opportunity to take over a large share of the market. Glide-Ease manufactures a somewhat lower quality line that is sold at a price at which it gives excellent value.

The sport has become ever more popular in recent years and Wing Ski has increased its volume and profits each year. Naturally, this profit is considerably less than it would be if Glide-Ease were not in the picture.

Questions

1. Did Wing Ski make an error?
2. What alternatives are available to Wing Ski?
3. Does Wing Ski have a moral responsibility to its dealers?

BIBLIOGRAPHY

American Marketing Association, *The Values and Uses of Distribution Cost Analysis.* Chicago: American Marketing Association, 1957.

Berg, Thomas L., "Designing The Distribution System," from *The Social Responsibilities of Marketing.* Chicago: American Marketing Association, 1962.

Cox, Reavis, *Distribution in a High-Level Economy.* Englewood Cliffs, N.J.: Prentice-Hall, Inc., 1965.

"Distribution Channels for Small Manufacturers," *The Small Business Reporter,* May, 1951.

"Distribution Getting Increased Attention from Top Companies," *Marketing Insights,* March 6, 1967.

Feder, R. D., D. F. Blankertz, and S. Hollander, Jr., "Channel Research," in *Marketing Research.* New York: The Ronald Press Company, 1964.

"How Companies are Cutting Distribution Costs," *Business Week,* May 1, 1965.

Mallen, Bruce, E., ed., *The Marketing Channel—A Conceptual Viewpoint.* New York: John Wiley & Sons, Inc., 1967.

McCammon, Bert C., Jr., and Robert W. Little, "Marketing Channels: Analytical Systems and Approaches," in George Swarz, ed., *Science in Marketing.* New York: John Wiley & Sons, Inc., 1965.

McCarthy, E. J., and R. J. Williams, "Simulation of Production—Marketing Channels," in Raymond E. Haas, ed., *Science Technology and Marketing.* Chicago: American Marketing Association, 1967.

McVey, Phillip, "Are Channels of Distribution What the Textbooks Say," *Journal of Marketing,* January, 1960.

Murray, Thomas J., "Dual Distribution vs. the Small Retailer," *Dun's Review and Modern Industry,* 1968.

Preston, Lee E., and Arthur E. Schramm, Jr., "Dual Distribution and Its Impact on Marketing Organization," *California Marketing Review,* Vol. 8, No. 2 (Winter, 1965).

"Selecting and Evaluating Distributors," *Studies in Business Policy, No. 116.* New York: National Industrial Conference Board, 1965.

MARKETING RESEARCH

7

INTRODUCTION

Decision making and problem solving are probably the most important aspects of marketing management. Should a new soft beverage be packaged in a reusable or disposable container? Will the addition of a new compact car to an automobile manufacturer's line find a new market to increase overall company sales, or will it cut into sales of the company's other, established models? In the late 1950s Corning Glass was faced with many problems concerning its prospective new product, Corning ware. One major problem was the effect on Corning's already successful line of Pyrex. One decision that had to be reached was whether or not to associate the new product with the Pyrex name, thereby possibly jeopardizing Pyrex's position, or to market Corning ware separately. It is quite obvious that in order to intelligently make such decisions a good deal of information is needed by marketers. Marketing research, broadly defined, involves investigation of marketing problems and formulation of the necessary recommendations to solve these problems. *Market research* and *marketing research,* although often used interchangeably, are actually different and should not be substituted for each other. *Marketing research* refers to the investigation of *all* marketing problems, whereas *market research* deals exclusively with problems associated with markets.

Marketing research had its formal beginning in the early 1900s. Throughout the years, businesses, having realized the value of the dollars spent for research in terms of improving their marketing positions, continue to increase their expenditures for marketing research. Companies spend millions of dollars each year to have those questions answered that will improve the chance success of their companies and products. Although, from every indication, marketers will continue to increase their research expenditures, it should be understood that even with extensive marketing-research programs some products have failed in the past and others will do so in the future. One need only to look to the Ford Motor Company's Edsel as an example. The Edsel and a number of other well-known marketing mistakes will be examined in Chapter 18.

CLASSIFICATION OF MARKETING RESEARCH ACTIVITIES

Research is not confined to a specific aspect of marketing but is part of every marketing function. Only a few very large businesses, doing upwards of one hundred million dollars of sales volume, have formally organized research departments equipped to deal with all the areas that require examination. Smaller companies, although able to research some specific areas, call upon private marketing-research companies if extensive investigation is necessary. Generally, the following classifications include all the activities of research.[1]

1. Research on Products and Services
   a. Customer acceptance of proposed new products
   b. Comparative studies of competitive products
   c. Evaluating competitive product developments
   d. Determining present users of present products
   e. Evaluating proposed new products or services
   f. Market tests or test market activities
   g. Determining sources of customer dissatisfaction
   h. Seeking new uses of present products
   i. Product line simplification
   j. Packaging studies
2. Research on Markets
   a. Competitive position of company products
   b. Analysis of market size
   c. Estimating demand for new products
   d. Sales forecasting
   e. Determining characteristics of markets
   f. Analysis of territorial potentials
   g. Studying trends in market size
   h. General business forecasting
   i. Studying relative market profitability
   j. Studying economic factors
   k. Studying shifts in market composition
   l. Changes in consumer-type importance
3. Research on Sales Methods and Policies
   a. Establishing or revising sales territories
   b. Measuring variation in territorial yield
   c. Evaluating present sales methods
   d. Competitive pricing studies
   e. Analysis of salesmen's activities
   f. Price studies
   g. Appraising proposed sales methods
   h. Measuring salesmen's effectiveness
   i. Distribution cost studies
   j. Setting sales quotas
   k. Development of salesmen's standards

[1] Richard D. Crisp, Research Study No. 35, *Organization and Operation* (New York: American Management Association, 1958).

      l. Sales compensation
     m. Effectiveness of promotional devices
4. Research on Advertising
     a. Advertising effectiveness
     b. Competitive advertising and selling prices
     c. Motivational or qualitative studies
     d. Selecting media

Although marketing institutions differ in their research emphasis, it is generally agreed that research on markets receives the greatest amount of attention from marketers. Without the determination of significant market information it is unlikely that marketing managers can proceed to any other marketing activities.

MARKETING RESEARCH EXAMPLES

In order to make the foregoing list more meaningful to marketing students, a specific example of a marketing-research problem will be discussed under each major classification.

Research on Products and Services

A well-known manufacturer of cookware was contemplating the addition of an electric coffee maker to its line of products. The company's design team developed many different styles, from which one was to be selected for production. Management narrowed the field down to two models. They then assigned the task to determine which one would be the most successful to their marketing-research department. The research staff felt the best-qualified person to make the ultimate decision should be the user of the product, the housewife. Briefly, the main approach employed in solving the problem was as follows: a test market (a city, town, and so on, with a population considered typical of the manufacturer's entire market) was selected and a number of housewives were chosen to use both coffee makers in their homes for a specified period of time. At the end of the time period each housewife completed a questionnaire that provided meaningful information with which a final choice could be made by the company. After tabulating this data (and measuring many other factors) the company decided upon the model they would market.

Research on Markets

A real estate developer tentatively decided upon a site on which to build a shopping center. From the real estate man's point of view the location was easily accessible by public and private transportation and the amount of land was sufficient for a subtantial number of stores plus ample parking. The last problem was to analyze the size of the potential customer market. A marketing-research firm was employed to assess the market. After careful analysis, the research firm suggested that the plan to develop the site be dropped because survey results indicated that due to the short distance to similar nearby shopping centers, the size of the potential market was not sufficient to warrant another venture.

Research on Sales Methods and Policies

It had been the policy of a high-priced men's coat' and suit manufacturer to sell its merchandise to retail outlets on an exclusive basis. That is, only major department stores, one in each city, could carry the line. For the past few years, management was confronted with declining sales, although each store was the finest in its respective city, and the stores' sales were steadily increasing. This was a problem for a marketing-research company. The study conducted by the research consultants showed that although department store sales were on the rise, men's high-priced clothing was being purchased, more commonly, from small specialty stores. It was recommended that in the future company policy should change from exclusive to selective distribution (a chosen few in each city) and that emphasis should shift from the department store to the specialty store.

Research on Advertising

A mail-order wholesaler had always received a large percentage of orders through advertising. The media he had continuously and successfully used were trade papers and direct mail. He had never really determined which medium was more successful in achieving results. In an attempt to measure media effectiveness, a new statement form (mailed to customers monthly) was prepared by the wholesaler. In addition to the amount due the wholesaler, a listing was incorporated that asked the customer where he learned about the various products. After a few months, tabulation of the data showed that trade-paper advertising accounted for an insignificant proportion of sales. Trade-paper advertising was suspended and the savings eventually led to an increased profit.

THE SCIENTIFIC METHOD

The term *scientific* is often loosely used in marketing. Often so-called research studies are merely the educated opinions of marketers. If a method of research is to be considered scientific, there must be a systematic procedure for the solving of problems. The scientific method is adequately defined as follows:

> We can distinguish that which actually is scientific by two criteria: that it is *systematic* and *impartial*. Nothing deserves to be called scientific unless it is carried out in a systematic fashion, which requires accurate problem definition and measurements, orderly data

gathering, organized arrangement of knowledge within the total frame-
work of knowledge, and systematic methods in all other respects.
Impartiality is of course the ability to place the meaning on evidence
without the distortion of preconceived notions of its nature or foregone
conclusions.[2]

THE RESEARCH PROCEDURE

Although the problems to be solved might employ different techniques,
the procedure used by marketing researchers is generally as follows:

Identification of the Problem

A number of factors might contribute to the eventual investigation of a
problem. It might be the decrease in sales of a line's particular product or
perhaps a decline of an entire line of goods. Although management could
be aware of the decline in sales, the actual cause of the problem might not
be apparent. Similarly, a wholesaler might be concerned with the effectiveness of his promotional campaigns and wonder whether or not they
substantially contribute to sales. Whichever area troubles management, it
must be clearly identified before research can begin.

Definition of the Problem

In the discussion of their business problems, executives usually resort
to generalities. Marketing researchers, however, are trained to solve specific
problems. What the problem is must be clearly determined. For example,
mentioning that the entire line of a manufacturer is declining in sales is
too general a statement. It should be specified how much it has declined and
where the decline has taken place.

Making the Study

Sometimes the costs to solve a problem are extravagant. Practicality
of searching for a solution must be decided in terms of dollars and relative
worth.

SECONDARY DATA. Once research has been decided upon, secondary
sources are usually studied for pertinent data. The data from these sources
have already been compiled and are called secondary data. Their information may play an important role in the solution and sometimes may be all
that is needed, so that original research can be omitted. Some of the common
sources of secondary data are:

1. *Company records.* Records of sales orders, sales according to territories, product returns, salesmen's periodic reports, and advertising expendi-

---

[2] D. Luck, H. Wales, and D. Taylor, *Marketing Research* (Englewood
Cliffs, N.J.: Prentice-Hall, Inc., 1971).

tures in some instances will provide sufficient information to solve the problem.

2. *Libraries.* An unlimited number of business periodicals is available to researchers in the public libraries, for example, *Marketing Insights, Advertising Age, Chain Store Age, The Journal of Marketing,* and *Business Week.* To facilitate finding the appropriate business literature a *Business Periodical Index* is available. These publications are significant in that they often provide survey results that might be similar or pertinent to the study being made. They may contain adequate data to render a new and original research project unnecessary.

3. *Trade Associations.* These organizations are groups of businesses with similar interests. Most industries have trade associations. One of the largest is the National Retail Merchants Association (formerly the National Dry Goods Association) with almost every important retail store a member. Trade association activities include regular meetings to discuss problems in the trade, training seminars, and sometimes the publication of journals.

4. *Government Agencies.* An abundance of material is available from all levels of government. At the federal level, the monthly catalog of the Government Printing Office is a publication constantly used by researchers. It provides an extensive listing of everything published by the government. The Department of Commerce, of which the Census Bureau is a part, provides a census of business, one of population, and one of agriculture. These may be etxremely valuable to marketing-research projects. Other federal sources of data are the many regulatory agencies, for example, the Federal Communications Commission, the Federal Trade Commission, the Bureau of Labor and Statistics, and the Food and Drug Administration. At the state and municipal levels, the consumer affairs departments provide information concerning consumer protection. With the big consumerism movement (previously discussed) these departments are being tapped more frequently for information.

5. *Private Agencies.* Many established service organizations provide data that otherwise might only be obtainable to original research. Compilers of such vital data are A.C. Nielsen Co.—noted for broadcast-audience measurement and other consumer data—and Dun & Bradstreet, leaders in credit information. These companies supply pertinent research data.

6. *Advertising Media.* The various media, such as newspapers, magazines, radio, and television make studies that are of interest to researchers. Studiles of population, readership, and income are examples of the statistics made available by the media.

PRIMARY DATA. Although careful examination of secondary data often provides valuable information, an original study is mostly still needed. If so, primary data (that is, compiled firsthand) must be collected. Primary sources include company salesmen, potential customers, regular customers, ultimate consumers, and advertising agencies. The methods by which the information is gathered are numerous. Final determination of the technique ·or combination of techniques to be employed is generally dictated by the particular problem.

METHODS USED TO GATHER INFORMATION. *Observation Method.* Probably the simplest of the methods used to collect raw data is the observation or counting technique. The individual assigned to the task merely counts and records what he sees without talking to those being studied. Traffic counts and fashion or style counts are often used by marketing-research teams.

Traffic Counts are used at various times. In the supermarket chain, top management, in trying to evaluate the location for a new unit, is interested in how much traffic passes the proposed site. It is unlikely that general traffic information is sufficient to satisfy the needs of the researcher. Classifications such as pedestrian traffic, automobile traffic, and traffic generated by buses and trains might be devised to see how important each one is. Similarly, recorders might be assigned to tabulate from which direction the traffic originates. Forms are constructed to make the task of recording simple. Usually, just a check mark placed next to predetermined categories is all that is necessary to record the information. The traffic observation might be used by a retailer to help determine store-entrance locations.

Fashion Counts are used by both manufacturers and retailers as aids in determining which styles are being purchased and worn by consumers. The shirt manufacturer, in determining which colors and styles he should produce, might make a fashion count. The retail buyer, in trying to determine additional purchases for the present season, might also use this method of research. These counts, which are merely recorded observations of people, are also helpful in recognizing trends. A survey of this type, checking a partical kind of merchandise and taken at periodic intervals in places where a company's clientele assembles, might reveal factors that would be of interest in future purchasing. For example, a shoe store catering to the jet set might want to determine whether both shoes and boots should be replenished in inventory and in which amount. By selecting various places where the jet set comes together the firm can rapidly learn what its clientele is wearing. Events like the opening night of the opera or the first horse show are sure to bring scores of jet setters. Through the use of a simple form, as pictured in Figure 7–1, all the pertinent information can be easily recorded. The exact number to observe in order to make the survey meaningful is figured by statistical formulas. After the data have been recorded and tabulated it is relatively simple to rank, in order of importance, what was studied. For example, if half the women wore boots, it would indicate that half the inventory should consist of boots to satisfy customer needs.

In order to determine trends, several counts could be taken to see whether there is a decline or increase. For example, 50 percent of the women wore boots at one observation; however, two weeks later another count might indicate that it was 53 percent. This increase in percentage should be reflected in the proportion of shoes and boots in stock.

FASHION COUNT

Item Counted: LADIES' FOOTWEAR

LOCATION: _____

CLASSIFICATION

SHOE
BOOT
OTHER _____

BOOT STYLE

ANKLE
MID-CALF
ABOVE THE KNEE
HIP
OTHER _____

SHOE STYLE

SANDAL
OPEN-TOE PUMP
CLOSED-TOE PUMP
T-STRAP
HIGH HEEL
MEDIUM HEEL
FLAT HEEL
OTHER _____

COLORS

TINTS

PINK
BLUE
YELLOW
GREEN
MELON
TAN
AQUA
OTHER _____

SHADES

BLUE
GREEN
GOLD (MUSTARD)
ORANGE
RED
PURPLE
BROWN
OTHER _____

NEUTRALS

BLACK
WHITE
SILVER
GOLD (METALLIC)

PLACE CHECK MARKS NEXT TO THE APPROPRIATE ITEMS

Figure 7–1

Questionnaire Method. Although observation is used by marketers, it is by no means as widely employed as the questionnaire. Whereas the counting technique is relatively simple, the questionnaire is more complex and therefore more costly and time consuming. One major difference is that observation can actually take place without consumer awareness, but that a questionnaire requires cooperation from those being studied.

Marketing managers can select the method by which they will collect data from three types of questionnaires: telephone, mail, and interview. The choice is based upon several factors. Among them are:

1. Size and location of the area to be surveyed.

2. Availability of manpower to be assigned to the project.

3. Availability of funds.

4. Amount of time allocated to gathering of the data.

A study of both the advantages and disadvantages of each type will show which method is the most appropriate for a particular project.

Telephone advantages

1. People cannot be reached faster in any other way.

2. Telephone calls are relatively inexpensive.

3. Questioning can be carried out from a central point, without sending people into the field.

4. Information is obtained very quickly.

Telephone disadvantages

1. People without telephones cannot be reached. Businesses catering to the lower socioeconomic groups may not be able to contact their customers using this method.

2. People are frequently reluctant to answer callers they cannot see.

3. People living in toll zones might not be called because of the high cost involved if the company's market is out of its local calling zone.

4. Calls might be annoying to customers.

Mail advantages

1. Postage is inexpensive.

2. Wide distribution (for trading areas of nationally distributed products) does not affect the cost for any person being questioned. Telephone costs would be different because of toll calls.

3. Time allotted for studying and answering questions is longer.

4. Interviewer cannot have influence as might happen in an interview.

5. Field staff is eliminated.

Mail disadvantages

1. Rate of return is very small. A 10 percent response is considered to be average.

2. Cost per return is very high, since the cost of the unanswered questionnaires must be considered part of the overall cost of the survey.

3. Questions might not be completely understood without an interviewer.

4. The time it takes to receive the answer is longer than for either interview or telephone.

RICHARD MANVILLE RESEARCH INC.
230 PARK AVENUE, NEW YORK, N.Y. 10017

<u>WASHING MACHINE SURVEY</u>

NAME:_____   TIME STARTED:_____

TELEPHONE
NUMBER:_____   DATE:_____

Hello, we're conducting a survey and I'd like to ask you a few questions.

1.   Do you have a washing machine in your home?

      4-1 ☐ Yes

      -2 ☐ No   (IF NO, DISCONTINUE -
               IF YES, ASK:)

2.   Did you buy it within the last six months?

      5-1 ☐ Yes

      -2 ☐ No   (IF NO, DISCONTINUE)

3.   Is it <u>filled</u> by one hose or by two hoses?

      6-1 ☐ One Hose

      -2 ☐ Two Hoses

      -3 ☐ Don't Know

4.   Where in your home or apartment do you keep the washing machine?

In what room?

      7-1 ☐ Kitchen

      -2 ☐ Basement

      -3 ☐ Washroom

      -4 ☐ Hallway

      -5 ☐ Other (Specify)_____

5.   Is it on rollers or is it permanently installed?

      8-1 ☐ Rollers

      -2 ☐ Permanently Installed

      -3 ☐ Don't Know

(IF ON ROLLERS, ASK QUESTION 6)

6.   Do you have to move the washing machine each time you use it?

      9-1 ☐ Yes   -2 ☐ No

7a   Is the washing machine regular size or compact size?

      10-1 ☐ Regular

      -2 ☐ Compact

      -3 ☐ Don't Know

b   (IF A COMPACT WAS PURCHASED, ASK:) Why did you purchase a compact
      machine rather than a regular size model? (PROBE)

11-   _____

      _____

      _____

Figure 7–2   Questionnaire for telephone survey

5. Persons responding might not be truly representative of the sample.

In order to overcome the disadvantages of the time lag and the small number of returns, businessmen sometimes offer premiums to those from whom information is being sought as a motivational device. The results are usually better when inducements are offered.

The personal interview may take place at the individual's home, on the job, at subway entrances, in front of a retailer's store entrance, or in other places where people come together. This is the only method employing face-to-face involvement. The questions may either be of the short-answer variety or open-ended, with the respondent giving a complete reaction to the question.

Interview advantages

1. Trained interviewers have great success in the percentage of people who will grant interviews.

2. Questions that are not completely clear can be explained.

3. Additional probing can be carried on by using the open-end question. This is not possible via the mail.

4. Observations may also be recorded.

Interview disadvantages

1. Responding to an interviewer may cause the interviewee to color his responses because of embarrassment; for example, the response to such questions as age and income.

2. Employment of experienced interviewers is costly.

3. Interviewer's bias might be reflected in responses.

4. Interviews in the home might come at an inopportune time.

Preparation of the Questionnaire Form. Although the researcher might select the most appropriate questionnaire technique to obtain information, the number and caliber of answers is directly dependent on the questionnaire design. It is necessary to make certain that a quality form has been produced. Sufficient time should be allocated to structuring the document to be used, or the survey could bring disastrous or no results. Among the factors to be considered are:

1. The occupations of those being questioned.

2. The educational level of those being questioned.

3. Prejudices of those to be interviewed.

In constructing the form to be used, the following requirements are vital:

1. Questions must be easily understood. The language must be com-

Dear Madam:

   In our efforts to serve you better and to provide you
with the best in shopping facilities, we periodically
ask some of our valued patrons to answer a few simple
questions. Your responses and suggestions guide us in
sme key decisions regarding store operations. Our sole
objective is to give you the type of store that you can
look forward to shopping in the year round.

   Please fill in the form below. After completion, fold
and insert the form into the attached self addressed,
stamped envelope.

   As a token of our appreciation, on receipt of your
questionnaire, we will send you a free premium for an
attractive gift that may be redeemed at any of our branch
stores. Please hurry since the supply is limited and
the cut off date is _____.

   May we thank you in advance for your answers, your
comments and your advice.

                    (Tear off)
1. Do you find the store layout convenient?

    ☐ Yes   ☐ No   (If no, please suggest some changes
                       you would like to see made. Comment
                       in the space provided below.)

_____

_____

_____

Figure 7–3   Mail questionnaire

2. Are our sales people always helpful?

    ☐ Yes   ☐ No   (If no, please mention some ways they can better serve you.)

_____

_____

_____

3. Are you satisfied with our checkout counters, particularly in terms of speed, handling of credit cards and charge accounts, and wrapping?

    ☐ Yes   ☐ No   (Please comment below)

_____

_____

_____

4. What other merchandise lines or service would you like to see added to our store?

_____

_____

_____

5. Are you satisfied with our adjustment and refund policy?

    ☐ Yes   ☐ No   (If no, please suggest ways we can improve this policy)

_____

_____

_____

Figure 7–3 (cont.)

<u>Classification Data</u>

6. Please tell us approximately how often you shopped here in the past six months.

Check the appropriate box below:

None   ☐

1-3 times   ☐

4-6 times   ☐

7-9 times   ☐

10-12 times   ☐

15 or more times   ☐

7. Of your total purchases what percent is:

       Cash   %

       Charge Account   %

       Credit Card   %

       Other (specify)   _%_

       _____100%

8. What is the occupation of the head of the household?

_____

9. What is the last grade of school you completed?

      Grade school or less   ☐

      Some high school   ☐

Completed high school   ☐

      Some college   ☐

      Completed college   ☐

Figure 7–3 (cont.)

10. Was your approximate family income last year under

$7500 or over $7,500

	Under $7,500	Over $7,500
Was it	- under $3,000	Was it - under $10,000
	or $3,000-5,000	or over $10,000
	or 5,000-7,500	

11. Would you please indicate in which of these age groups

you belong? Are you in your ...

20's ..... ☐

30's ..... ☐

40's ..... ☐

50's ..... ☐

60 and over ☐

Your Name (Please print) _____

Address (Please Print) _____

City _____ State _____Zip #____

(Do not abbreviate)

Figure 7–3 (cont.)

Questions Asked of Brant Walk-Outs

Pardon me . . . I am making a consumer survey for Brant's.

1. Did you buy anything at Brant's today? ___ Yes ___ No ___ Just passing through

   If respondent answers "yes," thank her for her patronage and tell her that

   the study you are making does not involve Brant customers.

   If she is just passing through the store, thank her for this information.

   If her answer is "no," go ahead with the rest of the questionnaire.

2. What departments at Brant's did you visit (indicate department and floor)?

3. Would you mind telling us your reason for not buying anything at Brant's?

Item	Didn't have what I wanted (size, color, brand, style, etc.)	Price too High	Salesperson not helpful	Out of Stock	Just looking	Other, specify
a)						
b)						
c)						
d)						

4. When you think of Brant's what is the first thing that comes to your mind?

Classification data –

   What part of town are you from? (Eastland, Riverview, etc.)

   Do you work downtown?   Yes   No

   Age (to be estimated by interviewer)   Under 30   30–44   45 and over

   Man   Woman

   Date and time

Store entrance (circle one)

Walnut Street Cosmetics	Walnut Street Men's Furnishings	Walnut Street Blouse
Euclid Street Purses	Euclid Street Hosiery	Main Street
Euclid Street Men's clothing		

Figure 7–4 Personal interview questionnaire (Robert H. Myers, "Sharpening Your Store Image," *Journal of Retailing,* Vol. 36, No. 3, Fall, 1960.)

patible with the intelligence of those to be interviewed. This is particularly true in the case of the mail questionnaire, where no interviewer will be available to clarify questions.

2. Generalities must be avoided by eliminating words as usually, frequently, generally, and occasionally, which tend to prohibit a clear-cut response. For example, an answer to the question, "Do you frequently shop at Value-Rite?" will not tell how often the customer shops at Value-Rite

and the percentage of purchases that are made there. This information may be important to the study.

3. Questions should be arranged in sequential order, so that each preceding question makes for a smooth transition to the next.

4. Questions should be concise and to the point.

5. Questionnaire should not be too long. This might discourage a response. For example, a one-page form is most satisfactory for use by retailers.

6. Design must be organized in such a manner that recording is simple. Caution must be taken to provide enough space for responses, particularly if the open-end question is used.

7. Questionnaire should be organized in such a manner that tabulation of the results is simplified.

8. Factual questions should be limited to obtaining data that can be clearly remembered by the respondents.

9. Leading questions should be eliminated.

10. Questions that are too intimate or that raise personal prejudices should be omitted.

11. Questionnaire should as much as possible be limited to obtaining facts or opinions.

12. Questions containing more than one element should be eliminated.

13. Questions should always provide for conditional answers.

Experimental Method. This method of gathering information employs either the observation method or the direct approach or both. In some instances marketers would like to see the results of a controlled experiment, which this method permits. Experimentation might be risky on a large scale, but management often experiments on a small scale. For example, a company might want to change the disposable container now used to package its soft beverage to a reusable container, in order to deal with the country's ecology problem. The tremendous amount of disposable containers present many problems that contribute to the destruction of the environment. Before calling for this major packaging change, which might seriously hamper sales, the company would select a test market in which it could sample the new package while the balance of its soft-drink distribution is normal. Theory has it that the results of these experiments will hold true in the overall distribution of the company's product.

This method is an excellent research procedure in that it actually simulates the company's complete marketing activities. The disadvantages involved are the high costs of experimentation and the length of time necessary to carry out the project.

Perhaps not a disadvantage, but rather a major difficulty with the experimental method is the control of relevant variables. When employing this research technique it is necessary to select markets that are identical in all significant aspects. For example, in the case of the above-mentioned change to reusable containers it might be impossible to find two distinct groups that possess all the significant identical factors. If only one out of all the factors is different, this might have an effect on acceptance of the proposed container. When the variables are uncontrollable, the results might not be truly comparable.

Sampling

After preparing the necessary forms to be used, a determination must be made regarding the number of people to be included for the survey to be meaningful. It is neither necessary nor practical to involve every conceivable individual in a group. For example, a manufacturer with a potential market of six million persons need only investigate a part of this population. The segment of the population selected is known as a sample. The sample is most effective when its members are truly representative of a group to be studied. The size and selection of the sample is based upon many considerations and should be carefully decided on with the help of a statistician.

Collection of the Data

The actual collection of data depends on the technique to be used. A choice must be made among available methods—mail questionnaire, interviewing, telephone questioning, and observations. Whichever technique or combination of techniques is employed, the investigators involved must be thoroughly trained. Companies employing the services of a professional research organization need not be concerned, but those using their own employees or college students (often used) to collect data must make certain that there is a thorough understanding of the investigative methods. Successful in training laymen to conduct personal interviews is role playing. For example, one individual assumes the interviewer's identity and the other the interviewee's. In this way an individual, trained in the art of questioning, can observe, criticize, and make recommendations to improve questioning techniques. In the area of observations, investigators must be familiar with what they are observing and recording.

Processing and Analysis of Data

After the investigators submit the raw data collected, they must be processed. Processing involves arranging data in proper form for analysis. All data sheets must be first inspected and corrected or modified to guarantee that the information is stated appropriately for tabulation. The data must then be classified into categories. This step is simplified if care was exercised in the preparation of the questionnaire. Without being classified into homogeneous groupings, the data cannot be analyzed. The next step, particularly if data-processing machines are to be used for the purpose of tabulation, is coding. This involves a code being devised for assignment to each type of reply. For example, code 6 might mean blue and code 12 might stand for red. These codes can then be fed into the computer for quick processing. Coding can be eliminated if the questionnaire was pre-coded, with each item having a number assigned to it on the original form. Actual tabulation can be done by machine, as mentioned, or by hand. Small samples that can be tabulated by hand are often employed by small retailers. More common, in marketing research, is the machine tabulation, which mechanically and more quickly and efficiently performs the steps involved in manual tabulation.

After the data have been compiled and summarized, analysis takes

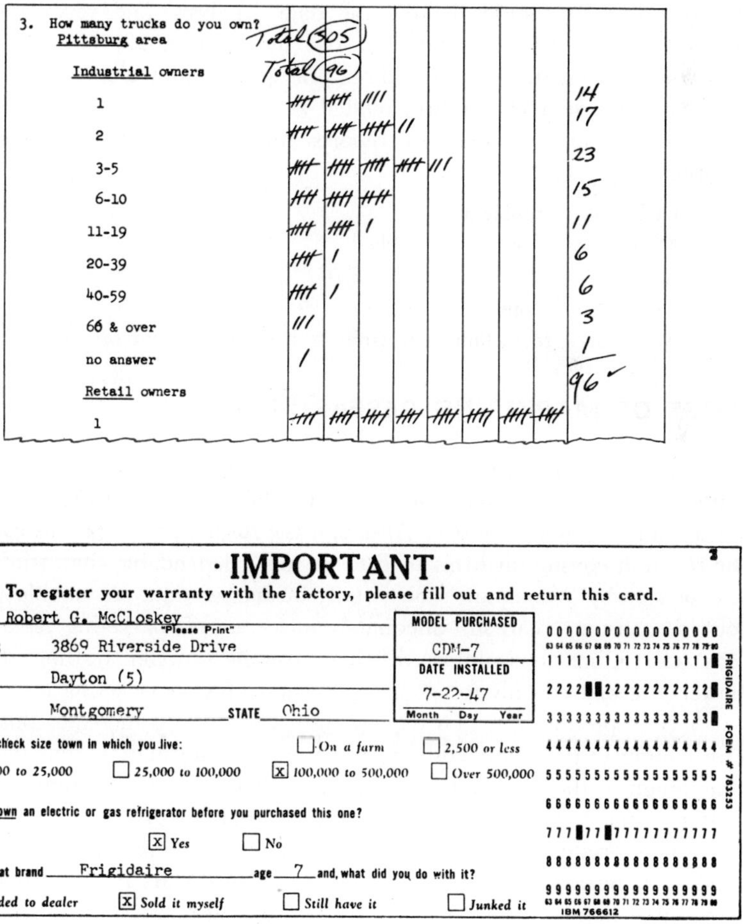

3. How many trucks do you own? Pittsburg area	Total (505)	
Industrial owners	Total (96)	
1	𝍸 𝍸 ////	14
2	𝍸 𝍸 𝍸 //	17
3-5	𝍸 𝍸 𝍸 𝍸 ///	23
6-10	𝍸 𝍸 𝍸	15
11-19	𝍸 𝍸 /	11
20-39	𝍸 /	6
40-59	𝍸 /	6
60 & over	///	3
no answer	/	1
		96
Retail owners		
1	𝍸 𝍸 𝍸 𝍸 𝍸 𝍸 𝍸 𝍸	

· IMPORTANT ·

To register your warranty with the factory, please fill out and return this card.

Please do not fold or bend this card

NAME Robert G. McCloskey "Please Print"

ADDRESS 3869 Riverside Drive

CITY Dayton (5)

COUNTY Montgomery STATE Ohio

MODEL PURCHASED CDM-7

DATE INSTALLED 7-22-47 Month Day Year

Please check size town in which you live: ☐ On a farm ☐ 2,500 or less

☐ 2,500 to 25,000 ☐ 25,000 to 100,000 ☒ 100,000 to 500,000 ☐ Over 500,000

Did you own an electric or gas refrigerator before you purchased this one?

☒ Yes ☐ No

If so; what brand Frigidaire age 7 and, what did you do with it?

☐ Traded to dealer ☒ Sold it myself ☐ Still have it ☐ Junked it

FRIGIDAIRE FORM # 783253

IBM 766612

Figure 7–5 Data tabulation forms. Top: form for hand tabulation, with tallies. Bottom: tabulating form for original recording.

place. The amount and kind of analysis depends upon the research project. Some studies, such as the fashion count, might only be used to determine which colors are most popular and in what percentages. Other studies might require more sophisticated statistical analysis and interpretation. This phase of the research project is most important, since future decisions will be based upon it. Knowledgeable research analysts are best used to evaluate all possible courses of action and make final recommendations. If a company is conducting its own study, it is advisable that everyone in management connected with the project review the recommendations of the chief researcher before implementing the suggestions.

Preparation of the Research Report

A written report should be prepared outlining the findings of the investigation. It should include the data, analysis, and recommendations bound in some permanent form. Also included should be any pertinent graphic displays, such as bar charts, line graphs, and pictograms. This can serve for future reference and related studies.

Most complete research reports follow the areas covered in this chapter. They are:

Definition of problem
Methodology used in the study
Analysis
Recommendations
Appendices, to include data from both secondary and primary sources

COST OF MARKETING RESEARCH

It is not uncommon for a research project to cost in excess of one hundred thousand dollars. Generally, the larger expenditures are allocated to the study of new products. Although the formal investigations carried out by research consultant firms tend to be more dependable than studies made exclusively by a company's own staff, businesses that are unable to afford outside assistance can still adequately make use of marketing research. The gas station, in determining whether customers prefer trading stamps or lower prices, need only to ask its customers. This is marketing research.

New product-research expenditures continue to increase. Businessmen are willing to pay these costs in exchange for information that might alter the design of their proposed product and therefore make it more successful. Often, after a study has been completed, manufacturers scrap their plans for a new product entirely. It is more sensible to spend a hundred thousand dollars in research than to lose several million dollars in the production of something that will not appeal to the consuming market.

THE FUTURE OF MARKETING RESEARCH

With the success businesses have enjoyed through marketing-research involvement, it is certain that there will be significant increases in research budgets. Companies that have heretofore limited making investigations to their own personnel will employ the services of research organizations.

Of particular significance to the future of research is the computer and its limitless applications. No doubt, the computer will make the greatest contribution to the continued growth and success firms have enjoyed through marketing research.

In Chapter 16, the Computer and Marketing, an extensive overview of computer application in terms of marketing research will be offered.

IMPORTANT POINTS IN THE CHAPTER

1. Marketing research relates to the investigation of marketing problems and the recommendations needed to solve the problems.

2. Marketing research is generally categorized into research on products and services, market research, sales methods and policies research, and advertising research.

3. The scientific method involves the systematic and impartial procedure for the solving of problems.

4. Generally, the research procedure followed by investigating teams is as follows:

    a. Identification of the problem
    b. Definition of the problem
    c. Investigation of secondary sources of information
    d. Securing primary information
    e. Sample selection
    f. Collection of data
    g. Processing and analysis of data
    h. Preparation of the report

5. The costs of marketing research are expected to continue to increase, since the results of research continue to make companies operate more effectively.

6. The computer, through its speed and accuracy, promises to make greater contributions to marketing-research management.

REVIEW QUESTIONS

1. Define *marketing research.*

2. Can the terms *marketing research* and *market research* be used interchangeably? Defend your answer.

3. What arrangements do large companies generally make for their research? Are the arrangements the same as those for small companies? Discuss.

4. Into how many categories is marketing research usually divided? List and briefly describe each category.

5. Which area of marketing research usually receives the greatest amount of attention? Why?

6. Briefly define *scientific method*.

7. What is the first step in the research process?

8. Differentiate between secondary and primary data.

9. How important are trade organizations to the research team?

10. Of which single governmental source can the researcher avail himself for the most complete listing of government publications?

11. Are the advertising media helpful to marketing researchers? How?

12. Describe the observation method employed in gathering information.

13. In what principal way does the questionnaire method differ from the observation method?

14. Compare the telephone and mail questionnaires. Which is less costly to operate? Which brings the quickest response?

15. Discuss some of the major disadvantages of the personal interview.

16. Briefly describe the areas to be considered in the preparation of a questionnaire.

17. Which research method often combines observation with the direct approach? Why do marketers often use this method?

18. Define the term *sample*. Why do marketers use a sample?

19. How are the data tabulated? Why are the data coded?

20. The costs of marketing research continue to increase. Why are marketers willing to spend such huge sums for research?

CASE PROBLEMS

Case Problem 1

David's Emporium is a large department store with six branches, all of which are located in the New York City area. For the past twenty years the organization has steadily increased its advertising expenditure and its sales.

The advertising dollar has been spent on newspapers, television, radio, direct mail, and magazines. The effort has been effective on an overall basis, but management has not really determined whether or not all the media employed have been producing results in direct proportion to the investment. For example, is radio with an annual expenditure of 5 percent of the advertising budget bringing in only half as much as television for which 10 percent is being spent?

In an effort to ascertain the true worth of the present allocation of the advertising money, a marketing-research consultant has been retained to help the company.

Questions

1. Should David's continue their present system, which has proved to be successful? Why?
2. Pretend you are the research consultant. What procedure would you employ in order to make sound recommendations to David's Emporium?

Case Problem 2

International Foods, Inc. have manufactured, processed, and distributed foreign and gourmet-type foods for the past five years. Initially, they successfully produced and sold Italian and French delicacies to supermarkets and gourmet food shops. Each year they added to their existing line food from one more nation. The last four years have seen the inclusion of popular Swedish, Japanese, British, and Chinese foods. All were sold to the satisfaction of the company.

Three months ago, they added a full line of products from Greece. With the enormous increase in travel to Greece, the company felt that introduction of Greek foods would be a natural. Techniques of packaging, promotion, distribution, and so on, that had been employed for distribution of the other products were used again. Immediate success was expected, but the results were dismal. Preliminary investigation showed that initially the Greek products were well received; however, repeat business was very low. International Foods, Inc. must decided how to rectify this undesirable situation.

Questions

1. Should the Greek foods be immediately withdrawn? Why?
2. What might be the problem?
3. What kind of research would you suggest if you were the director of research? Specify which techniques you would employ to discover the cause of the problem.

BIBLIOGRAPHY

Day, Ralph L., *Concepts for Modern Marketing*. Scranton, Pa.: International Textbook Co., 1968.

Dichter, Ernest, "Creativity—Based on Research, not Inspiration," *Marketing Insights,* February 17, 1969.

———, "Psychology in Market Research," in *The Environment of Marketing Behavior,* eds. Robert J. Holloway and Robert S. Hancock. New York: John Wiley & Sons, Inc., 1969.

Ferber, Robert, Donald F. Blankertz, and Sidney Hollander, *Marketing Research.* New York: The Ronald Press Company, 1964.

Heidingsfield, Myron S., and Frank H. Eby, *Marketing and Business Research.* New York: Holt, Rinehart & Winston, Inc., 1962.

Herzog, Donald R., "Research in New Product Planning," *Marketing Insights,* January 20, 1969.

Holmes, Parker, *Marketing Research: Principles and Readings.* Cincinnati, Ohio: South-Western Publishing Co., 1966.

Ladik, Frank, Leonard Kent, and Perham C. Nahl, "Test Marketing of New Consumer Products," originally in *Journal of Marketing.* Reprinted in *Readings in Marketing,* eds. Charles Dirksen, Arthur Kroeger, and Lawrence Lockley. Homewood, Ill.: Richard D. Irwin, Inc., 1968.

Luck, David J., Hugh G. Wales, and Donald A. Taylor, *Marketing Research.* Englewood Cliffs, N.J.: Prentice-Hall, Inc., 1971.

McConnell, J. Douglas, "Testing Brand Loyalty and Beer Quality," *Marketing Insights,* October 21, 1968.

Nordlie, Charles B., "In the Petroleum Field: Marketing Research Is a Promotional Tool," *Marketing Insights,* April, 1969.

Pamphlets and Brochures on All Aspects of Research. Chicago: Nielsen Consumer Research Services.

Phelps, Maynard, "The Place of Marketing Research in Economic Activity," in *The Environment of Marketing Behavior,* eds. Robert J. Holloway and Robert S. Hancock. New York: John Wiley & Sons, Inc., 1969.

"Putting a Measure on the Market," *Marketing Insights,* March 17, 1969.

Schreir, Frederick T., *Modern Marketing Research.* Belmont, Calif.: Wadsworth Publishing Co., Inc., 1966.

Talley, Walter, "Marketing Research and Development: Neglected Way to Profit Growth," in *Concepts for Modern Marketing,* ed. Ralph L. Day. Scranton, Pa.: International Textbook Co., 1968.

Uhl, Kenneth P., "Better Management of Marketing Information," in *Modern Marketing Thought,* 2nd ed., eds. J. Howard Westing and Gerald Albaum. London: Macmillan & Co., Ltd., 1969.

Wasson, Chester R., *The Strategy of Marketing Research.* New York: Appleton-Century-Crofts, 1964.

THE
PRODUCT

8

INTRODUCTION

Essentially, the success or failure of a business enterprise is contingent on customer acceptance of its product. It is impossible to select the most important of the four factors of marketing: product, promotion, price, and place. There is no question, however, that product is most basic. It all begins with product. Once product decisions have been made, marketing strategy can be woven around it until a total marketing program is achieved. The success of the final marketing program depends, in large part, the accuracy of the product decision.

DEFINITION—THE TOTAL PRODUCT

It should be emphasized that in this discussion, product refers to the total product, that is, all the elements that are necessary for customer satisfaction. The total product, in addition to the physical product, includes guarantees, installation, instructions for use, packaging, branding, and the availability of service. The total product is what the customer buys, and frequently the fringe characteristics such as guarantees and servicing are as important as the physical product itself. In the case of a prospective buyer of a home appliance, for example, the fact that Sears, Roebuck and Co. offers a one-year replacement, rather than merely service, may be the factor that clinches the sale.

REASONS FOR ADDING PRODUCTS

New products should never be added without a sound business reason. However, there are many situations in which new products are essential to a successful operation.

Company Growth

Since there is generally a limit to the amount of sales that a given article can produce, company growth may depend on the introduction of new products for an increase in sales. Besides sales volume, profits and capital may also be increased by new products. As a consequence, company growth is the most important or at least one of the principal reasons for introducing new products.

Maximum Use of Resources

Management is charged with the responsibility of getting the maximum use of the resources available. The term *resources available* covers many areas; if they are not fully utilized, profit opportunities may be overlooked.

Idle Plant and Equipment

When the manufacturing or distribution facilities do not have to work at full capacity to satisfy the demand for existing products, an attempt should be made to use the idle time by the introduction of new products. This will not only increase the potential sales volume of the company but improve its operating efficiency as well. The cost per unit produced of such fixed overhead expenses as rent is decreased as the number of units produced increases. When new products are produced by existing facilities rather than by specially constructed facilities, the cost of both the new product and the goods presently produced may be drastically cut.

Idle Personnel

When the personnel of a business is not working at its full potential, the resulting idle time is being wasted. As in the case of idle plant and equipment, new products that can be handled by existing personnel will improve both profits and efficiency.

Idle Capital

The main function of capital is return on investment. Any company that has more capital than it requires for the operation of its business should try to invest this capital to improve its return on the investment of its owners. New products are an excellent place for such investment, since management knows their impact and can exercise control over them.

Good Will

An important asset that does not appear on the financial statements of a company is its customer good will. In the area of new products, consumer good will may be a factor that enables new products to be introduced with relative ease. Some years ago, the Sunbeam Corporation produced a highly successful electric food mixer. Capitalizing on the resulting good will, the Sunbeam Corporation is now a successful marketer of a wide range of household appliances. The Green Giant Company is another good example of effectively using customer acceptance as a vehicle for expansion through the introduction of new products. During the last ten years, this fast-growing company has introduced nearly five new food products a year, most of which were readily accepted by its customers.

Distribution Channels

Another important nonfinancial asset consists of a company's channels of distribution. These are difficult and expensive to set up and maintain. If the distribution channels are capable of successfully marketing products in addition to those already handled, the introduction of new products should be considered.

Replacement of Old Products

Every product has a life cycle. This may be graphically illustrated as is shown in Figure 8–1. This cycle may be divided into four periods:

1. The *pioneer period* of introduction is characterized by slow sales growth as the company strives for distribution and customer acceptance.

2. The *period of growth* occurs as customers accept the product. This is a time of rapidly rising sales volume and profits. If there is a strong period of growth, the product is successful, and competitors are attracted. This causes price declines and a movement toward manufacturing efficiency. The competition results in a leveling off of the sales and profit. This signifies the end of the growth period.

3. The *maturity period* is marked by a further leveling off and gradual decline of the product's growth and profitability. It is a time of high competition that requires large outlays of promotional expenses that tend to reduce profits. During this period variations on the original product appear

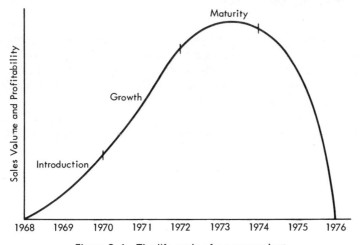

Figure 8–1   The life cycle of a new product

that appeal to specific segments of the market. These tend to increase costs and reduce the potential sales market. During the latter half of the maturity period the weaker producers are forced out.

4. The *period of decline* begins when the product is made obsolete by the introduction into the market of a new product that replaces the old. The necessary cutback in promotional expenditures to match the declining sales accelerates the decline. The time comes at which the product must be abandoned.

A study of the product illustrated in Figure 8–1 indicates that a product started in 1968 reaches maturity in 1972 and begins to decline by 1974. If the company wants to maintain its high sales and profit level, a new product must be introduced in 1970. The new product will then reach its maturity (and maximum profitability) by 1974, the date at which the product illustrated begins its decline.[1] Since nearly all products face a growth and decline cycle of one time span or another, management is required to be constantly researching new products to maintain the company's profitability.

THE DEVELOPMENT OF NEW PRODUCTS

As has been indicated, the development of new products is essential to the continuing success of a business organization. That most successful companies accept this idea is evidenced by the fact that some 70 percent of the food products available to today's housewife were not available ten years ago and fully 50 percent of the drugs available were not in existence five years ago.

Organizing for Innovation

Considering the importance of new-product development, it is obvious that product innovation is a top-management responsibility. Despite this, few companies, even the best-managed and most successful, are properly organized for new-product development. A recent survey indicated that four out of five outstanding firms had problems in this area. One author goes so far as to suggest that fewer than one-third of American manufacturing firms have an adequate organization responsible for new products.

The trend among the more agressively managed American firms is toward formally organized new-products departments. These are generally small departments, frequently consisting of not more than four or five people. Typically, the head of the department reports directly to the president.

[1] It must be understood that the chart pictured in Figure 8–1 relates to an imaginary product. Specific products will vary greatly.

DUTIES OF THE NEW-PRODUCT DEPARTMENT. *Getting and Screening Ideas.* Since the new-product department must depend, to a large extent, on outside sources for ideas, it may be necessary to offer incentive rewards to help generate such information. Salesmen, customers, employees, and inventors are only a few of the sources of new-product ideas that should be utilized. These ideas must be carefully screened to determine the ones that are worthy of further investigation.

Analysis of Ideas. The suggestions that survive the preliminary screening must be put to further tests before they can be placed in the developmental stage. Among these are estimates of customer demand, estimates of profitability, decisions on whether or not the idea falls within the company's goals and objectives, and decisions on whether or not the idea is within the capability of the company.

Development of the Product. The new-product ideas that meet all prior testing satisfactorily must, at this stage, be converted from an idea on paper to an actual physical product. This requires the construction of samples and models in small quantities that can be physically tested and adjusted. In this way, it can be determined what will be the best way to manufacture the article as well as what will be the most salable and profitable product. During the developmental stage the new-product department requires the cooperation of the production, engineering, cost-accounting, marketing, and many other departments. The final result of the developmental stage is a product that is ready to be test marketed.

Market Testing the Product. At this point the consuming public must be brought into the picture. This is generally done in limited geographical areas with the purpose of determining public interest in the product. The information provided by market testing is used to make design and production changes intended to improve the product's consumer acceptability. At the completion of the test-marketing program, top management must decide whether or not to go ahead with the project.

Production and Marketing. Those new products whose test marketing programs are favorable and that are given a "go ahead" signal by top management are now removed from the new-product department and turned over to the production and marketing departments as additions to the product line. (This does not mean that cooperation with the new-product department should stop at this point.)

It should be noted that the most important steps in the new-product development program outlined above are the early ones. The getting, screening, and analysis of ideas are the relatively inexpensive parts of the program on which the success or failure of a company's new-product development rests. Poor judgment in the early stages results in missed opportunities and costly errors.

The major problem that management faces in new-product decision making is the fact that whereas new products are essential to the life of a business, some 80 percent of all new products are costly failures. That these errors are not at all restricted to small, poorly managed companies is evidenced by the fact that even industry leaders whose customer good will and promotional facilities are second to none are constantly making new-product errors. Giant IBM is a good example. During an eighteen-month period, that company discontinued its operations in microfilm, offset duplicators, voting machines, and production control, all new products that did not make the grade.

Perhaps the most serious problem facing new-product development departments is the possibility that failure will be treated so harshly that innovation may be replaced by conservativeness. Top management must expect a great number of new-product failures and not allow such failures to stand in the way of an aggressive search for innovation.

THE BASIS FOR THE MANAGERIAL DECISION

The final decision on whether or not a new product should be included in the line is made at the top-management level. Since the chance of failure is great and the financial result of failure can be massive, this decision must be made with great care. The following are some of the considerations that should be taken into account in making this decision.

Demand

The demand for the item is by far the most important factor that management must consider. No matter how perfectly the new product meets every other standard, it must be discarded if the estimate of the demand is too low to assure profitability. Approximations of a product's demand are based on the results of market-testing programs.

Fit

The manner in which the new product fits into the company's operation is important to the success of a new item. Adequacy of fit must be considered in several areas.

Marketing Fit.   Cambell's can sell soups, but they better stay out of the paint business. The chance of an item's success is increased if it will be purchased by the same people who buy the company's other products. In some cases, the new product may actually conflict with the old, as in the case of a manufacturer of children's clothing who added a line of teen-age garments only to find that teen-agers refused to have any part of a label that was well known in the marketing of children's wear.

CHANNEL FIT. The existence of a successful distribution channel is an important asset. To set up new channels generally requires a considerable expense and effort, including the cost of establishing a separate sales force. For this reason, most companies limit product expansion to those areas that may be handled by their established distribution channels. In this way, General Mills has no trouble in introducing several new supermarket products each year.

PROMOTIONAL FIT. Promotional activities are both expensive and necessary. If the product under consideration is similar enough in nature to be included in the regular promotion campaigns, considerable savings can be made. In addition, the promotional dollar can be stretched if the promotion of one product helps the sales of allied products.

PRODUCTION FIT. Ideally, the capability to produce the new product should be within the capacity of the company's present production facilities. If this is not the case, the production of the new product should, at least, be within the know-how of the company's production experts.

Legal Problems

New products are particularly susceptible to such legal problems as patent infringements. All legal problems must be researched before the decision on adopting a new product is made.

Financial Problems

Before a new product reaches its developmental stage, management must answer two vital questions concerning finances: Does the company have sufficient capital to properly produce, promote, and maintain an inventory of the product? If so, will the expected profits derived from the product be worth the capital invested?

In conclusion, it appears that the success or failure of a new product depends, in large part, on how well it fits into the existing operation. This includes not only the production and distributional efforts of the company but its goals, image, and aspirations as well.

PRODUCT CHARACTERISTICS

Certain product characteristics require decisions that will affect the profitability of the item. Among these are quality, design, color, size, materials, and performance.

Quality

Naturally, the minimum quality that a product must have is the amount it needs to satisfactorily do the job for which it is intended. Since any increase in quality requires an increase in production costs that must ultimately be passed on to the consumer, the question of how much quality should be built into a product becomes a difficult one. It is possible to include a great deal of quality in a product, but the resulting high price might be more than a buyer is willing to pay. Before the decision on the amount of quality is made, the concept of useless quality must be considered. It is pointless to increase the cost of an item by setting the quality level at a point beyond the customer's desires. Unquestionably, General Motors could make a car that would last twenty years, but they would surely find difficulty finding customers willing to pay the cost of such a car. A better example may be found in the high-fashion industries. What woman, for example, would be willing to pay the excessive cost of a dress that was constructed to last for ten years? The quality built into a product should be at a level desired by the customer and for which the customer is willing to pay. It should be borne in mind that the quality of most products is determined by their weakest part. It would be wasteful to construct a lawn mower whose body will last for ten years if the motor will break down in five years.

Once a level of quality has been decided upon, it is important that every unit produced be as close as possible to that level. There is nothing more damaging to the good will of a company than a "lemon."

Design and Color

Not too many years ago, the importance of design and color was limited to a select few fields, such as apparel. Today, these characteristics are recognized as important sales factors in such widely diversified fields as kitchen appliances and vitamin pills. Decisions on design and color must be customer-oriented. That customer opinion must be constantly researched is evidenced by a test made by Rubbermaid, a manufacturer of sink mats, dish-draining trays, soapdishes, and so on. The company had been successfully marketing its products in bright colors only to find that its customers preferred dull colors. It would seem that the company's success was due to factors that offset the color disapproval by customers.

Size

Size, like the other characteristics of a product, must be fitted to customer needs. Consider the case of Thom McAn Shoes, where some 150 styles must be carried. Each style must be broken down into colors and sizes. Many marketers in similar situations simply do not try to carry all the sizes that customers desire, preferring to lose business in unusual sizes and keep their stock at a manageable level.

The manufacturer's estimate of size is not always correct and requires constant revision. For example, when television sets first came out, manufacturers competed to market the largest sets possible under the belief that the bigger the picture, the wider the public appeal. Most manufacturers produced twenty-seven-inch monsters before they learned that the twenty-one- to twenty-three-inch screen had the widest popularity.

Styles in size vary as much as styles in products. Several years ago, the twenty-five-pound packages of soap powder and sixteen- and thirty-two-ounce soft drinks, which are popular today, were not available.

Marketers prefer large-package selling, since the expense of selling a large package is no greater than the costs of marketing a small package, whereas the sales volume and profitability are increased.

Materials

Frequently, the manufacturer of an article is faced with a wide variety of available materials. Clothing can be made of fabric constructed of many different natural or synthetic yearns. Other manufacturers must choose between various plastics and metals. The choice of materials should be based on the functional value of the material (the material chosen must be adequate for the use to which it is put), the salability of the material (customers may prefer a particular material over others, for example, nylon stockings), and production problems that might arise from the various materials (it is difficult to manufacture a fine white shirt from pure nylon).

Performance

Here again, the producer must put out an article conforming to the customer's requirements. This is particularly true in the wholesale market, where the customer frequently places performance specifications on his desired purchases. Since improved performance raises the cost of the product, manufacturers generally fit performance to customer needs. Thus, most automobiles are not designed to travel at speeds of 120 miles an hour when are rarely used at speeds in excess of 70 miles an hour.

REASONS FOR NEW-PRODUCT FAILURE

The enormous failure rate of new products has led to many surveys to determine the reasons for such failure. One study of over eighty firms, each of whom had a high reputation for successful new-product development, led to the following conclusions:

Poor Market Testing

Included in this category is the inability to accurately predict the demand for the new products. Apparently, even the most sophisticated market-research programs cannot always judge the customers' buying habits and product preferences.

Defective Product

It is frequently difficult to determine a company's ability to properly design a new product. Occasionally a good, innovative idea is destroyed by production as a poorly designed, inferior-quality product.

Errors in Costing

Underestimates in the cost of production may result in a product for which the selling price is above the amount that customers are willing to pay. This may reduce the profitability to a point at which the product must be abandoned.

Obsolescence

Products are changing so frequently that on occasion a competitor may offer a product that makes the new item obsolete before it achieves market success. The proper timing of new products is vitally important.

Competitor's Action

Price reductions by competitors may ruin the chance of a promising new product.

Insufficient Effort

Shortages in the amount of capital a company is willing to invest in a new product may result in insufficient promotion, sales staff, or distribution.

It is obvious that many of the reasons for the failure of new products described above are the result of errors of judgment. Although errors like these must occur, they may be kept at a minimum by a careful selection of the personnel of the new-products department. It is not enough to select people with imagination who are capable of innovative ideas; they must also have the proper attitude. Some of the attitudes causing failure of potentially highly successful products are:

1. Assumption that everyone looks at a product in the same way the new-product department does. To offset this, the new product should be tested among the wide variety of people that will make up its eventual customers; this will show the attitude of each class of customers toward the item.

2. Tendency halt research on new-product design too soon, that is, as soon as what appears to be an adequate design is achieved. The fact is that adequate is not enough. Research and development must continue until the design has been proven successful by careful market research.

3. Attitude on the part of the new-product department that the production and marketing of the item is not its problem; in fact, this

department should be responsible for the manufacturing specifications as well as for the formulation of the selling pitch. This is a common error that is more the result of faulty organization than of personal attitude. It can be remedied by a revision of the duties and responsibilities of the new-products department.

4. Substitution of the everything-will-be-all-right attitude in estimating the adequacy of the budget for a scientific analysis of the funds necessary to properly launch the product.

5. Failure to have an attorney clear the patent and other legal aspects.

Not all of these errors are the fault of the personnel in the new-product department. Generally, the new-product department is under a considerable amount of pressure from management to get the product out on the market (where it can start earning money) as soon as possible. Giving in to this pressure before the product is ready may result in any of the reasons for failure that were described above. In Chapter 19, Marketing Mistakes, specific product failures will be examined.

MAKE OR BUY

As the present trend toward expanding the product line continues, management must face the decision of whether to make new products with the company's own manufacturing facilities or to contract the work out. Many firms compromise by doing part of the work in their own plants and contracting out the remainder. This is common among apparel manufacturers. In other industries, such as automobile manufacturing, the usual practice is to contract out almost all the manufacturing and do all the assembling and finishing at company-owned plants. When a company has the idle time and the skills required for manufacture of the product, it should unquestionably do its own work. On the other hand, if a company is capable of distributing more goods than it is able to manufacture, the difficult problem of whether to make or buy must be faced. That is, should new manufacturing facilities be constructed or should the work be contracted out? Several questions have to be answered before the make-or-buy decision can be made.

1. What is the cheapest way to obtain the product? Not too long ago high union-labor costs forced low-end ladies' clothing manufacturers to give up their New York City area plants. The merchandise could not compete with similar goods manufactured in nonunion southern shops. As a result, many manufacturers contracted their goods out to southern manufacturers. Recent labor increases in the South have forced overseas contracting in such low labor-cost areas as Puerto Rico, Hong Kong, and the Philippines.

2. Does the company know how to make the product? Many com-

panies whose personnel does not have the knowledge needed to produce the new item prefer to have the work done by experienced, knowledgeable contractors.

3. Is the capital available to set up a new plant? Frequently, the specialized equipment necessary for construction of the new product (or some part of the new product) is beyond the financial capabilities of the company and contracting becomes a necessity.

4. Do the estimated life cycle and profitability of the item warrant the necessary expenditure for plant and equipment? If not, the obvious answer is to contract the work out.

5. Is secrecy important? Particularly among nonpatented items, materials, techniques, and design must be kept secret. This can be best effected by self-manufacture.

6. Can you depend upon outsiders? There is always the possibility of late delivery, price raises, and cut-off relationships when outside sources are used. This is particularly a problem for small manufacturers who exercise minor control over their contractors. Such giants as Sears, Roebuck and Co.—an enormous user of contract manufacturing—are able to enforce rigid control over their contractors.

PRODUCT DISCONTINUANCE

In the life of each product there comes a point at which decline in terms of sales and profitability necessitates its abandonment. Alert management should be able to milk the declining product until it reaches its nonprofit level. This requires careful planning, since reductions of promotional and other expenses must be timed to coincide with the decline in sales volume.

Many products must be kept in the line despite loss of profits in order to round out the offerings and maintain customer convenience. Most supermarket operators feel that sugar is a losing proposition because its handling costs are greater than its markup. Naturally, they cannot drop sugar from their shelves.

Manufacturers who are considering eliminating a product from their line must keep in mind their obligations to customers who own the product. This may require them to maintain a supply of replacement parts for some time after the last sale of the item.

SERVICE AS A PRODUCT

No discussion of product can be complete without some reference to services, since they form the fastest-growing sector of our economy. The definition of *services* is the performance of activities and accommodations required by the public. The marketing activities related to services do not include any physical goods. They are insignificant and incidental to the services involved. Service industries include professional services (medicine, law, and accounting); recreational services (motion pictures, television, and bowling alleys); renting services (hotels, motels, homes, and offices); personal services (beauty parlors, dry cleaners, and laundries); insurance; finance; and public utilities.

The same principles apply to the marketing of services as to that of other goods. The success of a marketing plan for services depends upon the quality of the service (product), its availability to the consumer (place), and the appeal of its promotion. In short, the marketing mix is as valid for services as products as it is for commodities as products, and the discussions concerning the marketing of products refer to both services and physical products.

IMPORTANT POINTS IN THE CHAPTER

1. To a marketer, the definition of a product includes all the factors needed for customer satisfaction, that is, the physical product plus service, instructions, packaging, and so on.

2. New products are added to the line to get maximum use of manufacturing facilities, personnel, capital, good will, and distribution channels. As old products become obsolete, new products must be available to take their place and provide company growth.

3. The life cycle of a product consists of four stages: introduction, growth, maturity, and decline. To maintain a level state of income, new products must approach maturity as older products decline.

4. Well-managed companies set up new-products departments that analyze ideas for new products, develop and market test them, and cooperate with the production and marketing divisions to get the product to the market.

5. Management has the final decision on whether or not to adopt a new product. This decision should be based on the probable demand for the new product, the manner in which the new product fits into the company's operation, and the capacity of the company to product and market the new product.

6. Decisions on a product's quality, design, color, size, materials, and performance must be based on the consumer's desires. It should be neither better nor worse than the consumer demands.

7. New products fail because of weaknesses in market testing production, cost estimating, timing, competitor's action, and insufficient promotional and marketing efforts.

8. The pressure to get new products on the market often results in insufficient testing, design research, cost analysis, and marketing and promotional study.

9. The decision to make or buy must be based on comparative costs, capacity to produce, investment required in new equipment, and dependency of the contractor.

10. Products are usually discontinued when they are no longer profitable. As they go into their period of decline, costs should be reduced to prolong the period of profitability as much as possible. The company owes it to its customers to maintain a stock of service parts long after a product has been discontinued.

REVIEW QUESTIONS

1. Explain the importance of the product in relation to promotion, price, and place.

2. Management is responsible for getting the maximum use of available resources. Discuss various idle resources that may be utilized by new-product development.

3. Discuss the period of introduction and growth in the life cycle of a product.

4. Why are new products important to the life cycle of older products?

5. How should a new-product department get ideas?

6. What tests should be put to ideas that seem good before the decision to develop the product is made?

7. Explain the new-product department's role in the final production and marketing of a product.

8. Why are the getting, screening, and analysis of ideas the most important steps in new-product development?

9. List the elements that must be taken into account by management in making the decision for the adoption of a new product.

10. What legal problems may arise with new products?

11. Discuss the quality that should be built into a new product.

12. Why are design and color important to a new product?

13. Explain how competitor's actions can result in the failure of a new product.

14. How can errors by the engineering and accounting departments lead to the failure of a new product?

15. The attitude of "We now have an adequate design, let's stop researching" is dangerous. Why?

16. Discuss the feeling in the new-product department that sales and promotion of a new product are the concern of other departments.

17. Why is there pressure on the new-products department to rush its job?

18. Why should a company want to contract manufacturing out to other manufacturers?

19. What planning is required when a product reaches the decline stage of its life cycle?

20. Should a company retain an inventory of parts for its discontinued products? Why?

CASE PROBLEMS

Case Problem 1

Electronic Products, Inc. is the manufacturer of a line of electronic devices. Its alert, engineering-oriented management has been responsible for a steady growth rate during the fifteen years of the company's existence. The product line consists of electronic equipment that sells directly to the Department of Defense and the Atomic Energy Commission. In addition, some 10 percent of the company's sales arise through a subcontracting arrangement with a large manufacturer of household appliances.

Recent cutbacks in defense appropriations pose the threat of a reduction in the principal source of the firm's sales. Like many other companies in the same situation, the company is engaged in a frantic search for new consumer products. They have come up with a ship-to-shore receiver–transmitter radio for boating hobbyists. The consumer market for such equipment is large and rapidly expanding. The test models indicate that the company can profitably produce a better product than is presently available at the $250 price range. The financing, manufacture, and know-how of the radio is well within the company's capabilities.

Management understands that it must set up a marketing department to handle the promotion and distribution of the item. A young engineer who has been with the company for five years is anxious to take on the job. He is a graduate engineer with a master's degree in business administration. He is an intelligent, innovative, enthusiastic young man.

Questions

1. Should the company go ahead with the new product? Why?
2. If they decide to go ahead with it, how should they handle the marketing problem?

Case Problem 2

A leading manufacturer of grocery foods produces a very popular instant coffee. For years the firm has been troubled with the annoying and expensive problem of the disposal of the used coffee grounds that form the waste product of the manufacture of instant coffee.

Several years ago the problem was turned over to the research and development division to determine possible commercial uses for the waste material. After much testing, it was found that with small additional cost, the coffee grounds could be converted into an excellent mulch for home gardeners and farmers. Cost estimates indicate that the product could be sold at a price competitive with competing brands of similar quality. Although the profitability of the new product would be somewhat below the high return that is typical of the company's other products, it would be acceptable as a return on the investment required to set up a processing plant for the item.

At the present time, the company has no intention of further penetration into the home-gardening or commercial-farming fields.

Questions

1. Should the company go into the product?
2. Are there any other alternatives?
3. If the firm decides to go ahead with the product, outline—in order—the steps that should be followed.

BIBLIOGRAPHY

Alexander, R. S., "The Death and Burial of 'Sick' Products," *Journal of Marketing,* April, 1964.

Berg, Thomas L., and Abe Schuchman, *Product Strategy and Management.* New York: Holt, Rinehart & Winston, Inc., 1963.

Berton, Lee, "Firms Trying to Profit from Inventions Often Face Many Obstacles," *Wall Street Journal,* June 26, 1968.

Bours, William A., III, "Imagination Wears Many Hats," *Journal of Marketing,* October, 1966.

Buzzell, Robert D., and Robert E. M. Nourse, *Product Innovation in Food Processing, 1954–64.* Cambridge, Mass.: Harvard University Press, 1967.

Clifford, Donald K., Jr., "Leverage in The Product Life Cycle," *Dun's Review,* 1968.

"Creating a Climate for Employee Innovation," *Management of Personnel Quarterly,* Fall, 1967.

Fisk, George, *Marketing Systems—An Introduction Analysis.* New York: Harper & Row, Publishers, 1967.

"NICB Discusses New-Product Failure," *Printers Ink,* April 14, 1967.

O'Meara, Jr., John T., "Selecting Profitable Products," *Harvard Business Review,* January–February, 1961.

Pessemier, Edgar A., *New-Product Decisions.* New York: McGraw-Hill Book Company, 1966.

"Phasing Out Weak Products," *Harvard Business Review,* March, 1965.

"Setting a Timetable," *Business Week,* May 27, 1967.

Verma, Dharmendra T., "New-Product Planning and Development." Unpublished thesis, University of Utah, 1968.

Wasson, Chester R., "What Is 'New' about a New Product," *Journal of Marketing,* July, 1960.

PACKAGING AND BRANDS

9

INTRODUCTION FOR PACKAGING

The activities throughout the marketing process that are concerned with the design and construction of the container or wrapping of a product are called packaging. Not too long ago, packaging decisions were based solely on the physical characteristics of the product. Goods were moved from the producer to the final consumer in a manner that would insure product protection at the lowest possible cost. A prime example of this is the old general store in which merchandise such as flour, sugar, and crackers were received in bulk containers such as sacks and barrels and distributed to housewives in small unmarked containers by the storekeeper.

More recently, the package in which the goods are held has become as much of a sales tool as it is a container. At present, proper package design is one of the most important factors in the competitive battle for sales. The producer with the best package has a decided edge over his competitors and all progressive businessmen are contantly researching means to improve their packaging function.

PACKAGING CONSIDERATIONS

The problems of packaging design are not easy to solve. A good package poses many difficulties and many people are involved whose preferences may conflict. For example, the transportation and storage department may be primarily interested in the safety of the product and the ease with which it can be handled, whereas the main concern of the sales department is the package's eye appeal as a promotional device.

Packages must be individualized. That is, each type of goods has its own requirements and the design of the package must be unique to the specific goods involved. Several factors must be taken into consideration when packaging decisions are to be made.

The Retail Store

To design a package for a retail store, the designer must know the kind of store in which the package will be placed and the kind of customer that will buy the package. In a self-service supermarket, or any other self-service store, the package is an important selling device and the design of the package is vital to increased sales. The package must be visually competitive in order to facilitate the undecided shopper's choice.

The designer must keep in mind in which location of the store the package will be placed. Must it fit a supermarket shelf? Will it be part of a display? How will it be stored in the storeroom? (It must be strong enough to withstand storeroom handling.)

Transportation

Various transportation companies have standards and requirements that must be taken into account in packaging design. In addition, the size and weight of the shipping carton play an important role in the cost of transportation. Some goods require special treatment as to temperature control, moisture, pilferage, and vermin.

Warehousing

Goods that are warehoused may require special treatment relative to the manner of storage. The package design must depend upon the duration of warehousing, the way of handling the goods in the warehouse, the number of pieces that make up a typical shipment, and the method of taking warehouse inventories.

The Consumer

Packages, to be effective, must be designed for home use. A container that is immediately emptied and discarded has other requirements than one that is used to store the product until its consumption. The length of time that the contents will be stored and the method of use are also important. For example, it would be difficult to sell a pound of table salt in a flimsy container without a dispensing device. The packaging designer is also interested in whether or not the package is to be reused for the same product, reusable for another product by the housewife, returnable, stored in the kitchen or the basement, and so on.

PACKAGING AND SALES

The expansion of self-service shopping has placed an increased emphasis on packaging. If there is no salesman that can highlight the outstanding features of the product, only the package can be used to convince the customer to buy a particular product rather than that of a competitor. One method of achieving this is widely used by food companies. Their packages give such information as recipes, varieties of use, and number of servings in the package.

The use of transparent packaging material permits the supermarket customer to visually inspect the merchandise. Many products that are made of fabric carry a swatch of the goods on the package so that the customer may touch a sample.

Television and magazine advertising have increased the importance of packaging design by visual promotion. Prospective customers who cannot recall the brand name might still be familiar with a package because they have seen it and are more likely to buy it than an unfamiliar product. For this purpose, the package has to be uniquely designed.

Reusable Packages

Many plants package their products in containers designed for reuse. Cheeses, jellies, and similar foodstuffs are packed in containers that are suitable for drinking glasses. Many other items, for example, peanut butter and mayonnaise, are packed in glass or plastic jars that may be reused for leftovers, home canning, and so on. The aim of such packaging is to increase sales by giving the customer something in addition to the product itself. Packaging in reusable containers may lead to repeat business, since the customer may try to secure a complete set of drinking glasses or a plastic container of a particular size. Of course, the marketing drawback to collecting a complete set is that the customer may switch to another brand upon completion of the set. It is, however, effective as a short-term promotional device.

The problem that arises with reusable containers is whether or not customers are willing to pay the increased cost. An excellent example of a case in which the package is costlier than the product is a honey jar shaped like a bear, which later may be used as a coin bank. The customer is generally willing to pay far more for such an attractive, reusable container. Candy companies, for Valentine's Day, place more emphasis on the package than on the product.

Multiple Packs

Multiple packaging is the packaging of several units in one container. This practice has been steadily growing, since marketing research indicates that both total and unit sales may thus be increased. Products like handkerchiefs, beer, golf balls, cereals, dehydrated soups, and pillow cases are generally packed in multiples.

In addition to the obvious increase in sales, there are many other advantages to multiple packaging. For example, it reduces handling and price-marking costs. Many producers find that multiple packaging gives them an opportunity to effectively introduce new products. In this manner a manufacturer of dry breakfast cereals may package an assortment of six products, including a new item. The multiple pack almost guarantees that the new product will be tried by the consumer.

PACKAGING COSTS

It is obvious that good packaging is expensive. However, good packaging can result in an overall saving by improving product protection, ease of handling, and shipping costs. Moreover, by increasing the total sales volume, the costs per unit may be reduced. It should also be borne in mind that in large part packaging requirements insisted upon by the consumer result in higher costs. The packaging cost of a one-hundred-pound bag of sugar is only 1 percent of its selling price, but most shoppers prefer to buy sugar in two- and five-pound cartons and are willing to pay the 25 to 30 percent of the selling price that is involved with smaller lots.

ETHICS IN PACKAGING

One of the harshest criticisms of marketing concerns the misleading use of packaging. Each year the FTC receives an increasing number of complaints concerning the use of unnecessarily large boxes, false bottoms, overly thick walls, and so on, designed to give the consumer the impression that the package contains more of the product than it actually does.

It is true that many producers design their packages to mislead the consumer but this cannot always be determined by comparing carton size. The cost of packaging is ultimately paid by the consumer. Some producers are able to reduce the retail price of their product by gravity feeding, an inexpensive packing method that results in a considerable amount of air space at the top of the carton. Others reduce packaging costs by volume purchases of single-sized packages, which are then used for various quantities and densities.

Marketers argue that such packaging is done for competitive reasons rather than for fooling the public. They point out that the larger the package, the greater the customer eye impact and shelf space. For example, the toy industry, in an attempt to attract the eye of a child, often over-packages the product.

Another packaging complaint is that the amount packaged does not lend itself to the arithmetic necessary for comparison shopping. A customer who can easily compare the prices of the products of two manufacturers who package in one-pound lots cannot so simply make such comparison if one producer markets a 10½-ounce and the other and 11¾-ounce unit.

Some producers, for competitive reasons, reduce the amount in their package without reducing prices. In such cases an attempt might be made to change the container so that the change in quantity will not be noticed. (The law requires that the volume in the container must be clearly indicated on the label.) One large brewer uses an eleven-ounce container, whereas the industry standard is twelve ounces. Are the consumers aware of this?

Taking advantage of the fact that most shoppers do not calculate their costs on a price-per-ounce basis, many producers pack in large containers at a price equal to or higher than the sum of the prices of several smaller packages. Since most Americans have been conditioned to believe that savings are made by purchasing in the large "economy" size, this practice may improve profits.

The ethics of the practices described above are a constant source of debate. Truth-in-Packaging legislation, to make illegal some of the more flagrant packaging abuses, is constantly being brought up in Congress.

LEGAL ASPECTS OF PACKAGING

Federal legislation has placed certain controls on packaging. Laws such as the food and drug acts forbid the use of misleading and false information. More recently a law has been passed requiring a health warning on each pack of cigarettes.

The Fair Packaging and Labeling Act of 1966 requires:

1. Identification of product.

2. Name and address of manufacturer or distributor.

3. Indication of net contents.

4. Indication of weight in ounces and pounds for packages under four pounds.

5. Indication of the exact size of each serving if statements on servings of food product are made.

6. Voluntary, industry-wide standards for package sizes.

ECOLOGY

In recent years a great deal of attention has been focused on the disposal of waste matter and litter. Since a very substantial proportion of such litter consists of discarded packages, the issue is of vital importance to package designers.

The discontinuance of the reusable container that paid the user a premium to return the container to the store has resulted in a situation in which many such containers are either littering our streets and countryside or are overtaxing our garbage disposal facilities.

The core of the problem is that metal, glass, and plastic containers take up a great deal of space, require expensive garbage disposal equipment, and, when left in an open field, require many years to disintegrate.

At present, seemingly fruitful research is under way in the following areas:

1. Construction of new materials for containers that will shorten decay time and ease garbage incineration. The Jos. Schlitz Brewing Company is considering edible, soluble, and self-destructing bottles as a solution to the disposal problem created by throwaway bottles.

2. Uses for reclaimed glass and metal cans that will make the purchase of such waste an economically sound proposition. The Reynolds Metal Company pays one-half cent for each aluminum can. The company's Los Angeles reclamation center receives one million cans per month. These cans are melted down and reused.

3. Citizen education in the best means of disposing of such products and in the importance of disposal.

INTRODUCTION FOR BRANDS

An important factor in marketing success is product identification by customers. Many large firms accomplish this by establishing brands for their products. The American Marketing Association defines *brand* as follows:

> A name, term, sign, symbol, or design, or a combination of them, which
> is intended to identify goods or services of one seller or group of sellers
> and to differentiate them from those of competitors.

With the exception of certain bulk, standardized goods, such as cotton, coal, or wheat, almost all goods have an identifying name or brand. For example, Chevrolet is a brand owned by General Motors and Citgo is the brand name owned by the Cities Service Corporation.

By branding his goods and promoting the brand name, the producer or distributor hopes to develop an attitude in users that will give his goods a better marketing position than competing goods. If this acceptance can be achieved, it will result in increased sales and possibly also in increased selling prices. Frequently, the brand may be the most important asset of a firm and its only asset that cannot easily be reproduced by competitors.

MANUFACTURERS' BRANDS

Since the promotion of a brand requires a considerable amount of financing, usually only the largest companies own important brands. Some of the advantages derived from their established brands are:

1. Sales promotion depends upon customer identification with the specific product. Therefore, an established brand can act as a central point around which sales promotion can be built.

2. Branded merchandise is easily recognized by a customer, particularly if the brand is familiar through sales promotion. This encourages repeat sales, since the customer can find the product without searching or by mistake taking a competitor's product.

3. Brands build up their own customer following, so that it is difficult for a store to replace the brand with another product. A customer

who is interested in a particular brand will generally not accept a substitute and will resent being offered one.

4. Customers for present products will potentially buy similar new products. Customer confidence in a brand name can be transferred to a new product with relative ease because the customer feels certain that the quality will be up to the same standards.

5. Established brands have a tendency to maintain their prices in a falling market when nonbranded merchandise is likely to require drastic and frequent price cuts.

6. Manufacturers are prohibited by law to set the retail price of their goods except for "commodities identified by the trademark, brand, or the name of the producer or owner." In other words, manufacturers who use brand names are able to exercise control over the retail price of their goods.

7. Middlemen in many industries are eager to handle branded merchandise, since customer acceptance of such goods is already high and selling is relatively easy. Wholesale liquor dealers, for example, can rarely exist without including accepted brands in their line.

Manufacturers of branded merchandise face certain disadvantages as well. Some of these problems are:

1. A completely successful brand is one whose name becomes synonomous with the product itself. By law, when the "brand name may be identified so completely with an article of merchandise by the consuming public that it becomes the common or 'generic' name for the product itself," the producer's legal right to the brand name is ended. If the brand is too well established, it is no longer a private brand and may be used by all producers. Among the brands lost in this fashion are aspirin, milk of magnesia, cellophane, linoleum, lanolin, and shredded wheat. For this reason, branders must be extremely careful in promoting their brands to emphasize that there is a difference between the name of the brand and the name of the product. The Coca-Cola Company was not careful enough and the word *cola* has been ruled to be generic and may be used by any producer of that particular type of drink. Orlon is always advertised as a type of acrylic fiber and has not been declared generic. Borderline cases are Kleenex, Band-Aid, and Frigidaire. Strategies used by companies to protect their brand against being ruled generic are the use of two names including the firm name (Eastman-Kodak) and the changing of the name of the firm to coincide with the brand (Sunbeam, Sunkist, and Talon).

2. Some retailers resist nationally advertised brands because their profit margin is generally smaller on sales of such items. They either refuse to carry those brands or—if forced by their customers to carry such goods— they do not promote them.

3. Branded goods are easily identified, so that any customer unhappiness over the quality of the goods results in immediate sales loss. Effective quality control is absolutely necessary to a branded producer.

4. The advertising and sales promotion required to establish and maintain a brand name are extremely expensive.

CUSTOMERS AND BRANDING

To the customer, the most important characteristic of branded merchandise is that, unlike nonbranded merchandise, a branded item is guaranteed to be consistently of high quality. Manufacturers who have spent large sums of money in establishing a brand cannot afford to allow the quality of their merchandise to vary.

Another advantage of brands to the consumer is that the creation of a brand establishes a certain amount of prestige, which may give added consumer satisfaction.

PRIVATE BRANDS

Not all brands are owned by producers. Private brands are owned by distributors who do not own the manufacturing facilities for the product. A typical user of private brands is Sears, Roebuck and Co., which owns the brands Coldspot, Kenmore, Craftsman, Homart, and others. The major supermarket chains also promote a great number of their own brands.

Advantages of Private Brands

Distributors derive the following advantages from private brands:

1. Private-brand merchandise is less expensive than manufacturer's-brand merchandise because the manufacturer does not include the cost of promoting his brand when he produces goods under a distributor's brand. As a result, the distributor may sell his own brand, equal in quality to the manufacturer's brand, at a price below that charged for the manufacturer's brand and still work at a better profit margin than is made by selling the manufacturer's brand.

2. The private brand is controlled by the distributor. Not only does he control the quality and price but it cannot be taken away from him at the whim of the manufacturer.

3. It is very difficult for a customer to compare private-branded merchandise with similar goods sold by a competitor because the buyer can never be sure that the products are the same. For this reason private brands are not price-cut as frequently as unbranded merchandise. Private brands

are frequently used in retail stores that are faced with discount-house competition.

4. High-value private brands can build a following that will increase a dealer's total sales volume. Manufacturers' brands can generally be found at many competing establishments.

5. Private brands can be tailored to the tastes of a dealer's specific customers. Manufacturers' brands, on the other hand, are designed to suit a nationwide clientele.

Disadvantages of Private Brands

1. The private brand requires quality control at a manufacturing facility not owned by the distributor. This may result in less consistency in quality than is required of all branded merchandise.

2. The promotion necessary to achieve customer acceptance of private brands is very costly.

3. Owners of manufacturers' brands resent the competition of private brands and may in some instances take their brands away from distributors who sell private brands.

4. Unless the private brander's volume is very high, the material and manufacturing cost may be too high for him to offer a competitive product. In addition only large distributors have the prestige required to put a private brand across.

Manufacturers' Attitudes towards Private Brands

Since there is competition between manufacturers' brands and private brands, one would hardly expect manufacturers of their own brands to produce merchandise for private branders. In practice, this is not the case at all. For example, General Electric makes appliances for J. C. Penney, and Whirlpool Corp. for Sears. There are several reasons for the brand-owning manufacturers' willingness to produce for private branders.

For one thing, private branders are usually high-volume firms (Sears, Roebuck and Co., Montgomery Ward) whose orders are enormous. The manufacturer knows that if he does not take the order, someone else will, and the business will be lost. In some instances where no manufacturer could be found, the private brander may set up his own factory. Sears has done this many times. In short, if Sears wants goods to be manufactured, they will be manufactured. It would be foolish to turn away this business because of fear of competition, which will come about whether or not the order is taken.

Frequently, when the number of units manufactured increases, the cost of all the units manufactured decreases. General Electric, by producing appliances for J. C. Penney, not only makes a profit on the goods sold to J. C. Penney, but reduces the cost of the General Electric goods as well.

Finally, many manufacturers question whether or not the private brand is in direct competition with their own manufacturer's brand. The position they take is that a customer who is interested in a Sears Coldspot refrigerator only rarely considers a Whirlpool refrigerator at the same time.

Battle of the Brands

The competition between manufacturers' and distributors' brands seems to be favoring private brands because some of the retailing giants are putting more and more of their offerings under their own labels. In many large department stores 10 percent of total volume is done under the store's own brands. A&P has reached 25 percent and Montgomery Ward is aiming at 80 percent of total sales volume.

Family Brands

A manufacturer or distributor who is interested in establishing a brand for his merchandise must decide whether to set up an individual brand for each item in his line or have one family brand for all his products.

Family brands are generally used for products that carry a similar price and market. General Motors uses the family brand Chevrolet for a variety of cars of similar price that are aimed at a similar market. Their Cadillac brand is a separate price range keyed to a different consumer. If both Chevrolet and Cadillac were combined under one brand name, the lower-priced, lower-quality Chevrolet line would damage the image and prestige of the Cadillac models.

Wherever possible, family brands are used, since the advertising and promotion of any item within the family will help promote all of the family members. However, the various products in the family must be similar. That is, a successful family brand for canned fruits would not help the sale of appliances.

Many producers package a whole line of similar products in a family of brands. This is done by designing all the packages within the family in a nearly identical fashion. Heinz and Campbell soups are typical of family branding and packaging. The advantage of family branding is that new products added to the line reap the benefits of the goodwill and customer acceptance that has already been established for the old line. For family branding to be worthwhile, the line must have wide customer acceptance and the varous items in the line must be similar in cost, use, and quality. The disadvantage in family branding is that customer acceptance goes both ways. Acceptance of the older products will undoubtedly help win approval for the new item, but a weak new product may have a damaging effect on the older, established merchandise in the line. Producers that use family branding are mostly extremely careful in their research involving customer approval for new products.

Individual Brands

Although the case for family branding is a very strong one, many manufacturers prefer individual branding. That is, they market identical, nearly identical, or similar products under separate brand names. Procter & Gamble Co., for example, uses individual branding for such similar products as: Tide, Dreft, Oxydol, Ivory, and Joy. Since these are all household soaps or detergents, they could easily be placed under a family brand name. Producers use individual branding for the following reasons:

1. Producers can saturate the market by individual branding. There is a limit to the size of the product market an individual brand can achieve. A housewife who uses Tide to wash work clothes may feel it is too strong for her lingerie; she therefore selects Dreft, another P&G product, for delicate laundering.

2. Producers who grant exclusive territories can increase their number of outlets by individual branding. In this way a territory can be saturated without antagonizing the original dealer.

3. To meet price competition without reducing the price of his principal brand a producer may introduce a new "fighting brand."

4. When there is a chance of failure of a new product, an individual brand will protect the good will of the established brand.

5. Products aimed at different markets should be branded individually. The Gillette Company uses Papermate for pens, Toni, Prom, and Bobbi for home permanents, and Gillete for razor blades. It is doubtful if a woman would be attracted to the brand name Gillette for a home permanent.

6. Different quality levels should be branded separately. General Motors uses different brands for its various price lines. How many people would spend $7,500 for an automobile when the same brand name could be bought for $2,500?

SELECTING A BRAND NAME

Selecting a good brand name can be a very important factor in the success or failure of a brand.

The first important feature of a good brand name is that it is easily pronounced, spelled, read, and recognized. If the brand must be sold abroad, these characteristics should hold true for the languages of all countries in which the product will be offered for sale. The simplicity of reading, spelling, and recognition is important if the customer is to be able to find the item on a shelf with a minimum of effort. Since many customers hesitate to ask for a brand name if they are not confident of the pronunciation, the name must be easy. Kodak is an excellent example of a brand name that meets the requirements of pronunciation, spelling, recognition, and the necessities of the foreign market.

Short names are easy to pronounce. They have the additional value that they can be placed in large letters on the package. Major soap companies take advantage of this.

Good brand names are usually unique. Such names are easily remembered and do not run into the problem of being overused as is the case with General, United, or National. The use of personal names frequently causes trouble as in the case of Mr. Gerber's "Gerber Baby Food Company" having to buy out a furniture manufacturer named Gerber.

A brand name should have the proper relationship to the product. Sears "Craftsman" brand of tools is exactly right, as is Frigidaire, Sunkist, and Safeguard (a deodorant soap).

Brand names must be legally protected. Before going into an expensive promotional campaign, a company must make certain that the same name, or a similar one, is not already the property of another firm.

IMPORTANT POINTS IN THE CHAPTER

1. Packaging consists of the activities—throughout the marketing process—concerned with the design and construction of the container of a product. In recent years packagers are as much concerned with sales promotion as they are with product protection.

2. Since the characteristics of products vary, each package must be designed to fit the needs of the specific merchandise. Complications arise because consideration must be given to a variety of problems, for example, transportation, storage, type of customer, and use in the home.

3. The expansion of self-service shopping has placed strong emphasis on the use of the package as a "silent salesman." Since in many cases the package must sell itself, it must be designed in an unusual eye-catching fashion.

4. Packaging must perform a wide variety of functions; therefore, packaging costs are high. The customer is willing to pay extra for the convenience of a reusable container, and so on. Multiple packaging is a means of reducing packaging and handling costs while increasing sales volume.

5. Misleading packaging designed to exaggerate the contents in the

container or make price comparisons difficult has resulted in legislation that attempts to improve packaging ethics.

6. America's garbage and litter-disposal problems are in large part the result of discarded packages that do not lend themselves to rapid disintegration. Considerable research is under way to make packaging materials more readily disposable.

7. A brand is a means of identifying a producer's or distributor's goods from the product of his competitor. A brand with a good customer following has a marketing edge over its competitors. As a result, companies that are financially strong enough to promote a brand name generally do so.

8. The maintenance of a successful brand requires a guarantee of consistent quality. Failure in this area will offset all the costs and benefits of an established brand name.

9. Customers prefer branded to unbranded goods because they are not gambling when they purchase branded goods. They know exactly what are getting.

10. Manufacturers' brands are the property of the producers. Private brands are owned by distributors who contract with manufacturers for the production of their branded merchandise. The competition between private and manufacturers' brands is swinging in the direction of the private branding among high-volume retailers.

11. Family brands are used for similar items that fall within the same range of price and quality. They have the advantage of carrying each other. That is, when one item in the family is promoted, all the other products benefit.

12. A brand name should be easily pronounced, spelled, read, and recognized. It should also be unusual and related to some quality in the product. Care must be taken in promoting brand names, since they become generic when they are used as a synonym for the product. When a name becomes generic, its use is no longer restricted to the owner.

REVIEW QUESTIONS

1. Define *packaging*. Explain the use of packaging as a sales' promotion device.

2. Is transportation a problem in package design? Discuss.

3. What factors must be considered in the packaging of goods for home use?

4. Discuss the package as a sales-promotion tool. Why is it increasing in importance in this area?

5. Explain the effect of television advertising on packaging.

6. Discuss multiple packaging. What are the advantages of multiple packages? Give several examples.

7. Why are consumers willing to pay for the high cost of packaging?

8. How do distributors and manufacturers respond to the charge that they use large packages to mislead their customers?

9. In your opinion, will the provisions of the Fair Packaging and Labeling Act of 1966 improve packaging ethics? Discuss.

10. What is being done to help the garbage-disposal problems partly brought about by discarded packages?

11. Define *brand*.

12. What are the advantages of owning a brand?

13. Discuss the types of businesses that should not attempt to establish their own brands.

14. What type of business is most frequently involved in private branding? Why?

15. Discuss the disadvantages of owning private brands.

16. Why do some manufacturers turn down business from private branders?

17. What is the difference between family brands and individual brands?

18. Why do manufacturers choose to use family brands?

19. List and discuss the characteristics of a good brand name.

20. Explain the use of the term *generic* as it applies to branding. Give examples of brands that have been ruled to be generic.

CASE PROBLEMS

Case Problem 1

The S&H Kimmel Company is a family business that operates four food markets in high-rent areas in New York City. The stores are partially self-service, with clerks available to make suggestions and offer help when needed. The clientele is wealthy, and Kimmel's carries several well-known brands of gourmet and other high-quality foodstuffs. The service given customers, including deliveries, is excellent and has resulted in a strong, loyal group of customers who provide a handsome living to the owners. The annual sales of the chain are about two million dollars and are expanding, both through improvement in individual stores and the opening of new units. Management is conservative about opening at new locations, with a growth rate of about one store every four or five years.

Recently, Quality Foods, a West Coast canner of gourmet foods whose line is not carried by the store has approached the owners with the suggestion that Kimmel's take in their line under a private label. Quality Foods is a well-established, high-quality producer, whose products are widely advertised and certain to be acceptable to Kimmel's customers.

If Kimmel's decides to go ahead with the deal, they will be able to buy the line at a price about 10 percent less than they pay for foods of similar quality.

Question

1. Discuss the advantages and disadvantages of private labeling in this case.

Case Problem 2

Green Fields, Inc. is one of the giants in the fruit- and vegetable-canning industry. Their products are to be found in almost every food store in the country. The company's advertising and promotional policy is aggressive and it would be hard to find an American housewife who has never tried a Green Fields product.

There are twenty Green Fields canneries throughout the country, and their four hundred warehouses and distribution centers keep grocery shelves filled in every corner of the land.

At present, the company does not carry a frozen-food line. A recent market-research study has indicated that there would be wide public acceptance of frozen food packaged under the Green Fields brand name, and the board of directors has authorized construction of the necessary manufacturing facility.

The packaging director has been informed of this development and instructed to design packages for the new line. To get help with his problem, he has held discussions with the following people:

Production manager

Manager of sales promotion and advertising

Distribution and warehousing manager

Manager of customer relations

His wife

Questions

1. What questions should he ask of each of these people?

BIBLIOGRAPHY

"A Continuing Trend: Large Package Sizes," *Printers' Ink,* February 12, 1965.

Boyd, Harper W., Jr., and Ronald E. Frank, "The Importance of Private Labels in Food Retailing," *Business Horizons,* Summer, 1966.

Cook, Victor J., *Brand Policy Determination.* Boston: Allyn & Bacon, Inc., 1968.

Diamond, Sidney A., "Product Your Trademark by Proper Usage," *Journal of Marketing,* July, 1962.

Hancock, Robert S., "Factors Motivating Consumer Choice of Private Brands," *Marketing Concepts in Changing Times,* December, 1959.

Mason, William R., "A Theory of Packaging in the Marketing Mix," *Business Horizons,* Summer, 1958.

Modern Packaging, Encyclopedia Issue, 1967.

Morse, Leon, "The Battle of the Brands," *Dun's Review* and *Modern Industry,* May, 1964.

"Name of the Game: The Name," *Newsweek,* October 25, 1965.

"Private Brands Score Well," *Printers' Ink,* May 12, 1967.

Sanchagrin, Ted, "The New Power of Packaging: Management Takes Control," *Printers' Ink,* June 11, 1965.

"The Case of the Crumbled Cookie," *Printers' Ink,* January 13, 1967.

"The Power of Proper Packaging," *Business Week,* February 20, 1965.

Webster, Benjamin L., "First Steps in Package Design," *Distribution Age,* June, 1957.

PRICING

10

INTRODUCTION

The success or failure of a business depends on its ability to have available for sale a unique, properly promoted product at an attractive price. This combination of factors is called the marketing mix. The selection of the most important of the four factors (product, promotion, availability, and price) depends on the specific product. However, it is likely that it generally is price.

Price, by definition, is an offer to sell for a certain amount of currency. The important word is *offer,* since it indicates that price is subject to change if insufficient buyers can be found at the original price. That is, prices are always on trial, and if they are found to be wrong, they must be immediately changed or the product must be withdrawn from the market.

PRICING OBJECTIVES

Before prices can be set, it is important that management have an overall marketing goal. A survey of the pricing goals of twenty large industrial corporations indicated that prices were set with the following targets in mind:

To Achieve a Specific Return on Investment or Net Sales

When prices are set with the purpose of achieving a specific return, the targest return may be a short- or long-term goal. Targets of this type are generally found among enterprises that are leaders in their field, for example, General Motors, International Harvester, Aluminum Corporation of America, or Du Pont. These firms are generally the price leaders in their industries and as such are able to set prices without undue worry about competitors. It is important for these industrial giants to set prices that are "fair and reasonable," since "fair and reasonable" is the yardstick by which the Antitrust Division of the Justice Department, the labor unions, and the general public measure monopolistic practices or charges of restraint of trade. Smaller firms can only use prices to achieve targets of return on investment or sales for new or unique products because the price of run-of-the-mill products must be set to meet the competition of the rest of the industry.

To Stabilize the Market—Price Leaders

Another important pricing objective available to industry leaders is price stabilization. Companies that already control a large share of the market are frequently interested in a stability of price that will enable them to maintain their level rather than to increase it. U.S. Steel, Kennecott Copper, American Can, and Aluminum Corporation of America are typical of price leaders whose target is stabilization.

Price leadership does not indicate that all companies in the field will follow the leader by charging the same price as that set by the price leader. It rather means that a relationship is set between the price leader and the others in the industry. For example, minor oil companies generally price their product at one or two cents a gallon less than the prices charged by the major company in the field.

Price leadership requires careful policing by the leader if it is to be effective. If smaller firms cut their prices in an effort to increase their share of the market, the leader must be ready to keep them in line by means of a drastic, if temporary, price cut.

As the smaller firms in an industry grow in size, price leadership may shift. In the aluminum industry, the past twenty years have witnessed a gradual decrease in the importance of the Aluminum Company of America as the price leader, with the corresponding growth of Reynolds Aluminum and Kaiser Aluminum.

If a price leader sets price to stabilize the market and achieve a status quo, it does not necessarily follow that conservatism is the rule throughout its endeavors. For example, General Electric, Johns Manville, U.S. Steel, and other conservative price leaders are very aggressive in areas of product promotion and research.

PRICING CONSIDERATIONS

Unquestionably, the major objective of pricing is the earning of maximum profits. This may be done by a pricing policy that will attempt to achieve a high return, or by a pricing policy that seeks stability of price while the company seeks to maximize profits by means of research or promotion. Whatever pricing policy is decided on, for maximum effectiveness certain considerations must be taken into account before prices can be set.

Consistency

It is important to bear in mind that pricing is only one part of the marketing mix and that the profitability of an enterprise depends on the total mix rather than on prices alone. For marketing success, all the marketing elements must be handled consistently. For example, Lord and Taylor's (a retailer) promotion policy is to establish itself as a high-image prestige operation. Consequently, the product, price, and other factors must be consistent witth the high-image concept.

The Long-Run View

Setting prices that will maximize profits requires a long-run point of view. A new product that might be sold at a price that is designed to bring in a very high profit might also result in the attraction of competitors, which would minimize long-run profitability. Frequently, it may be to the long-run advantage of a firm to sell new products at a loss in order to get into a new field or gain customers for the firm's other offerings. New products on which production is limited generally have high production costs. The General Electric Company sets a low introductory cost on such items by calculating the production cost of the new item at the estimated cost of full-volume production. This policy may lead to short-term losses that will turn into maximum profits in the long run.

Pricing by Individual Items or by Total Profit

Many organizations find that their overall profits may be improved by varying the profitability of the individual items in their line. This procedure is quite apparent among retailers, who frequently employ the concept of loss leadership, that is, the drastic reduction of the price of one or more items to attract customers to the store in the hope of selling them more profitable merchandise. The drug department of R. H. Macy & Co., Inc. operates at a minimal profit to increase store traffic. Loss leadership can be achieved on individual items as well. Thus, a razor sold at cost will bring no profits, but the associated sale of razor blades may make up for it.

One Price versus Variable Price

A one-price policy, in which all buyers are charged the exact same price at any specific time, is the most common type of pricing. There may be provision under a one-price policy for varied prices for different classes of customers, quantity discounts, and price changes. This policy has the following advantages:

1. A buyer may be confident that the price he pays is exactly the same as the price any other customer must pay.

2. By eliminating negotiation for price, the sales personnel is able to concentrate its selling efforts on the positive qualities of the goods.

3. A one-price policy eliminates possible conflicts with the law.

Despite these obvious advantages, many large industries use variable pricing. Under such conditions, each customer is expected to haggle over price in an effort to make the best deal possible. This situation results in excessive shopping for the best price and loss of goodwill through favoritism. Variable pricing is much more common on the wholesale market than among retailers, but even at retail, purchases of automobiles and major appliances are tests of the buyer's skill at price negotiation.

Prices and the Standard of Living

During inflationary periods it is considered the responsibility of price leaders to do all they can to keep prices at a stable level. Great pressure is applied by the public and government to influence major industries to forego price increases for the good of the economy. This was dramatically illustrated when President Kennedy applied pressure to the steel industry to achieve the cancellation of a price increase.

PRICING PROCEDURES

Before arriving at a specific price, certain procedures must be undertaken. This is true for new as well as established products.

1. The demand for the product and the company's share of the market must be estimated.

2. Competitive reaction must be taken into account.

3. A decision must be made on the pricing strategy to be adopted to insure that the target share of the market will be achieved.

4. Consideration must be given to the company's image, promotion policy, channels of distribution, and a host of other company policies.

The Traditional Price

Customers traditionally expect to pay a certain price for a certain type of article. Lipsticks of a certain grade sell between one and three dollars. A price of more than three dollars would probably result in customer rejection and a price below one dollar would cause customers to question the quality of the merchandise. Consequently, for all but completely new products, a definite range must be researched before a specific price is established. The lower end of the price range (one dollar in the case of the lipstick illustration) is generally the cost of the product. This does not mean that the cost of the goods need have any effect on the selling price. Rather, if the cost is above the traditional price range, the article must not be included in the company's line of products.

The traditional or expected price can be determined by submitting the product to a knowledgeable retailer or wholesaler who knows the competitor's product. It may also be done by interviews or questionnaires given to wholesale or retail customers. Perhaps the best way to estimate demand at varying price levels is to test the product in a few areas at various prices. This sort of testing, although expensive, provides management with demand estimates at varying prices, which is extremely valuable information for the decision on specific price.

Competitive Reaction

In pricing an article it is vital to estimate the reaction of competitors to the price selected. A highly priced new article may attract competitors in droves. An established article with a low price may force the competition to cut prices, which may result in a price war or in a product with an unrealistically low profit margin. In industries that have price leadership a price cut by a small firm may result in a sharp painful response from the price leader.

Competition decreases as the difficulty to manufacture increases. That is, an item that is easily and inexpensively produced is likely to attract competition if the price and consequent profitability make it worth the competitor's effort. Those items that are not easily manufactured must be priced with an eye to the competition available through substitutes. Thus, as the price for steel increases, more use is made of aluminum and plastics.

PRICING STRATEGY

Several marketing strategies are available to management to achieve the target share of the market.

Skim the Cream

The skim-the-cream pricing policy is generally used for new, unique products such as color television. Ideally, it will get the maximum return from a new product by setting a price at the top of the expected range until all consumers willing to pay that price are used up, and then gradually lowering the price by steps to bring in new groups of buyers. Advantages of the skim-the-cream strategy are:

1. Frequently errors are made in the selling price of a new item. For example, production costs may be higher than anticipated. The selection of a low selling price that required an upward revision because of a faulty estimate is poor marketing practice. Consider an appliance that should sell for twenty dollars. It would be better marketing to begin with a twenty-five dollar price that would eventually be reduced to twenty dollars than to begin with a fifteen dollar price that would later be raised to twenty dollars.

2. New items require high production costs, high promotion costs, and high profits for channel members to stimulate their interest.

3. The production rate of new items is generally low and uneven. A skim-the-cream policy reduces demand while maximizing profits.

4. New items are frequently undercapitalized. High early profits, before the item attracts competition, will enable the producer to accumulate a sound financial bases for the article before it becomes competitive.

5. A high opening price on a product frequently has the effect of improving the sales appeal when the price is ultimately lowered.

6. The customers who are willing to buy the new product when it first becomes available are generally not price conscious and willing to pay a price that will yield high profits to the producer.

A skim-the-cream pricing policy is generally reserved for products that are difficult for competitors to produce. The policy may also be used for short-lived products (fads); in the latter case, the producer expects to be through with the item before any serious competition can develop. The Hula-Hoop is a classic example of this situation.

The chief disadvantage of the skim-the-cream policy is that it attracts competition. For those items that are easily produced excessive competition can be disasterous. When electric rotisseries first hit the market they were priced at seventy dollars. This was so profitable for an easily produced item that many competitors were attracted and the price went down to twenty dollars, so that the item's profitability became marginal. A more realistic opening price might have resulted in a very profitable item, since consumer appeal was excellent and competitors would not have been attracted.

Penetration Pricing

Penetration pricing is the direct opposite of skim-the-cream pricing. Instead of aiming for a market of few non-price-conscious customers, it emphasizes maximum exposure. It is felt that if enough people try the product, its chance of success is excellent. Penetration pricing is effective under the following circumstances:

1. The quantity sold must vary with the selling price. Such products as toothpaste and soap, whose demands vary strongly as prices change, are typically sold under a penetration price policy.

2. For penetration pricing to be effective, the product must have a substantially lower unit cost when produced in high volume since only reduced production costs will result in profits under penetration pricing.

3. The producing company must be financially strong enough to set up production and carry large inventories prior to the time the product hits the market. This is necessary because effective penetration policy results in an immediate high-volume demand.

4. The competition for the product must be so high that skim-the-cream pricing is impossible.

5. The demand for the product at skim-the-cream pricing must be so low that such pricing is out of the question.

6. Promotion must be geared to insure the maximum demand at which penetration pricing is aimed.

Penetration pricing is designed to limit competition. It is generally used for products that are expected to have a long market life and that can be produced easily by competitors.

Premium Pricing

Premium pricing must begin with a strong product. This, coupled with high-image promotion and quality customer service, can result in higher than normal prices. In this way, Saks Fifth Avenue can get more for a product than a discounter, and the Cadillac division of General Motors can sell at a better markup than the Chevrolet division. It should be emphasized that premium pricing must begin with a quality product. The finest and most effective promotion cannot sustain a premium price if the quality of the product is mediocre.

Promotional Pricing

To attract attention to certain products, prices are frequently set to give bargains, or at least to appear as bargains. Promotion pricing should be coupled with a promotional policy in keeping with the product and its price. Polaroid's low-priced *Swinger* is advertised to appeal to the young, price-conscious buyers. Among automobile manufacturers it is commonplace to offer the same basic products under different names and a variety of trims. In this way the lowest-priced model may be available for a promotion price whereas the more elaborately trimmed models may be regularly priced; that is, four or five hundred dollars higher.

THE COMPANY'S MARKETING POLICIES

No discussion of pricing can be complete without reference to the great number of other factors that affect pricing decision. Among these are a great variety of company policies that must be taken into account when prices are set. Some of these policies are:

Relation to other products in the line
Guarantees to the purchaser
Services offered by the company
Channels of distribution

Relation to Other Products in the Line

Those companies that offer a line of related products must price new products with an understanding of the effect the new product will have upon the other items in their offerings. In other words, General Motors, in setting a price on a newly developed Pontiac, must consider the competitive effect the new item will have on its Chevrolet, Oldsmobile, and Buick division. In such a situation, the range of prices for which the new Pontiac must be sold is dependent on the prices that have been set for the other products in the line. In some cases, the same product may bear different labels and different prices to appeal to different segments of the market. The cosmetic industry provides many examples of this situation.

Guarantees to the Purchaser

When product guarantees are made to the purchaser, as is the case with most automobiles and appliances, the cost of fulfilling such guarantees must be included in the price.

Services Offered by the Company

Prices must be high enough to cover any associated services that are offered by the company. For example, Bonwit Teller is a high-fashion-image specialty store in which the major portion of the selling is handled by carefully trained personnel. Consequently, one would expect to find higher prices at Bonwit Teller's that at Korvette's, a self-service discount department store. If customer alterations are free in a clothing store, the price must include this cost. The point is that when more than the bare product is being sold, the price must be set to cover such additional expenses.

Channels of Distribution

Prices must be set at a level that offers an adequate profit for each channel member to insure his enthusiastic cooperation. Those channel members who are responsible for the advertising and promotion of the item must have sufficient markup on the product to cover these expenses. In many instances producers set prices not only for themselves but also for every channel member up to the final consumer.

SETTING THE PRICE

After all the various considerations that affect price have been taken into account, the actual setting of the price must be effected. The price must be high enough to cover all costs plus the hoped-for profit.

Markup on Selling Price—Retailers and Wholesalers

Most retailers and intermediary channel members figure their price by using a markup based on selling price. It works this way: an item that costs $1.00 is sold for $1.50. The markup is $0.50. In terms of a percentage of selling price, the markup is $\frac{0.50}{1.50}$ or 33⅓ percent. In other words:

Selling price	$1.50
Cost	1.00
Markup	0.50

$$\frac{\text{Markup} \quad 0.50}{\text{Selling price } 1.50} = 33\tfrac{1}{3}\% \quad \frac{\text{Markup on}}{\text{Selling price}}$$

Markup is generally based on selling price rather than on cost. For one thing, it is in accord with accounting reports and terminology. In addition, if the average markup percentage is known, it can be applied to the sales for a period and an estimated profit can be determined.

In practice, wholesale channel members are generally limited in their pricing by the discounts set for them by prior channel members. For example, in the medical-accessory business, the producer or price leader might mark a piece of equipment at the retail price and sell it to a wholesale channel member at 60 percent below retail. The difference between the retail price and the retail price less the 60 percent discount to the wholesaler is the amount of profit to be shared by the remaining channel members.

An important aspect in retail pricing is the number of times the average inventory is sold during the year. This is called turnover. A retail jewelry store that has a turnover of one or two times a year must, of necessity, make more profit per item sold than a fresh-fruit-and-vegetable store that has a turnover of forty or fifty times per year.

The notion that high retail profits result from high markups is erroneous. Low prices can improve the turnover and frequently yield higher profits than the high price resulting from large markups. The growing success of discount retailing operations is proof that profits can be increased by a high turnover caused by low markups and the resulting low prices.

Markup on Cost—The Producer

Most producers compute their selling prices by adding a percentage or specific amount to the estimated cost of product. Various producers use different methods of calculating the selling price, but it is generally done on the basis of cost. For example, one manufacturer may determine the selling price of his product by adding 50 percent to his cost to cover his general and administrative expenses (expenses other than those concerned with manufacturing, for example, officer's salaries) and profit. Another manufacturer, whose pricing target is to achieve a 20 percent return on investment, would add a specific amount to his cost that would result in the target profit. A producer whose investment is five hundred thousand dollars and whose target is a 20 percent return on investment or one hundred thousand dollars would estimate the number of units he will sell for the year and add sufficient profit to the unit price to achieve the desired target. (If estimated sales were one hundred thousand units, each unit would be priced to yield one dollar of profit in order to reach the target profit of one hundred thousand dollars.)

Pricing based on cost is simple and readily understandable. Unfortunately it has some serious limitations. This can be explained by the following example.

A manufacturer of upholstered couches decided that he could sell one hundred pieces of a certain style. His workers were paid on a piecework basis, so he was certain of his labor cost. By careful analysis he was able to calculate his material cost exactly. His only other costs were rent, his salary, and other overhead expenses that were easily determined. He set his selling price in this manner:

Total labor cost $60 per couch × 100 couches	=	$6,000
Total material cost $40 per couch × 100 couches =		4,000
Total labor and material cost		$10,000

By dividing the total labor and material cost by the one hundred counches that were to be produced he found his labor and material cost to be one hundred dollars per couch ($10,000 ÷ 100 = $100). Since the job would take one month, and his average month's overhead was two thousand dollars, he determined his overhead cost per couch to be twenty dollars ($2,000 ÷ 100 = $20). His total cost per unit was:

Labor and materials	$100
Overhead	20
Total	$120
Since his profit was to be 25 percent of cost he added ($120 × 25%)	30
and determined his selling price to be	$150

Let us assume now that he only sold sixty couches. His income statement would be as follows:

Sales (60 couches × $150 selling price)		$9,000
Labor and material cost (60 couches × 120 L&M cost)	$7,200	
Overhead cost for the month	2,000	
Total cost		$9,200
Loss		$ 200

The problem is that there are two kinds of costs: variable costs (that vary with the sales volume) such as labor and materials, and fixed costs (that do not change with sales volume) such as rent and officers' salaries. The difficulty with figuring selling prices based on cost is that whereas the variable cost per unit (materials and labor) remains constant regardless of volume, the fixed cost per unit changes according to the volume. In other words, it is impossible to calculate fixed costs on a per unit basis unless the estimated number of units sold can be accurately predicted.

Marketing specialists construct graphs to illustrate the effect of volume

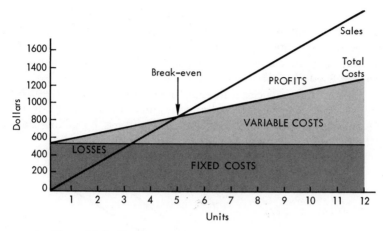

Figure 10-1 Break-even chart—Selling price $160 per unit

on costs and profits. The graph is called a break-even chart, since it indicates the number of units that must be sold at a particular selling price in order for the firm to break even. Figure 10–1 illustrates the break-even chart of a company with fixed costs of $500, variable costs of $60 per unit, and a unit selling price of $160 per unit.

The chart pictured in Figure 10–1 was prepared as follows:

1. The graph was designed with the number of units that might be sold arranged horizontally, and dollars of sales and costs arranged vertically.

2. The fixed costs of five hundred dollars, which will remain the same regardless of the number of units sold, was shaded in. (Remember, officers' salaries, rent, and so on do not vary with sales.)

3. A line was drawn that indicates the variable cost for each number of units sold. Since variable cost must be added to fixed cost to calculate total cost, $500 (total fixed cost) was added to the variable costs. For example, the variable cost of selling three units is $180. In a situation in which three units are sold, the total cost would be $180 variable cost plus $500 fixed cost or $680. After calculating the total cost for several levels of volume, the total cost line could be drawn on the chart.

4. The sales line was drawn by indicating the total sales volume, which is the result of multiplying the units sold by the selling price per unit ($160). For example, the sale of ten units would yield $1600 (10 × $160).

ANALYSIS OF THE BREAK-EVEN CHART

The break-even chart indicates the fixed cost, the variable cost, the sales volume, and the profit and loss at every level of sales volume. If three units are sold, the total sales equal $480 (3 × $160), the total cost equals

$500 fixed cost plus $180 variable cost or $680, and the loss equals $200, total cost $680 minus total sales $480. In addition, the break-even chart indicates that the break-even point is reached when five units are sold, since total sales (five units at $160 equal $800) and total costs equal $800, (fixed cost $500 plus variable cost five units at $60 equal $300).

When a pricing decision must be made among several possible prices, the break-even chart can be adjusted to indicate the break-even point, profits and losses, sales, and costs for various levels by adding additional sales lines to the chart. Figure 10–2 illustrates this.

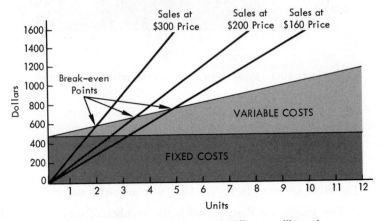

Figure 10–2   Break-even chart with different selling prices

The difference between the break-even charts illustrated in Figures 10–1 and 10–2 is that consideration has been given in Figure 10–2 to the effect of various selling prices on profits, losses, and the break-even point.

The major difficulty with the break-even charts that have been discussed so far is that customer demand at the various prices has been ignored. The charts are based upon the unrealistic idea that the product can be sold in unlimited quantities at various prices. In other words, although showing what must be sold to break even, the chart gives no estimate of what can be sold at the various price levels. This can be overcome by estimating the sales of the product at the various price levels.

As we have seen, break-even charts are easy to understand and construct. They are, however, anything but a perfect pricing tool. The problem is that the charts are based upon estimates of future fixed costs, variable costs, and sales levels at several different selling prices. Each of these factors is subject to uncontrollable factors that make accurate estimation very difficult. For example, variable costs tend to decrease at a certain level of production. However, since all pricing must be based on estimates of costs and sales, the break-even chart offers a means of indicating these estimates with maximum simplicity.

Pricing based on cost is widely used among manufacturers and producers. However, the term *cost-plus pricing* is somewhat misused. The price that must be charged for a product is actually the amount the customer is willing to pay. It is ridiculous to assume that a customer would be willing to pay a high price for a product because its cost is high. Cost-plus is used to determine whether or not a business organization should go into the production of a particular product. If the merchandise can be produced at a cost that will result in an adequate profit, the organization might decide to produce it. Once the decision of to produce or not to produce is made, the actual price of the product must be based on customer attitudes rather than on the cost of the merchandise.

PRICE DISCOUNTS

Many sellers permit their customers to purchase merchandise at a reduction from the stated list price. Such reductions in price are called discounts. Although it is rarely obvious, discounts are generally given to channel members in return for their taking over a part of the marketing function. For example, a wholesaler who buys merchandise for later sales is in fact taking over the function of carrying inventory for the producer. In return for assuming this important marketing function, he is entitled to a discount. The following are the most commonly used types of discounts:

Cash discount—a deduction for prompt payment

Quantity discount—a deduction based on the size of the purchase

Trade discount—a deduction that is given to differentiate between different types of customers (wholesale versus retail)

Seasonal discount—for off-season orders

Cash Discounts

A cash discount is a reduction in price allowed to a buyer for payment of his bill before it is due. For example, a manufacturer might sell one hundred dollars worth of goods, with payment due in thirty days. As a reward for prompt payment, the manufacturer allows his customer to deduct 2 percent if he pays within ten days. In this manner, the manufacturer is willing to take less money for his merchandise if the buyer is willing to pay his bill before the due date. A 2 percent discount for payment within ten days of a bill that is due in thirty days may be stated as: 2/10, N/30 (2 percent discount for payment in ten days, total net amount due in thirty days).

The size of the cash discounts varies from industry to industry. Whereas 2/10, N/30 is common for food sales, dress manufacturers offer their customers 8/10 e.o.m. That is, the customer may deduct 8 percent for payment within ten days after the end of the month in which the purchase was made.

Quantity Discounts

To encourage customers to buy in large quantities, many sellers offer discounts that are scaled to the number of units ordered. As far as the seller is concerned, the larger the order, the smaller the selling and shipping costs and the greater the sales. To achieve this, the seller is willing to offer discounts. To the buyer, quantity discounts offer the opportunity of a reduction of the cost of merchandise.

Quantity discounts may be noncumulative (on a per order basis) or cumulative (over a specific period of time).

Noncumulative quantity discounts are based on individual orders. An example of such a discount would be men's shirts sold either at four each or at three for eleven dollars. At the wholesale level noncumulative quantity discounts might be offered as follows:

Pieces Ordered	Price per Piece
1–20	$10.00
21–50	9.50
51–100	9.00

Large orders result in savings in such areas as packing, shipping, bookkeeping, and production planning. Noncumulative quantity discounts encourage large orders by passing along some of the savings to the purchaser.

Cumulative quantity discounts are based on volume of purchases over a specified period of time. They are a means of encouraging business by offering increasing discounts as the total volume from a customer increases. Cumulative quantity discounts might be offered as follows:

Total Annual Purchases	Cumulative Discount
$0– $5,000	1%
$5,001–$10,000	1½%
$10,001–$20,000	2%

Trade Discounts

Trade discounts (sometimes known as functional discounts) are a means of reducing the price charged to certain buyers in return for the performance of specific marketing functions. For example, a manufacturer selling to wholesale and retail customers may give a trade discount of 40 percent to the wholesaler (who will have to resell the goods to retailers) and a trade discount of 25 percent to the retailer.

Seasonal Discounts

Manufacturers of highly seasonal products such as toys, furs, and lawn mowers are plagued with the problem of keeping their factories running during the slack season. Seasonal discounts are a means of attracting orders during the slack season by reducing prices on goods sold in the off-season. Frequently, such orders are given forward dating as well. That is, although the manufacturer's regular terms may be 2/10, N/30, much longer terms are offered to those customers that place their orders during the slack season.

GOVERNMENT REGULATIONS ON PRICING

Federal and state governments have been active in passing legislation that affects price. The laws have frequently been poorly written, complex, and difficult to understand or administer. However, some of the laws are important and play a significant role in pricing. For example, in an effort to slow down the economy a price control board limited price increases to an average of 2½ percent in November 1971.

The Robinson-Patman Act

Perhaps the most important type of federal legislation involved with pricing is the government's attempt to limit price discrimination. Any buyer who can make a purchase at a lower price than his competitors has an advantage. His lower cost enables him to either increase his profits by maintaining the regular selling price or to increase his share of the market by reducing his selling price without affecting his profit per sale. To protect buyers who do not get a price edge from this sort of discrimination, the Robinson-Patman Act of 1936 (an amendment to the Clayton Act) was passed. In addition, the act states that there cannot be any unfair advertising allowances that would give the larger user an advantage. Advertising allowances should be given in direct proportion to total purchases to prevent discrimination against tthe smaller business.

Price discrimination is prohibited by the Robinson-Patman Act when:

1. "The effect of such discrimination may be substantially to lessen competition or...

2. To create a monopoly."

The Robinson-Patman Act does not control all price variations. In the following situations price reductions may be legal:

1. When the price reduction was made to meet the low price of a competitor.

2. When the price reduction was based upon cost savings incurred in selling the favored customer.

3. When the price reduction was made on goods that were either obsolete or about to become obsolete.

The workings of the Robinson-Patman Act can be illustrated in the following example.

A shoe manufacturer sells to many stores within a certain city. Included among the customers is a member of a large national department-store chain. Since the shoe manufacturer is anxious to sell other units in the department-store chain, he agrees to grant a 12 percent discount to the department store. This discount enables the department store to undersell its competitors. The discount will be considered in violation of the Robinson-Patman Act unless one of the following defenses can be shown:

1. The discount is based on a reduction in cost. The large sale to the large store resulted in cost savings (delivery, bookkeeping, and so forth).

2. The discount was a response to a similar cut made to the department store by a competitor.

3. The shoes in question had to be sold at once due to style changes.

IMPORTANT POINTS IN THE CHAPTER

1. Price leaders, who need not be concerned with competitors, fix prices on their products with definite goals in mind. Such goals may be to earn a specific return on investment or to stabilize the market.

2. Pricing is one of many elements upon which commercial success depends. Intelligent pricing requires prices that fit consistently with the other market elements.

3. The procedures used for setting prices include consideration of customer demand, competitive reaction, and other policies of the company.

4. Skim-the-cream pricing is generally reserved for relatively non-competitive items. This policy attempts to maximize profits by setting high prices that are gradually reduced as the demand at the price set dries up.

5. Penetration pricing attempts to give a product maximum exposure by setting prices at a very low level.

6. Markup is the difference between cost and selling price. When markup is calculated as a percentage, it is generally based on the selling price for retailers and other channel members and on cost for producers.

7. Variable costs are those that change as sales volume changes. Fixed costs remain constant regardless of sales volume.

8. A break-even chart is a graphic way of illustrating the number of units that must be sold at a particular selling price if a firm wants to break even.

9. Discounts are price reductions that are given to channel members in return for their taking over a part of the marketing function.

10. Price discrimination is illegal under the Robinson-Patman Act if it results in lessened competition or monopoly, unless it can be shown that the deduction was made to meet competition, from cost savings to a particular customer, or on old goods.

REVIEW QUESTIONS

1. Differentiate between the pricing problems faced by price leaders and those faced by smaller firms.

2. Explain the statement, "pricing must be consistent with other company policies."

3. Discuss loss leadership as a means of increasing overall profits.

4. Compare one price and variable price. What are the advantages and disadvantages of each policy?

5. How can the traditional price range within which the price must fall be established?

6. Why is competitive reaction an important factor that must be taken into account in price seting?

7. Explain the skim-the-cream pricing policy. When is it most effective? When least effective?

8. Explain the penetration pricing policy. When is it most effective? When least effective?

9. What type of product would be suited to premium pricing? Promotional pricing?

10. How do company policies such as guarantees or customer service affect pricing?

11. A table that cost sixty dollars is sold at one hundred dollars. Calculate the markup percentage and the markup percentage on retail and on cost.

12. Differentiate between variable and fixed costs.

13. What information is illustrated by a break-even chart?

14. What are the shortcomings of a break-even chart?

15. How much cash will be needed on July 10 to settle a purchase of $150, with terms 2/10, N/30 dated July 3?

16. Discuss the reasons for which discounts are given.

17. Explain quantity discounts. What is the difference between cumulative and noncumulative equantity discounts?

18. Why are seasonal discounts given?

19. Under which two conditions is price discrimination prohibited by the Robinson-Patman Act?

20. Indicate three instances in which prices may be reduced for special customers without fear of a violation of the Robinson-Patman Act.

CASE PROBLEMS

Case Problem 1

Prepare a break-even chart from the following information:

Fixed costs	$1,000
Variable Costs	120 Per unit
Selling Price	320 Per unit

Questions

1. How many units must be sold for the company to break even?
2. Indicate the profits or losses under the following sales assumptions:
   a. None
   b. 4 units
   c. 8 units

Case Problem 2

The Research Department of one of the country's largest cosmetic manufacturers has developed a hair straightener that is far better than any similar preparation presently on the market.

The formula is nonpatentable but requires very expensive equipment. It is considered likely that six of the company's competitors have the financial strength to go into the new product. Expectations are that competitive products will be on retailers' shelves within twelve to eighteen months of the time the product hits the market.

The company's marketing division is split over the pricing of the new item. One group favors a low price that will encourage universal acceptance of the product before any of the competitors' products arrive on the scene. The second group feels that because the product is of high quality, the demand will be so great that price will be of little importance and prices should be set to yield maximum early profits.

Questions

1. List all arguments you can think of in support of the penetration-price group.
2. List all arguments you can think of in support of the skim-the-cream-price group.
3. As the-vice president in charge of marketing, the ultimate decision is yours. Which policy do you prefer?

BIBLIOGRAPHY

"The Anatomy of a Price-Fixing Conspiracy," *Business Week*, September 8, 1962.

Bachman, Jules, "Pricing: Policies and Practices," *Studies in Business Economics*, No. 71 (1961).

Doan, Joel, "Pricing a New Product," *The Controller*, April, 1955.

Griffin, Claire E., "When Is Price Reduction Possible," *Harvard Business Review*, September–October, 1960.

Harper, Donald V., *Price Policy and Produce*. New York: Harcourt Brace Jovanovich, Inc., 1966.

Kaplan, A. D. H., Joel B. Dirlam, and Robert F. Lanzillotti, *Pricing in Big Business*. Washington, D.C.: The Brookings Institution, 1958.

Leavitt, Harold J., "A Note on Some Experimental Findings about the Meaning of Price," *Journal of Business,* July, 1954.

Machlup, Fritz J., Howard Westling, and Gerald Albarem, *Resale Price Maintenance*. New York: The Macmillan Company, 1964.

"Management Often Kills New Products with Poor Policies," *Marketing Insights,* October 2, 1967.

Moranian, Thomas, Donald Grünewald, and Richard C. Reidenbach, *Business Policy and Its Environment*. New York: Holt, Rinehart & Winston, Inc., 1965.

Mortimer, Charles G., *The Purposeful Pursuit of Profits and Growth in Business*. New York: McGraw-Hill Book Company, 1965.

"New Strategies to Move Goods," *Business Week,* September 24, 1966.

"Rambler Takes a Gamble," *Business Week,* February 25, 1967.

Udell, Jon, G., "How Important Is Pricing in Competitive Strategy," *Journal of Marketing,* January, 1964.

Welsh, Stephen J., "A Planned Approach to New-Product Pricing," American Marketing Association Management Report No. 66.

TRANSPORTATION AND STORAGE

11

IMPORTANT POINTS IN THE CHAPTER
REVIEW QUESTIONS
CASE PROBLEMS
BIBLIOGRAPHY

INTRODUCTION

From a businessman's standpoint, transportation has the function of moving goods from the place of production to that of consumption. To be effective, a system of transportation must be able to deliver the correct quantities at the right time at a reason able cost.

In marketing, transportation is essentially a tool for carrying out the place function. As such, it is extremely important, since it affects both the time and price functions: time because transportation must insure that the product is in the proper place when it is needed; and price because the cost of transportation should not exceed the level at which the goods may be sold in a competitive market. The importance of transportation to marketing cannot be overemphasized. Physical distribution of goods accounts for nearly 50 percent of total marketing costs.

The wide variety of methods by which goods may be transported at different costs creates rather complicated transportation decisions. Success

TABLE 11–1

ESTIMATED DISTRIBUTION OF INTERCITY FREIGHT TRAFFIC
IN UNITED STATES: IN MILLIONS OF TON-MILES

Railroads are still the major carrier for intercity freight. Although the physical volume of rail freight has increased substantially, the railroads' share of the market has declined considerably since 1940. Freight shipped by truck or pipeline has increased from 10 percent of the total in 1940 to 22 percent in 1969. If we consider intracity freight, which carrier is most important?

Carrier	Ton-miles, 1969	Percentage of Total			
		1969	1960	1950	1940
Railroads	780,000	41.2	44.1	56.2	61.3
Great Lakes	111,000	5.8	7.6	10.5	15.5
Rivers and canals	185,000	9.8	9.2	4.9	3.6
Motor trucks	404,000	21.3	21.7	16.3	10.0
Oil pipeline	411,000	21.7	17.4	12.1	9.6
Air carriers	3,200	0.2			
Total	1,894,200	100.0	100.0	100.0	100.0

Source: *Yearbook of Railroad Facts*, Association of American Railroads, Washington, D.C., 1970, p. 42.

or failure of the product may depend in large part on selection of the most suitable transportation method. Naturally, the type of goods involved is the most important factor in this decision.

METHODS OF TRANSPORTATION

Railroads

Despite the growth of various competitive means of transportation, the railroads are still the major carriers of goods in terms of ton-miles (five tons of goods moved two miles equals ten ton-miles). The reasons for this success are:

Fairly quick service
Fairly low cost
Fairly extensive coverage (there are in excess of 400,000 miles of track in the United States)

Although the railroads do not lead in any of these respects, their combination is unique and enables them to maintain superiority. For example, waterway carriers are less expensive than railroads, but they offer far less speed and geographical coverage; trucks give more extensive coverage, but at a higher cost.

The rates charged by railroads vary considerably with the size of the shipment and the distance the goods must travel. Thus, the full-carload (CL) rate is much lower than the less-than-carload (LCL) rate and the through rate (relatively long distance) is less expensive than the local rate (short distance). These characteristics of railroads make them ideally suited to the transportation of heavy, bulky goods such as coal, sand, and ores over long distances.

In recent years, shippers have been inclined to bypass the railroad carriers in favor of other means of transportation. To offset this, the railroads have instituted certain innovations designed to keep old customers and attract new users.

PIGGYBACK SERVICES. One of the disadvantages railroads face is the fact that they are limited to tracks. As a result, a shipper using the railroads frequently must allow the time and bear the expense of unloading a freight car and loading the merchandise on a truck before it reaches its destination. Piggyback service entails loading the goods on a truck trailer, which in turn is loaded on a freight car. When the freight car reaches its destination, the truck trailer can be quickly attached to a truck cab and the delivery can be completed. In this way the shipper is not bothered with unnecessary unloading of the freight car and loading of the truck trailer.

POOLING SHIPMENTS. To try to overcome the competition offered by other carriers for LCL shipments (with a relatively high railroad cost), the railroads have developed procedures for LCL shippers to pool their shipments into CL quantities. This results in lower shipping rates and faster service. One requirement for pooling LCL merchandise into CL quantities is that the goods must have the same point of origin and destination.

IN-TRANSIT PRIVILEGES. In another attempt to make rail transportation more attractive to customers the railroads permit their customers, at no extra cost, to change destinations while en route. In this fashion a shipment of oranges from California to Omaha may be diverted to Kansas City and be charged as if the shipment were made directly from California to Kansas City. Another in-transit privilege permits goods to be processed en route, with a rate from the point of origin to the ultimate destination (a longer haul, therefore a cheaper rate). Under this provision, wheat may be shipped from Kansas City, converted to flour in Detroit, and shipped on to New York, with a freight rate based on the through rate from Kansas City to New York.

SPECIALIZATION OF EQUIPMENT. Railroads are able to attract business by specializing their equipment to the needs of specific customers. Triple-deck carriers for automobiles, refrigerator cars, and tank cars are typical of the types of equipment used by railroads to suit the needs of certain target customers.

FAST FREIGHT. In order to compete with other carriers who move goods more quickly than the conventional freight service, many railroads offer fast-freight service. This is a nonstop 60-miles-per-hour freight service designed to compete with trucks for shippers of perishables and goods that require rapid transit.

Trucks

The enlargement of the American network of roadways and the technological improvement of motor vehicles has brought about a tremendous expansion in the use of trucks as means of transporting goods. There are three types of motor transportation:

1. *Common carriers* serve the public at large. They move any type of goods to any part of the country. Generally, common carriers specialize in particular types of goods, such as refrigerated trucks and moving vans.

2. *Contract carriers* serve particular customers by entering into formal contracts with their customers for specific periods of time.

3. *Private carriers* are owned and operated by individual firms for the transportation of their own goods.

The reason for the competitive success of motor vehicle transportation is that it offers the following advantages over transport by railroad:

1. Trucks are not restricted to railroad tracks. Unlike railroads, they can go to any place that has available roads. The network of roads in America is vastly more extensive than the network of railroad tracks.

2. Goods shipped by truck sustain less damage, since their handling is limited to loading at the shipping point and unloading at the destination. This results in savings in expensive packing materials and in insurance.

3. Merchandise can be picked up at any time and delivered directly to the customer. There is never any unnecessary unpacking and repacking.

4. Railroads cannot begin a trip until a full load of freight cars has been assembled. Trucks, on the other hand, can leave at any time.

5. Transportation for short distances is considerably cheaper by truck than by railroad.

No comparison of trucks with railroads can be complete without mentioning the fact that trucks benefit from the building and maintenance of highways by public funds, whereas railroads must build and maintain their own tracks. Therefore, in part at least, motor transportation receives governmental subsidy in its competition with railroads. This puts the railroads at a significant disadvantage, which is apparent in their reduced profits and increasingly less-effective passenger service.

Pipelines

Although rarely noticed by travelers, pipelines rank third in America as means of transportation of goods. They are used chiefly for the movement of natural gas and crude oil and derived products. Continued improvement in the construction and operation of pipelines has considerably increased their efficiency and extended their use to other types of liquids.

For suitable products pipelines offer an economical way of transportation. Like railroads, pipelines are limited in their use by the availability of facilities; railroads and trucks are still widely used to transport goods that could be more efficiently handled by pipelines. Presently, there is widespread construction of pipelines going on; this will further increase their use at the expense of other means of transportation.

Waterways

The cheapest transportation available to American industry is via the coastal and inland waterways. Regrettably, the waterways are also the slowest means of transportation. However, there are many industries to whom price is more important than speed. They locate their facilities to take advantage of the low freight cost offered by the waterways. Typical is the location of steel mills in the Great Lakes area, where the barge rate for iron ore is about one-tenth of the rail rate.

The construction of the St. Lawrence Seaway resulted in important savings to midwestern shippers and increased the use of the waterways for shipping goods. At the same time, the St. Lawrence Seaway points up one of the serious disadvantages of this use, namely that freezing, floods, or drought increase the risk of delay. Despite these drawbacks, the petroleum, chemicals, sugar, coffee, cotton, and grains industries use the waterways extensively for transportation of their products.

FISHY-BACK.   Water transportation suffers from a similar disadvantage as does rail transportation: merchandise must be unpacked from the barge and repacked on a truck before reaching its destination. This is made unnecessary by the so-called fishy-back method of packing, which involves packing the goods into a truck trailer and the truck trailer onto the barge. At the end of the waterway the truck trailer is attached to a truck cab; this eliminates unnecessary packing.

Air Carriers

Although recent years have seen enormous growth in the use of the air carriers for transporting merchandise, they are still relatively insignificant in terms of total ton-miles shipped. The most important features of air transport are:

1. They are much faster than any other means of transportation. As a result, the air carriers are excellent for the shipment of perishables, high-fashion goods, and small, high-value industrial goods.

2. Thanks to their speed air carriers have opened markets never before used because of the perishability of the product. This is particularly ture for overseas shipments. For example, Hawaiian orchids, too perishable to be sent to the continental United States by boat, are now being flown in.

3. The careful handling given freight by air carriers reduces damage and packaging costs. One California producer of equipment merely wraps his product in paper for airfreight. In the past, when his goods were shipped by rail or truck, costly wooden containers were required.

4. Many shippers who previously maintained warehouses at central points throughout the country to assure prompt delivery to customers are finding that airfreight can get the goods to the customer as fast without the expense of maintaining warehouses.

Undoubtedly air transportation of merchandise will maintain its enormous growth rate.

Containerization

In recent years, there has been a promising attempt to reduce transportation costs by shipping all goods in standardized containers. If a group of small packages going to a single destination is packed into one container, considerable reduction in the amount of handling, pilferage, and time will result. In addition, specially designed merchandise-handling equipment can be used, which will further reduce costs.

Regrettably, the packaging requirements of shippers and the preferences of carriers have made agreement on standardization difficult. Consequently, containerization is less widespread than would be expected.

REA Express

REA Express is the name given the reorganized Railway Express Agency. It is an organization that under a monopoly owned by the major railroads provides rail, air, and truck service to all parts of the country. The REA Express is used chiefly for small-sized, perishable consumer goods. Its offices throughout the country provide a coordinated pickup and delivery service, both C.O.D. and prepaid.

Parcel Post

In 1912 the federal government established the parcel post under the Post Office Department to stimulate transportation by mail. As is the case with REA Express, parcel post is generally used for small consumer articles. Parcel post puts some restrictions on size, weight, and perishability that are not in force for REA Express. Mail-order companies make considerable use of parcel post.

TRANSPORTATION RATES

As we have seen, the shipper can choose from several competing transportation facilities; each performs a somewhat different service for a different rate. The cost depends chiefly on the amount and type of goods to be shipped and the travel distance. However, numerous factors within those two classifications affect the cost of transportation.

Type of Goods

1. Loading problems. The difference between the loading costs of, for example, canned foods and iron ore affects the total cost of their transportation.

2. Carrier's liability for loss or damages.

3. Volume and frequency of shipments.

4. Special requirements of the goods and type of equipment needed.

Travel Distance

1. Longer hauls are relatively less expensive.

2. Switching from one line to another and reloading (for LCL) affects the cost.

3. Amount of other traffic in the same direction. Generally, the more heavily traveled routes have a lower rate.

4. Competition among carriers frequently results in considerable price variations.

FREIGHT FORWARDERS

Freight forwarding is a service industry specializing in handling LCL shipments. By appealing to a wide variety of small customers freight forwarders are able to consolidate small lots into full-carload or full-truckload size shipments and to reduce freight costs. For customers with occasional export business they offer the know-how and paper work for combining train, truck, and transoceanic shipments. They also provide the technical skill and traffic-management services for small shippers. It is estimated that about 75 percent of the general cargo shipped from U.S. ports to foreign countries is handled by freight forwarders. Their expertise in processing the required export paper work makes them valuable to even the largest exporters. As a result, more than 90 percent of all exporters use freight forwarders.

FUTURE TRENDS IN TRANSPORTATION

During the past thirty years there has been a consistent trend in the relative importance of the various types of transportation available to shippers. There is no reason to believe that this trend will not continue.

The future of transportation will probably be along the following lines:

1. Railroads will continue to lose their relative importance as freight movers while continuing to increase their ton-mileage.

2. Waterway traffic will continue to increase both in ton-mileage and relative importance, despite the construction of new pipelines for the petroleum industry.

3. Pipelines will increase in relative importance due to continued increase in the consumption of the products they serve and the construction of new pipelines.

4. Motor trucks will be used more and the relative importance of the trucking industry will expand.

5. Airfreight will have the most dramatic growth, both in terms of ton-miles and in relative importance.

TRANSPORTATION AND THE COMPUTER

As has been discussed, the variety of carriers and rates can pose a complicated problem to a shipper. As for many problems in which a wide variety of factors must be considered, modern business is turning to the computer for rapid solution. By putting all pertinent data into the memory banks of a computer and requesting information as to the best route between two points, many firms have succeeded in simplifying an otherwise knotty transportation problem.

STORAGE

The time function is created by storage. Storage is involved with the holding of goods from the time of their production to that of their final sale. Some of the reasons for storage are:

1. Agricultural products and other seasonally produced goods must be warehoused between the production and final sale or use.

2. Goods that are produced regularly throughout the year but sold seasonally, such as sporting equipment, toys, furs, and so on, require storage.

3. Excess goods, that is, goods bought in excess of immediate needs of the purchaser because of quantity discounts offered by producers and the transportation savings that result from full-carload shipments require storage.

4. Goods not purchased for current use must be stored. Frequently price increases can be anticipated. In such cases it is common for buyers to place large orders prior to the price increase.

5. Some products require an aging period after they are produced to improve their quality, such as tobacco, liquor, meats, and cheeses.

6. When the selling price of goods can be increased by withholding them from the market, storage becomes necessary.

METHODS OF STORING GOODS

Since the types of merchandise that require storage differ widely as to their physical requirements, their storage requirements differ as well. Storage facilities include cold storage (for meats, fruits, and vegetables), grain elevators, and warehouses.

Warehouses are the most common type of storage facility. These may be privately owned by industries who maintain, control, and supervise the storing of their merchandise to suit their own specific needs, or be public warehouses.

Public warehouses are regulated by the government and may be found all over the country. For a fee they provide all the services required in the storage of goods. There are five types of public warehouses:

1. *General-merchandise warehouses,* used to store a variety of goods for a relatively short time. General-merchandise warehouses may be bonded, in which case they control merchandise on which a tax must be paid before the goods are released. There is, for example, a tax on whiskey. Rather than pay the tax during production and storage, the producer sends the finished product to a bonded warehouse that provides for the payment of the taxes only when the goods are shipped to customers.

2. *Special-commodity warehouses,* designed for the specific requirements of such merchandise as grain, tobacco, and cotton.

3. *Furniture warehouses,* specially designed for furniture, household goods, and other personal property.

4. *Cold-storage warehouses,* for goods whose preservation requires carefully controlled, low temperatures.

5. *Field warehouses,* set up on the premises of the owner of the goods, but completely controlled by an independent warehouseman.

SERVICES OFFERED BY PUBLIC WAREHOUSES

Public warehouses generally offer their customers the following services:

1. Receipt, unloading, and placement in storage of goods.

2. Inspection of all incoming goods in accordance with the standards set by the owner.

3. Packing, shipment, and performance of the necessary paper work of goods sold by the owner.

These services are generally performed in well-constructed, often fireproof buildings, provided with sprinkler service and twenty-four-hour-a-day watchmen. (These provisions reduce insurance rates). Public warehouses are generally used by manufacturers who lack storage space and whose requirements for storage are too small to make owning or leasing private warehouse facilities practical. Another important reason for public warehousing is to secure a warehouse receipt.

WAREHOUSE RECEIPTS

When goods are stored in a public warehouse, the owner of the merchandise is given a warehouse receipt. This receipt is proof of ownership of the goods and its importance lies in the fact that it is negotiable. That is, the warehouse receipt may be transferred to a third party. The significance of the negotiability is that because the warehouse receipt carries with it the title to the goods, it may be given as collateral for bank loans. Each year banks lend hundreds of millions of dollars on inventory secured by warehouse receipts. In this way warehousing provides an important source of working capital to American businessmen.

Warehouse receipts that are later used as collateral for loans are the most important reason for the maintenance of field warehouses. Because the merchandise stored in such a facility is controlled not by the owner but by a warehouseman who is completely independent of the owner, the banker making the loan on a field-warehouse receipt may be confident that his security (the inventory covered by the field-warehouse receipt) will remain intact.

WAREHOUSING AND TRANSPORTATION

Many manufacturers who do business on a national scale maintain warehouses throughout the country. This results in savings in transportation and improvement in customer services. Many large supermarkets maintain distribution centers (in effect, large warehouses from which shipments are made) in or near every large population center that is served by their retail outlets. This enables them to replenish stock on the store shelves within a day or two. Similarly, manufacturers locate warehouses near their markets, guaranteeing their customers improved delivery service.

The above-mentioned savings in transportation can be effected because businesses using distributions centers for shipping to customers are never forced to send expensive, small lots from the factory to far-off customers. Instead they send inexpensive, large-volume shipments to their distant warehouses, store the merchandise there, and make small, expensive shipments only for the relatively short distances between the distribution center and its local customers.

Since transportation and storage are closely related, they must never be considered separately. Instead, the overall picture must be carefully studied in terms of the effect on timely delivery and transportation costs before the location of distribution centers can be decided.

Improvement in the speed of transportation, particularly airfreight, has led many companies to reconsider their warehousing systems. Some examples of this are:

1. Raytheon replaced four New England warehouses with one large distribution center. By relying heavily on airfreight and using a computer for order filling they were able to reduce the amount of capital tied up in inventory, cut their distribution costs by 20 percent, and improve customer service.

2. Libby, McNeill, and Libby replaced 214 warehouses with five distribution centers as a result of a careful study of their warehousing and

transportation needs. Savings in this area lead to increased profits and lower customer prices.

Progressive management is constantly studying its warehousing and transportation problems. The present trend seems to be away from small warehouses and toward major distribution centers. This pattern has been followed by the Borden Company, Whirlpool Corporation, Bigelow-Sanford, and many others.

REDUCING TRANSPORTATION COSTS

Considering the fact that transportation costs are almost half of the total cost of marketing, it is strange that many firms ignore the opportunity to cut their transportation costs. Even those firms that employ the most scientific methods of shaving pennies from their manufacturing costs are frequently blind to the important savings opportunities resulting from improved transportation planning. Some suggestions follow.

Proper Location of the Manufacturing Plant and Warehouses

The location of the manufacturing facility of a business organization has an effect on both the transporting of raw materials into the plant and the movement of finished goods out of the plant. Thus, the geographical site picked for manufacturing is most vital with regard to transportation costs. In general, it is wise to manufacture as close to the raw materials as possible because they frequently contain waste materials, transportation of which should be minimized.

Warehouses and warehouse distribution centers should be located near the markets they must serve. Transportation facilities at the warehouse sites should be adequate to their needs both in terms of incoming bulk shipments and outgoing small shipments.

Proper Use of Inexpensive Transport

Not all shipments require rush service. This is particularly true if production planning takes shipping problems into account. Production should be early enough so that inexpensive bulk rates may be used wherever possible.

The opening of the St. Lawrence Seaway provided the opportunity for tremendous savings on transportation to many businesses. However, some businessmen, unaccustomed to this form of transportation, have not yet made a proper survey of the effect of using the waterways in order to reduce their transportation costs.

The pooling of small orders into carload lots is another frequently ignored method of reducing transportation costs. Businesses that have occasional opportunities for pooling should turn to freight forwarders for help in arranging such pools.

Proper Packaging

Too often businesses are using specific packaging containers that are unwieldy and expensive to ship. Studies should be made of the possible transportation savings that can be made by a change in· the packaging design.

Proper Authority for the Traffic Manager

In most firms, the responsibility for transportation and warehousing is divided among many individuals, who are under the direction of various executives. When the importance of traffic in terms of the total cost of the product is considered, it becomes obvious that transportation is as important as any other major business function. Transportation and warehousing should be under the control of a distribution manager who reports directly to the president, and who is on a par with the sales manager, the factory manager, and other similar executives.

IMPORTANT POINTS IN THE CHAPTER

1. Transportation is a tool for moving goods from the place of production to the place of consumption. As such, it creates the place function. Since transportation constitutes about one-half of the total cost of most goods, it is a vital element in the price function as well. In addition, the time function (that is, availability of the goods at the right time) depends largely on the effectiveness of the system of transportation used.

2. Transportation problems are complicated by the large variety of methods of transportation, each of which has a great number of advantages and disadvantages.

3. Technological advances have reduced the importance of railroads while improving the relative significance of other means of transportation. In an attempt to keep their competitive position, the railroads have instituted certain innovations, such as piggyback and specialized equipment. Although they are still the transportation leaders, particularly for long-distance bulk shipments, the importance of railroads for transportation of merchandise is decreasing.

4. Trucks are steadily becoming more important. Our enormous network of roadways permits trucks to be anywhere. Trucks dominate the short-haul transportation market.

5. Pipelines are growing in importance as means of moving petroleum products and other liquids.

6. The waterways, though slow, are the cheapest means of transportation. The opening of the St. Lawrence Seaway resulted in their increased use. Bulk shipments for which speed is not vital are frequently shipped by boat.

7. Airfreight, although still relatively small in volume, is the fastest-growing method of shipping. The airways are very expensive, but their speed makes them attractive for high-value, urgently needed goods.

8. Transportation rates are controlled by governmental agencies and based on the characteristics of the goods and the travel distance.

9. Storage creates the time function. It is involved with the holding of goods from the time of their production to that of their final sale.

10. A wide variety of public warehouses is available for storing merchandise; warehouses also provide other services, such as unpacking and shipping.

11. Warehousing and transportation must be considered jointly, since the proper location of a warehouse may result in important savings on transportation costs.

12. Large distribution centers are replacing groups of smaller warehouses. The large distribution center, coupled with rapid means of transportation such as air freight, can be located farther from the markets without a loss in customer service, but with considerable savings in distribution expense.

13. It is important that all storage and transportation functions be combined into one department; its manager should be equal to other executives.

REVIEW QUESTIONS

1. Explain the effect of transportation on the place, time, and price functions.
2. Discuss the use of railroads for moving goods, indicating its advantages and disadvantages.
3. What are pool shipments? Why are they used?
4. Railroads offer specialized equipment to their customers. Discuss fully.
5. Why are trucks able to compete successfully with railroads?
6. Compare the effect of governmental subsidy on the trucking and railroad industries.
7. What are the advantages and disadvantages of shipping by waterways?
8. Describe the type of merchandise that is likely to be shipped by airfreight.
9. Define and discuss REA Express as a way of moving goods.

10. Discuss some of the characteristics of goods that would have an effect on transportation rates.

11. Give instances in which the travel distance will affect transportation rates.

12. Discuss the future of trucks and of airfreight.

13. Define *storage* and differentiate between private and public warehouses.

14. What sort of services are offered by public warehouses?

15. Field warehouses are located on the premises of the manufacturer; why are independent warehousemen brought in to control them?

16. Explain the relationship between warehousing and storage.

17. What is the effect of the location of manufacturing and warehousing facilities on transportation costs?

18. How can packaging affect the cost of transportation?

19. Discuss the use of a computer for the solution of transportation problems.

20. Why is it important for the person in charge of transportation and storage to be equal to the sales and production managers?

CASE PROBLEMS

Case Problem 1

The Royal Company is a large, well-established manufacturer of household appliances. It boasts nationwide customers and it maintains twelve warehouses throughout the country to store goods, reduce transportation costs, and provide quick customer service.

A survey of transportation and warehousing costs has indicated that the expense involved in physical distribution exceeds the amount considered normal for the industry. The organization chart of the company indicates that the responsibility for transportation is divided among departments, as follows:

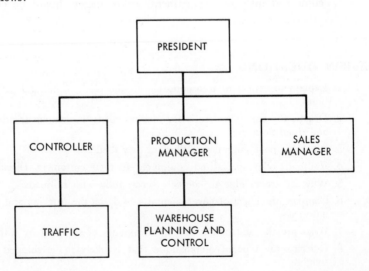

Inventory is carefully controlled by a computer that provides weekly information on low-inventory items. Production schedules are based on the indicated inventory shortages.

A management-consulting firm called in to study the distribution problem proposes that the organization of the firm be changed as follows:

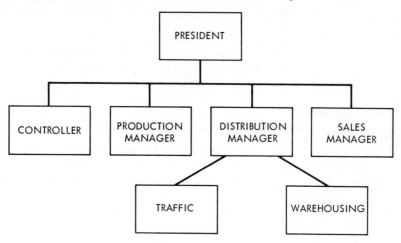

Questions

1. Why should all matters of transportation, both incoming and outgoing, be handled by the same department?
2. Why should both traffic and warehousing be placed under the responsibility of the distribution manager?
3. Why should the distribution manager be equal to the controller, the production manager, and the sales manager?
4. Comment on the effect of the system of production planning on transportation costs.

Case Problem 2

Sunflower Stores, Inc. is a large, rapidly expanding supermarket chain. At present, Sunflower Stores operate at 712 locations throughout the country.

The method of expansion used by Sunflower Stores is to construct six to eight large outlets in a specific area, and to support these stores with a centralized warehouse. There are now 102 warehouses throughout the country, providing rapid service in keeping the supermarket shelves filled. This system works very well, as is evidenced by the fact a store rarely has to wait more than three days after a request for merchandise until the goods arrive.

There is a proposal before management to replace the 102 warehouses with twelve large distribution centers. It is felt that considerable savings can be effected by this move.

Questions

1. What would be the effect of the change on transportation costs to the distribution center? To the stores?
2. What would be the effect of the change on warehousing costs?

3. What would be the effect of the change on the amount of inventory that Sunflower Stores would have to carry?
4. Since the distribution center would generally be located further from the existing supermarkets than the present warehouses, how could delivery time be speeded up?
5. Comment on the importance of a computer to a distribution center.
6. What would be the effect of this new system of warehousing and distribution on expansion into lightly populated areas that cannot support more than one or two stores?

BIBLIOGRAPHY

"Big Load Afloat," American Waterways Operators, Inc., 1965.

Bowersox, Donald J., Edward W. Smykay, and Bernard J. Lolonde, *Physical Distribution Management,* rev. ed. New York: The Macmillan Company, 1968.

Constantin, James A., *Principles of Logistic Management.* New York: Appleton-Century-Crofts, 1966.

"Containers Widen Their World," *Business Week,* January 7, 1967.

"Doubling the Freight Car's Workday," *Business Week,* December 18, 1965.

Gobel, Arthur E., and L. C. Schmetzer, "Reducing Transportation Costs," *Small Business Administration,* April, 1962.

"How to Manage Physical Distribution," *Harvard Business Review,* July–August, 1967.

Kotler, Philip, *Marketing Management: Analysis, Planning, and Control.* Englewood Cliffs, N.J.: Prentice-Hall, Inc., 1967.

Langhoff, Peter, *Models, Measurement, and Marketing.* Englewood Cliffs, N.J.: Prentice-Hall, Inc., 1965.

Lazer, William, "A Systems Approach to Transportation," in N. C. Marks, and R. M. Taylor, eds., *Marketing Logistics.* New York: John Wiley & Sons, Inc., 1967.

Magee, John F., *Physical Distribution Systems.* New York: McGraw-Hill Book Company, 1967.

"Pepsi Cuts Costs through Hawaiian Canning Operation," *Marketing Insights,* October, 1967.

Stewart, Wendell M., "Physical Distribution: Key to Improved Volume and Profits," *Journal of Marketing,* January, 1965.

"Two Ways to Look at Landed Costs," *Chain Store Age,* February, 1965.

"Waterways of the United States," National Association of River and Harbor Contractors, 1963.

WHOLESALING

12

INTRODUCTION

Wholesalers play an important role in the distribution of goods. Although it has often been suggested that elimination of the wholesaler will bring greater profits to the producer and perhaps lower prices to the consumer, statistics show clearly that the activities of wholesalers are continuously increasing. Obviously, the marketing experts do not wish to eliminate the wholesaler. In order to understand the significance of wholesaling for the marketing of goods, it is necessary to study the various types of wholesalers and the services they provide for producers and consumers alike.

This chapter shows charts provided by the Census Bureau that incorporate both consumer and industrial goods. However, wholesaling principles and methods in Chapter 12 apply strictly to consumer classification of goods and services. The industrial market is covered in Chapter 5.

DEFINITION OF WHOLESALING

The American Marketing Association defines *wholesaler* as

> ...a business unit which buys and resells merchandise to retailers and other merchants and/or to industrial, institutional, and commercial users but which does not sell in significant amounts to ultimate consumers.

Wholesalers are primarily middlemen who buy for the purpose of resale. Technically, however, the retailer, whose main function is to sell to the ultimate consumer, may be classified as a wholesaler if the goods he sells are not intended for personal use of the buyer. For example, a retail stationery store that sells ledgers to other retailers for their record keeping is engaged in a wholesale activity. Thus the *purpose of the sale* determines whether it is a wholesale or retail transaction.

DIFFERENCE BETWEEN WHOLESALING AND RETAILING

Wholesalers differ from retailers in many ways. Neither group is involved in manufacturing goods and they both engage primarily in selling, but to separate and distinct markets. Basic differences are:

1. *Markets Served.* Retailers sell goods and services to ultimate consumers for their own use. Wholesalers sell primarily to retailers (or other wholesalers) whose purpose it is to resell the goods.

2. *Size of Purchases.* Wholesalers buy in significantly larger quantities than retailers. One of the wholesaler's main functions, in fact, is to afford the retailer the opportunity to buy in small quantities.

3. *Methods of Operation.* Wholesalers generally operate in lofts and warehouses, which are typically located in out-of-the-way places. This is possible without being detrimental to business because they sell their goods either by means of orders placed with salesmen who make retail-store visits, or via telephone or mail orders. Retailers, on the other hand, generally operate from stores located in areas that are easily accessible to the ultimate consumer.

4. *Area Served.* The trading area of the wholesaler is typically larger than that of the retailer. There are exceptions to the rule. For example, by way of mail or telephone orders, the retailer's trading area can increase enormously.

5. *Cost of goods.* Although wholesalers and retailers can often purchase from the same manufacturer, the wholesaler generally is charged a lower price because of the nature of his business. Of prime importance is that he buys in much larger quantities than the average retailer. Giant retail chains are able to place orders larger than those of wholesalers. They frequently buy directly from the manufacturer, bypassing the wholesaler, and obtaining a price advantage. Examples of such retailers are Sears, Roebuck and Co. and R. H. Macy & Co., Inc.

HISTORY OF WHOLESALING

Wholesaling of goods dates back at least five thousand years. At that time the Chinese emperor Shen Nung established "the practice of holding markets for the exchange of commodities."[1] Early wholesaling was also in evidence in such far-off lands as Sumeria, Egypt, Babylonia, Phoenicia, Greece, and Rome. Much of the trade, wholesale as well as retail, took place at fairs.

[1] H. H. Gowen, *An Outline History of China* (Boston: Sherman, French & Co., 1917), p. 26.

During the Middle Ages, great fairs were held in Russia, France, Italy, and China. Manufacturers and merchants from distant lands came to these fairs to buy and sell merchandise. In the thirteenth and fourteenth centuries the fairs were held at intervals of three to twelve months and often lasted a full month.

From 1500–1800, wholesaling activities in foreign countries increased. Exchanges were organized to trade commodities, auctions were flourishing as means of selling certain goods, and the number of wholesale middlemen multiplied greatly.

In the United States, wholesaling activities expanded following the Civil War. Before that time the general-merchandise wholesaler was busy servicing the needs of the general store. The decline of the general store and its eventual replacement by the specialty retailer (limited-line store) prompted wholesalers who heretofore carried wide assortments of general merchandise to specialize in turn. Large-scale production helped to change the complexion of the wholesaler's wares. Formerly he dealt substantially in imported merchandise, but now his goods were primarily domestic.

Since 1929, a more accurate appraisal of wholesaling has been possible. In that year the wholesale trade was made part of the first census of distribution. Periodically censuses of business are taken. They offer invaluable statistics with regard to the various trends of wholesaling.

CLASSIFICATION OF WHOLESALING IN THE UNITED STATES

The census of business classifies wholesalers into five major categories (see Table 12–1). They are merchant-wholesalers, manufacturers' sales branches and offices, petroleum bulk plants and terminals, merchandise agents and brokers, and farm-products assemblers. An explanation of each classification follows for an understanding of their significant differences.

MERCHANT-WHOLESALERS

By a wide margin, the merchant-wholesalers comprise the most significant of the wholesaling classifications. Aside from their importance in terms of the mere number of establishments, they account for greater sales volume than any of the other categories. Basically, the merchant-wholesalers buy, take title to, and store goods for the purpose of resale.

Merchant-wholesalers are separated into two basic types and are further subclassified as follows:

Service wholesalers
  a. General-merchandise wholesalers
  b. General-line wholesalers
  c. Specialty wholesalers

TABLE 12–1

WHOLESALE TRADE: COMPARISON BETWEEN 1963 AND 1967

	1963		
Type of Operation	Establishments (Number)	Sales (000,000)	Operating Expenses (Including Payroll) Percentage of Sales
United States, total	308,177	$358,386	
Merchant-wholesalers' total	208,997	157,392	13.5%
Service wholesalers:			
Wholesale merchants' distributors	194,121	135,857	14.6
Importers	5,724	9,243	8.9
Exporters	2,664	8,282	4.4
Terminal grain elevators	633	3,000	5.6
Limited-function wholesalers:			
Wagon, truck distributors	5,825	1,010	13.0
Manufacturer's sales offices, sales branches, total:	28,884	116,443	7.2
Manufacturers' sales branches (with stock)	16,408	54,857	10.6
Manufacturers' sales offices (without stock)	12,476	61,586	4.2
Petroleum bulk plants, terminals, LP gas facilities, total	30,873	21,485	N. A.
Merchandise agents, brokers, total	25,313	53,245	3.6
Auction companies	1,894	5,141	2.6
Merchandise brokers	5,083	13,855	2.8
Commission merchants	3,416	9,524	2.7
Import agents	393	2,112	2.2
Export agents	544	2,179	2.8
Manufacturers' agents	11,189	10,941	6.0
Selling agents	2,574	8,292	3.9
Purchasing agents and resident buyers	220	1,201	2.6
Assemblers of farm products, total	14,110	9,820	9.0

(*N.A.*) *Item not applicable.*
Source: 1963 Census of Business.

Limited-function wholesalers
   a. Cash-and-carry wholesalers
   b. Drop shippers
   c. Mail-order wholesalers
   d. Truck-and-wagon distributors
   e. Rack jobbers

SERVICE WHOLESALERS. As the name implies, the service wholesaler, often known as the regular or full-function wholesaler, in addition to goods provides a host of services for both his customer—the retailer—and for the manufacturer. The limited-function wholesaler, on the other hand, provides

TABLE 12–1 (cont.)

1967

Type of Operation	Establishments (Number)	Sales (000,000)	Operating Expenses (Including Payroll) Percentage of Sales
United States, total	311,464	$459,476	
Merchant-wholesalers' total	212,993	206,055	13.8%
Wholesale merchants' distributors	204,783	181,776	14.8
Importers	5,171	10,354	10.3
Exporters	2,272	9,508	4.1
Terminal grain elevators	767	4,418	4.5
Manufacturer's sales offices, sales branches, total:	30,679	157,097	7.2
Manufacturers' sales branches (with stock)	16,709	67,175	11.3
Manufacturers' sales offices (without stock)	13,970	89,922	4.1
Petroleum bulk plants, terminals, LP gas facilities, total	30,229	24,822	0.3
Merchandise agents, brokers, total	26,462	61,347	4.0
Auction companies	1,594	4,792	2.9
Merchandise brokers	4,373	14,030	3.2
Commission merchants	5,425	14,068	3.4
Import agents	270	1,791	2.2
Export agents	548	3,372	1.9
Manufacturers' agents	12,106	15,257	6.4
Selling agents	1,891	6,890	4.2
Purchasing agents and resident buyers	255	1,147	3.6
Assemblers of farm products, total	11,101	10,156	8.6

Source: 1967 Census of Business.

relatively few services. The following is an extensive list of services; not every wholesaler provides every service discussed.

Services Afforded the Retailer

1. By carrying a sufficient supply of merchandise, the wholesaler makes it possible for the retailer to operate with a limited inventory. Since one of the major functions of the wholesaler is storage, the retailer can feel confident that stock replenishment will be quick and easy.

2. In order to make certain that the proper merchandise will be offered, ultimately, to the consumer, the wholesaler attempts to ascertain the needs of the retailer. Thus the wholesaler actually involves himself in the forecasting of consumer demands and plans his purchases accordingly. With the wholesaler researching the needs of the ultimate consumer, some of the burden is taken away from the retailer. The wholesaler will only be success-

ful if he makes certain that the retailer's shelves are stocked with the appropriate goods.

3. The prompt delivery of goods is often vital to retailers. Service wholesalers generally provide transportation at nominal costs plus quick delivery. The importance of quick delivery can be better understood with a practical situation. When a retailer advertises an item of merchandise that sells better than initially anticipated, the inability to quickly replenish the item becomes the store's loss. Reliance upon immediate direct shipment from the manufacturer is often impossible. Wholesalers, who have little to offer except service, often provide delivery within twenty-four hours. In the case of the advertised merchandise, customers can almost immediately be satisfied.

4. Merchandise is offered in small quantities and in various assortments. The retailer, when purchasing directly from the producer, might be confronted with minimum orders and must spend significant time seeking the best merchandise for his customers. Service wholesalers ease these two areas of purchasing for the retailer. Restrictions concerning the size of the order are generally nonexistent. The purchase of any quantity is usually permitted. In addition, the time and effort involved in shopping many producers' lines are eliminated because of the merchandise collected by the wholesaler from several sources of supply. Just as the consumer is afforded the luxury of one-stop shopping in department stores, so is the retailer when purchasing from the service wholesaler.

5. Wholesalers, by and large, provide better credit assistance to retailers than producers do. Traditionally, periods ranging up to several months are commonplace. Small retailers with insufficient amounts of capital could not function without the extension of credit. Although manufacturers often provide credit for their customers, wholesalers are generally more lenient. Perhaps this reason, more than any other, is the basis of the popularity of wholesalers with small retailers.

6. The prompt delivery of a large assortment of goods affords the retailer a faster stock turnover. This is a great advantage to the retailer in that it allows for a continuous fresh supply of merchandise with a much smaller working capital. Retailers often measure their success on their turnover rate, that is, the number of times the inventory has been completely sold out and repurchased during one year.

7. By purchasing through a wholesaler, the retailer gets a guarantee concerning the quality of the goods. Since wholesalers buy in very large quantities, it is important for them to make certain that the merchandise will live up to expectations. Through trained and knowledgeable buying personnel, the wholesaler is able to ascertain the quality of the goods and the reputation of the manufacturers from whom they purchase. The small retailer who is neither able to make the investment of time nor of money

to determine the value and quality of merchandise, depends on the whole-saler's ability to make sound judgments. It might be said that the purchase of goods through the wholesaler provides the retailer with a double guarantee, one from the wholesaler and the other from the producer.

8. Complaints are more easily adjusted through the wholesaler. If the retailer had to personally contact the many hundreds of manufacturers whose merchandise he stocks, the bother could be a monumental task. Purchasing through a wholesaler affords the luxury of having the middleman act as a clearinghouse for complaints.

9. The wholesaler's success is completely dependent on the success of the retail outlets he services. Thus, to insure his own maximum success, the wholesaler must see to it that the retailer succeeds. Continuous advice and counsel is an important role played by the wholesaler. This assistance is almost completely provided by the wholesaler's salesmen. Since the sales-men are technically oriented to the merchandise they offer for sale, they are invaluable sources of aid for the retailer. Among the areas of information and assistance provided by the wholesaler are:

a. *New-product development*
b. *Inventory checks* Salesmen may actually take a physical inventory of their goods in order to properly advise about stock replenishment.
c. *Merchandise planning* This may include special store promotions, advertising, and display.
d. *Markup* Suggestions are made concerning the proper markups to arrive at proper pricing levels in order to adequately meet competition.
e. *Store modernization* Complete assistance is given regarding store fixtures, lighting, layout, service managements versus self-service, and so on.
f. *Training* Through the use of brochures, manuals, films, and even in-person lectures and discussions, proper training of sales clerks and other personnel is supplied in order to improve the efficiency of the operation.

10. The use of salesmen to call upon retail customers is a very definite service. Without the visits from salesmen, it would be necessary for the store buyer to go to the market. Aside from being considered a convenience for the retailer, this also serves as a way of reducing expenses. That is, if the retailer had to visit the wholesaler when purchasing was necessary, he might need additional store personnel in his absence.

Services Afforded the Manufacturer

1. By providing the sales force to seek out and service retail customers, the wholesaler makes it possible for the manufacturer to employ fewer sales people. Store contact is now the wholesaler's task, so the manufacturer's salesmen have only to solicit wholesale business.

2. Wholesalers purchase in large quantities, whereby the manufacturer's shipping and packing problems are decreased considerably. Manu-

facturers need only to ship the larger orders to the wholesalers, who in turn break down the goods into smaller orders for the retailer. This enables the manufacturer to save on shipping, packing and billing expenses.

3. Through the maintenance of storage facilities for the manufacturer's goods, the wholesaler helps to alleviate many warehousing problems. In peak-production seasons, for example, it is likely that the producer would have to lease additional space for his manufactured goods if it were not for the wholesaler's warehouse facilities. Purchasing and maintaining permanent additional storage space especially for the peak-production periods is unsound, since these premises would be likely to remain empty in times of low production. Thus, the wholesaler aids the manufacturer by providing the warehousing function. It should be noted that public warehouses constitute an alternative for the manufacturer. However, wholesalers continue to serve manufacturers in this capacity.

4. The wholesaler typically purchases well in advance of the usual retail purchasing, thereby giving the manufacturer business soon after the goods are produced and simultaneously affording him the necessary money for continued production. Thus, the manufacturer's working capital is reduced.

5. Because he is closer to the consumer, the wholesaler is able to make meaningful market information available to the manufacturer, resulting in less involvement on his part in marketing research than would otherwise be required to determine consumer demand and reactions.

6. Transportation costs are lower because of the size of the wholesaler's purchases. A few large shipments cost considerably less than smaller shipments of the same amount of goods would. This is economical for the manufacturer.

7. The number of transactions is tremendously reduced when manufacturers deal with wholesalers; therefore, their bookkeeping is simpler.

8. Because manufacturer has fewer customer contacts, his credit risks are reduced.

In summary, the wholesaler provides many services for both his suppliers and customers. We have examined the following:

Services for the retailer
  a. Elimination of need for large inventory
  b. Determination of consumer demands
  c. Prompt delivery
  d. Smaller-quantity purchases
  e. Credit assistance
  f. Higher rate of stock turnover
  g. Double guarantee of merchandise
  h. Adjustment of complaints
  i. Advice and counsel
  j. Visits by salesmen

Services for the Manufacturer
   a. Provision of sales force
   b. Fewer shipping and packing problems
   c. Storage facilities
   d. Reduction of working capital
   e. Market information
   f. Lower transportation costs
   g. Simplified bookkeeping
   h. Decreased credit risks

As indicated, service wholesalers are subclassified according to the product lines they carry.

General-Merchandise Wholesalers. As the name indicates, this group of wholesalers offers for sale an assortment of unrelated merchandise. They carry such items as appliances, drugs, cosmetics, sporting goods, farm implements, and other nonperishable goods. Occasionally, they sell limited assortments of groceries. The importance of this wholesaling group has decreased significantly to a position of less than 1 percent of sales accounted for by wholesalers. Once general-merchandise wholesalers satisfactorily served the needs of general stores that stocked numerous unrelated items, but the waning importance of general stores led to the decline of general-merchandise wholesaling as well.

General-Line Wholesalers. Unlike the preceding group, which handled an unrelated assortment of goods, the general-line wholesaler carries a wide assortment of a specific type of merchandise. One might limit his lines to groceries and stock a complete selection of canned goods, coffee, sugar, cheeses, soap powders, and so on. Another might confine his merchandise to hardware and sell, for example, pots and pans, conventional tools such as hammers, power equipment such as rotary saws and lawn mowers, home electrical appliances such as coffee makers and toaster ovens, and other related items. Whereas the general-merchandise wholesaler serves the needs of the gneral store, this group of wholesalers sells primarily to limited-line stores. Among others, hardware stores, stationery stores, groceries, and delicatessens patronize the general-line wholesaler.

Specialty Wholesalers. The general-line wholesaler specializes more than the general-merchandise wholesaler, but the specialty wholesaler is involved in the highest degre of merchandise specialization. Wholesalers of coffee, tea, canned goods, fabrics, millinery, or some other specific line are considered to be specialty wholesalers. This classification of wholesalers offers the narrowest range of goods. Consequently, the specialty wholesaler offers the most complete assortment of his particular line.

A comparison of the three kinds of service wholesalers might facilitate better understanding:

1. Wholesaler A sells all kinds of merchandise, including fabrics, hardware, sporting goods, furniture, and canned goods. He is a *general-merchandise wholesaler.*

2. Wholesaler B operates on a more specialized basis and carries only furniture. In this assortment he offers chairs, beds, sofas, lamps, tables, and mirrors. He is a *general-line wholesaler.*

3. Wholesaler C specializes to the fullest. He carries lamps exclusively. In his assortment he features French, Italian, Spanish, oriental, and contemporary lamps. He is a *specialty wholesaler.*

LIMITED-FUNCTION WHOLESALERS.   Unlike service wholesalers, limited-function wholesalers make few wholesaling services available to their customers. They are not numerous and they deal primarily in a couple of product lines. Their small number is perhaps evidenced by the fact that they are not separately listed in the 1967 census of business. The major types of limited-function wholesalers will be examined to show the role that each plays in the wholesaler market.

Cash-and-Carry Wholesalers.   Typically, the cash-and-carry wholesaler, aside from operating on a cash basis (that is, no extension of credit) does not delivery the goods he sells to the retailer. Probably the most important product line offered by this type of wholesalers is the grocery line. They sell to small grocers, who are often unable to purchase from service wholesalers because the amounts they buy are too small. Some service wholesalers operate cash-and-carry departments specifically to serve the small retailer. This department provides immediate cash for the wholesaler.

Drop Shippers.   Often referred to as a desk jobber, the drop shipper does not perform warehousing. His function is to obtain orders from retailers (or other wholesalers) and to process these orders through producers. The producer then ships the merchandise directly to the customer. Although the drop shipper does not physically handle or store the goods—as do most wholesalers—he nonetheless takes title to the goods, which makes him the owner. With the elimination of warehousing and reassembling the goods for shipping, his operating costs are reduced. Most drop shippers deal in coal and lumber.

Mail-Order Wholesalers.   Very much like the mail-order retailer, the mail-order wholesaler operates through the use of catalogs, with orders placed by mail. The only difference between the two kinds of mail-order houses is the type of customer being served. The former sells to the ultimate consumer, whereas the latter sells to retail stores. Merchandise wholesaled in this fashion includes jewelry, novelty items, sporting equipment, and piece goods.

Truck-and-Wagon Distributors.   Immediate delivery and cash payment are generally characteristic of the truck-and-wagon distributors. These wholesalers are actually a combination of salesmen and delivery men. They deliver both perishable and nonperishable products, such as candy, cheeses, tobacco products, and processed meats. The delivery of goods is immediate because they are carried right on the truck.

Rack Jobbers. The newest type of limited-function wholesalers consists of the rack jobbers. They sell merchandise other than food items primarily to supermarkets. Products such as toys, housewares, greeting cards, paperbacks, toiletries, and stationery, found in ever increasing numbers in supermarkets, are usually merchandise maintained and owned until sold by the rack jobber.

The store provides space in which the rack jobber sets up racks for the display of his merchandise. He is responsible for the display and the replenishment of his merchandise and gets paid only for the merchandise that has actually been sold. Supermarkets, on the whole, have experienced greater success in the merchandising of these nonfood items when handled by a rack jobber than by their own staff.

Rack jobbers are sometimes considered to be service wholesalers. However, since they are generally paid on a cash basis when the merchandise is sold (in some cases on delivery) they are technically considered as limited-function wholesalers.

Manufacturer's Sales Branches and Offices

Although they comprise only about 10 percent of the total number of wholesale organizations in the United States, the manufacturer's sales branches and offices account for approximately one-third of the total wholesale industry in terms of sales.

The establishment of this type of branches and offices has cut substantially into the traditional methods of wholesaling. Examination of statistics since 1929 has shown a significant periodic increase in the manufacturer's determination to wholesale his own product. One of the major reasons for bypassing the traditional wholesaler is the belief that lower marketing costs will be incurred. Moreover, the fact that some wholesalers do not satisfy all the requirements of manufacturers regarding the distribution of their goods makes this 'kind of wholesaling popular.

Typically, the branches and sales offices are at some distance from the production point. They are located at various places throughout their market; customers may come there to write orders. Some branches also maintain inventories in order to facilitate the filling of these orders.

Petroleum Bulk Plants and Terminals

Petroleum bulk plants and terminals are dissimilar from other types of wholesale operations. They are distinguishable by the physical facilities incorporated in their wholesaling activity. Primarily, they provide storage for gasoline, oil, and other petroleum. The amount of sales credited to this wholesale classification is steadily increasing.

Merchandise Agents and Brokers

Aside from the various ways in which they perform their wholesaling functions and the different types of services rendered, all merchant-wholesalers take title to the goods; this is not true of the merchandise agents and brokers. The principal service rendered by this group of wholesalers is the facilitation of buying and selling.

There are several kinds of agents and brokers. They are characterized by the customers they serve and by the products in which they deal. A brief examination follows to underscore their different roles.

MANUFACTURER'S AGENTS. The manufacturer's agent—or manufacturer's "rep" (representative) as he is commonly called—works for a manufacturer on a commission basis. He is assigned a specific territory in which to transact business. His work is not to be confused with the job of a regular salesman (although he is primarily engaged in selling): the manufacturer's representative is in business for himself. Generally, he carries a number of different, noncompeting lines of merchandise. Manufacturers usually enter into contractual agreements with several reps because each is assigned to a limited geographic area.

Manufacturers and customers alike seem to enjoy this kind of arrangement, as is evidenced by the growth in this type of wholesaling. It affords the manufacturer the advantage of larger orders (because the reps accumulate orders of many small customers) and it gives the buyer the convenience of purchasing many items from one firm rather than having to be inconvenienced by visiting each manufacturer's showroom for individual lines of merchandise.

The manufacturer's agents deal in many different types of goods; included are home furnishings, electrical appliances, fashion apparel, sports equipment, and piece goods.

Buying from a manufacturer's agent does present some disadvantages as compared with purchasing from other wholesalers. Significant among the disadvantages are the possibility of slower delivery (this wholesaler does not stock merchandise) and the inability to obtain repair services on some technical merchandise that wholesalers frequently supply.

SELLING AGENTS. The selling agent usually provides more marketing services than all other agents and brokers. For the manufacturer, he normally takes the place of an entire marketing department. Unlike the manufacturer's rep, who primarily sells, the selling agent guides the manufacturers along styling lines (where pertinent), establishes prices, and often supplies financial aid to the manufacturer. In addition, he is the manufacturer's only agent without territorial restrictions. Selling agents deal in textiles, coal, lumber, some food products, and clothing.

BROKERS. Dealing mainly in information, the broker's role is to bring buyers and sellers together. He is strictly concerned with the needs of buyers and the offerings of suppliers. The majority of brokers work for sellers, although some do work for buyers. Their fee is based on a commission paid by the party that engaged their services after the terms of the sale have been negotiated and the deal has been consummated. Brokers work for a variety of producers, most often in the food industry. They might represent a small canner during the canning season and then move onto another industry in need of their services. It should be noted that, unlike the manufacturer's and selling agents, brokers do not enter into lasting or permanent relationships.

COMMISSION MERCHANTS. Generally confined to agricultural markets, commission merchants serve the producer who does not wish to dispose of his goods through local auctions. Since the farmer is to accompany his goods to the big cities, the commission merchant is engaged to sell the goods and make all the necessary arrangements in connection with the sale.

These merchants have some latitude as to the eventual price the goods will bring but usually are governed by a minimum price determined by the producer they represent.

AUCTION COMPANIES. Auctions are commonplace in a number of industries. They provide a place at which buyers and sellers can come to negotiate sales. For furs, used automobiles, tobacco, livestock, and produce, auctions are the usual means of sale. The prices of merchandise sold at auctions vary considerably depending on supply and demand. The auction company is either paid a flat fee or a commission for the use of its premises and the auction services supplied.

FARM-PRODUCTS ASSEMBLERS. Small producers of farm products employ the services of assemblers, who, as their name implies, accumulate and sort the farmers' offerings into a large unit that is more economical for shipping. Local farmers use assemblers because they are then often paid cash for their products. The local assembler ships the assembled farm products to central markets for disposal.

GEOGRAPHIC DISTRIBUTION OF WHOLESALING

The location of wholesaling establishments is influenced by the available transportation facilities and the nature of the products to be marketed. This is unlike retailing that must locate where the population is concentrated. Examination of Table 12–2 shows the heaviest wholesale concentra-

TABLE 12–2

GEOGRAPHIC DISTRIBUTION OF WHOLESALE TRADE

	1963		1967	
State	Total Wholesale Trade		Total Wholesale Trade	
	Establishments	Sales	Establishments	Sales
		Mil. dol.		Mil. dol.
United States	308,177	358,386	311,464	459,476
New England	16,685	16,816	16,830	21,611
Maine	1,495	980	1,440	1,234
New Hampshire	794	505	822	689
Vermont	482	264	513	382
Massachusetts	8,730	10,392	8,715	13,158
Rhode Island...........	1,436	1,199	1,465	1,475
Connecticut	3,748	3,476	3,875	4,673
Middle Atlantic...........	66,576	97,020	65,673	119,369
New York	40,160	66,208	39,205	77,957
New Jersey	9,626	12,769	10,098	17,932
Pennsylvania	16,790	18,044	16,370	23,480
East North Central	58,621	73,351	58,410	97,694
Ohio	14,299	18,208	14,497	23,706
Indiana	7,257	6,452	7,162	8,349
Illinois	18,691	29,262	18,689	39,539
Michigan	11,635	14,055	11,436	18,800
Wisconsin	6,740	5,502	6,626	7,300
West North Central	33,236	34,408	32,626	43,145
Minnesota	6,953	8,390	6,901	10,617
Iowa	6,025	4,724	5,824	5,950
Missouri	8,642	12,307	8,600	15,046
North Dakota	2,035	1,220	1,995	1,492
South Dakota	1,740	975	1,688	1,251
Nebraska	3,199	3,403	3,158	4,385
Kansas	4,642	3,390	4,461	4,405
South Atlantic	36,531	37,958	38,617	51,655
Delaware	565	1,090	588	1,430
Maryland	3,658	4,474	3,943	5,958
District of Columbia	1,184	2,059	988	2,376
Virginia	4,317	4,376	4,577	6,162
West Virginia...........	2,028	1,396	2,001	1,691
North Carolina	6,615	6,983	7,010	9,530
South Carolina	2,738	1,993	2,918	2,745
Georgia	6,530	8,100	6,941	11,459
Florida.................	8,896	7,487	9,650	10,303
East South Central	15,211	15,070	15,972	19,369
Kentucky	3,632	3,211	3,715	3,994
Tennessee	5,100	6,677	5,381	8,628
Alabama	3,935	3,395	4,253	4,437
Mississippi	2,544	1,787	2,623	2,309

TABLE 12–2 (cont.)

State	1963 Total Wholesale Trade		1967 Total Wholesale Trade	
	Establishments	Sales	Establishments	Sales
West South Central	29,888	27,915	31,213	36,688
Arkansas...............	2,566	1,546	2,659	1,956
Louisiana	4,852	4,598	5,243	6,559
Oklahoma	4,175	3,465	4,175	4,263
Texas	18,295	18,305	19,136	23,910
Mountain	13,238	9,926	13,265	11,843
Montana...............	1,590	844	1,509	1,081
Idaho	1,473	779	1,467	912
Wyoming	672	249	626	288
Colorado	3,720	3,623	3,713	4,386
New Mexico	1,406	779	1,425	910
Arizona	2,199	1,791	2,281	2,144
Utah	1,628	1,470	1,635	1,661
Nevada	550	390	609	461
Pacific	38,191	45,923	38,858	58,103
Washington	5,593	5,173	5,512	6,696
Oregon	3,768	4,448	3,855	5,873
California	27,565	35,386	28,096	44,234
Alaska	291	181	365	286
Hawaii	974	735	1,030	1,014

Source: Dept. of Commerce, Bureau of the Census; U. S. Census of Business: 1963 and 1967.

tion in the Middle Atlantic states, followed by the East North Central region. New York State continues to enjoy its status as the most important wholesaling state, with New York City accounting for 13 percent of total sales at wholesale. Although the two previously mentioned regions continue to lead in sales at wholesale, we see a small but disproportionate increase in sales of such regions as the South Atlantic and the West South Central states.

IMPORTANT POINTS IN THE CHAPTER

1. Wholesalers are basically middlemen who act as intermediates between producers and retailers or other commercial users.

2. Wholesalers differ from retailers with regard to the markets and areas they serve, their purchasing power, and their methods of operation.

3. Most important of the wholesalers is the merchant-wholesaler. Merchant-wholesalers are classified according to their services and

are called either service or limited-function wholesalers. They are further catagorized according to the product lines they offer.

4. Some of the services supplied by wholesalers to retailers are quick delivery, credit assistance, handling of complaints, operation with a smaller inventory, and advice.

5. Wholesalers afford manufacturers such services as a complete sales force, warehousing, market information, and simplified bookeeping.

6. Some manufacturers engage in wholesaling through the operation of their own sales branches and offices.

7. Merchandise brokers, unlike other wholesalers, service producers but do not take title to the goods they sell.

8. Most wholesale business is concentrated in the Middle Atlantic states and the East North Central part of the country.

REVIEW QUESTIONS

1. Define *wholesaling* in your own words.
2. Which group serves a larger market, the wholesaler or the retailer? Explain.
3. How does the method of operation for the wholesaler differ from that of the retailer?
4. Why have marketers been able to more satisfactorily appraise wholesaling since 1929?
5. According to the listing of the Census Bureau, which wholesaler is most important?
6. In which case is the service of quick delivery, available through the service wholesaler, extremely meaningful to the retailer?
7. Compare the consumer's one-stop shopping in department stores with the retailer's one-stop shopping at wholesalers' establishments.
8. How does purchasing from wholesalers affect the retailer's rate of stock turnover?
9. Discuss the importance of the storage service for manufacturers as provided by wholesalers.
10. What is the major difference between the general-line wholesaler and the specialty wholesaler?
11. General-merchandise wholesalers are declining in popularity. Why?
12. Differentiate between the drop shipper and the rack jobber.
13. Should the manufacturer's sales branch be considered a wholesale establishment? Why?
14. Compare the major function of the manufacturer's agent and that of the selling agent.
15. What is the role of brokers in the transfer of goods?
16. For which type of farmer does the commission merchant generally provide service?

17. How does the commission merchant, dealing basically in farm products, differ from the farm-products assembler?

18. Which region is extremely important in wholesaling, aside from the Middle Atlantic states?

19. Which two regions have recently shown disproportionate gains in wholesaling?

20. What is another, more popular title for the manufacturer's agent?

CASE PROBLEMS

Case Problem 1

Louis Blank and Mel Weinstein have been equal partners of Glo-Gems for the past ten years. Glo-Gems is a jewelry business where semiprecious stones such as amethyst, aquamarine, coral, and quartz are made into pins, necklaces, rings, and so on. Since the company's inception, Mr. Blank has been responsible for the purchase of the stones, a task that frequently takes him to the Far East and Europe. Mr. Weinstein, on the other hand, is responsible for production and also supervises the sales.

For the past few years, selling has been under the direction of Mr. Weinstein, with the bulk of sales attributed to his personal efforts. Mr. Blank, when not away on his foreign buying trips, has helped with selling too. As the business continued to grow, Glo-Gems hired salesmen: they now have three. The salesmen work exclusively for Glo-Gems, each in his own assigned area. The regions covered are the Middle Atlantic states, the New England states, and the East North Central states.

At this time Glo-Gems has a tremendous market. Its products include school rings, which are sold to students from the junior high school up through the university. Expansion of the presently covered territories seems to be a perfect way to transform the business into a large operation. Both partners agree to the expansion, but they are in disagreement as to how they should sell their products. Mr. Weinstein insists upon hiring twelve additional full-time salesmen to work exclusively for Glo-Gems. Fifteen salesmen could adequately cover the United States. Mr. Blank's opinion is that sales should be the responsibility of outside agents, specifically manufacturer's agents or representatives. Mr. Weinstein argues that company salesmen could be better trained and supervised under his direction and would devote their efforts to Glo-Gem's products exclusively. Of equal merit is Mr. Blank's argument that, with the anticipated growth, Mr. Weinstein would be needed to supervise production in a full-time basis.

Questions

1. Compare the advantages of each partner's recommendation.

2. With whom do you agree?

3. Is there still another method they could employ in order to distribute their goods? Discuss.

Case Problem 2

Sherry Kuhn and Estelle Barish have made all necessary arrangements to open a retail store called Party Boutique. Their business will be located in a suburban shopping center approximately ten miles from New York City. Having signed the lease and selected the necessary fixtures, they expect to open in eight weeks. Their working capital is limited, partly owing to the fact that they underestimated the costs involved in starting a retail business. Nonetheless, they plan to go ahead as scheduled with a complete assortment of merchandise.

After thorough investigation of similar stores, they have decided on the type of inventory to carry. Initially they will sell party goods (plates, table cloths, napkins, cups), greeting cards, gift-wrap (paper, ribbons, bows), and packaged chocolates. Arrangements have already been made with suppliers for the purchase of the greeting cards, gift-wrap, and chocolates. Although this merchandise is available through wholesalers, traditionally it is bought directly from manufacturers; they want to follow this rule. Party goods, however (which they expect to account for about 50 percent of their sales), are often purchased from wholesalers.

Sherry and Estelle have looked around everywhere for a supplier for their party goods. Ten of the best-known party goods manufacturers are located in New York City. About fifty miles from their shop is a service wholesaler who could serve them at a price about 5 percent higher than that of the manufacturers.

Questions

1. List all important factors that the partners should consider before coming to a conclusion.
2. From whom should they purchase? Why?

BIBLIOGRAPHY

Applebaum, William, "Management Responsibilities Facing the Wholesale Grocer," *Journal of Marketing.* Reprinted in *Readings in Marketing,* eds. Charles J. Dirksen, Arthur Kroeger, and Lawrence C. Lockley. Homewood, Ill.: Richard D. Irwin, Inc., 1968.

Beckman, Theodore N., and A. F. Doody, "Wholesaling," Small Business Bulletin No. 55. Washington, D. C.: Small Business Administration, 1965.

Beckman, Theodore N., Nathanial H. Engle, and Robert D. Buzzell, *Wholesaling,* 3rd ed. New York: The Ronald Press Company, 1959.

"Food Brokers Broadening Their Role in Food Distribution," *Progressive Grocer,* February, 1965.

Frederick, John H., *Using Public Warehouses.* Philadelphia: Chilton Book Company, 1959.

Hill, Richard M., *Wholesaling Management: Text and Cases.* Homewood, Ill.: Richard D. Irwin, Inc., 1963.

Lazar, I. W., "Nonfood Sales and the Rack Jobber," *New York Retailer,* May, 1966.

"Measuring Market Potential for Wholesalers," Bulletin No. 820. Urbana, Ill.: University of Illionis, Bureau of Business Management.

Revzan, David A., *Wholesaling in Marketing Organization.* New York: John Wiley & Sons, Inc., 1961.

"Selecting and Evaluating Distributors," Studies in Business Policy, No. 116. New York: National Industrial Conference Board, Inc., 1965.

Warshaw, Martin A., *Effective Selling through Wholesalers.* Ann Arbor, Mich.: The University of Michigan Press, Bureau of Business Research, 1961.

Washington, D.C.: National Association of Wholesalers. Excellent source of information on every facet of wholesaling.

RETAILING

13

INTRODUCTION

Retailing is the aspect of marketing that is most familiar to the ultimate consumer. The goods purchased by household consumers are bought through various retail institutions. Retailing, simply defined, is that from of business that starts with purchasing goods from vendors and ends with reselling them to the ultimate consumers. The activities included in this transfer of goods from the producer to the user (sometimes called merchandising) are buying, advertising, display, promotion, and selling.

Retailing has changed considerably since its inception. A brief overview of its history will enable marketing students to appreciate its fantastic growth.

HISTORY OF RETAILING

Retailing as we know it today, with its sophisticated research methods and such decision-making devices as the computer, had its meager beginning in the United States at the trading post in the early 1600s. Instead of purchasing goods from retailers by means of money, a barter system was employed. Merchants would exchange their own goods for those brought to the post by others. More specifically, fur trappers and farmers would exchange their merchandise for imported wares.

In the mid-1700s the trading post began to expand its operation to better serve the needs of the colonists. With large amounts of new merchandise desired, the trading post could no longer fulfill these needs. To accommodate the settlers, the general store was established. Unlike the trading post that was dominated by an exchange system, the general store operated on a cash basis.

The variety of goods in the general store was much larger than that of the trading post. The general store carried fabrics, manufactured clothing, shoes, cattle feed, harnesses, and so on. Contrary to the orderly arrangement in modern retail stores, merchandise was haphazardly placed wherever there was sufficient space. Today general stores are still found in rural areas, but they are no longer important retail establishments.

In the mid-1800s the number of manufacturing establishments increased rapidly, resulting in a larger quantity and variety of merchandise. The general store could no longer stock everything that was produced in the United States. This necessitated the beginning of specialization in retailing and the introduction of the limited-line store. The limited-line store— or specialty store, as it is frequently referred to—carried a particular category of merchandise exclusively. Shoe stores, ladies' specialty shops, jewelry stores, groceries, and so on are examples of limited-line stores. Today the limited-line store remains an important retail enterprise. Although initially these businesses were established by families or individuals as single-unit shops, a great number have grown into prestigious and successful chain operations. Among the most familiar nationally are Lerner's, A&P, Friendly Ice Cream, Ohrbach's, and Thom McAn Shoes.

The chain organization, the first venture into large-scale retailing in the United States, began in the late 1800s. It is generally defined as ten or more stores, similar in nature and having common ownership. Many operators of successful limited-line stores opened second, third, and more units in other areas. Among the early chain organizations were J. C. Penney Co., A&P (the food giant), and F. W. Woolworth Co. (the five-and-ten-cent store).

In the late 1800s and early 1900s Americans also witnessed the beginning of the department store, which was to become one of the most popular and successful organizations in retailing. It carried a full complement of hard and soft goods under one roof, so that the customer no longer needed to shop in many limited-line stores. It might be said that the department store provided the unrelated items offered by the earlier general store (with many more lines) and the assortment afforded by the limited-line store. The merchandise was arranged in an orderly fashion, in separate departments. In addition to the usual merchandise, modern department stores also have departments that specialize in travel, gourmet foods, baked goods, optics, pets, entertainment arrangements, and garden supplies.

Branch stores, smaller units of the department store carrying a representation of the main store's offerings, became popular as the population moved to the suburbs. Today, in the retail field, few new department stores are being established; instead we see a great expansion of the established stores through additional branches.

In an effort to better serve the needs of those people unable to patronize the existing retail institutions, either because of their distance from the stores or their lack of time to buy in person, the mail-order retailer began to attract attention. At first, in the late 1800s, little was available to the mail-order customer. Therefore, extensive catalogs—since then enjoying great popularity—were prepared and sent to customers. Thus, the mail-order business became an important part of retailing. Montgomery Ward & Co., Inc. and Sears, Roebuck and Co. were early mail-order houses. Even with mass transportation, the extensive chain organization, the branch store, and so on, mail-order retailing continues to flourish.

The supermarket, a large departmentalized food store, became popular in the late 1930s. In addition to the large variety of foodstuffs, it carries an abundance of miscellaneous items, such as drugs, toys, accessories for men, women, and children, plants, hardware, and so on. Just as the department store provides one-stop shopping for the consumer, the supermarket affords the housewife the luxury of being able to purchase all her food needs at one location instead of having to make separate trips to the grocer, the butcher, the baker, and the produce dealer. Although the great majority of supermarkets are chain organizations, many independent markets are in operation.

The latest major innovation in retailing has been the discount operation. At its inception, unlike the conventional retail store with all its services, the discounter offers limited service in exchange for lower prices. This method of merchandising is not restricted to one type of retailing organization but is found in chain-store, department-store, and specialty-store operations.

Discounters versus Traditional Retailing

There is much evidence today that there is conflict between the traditional retailer, for example Macy's, and the discount houses. Traditionally, as we remarked, discounters (often known as mass merchandisers) offer low prices in exchange for limited service and conventional retailers maintain higher prices in an effort to offer a wide variety of services, but there seems to be a leveling off that is affecting both groups of retailers. When visiting, for example, the new units of E. J. Korvette's—originally considered by many to be a discount operation—one notices the nice interiors and sees such services as charge plans offered. Similary, advertisements show that such traditional giants as Macy's, Gimbels, and Abraham & Straus continue to reduce their prices on, for example, appliances and records in order to meet the competition of the discounters. It seems obvious that this leveling off of prices and services is bringing the traditionalist and the discounter closer together.

Further descriptions of those retail institutions still flourishing will be discussed in the next section of this chapter.

MAJOR CLASSIFICATIONS OF RETAILERS

The era of the trading post belongs to history, but the other types of retail institutions that have been organized since then are still very much in evidence. Except for the general store, they all are flourishing throughout the United States.

Retailers may be classified in many ways. They can be grouped according to merchandising activities (activities in the buying–selling cycle), merchandise carried, dollar volume, number of employees, and so on. Although the study of each classification may be valuable, we feel that the investigation of small retailers and large retailers as separate categories, with further expansion into the variety of large retailers, presents the most complete overview of retailing institutions.

The Small Retailer

The small retail business usually grosses under one hundred thousand dollars annually. Typically, there is very little job specialization. The store owner is generally responsible for the overall management and merchandising tasks. He buys, sells, sets work schedules, plans sales promotions, secures personnel, and so on. The "larger" small retailer, doing business at the one hundred thousand dollar level, has more specialized personnel working in the organization. There might be a person responsible only for merchandising duties, which include the entire buying–selling cycle. A part-time display person might be hired for window decoration. Or a store manager might be responsible for the management of the physical layout of the store and the supervision of personnel. In stores of limited gross sales it is obvious that the owner must perform all activities.

The majority of small retail stores are individual proprietorships. However, included in the group are partnerships and corporations. The general store and the specialty store are types of small stores, with the latter accounting for almost all small retailing institutions.

THE GENERAL STORE. The age of specialization, the success of the chain organization, movement to urban and suburban communities, the automobile, and the continued growth of the mail-order house are some factors that have contributed to the decline of the general store.

In the rural areas, the general store is still in operation. Management is generally haphazard. The sophisticated tools and aids of modern retailers are rarely employed. The proprietor engages in purchasing merchandise, the variety of which is so great as to include cracker-barrel goods and ready-made apparel. His knowledge in any single area is sometimes so limited that he lacks the ability necessary to make the right decisions. How can one individual have the product knowledge for so diversified an inventory?

The limited floor space does not allow for wide assortment within a merchandise classification. The general store has the questionable distinction of being the most mismanaged type of retail organization. Retailers, although reluctant to agree on many things, usually concede that the general store will never regain its popularity.

THE SPECIALTY STORE. The limited-line store—or the specialty store, as it is usually referred to today—is an establishment carrying one line of merchandise. Stores specializing in jewelry, furs, shoes, hardware, groceries, baked goods, and broader classifications of women's clothing, men's accessories, and so on are examples. The greatest number of successful small retailers operate specialty stores. Some of the factors that have led to the success of this type of operation are:

Personalized service

Wide assortment of merchandise

Knowledgeable buying—the buyer must only be educated in certain lines of merchandise

The chain organization is the major competitor of the small specialty store. The chain is actually a retail organization with many units carrying specialty merchandise. The chain's wider advertising to the consumer and its ability to offer lower prices because of greater buying power pose the greatest threat to the small retailer.

In an attempt to meet the "unfair" competition of the chain, many small merchants have informally united. The combining of small orders to qualify for quantity discounts—particularly in groceries, small hard-goods and staple men's-wear (shirts and other accessories) has enabled the small merchant to become more competitive by lowering prices. Lately, advertising —an area that the small retailer often avoids because of the costs involved— has become popular as a group activity. Instead of one merchant spending a large sum for an advertisement, the group now shares the costs. A complete listing of all the stores involved in the advertisement indicates to the consumer which merchants offer the advertised merchandise. In both group-buying and group-advertising activities, noncompeting stores are generally involved.

More formalized groups of small retailers are evidenced by the voluntary chain or the cooperative chain. The former is usually organized by a wholesaler who enters into contractual arrangements with the individual retailers, requiring that all purchases be made from him. In that case, promotional plans, point-of-purchase display arrangements, advertising materials, merchandising advice, counter and shelf setup and location selection are typical aids provided by the wholesaler. The cooperative chain is different in that the retailers join together and operate their own warehouse. They too are involved in many group activities that tend to lower the cost of individual operations and increase individual efficiency.

In retailing today, with the giant chain- and department-store organizations, small retailers can compete more effectively through group activities. Of paramount importance in the field is knowledgeable advice on management and merchandising. The large retailer can afford the luxury of specialists. Through their combined efforts, the small merchants avail themselves of an exchange of ideas. One store owner may be expert in designing the best store layout, another might excel in the buying activity, still another might have a talent to prepare advertising copy. In this way, the exchange of information and ideas provides the special knowledge so necessary for success in retailing. Since the merchants are not direct competitors, this free exchange can be open and beneficial to all.

The nature of some small stores dictates a different type of management. Therefore, retailing today still includes completely independent retailers who are not involved in any group arrangement.

The Large Retailer

Today retailing is dominated by the large organization. Department stores, chain organizations, supermarkets, and mail-order houses provide the majority of retail sales.

THE DEPARTMENT STORE. The department store is a departmentalized retail institution that offers a large variety of hard goods and soft goods and numerous customer services. It has huge sales volume and employs a great number of people, specializing in various tasks.

The merchandise assortment varies according to the size of the store. Organizations such as Macy's, Gimbels, and the Allied Stores offer enough types of merchandise—in a range of prices—that a consumer family can satisfy just about any of its needs, for example men's, women's, and children's clothing, apparel accessories, musical instruments, sporting equipment, toys, furniture, hardware, perfumes, toiletries, gourmet foods, liquor, floor covering, bedding, draperies, and appliances. A Macy shopper can buy anything from an iguana to a painting by Joan Miro, from a set of Tom Swift books to fresh Beluga caviar. In many stores, optical goods, beauty-salon services, precious jewelry, religious articles, meat and poultry, silverware, and so on are available through leased departments. These departments are operated by independent or chain owners generally because the nature of the goods or services warrants unusual specialized ability. The department is usually leased on the basis of a square-foot rental or a percentage of sales. Department stores have found that a greater profit for the store can be realized in this way than if they operated these departments themselves. An important reason for offering these specialized goods and services is to provide the customer with one-stop shopping.

The department store offers the greatest variety of services in retailing. Free delivery, gift wrapping, charge accounts, return privileges, extended credit plans, and provision of meeting rooms for clubs are among the usual services. Unusual ones include personal shoppers for people speaking a foreign language, baby sitting for shopping mothers, special openings for children-shoppers before holidays, and procurement of tickets for theatrical and sporting events.

Department stores are individually owned, belong to ownership groups such as the Allied Stores Corporation, or are chains such as Macy's (a nationwide organization of fifty-two stores in six regional divisions).

Branches and Twigs. In view of the increase in the number of families leaving the cities and moving to the suburbs, the almost hopeless traffic congestion, the shortage of adequate parking facilities, and the development and growth of suburban shopping centers, department stores have opened additional units away from the city. The branch is a store usually smaller than the main store, carrying a representation of the parent store's merchandise.

It is geared to the needs of the community in which it is located. Some branch stores have exceeded the sales volume of the main store. Twigs, relatively rare in retailing today but still in existence, are very small units belonging to a department store, that unlike the branch, carry only one classification of merchandise. For example, a department store might operate a shop in a college town featuring merchandise worn on the campus. This sort of operation is called a twig store.

THE CHAIN STORE. The chain store may be defined as a centrally owned and managed organization with two or more similar units, each carrying the same classification of merchandise. The merchandise categories include drugs, hardware, shoes, restaurants, jewelry, variety goods, groceries, baked goods, and so on. For example, S. S. Kresge is a variety chain, A&P is a supermarket chain, J. C. Penney is a general-merchandise chain, Edison Brothers a shoe chain, Lerner Shops a women's chain, and so on. Each unit in these chains is similar in nature to the other units. The management of all chain operations is similar enough in nature that it does not necessitate separate investigation into the different kinds of chains according to merchandise sold.

The department store considers the main store its base of operations; it plans its purchases there. The chain organization operates from central headquarters, a location that houses merchandisers, buyers, personnel administrators, advertising executives, and so forth. Large chains have regional offices in addition to central headquarters. The units of the chain are generally charged with the responsibility of selling merchandise, whereas the central team is the decision-making body of the organization. Store managers usually do not formulate policy. Instead, they carry out the policies of the central staff.

In addition to the usual roles of central management, chains occasionally are centrally involved in other than the usual areas. For example,

Lerner Shops, a large women's specialty chain with stores throughout the United States, has at its main offices in New York City a display department that plans window displays centrally. Windows, similar to those in its many units, are arranged with merchandise, photographed, and distributed for duplication by each store. Supplementary materials and directions for ease of execution are included with each photograph. In this manner, all stores are assured of high-quality, similar displays. As a result, the company projects a uniform image and has control over the individual stores' displays. At the same time display costs are decreased, since not every store needs high-salaried window dressers. A store manager can easily follow the simplified plan.

The trend indicates that chains will expand and that the individual units will increase in size.

SUPERMARKETS.   The supermarket is a large departmentalized, self-service retail organization selling primarily food but also other merchandise. The merchandise assortment has grown from the usual grocery, meat, poultry, and produce categories to include hardware, toys, hosiery, drugs, books, greeting cards, and so on. Supermarkets are independently owned, operated individually, voluntary or cooperative chains, or part of regular chain organizations. The greatest number of supermarkets belongs to the latter category. Emphasis on lower prices, parking facilities to customers, and the luxury of one-stop food shopping are some of the more important factors that lead to their success. A&P, Safeway, and Kroger Company are presently the three largest supermarket chains.

THE MAIL-ORDER RETAILER.   This operation, although not as important as the chain or department store, does contribute enough to warrant further discussion. Selection of merchandise through the use of a catalog, ordering through the mail, and delivery by similar means are the major characteristics of the mail-order house. The merchandise offerings of some mail-order houses are so large and diversified that as wide an assortment can rarely be found in a merchandise-stocking store. In addition to those retailers that sell exclusively by mail, a large percentage of the total sales of department and specialty stores can be attributed to this method of retailing. Montgomery Ward & Co., Inc., Spiegel, Inc., and Sears, Roebuck and Co. are leading mail-order retailers. Sears presently enjoys the status of being the world's largest retailer. The more than 140,000 items now sold by Sears include mink stoles and sculpture priced as high as $39,500. With the exception of food, liquor, and automobiles, almost any article can be bought from Sears.

The chain has moved retail stores closer to the people and has perhaps made buying through catalogs not as necessary as it was in earlier times,

TABLE 13–1

RETAIL TRADE—SALES, BY KIND OF BUSINESS: 1965 TO 1969
(IN MILLIONS OF DOLLARS)

Kind of Business	1965	1967	1968	1969
All retail stores	**284,128**	**313,809**	**339,324**	**351,633**
Durable goods stores	**94,186**	**100,173**	**110,245**	**112,779**
Automotive group	56,884	58,273	65,261	66,911
Passenger car, other automotive dealers	53,484	53,966	60,660	62,048
Tire, battery, accessory dealers	3,400	4,307	4,601	4,863
Furniture, appliance group	13,352	15,267	16,540	16,719
Furniture, homefurnishings stores	(NA)	(NA)	10,227	10,439
Household-appliance, TV, radio stores	(NA)	(NA)	5,235	5,223
Lumber, building, hardware, farm equipment group	17,101	12,675	19,129	19,246
Lumber yards, building-materials dealers	9,731	9,781	10,984	11,278
Hardware stores	2,637	2,894	(NA)	3,284
Nondurable goods stores	**189,942**	**213,636**	**229,079**	**238,854**
Apparel group	15,765	18,123	19,265	20,158
Men's and boys' wear	(NA)	(NA)	4,424	4,761
Women's apparel, accessory stores	(NA)	(NA)	7,429	7,606
Shoe stores	(NA)	(NA)	3,196	3,505
Drug and proprietary stores	9,186	10,721	11,458	11,863
Eating and drinking places	20,201	23,473	25,285	25,849
Food group	64,016	69,113	72,881	75,866
Grocery stores	(NA)	(NA)	67,925	70,955
Gasoline service stations	20,611	22,739	24,526	25,116
General merchandise group, including nonstores	42,299	(NA)	54,493	58,615
Department stores	25,014	29,589	33,323	36,411
Mail-order (dept. store merchandise)	(NA)	(NA)	3,256	3,519
Variety stores	(NA)	(NA)	6,152	6,548
Liquor stores	5,674	6,409	6,969	7,403

NA Not available.

Source: Dept. of Commerce, Bureau of the Census; *Monthly Retail Trade Report.* Monthly data in Office of Business Economics; *Survey of Current Business,* February 1970.

when farmers and others in isolated areas depended heavily on mail order for merchandise. However, this method of doing business has not disappeared from the retailing scene. Perhaps the large number of women in the work force results in less time for shopping and encourages mail-order purchasing. Judging from the great sales volume of mail-order houses, this form of retailing is still important.

TABLE 13–2

LARGEST TWENTY RETAILERS IN UNITED STATES, 1969:
BY SALES VOLUME

The $49 billion total sales of these giant retailers represented one-seventh of all retail sales in the United States, and yet their average profit was only 2.4 percent of net sales. What are some of the marketing implications of this concentration for a maker of department-store merchandise?

Company	Sales ($000,000)*	Net Profit as Percent of Sales†
1. Sears, Roebuck	8,863	5.0
2. Great Atlantic & Pacific Tea	5,700	0.9
3. Safeway Stores	4,100	1.3
4. J. C. Penney	3,756	3.0
5. Kroger	3,477	1.1
6. Marcor (Montgomery Ward)	2,715	2.5
7. F. W. Woolworth	2,273	3.1
8. S. S. Kresge	2,185	2.5
9. Federated Department Stores	1,999	4.3
10. Food Fair Stores	1,555	0.8
11. Acme Markets	1,471	0.7
12. Jewel Companies	1,464	1.5
13. Lucky Stores	1,259	1.7
14. Gamble-Skogmo	1,258	1.1
15. Winn-Dixie Stores	1,250	2.1
16. W. T. Grant	1,215	3.4
17. Allied Stores	1,202	1.8
18. National Tea	1,193	0.6
19. May Department Stores	1,134	2.5
20. Grand Union	1,113	1.4
Total	$49,182	2.4

*Net sales, including all operating revenues. For companies not on a calendar year, the 1969 figures are for any fiscal year ending not later than March 1, 1970. Sales of subsidiaries are included when they are consolidated.
†After taxes.
Source: Fortune, May, 1970, pp. 208–209.

CURRENT TRENDS

Although many of the retailing practices of the past are still in evidence today, no period has seen as many innovations and as much research as the present. Through investigation of these trends, it clearly shows how diversified retailing is today.

Franchising

This is an arrangement wherein an organization (the franchiser) that has developed a successful retail product or service sells to individuals (the franchisees) the right to engage in the business, provided they follow the established pattern. The probability of success for the individual opening a franchise operation is greater than it would be if he ventured into a completely new independent enterprise, thanks to the competence and experience of the franchisers. The areas of service offered by the franchiser include location analysis, tested managerial techniques, knowledgeable merchandising, training plans, financial instruction, and counseling in other pertinent areas. Most retailers agree that inexperience and incompetence account for the great majority of store failures. With the previously mentioned services provided by the franchiser, the risk of failure is greatly reduced. Although franchising was started in 1898 by General Motors, it is currently making its most important mark to date. Franchising today accounts for 10 percent of the Gross National Product through 340,000 outlets.

Carvel, Howard Johnson, Chicken Delight, International House of Pancakes, AAMCO Automotive Transmissions, Rexall Drug Co., Hickory Farms, and Baskin Robbins 31 Flavor Stores are examples of franchise operations that bring a variety of goods and services to the consumer.

Automation

Automatic Vending Machines are responsible for the sale of many products that were originally sold the conventional way, in a retail store. Today these machines, in addition to their usual merchandise, such as newspapers and cigarettes, contain cooked foods, flight insurance, ladies' hosiery, sandwiches, and so on. Coin-operated machines are particularly successful in areas where stores are unavailable, for example, at railroad stations and in movie theaters. The vending machine offers the customer the opportunity to purchase at any time. In the conventional retail store, the hours for purchasing are limited. Since the consumer usually requires service for expensive merchandise, the vending machine is best suited for selling inexpensive items.

AUTOMATIC STORES.   Within the next five to seven years, installation of the automatic checkstand will take place in some supermarkets. In addition to a more accurate tally of the merchandise purchased by the shopper, the bill will be determined more quickly. Better inventory control will result in automatic orders being placed with the warehouse for the replenishment of stock. In addition, customers will be able to have money automatically withdrawn from their checking accounts and transferred to the store's account by presenting an identification card to the store's computer.

Today, some stores automatically move the goods along a conveyor belt until it reaches the customer's car. With the introduction of the new automatic services, the supermarket will certainly move toward more complete automation.

ELECTRONIC DATA PROCESSING. In many stores, the routine clerical duties involved in inventory control and accounting procedures are more efficiently handled through electronic data processing. In addition, the computer is used as a tool by merchandisers to forecast sales, fashion, color, consumer trends, and patterns. Because of its great impact on marketing, Chapter 16 is devoted to electronic data processing.

Enclosed Shopping Centers

In an effort to add to the customer's comfort and improve accessibility to stores in the shopping centers, many centers are enclosing their malls. The stores have the appearance of a huge unit selling a wide variety of merchandise under one roof. Customers can park their cars, enter the enclosed center and move freely from store to store without being bothered by extremely hot or cold weather. Two of the large shopping centers in the East, Green Acres and Roosevelt Field, Long Island, have enclosed their malls as a result of the success of another center in nearby Huntington, Long Island.

Leased Departments

This is an arrangement whereby a store leases space to an individual or chain organization to operate a separate business on the store's premises. The leased departments deal in merchandise or services that require specialized merchandising.

Optics, travel agencies, beauty salons, food stands, and liquor sections are typical examples of leased departments.

Shift in Hours

Most shopping is done by women, so that the growing number of women in the labor force has caused a shift in retail-store hours. Many retailers open later in the day and remain open during the evening hours. Even when the typical opening time for the store has not been adjusted, evening hours are being added to the schedule. In many stores, two shifts of employees are necessary to run the operation. In states where local laws permit, Sunday openings are common. On the West Coast, some supermarkets are open twenty-four hours a day. This arrangement allows factory workers, on different shifts, to shop at any convenient time.

Research

The retailer, to more efficiently meet competition and satisfy the customer's needs, is greatly involved in research methods. Questionnaires, interviews, fashion and traffic counts are some devices used to bring pertinent data to the retailer. By better understanding of what the consumer wants, management should be more efficient, and thus more productive. Marketing research procedures were discussed in Chapter 7.

IMPORTANT POINTS IN THE CHAPTER

1. The growth of retaling in America can be traced from colonial trading posts, where barter was used as the process for exchange, to the modern retailing giants.

2. The history of retailing parallels the growth of American consumer demand. As society became wealthier and more sophisticated, retailers responded by offering a greater variety of goods and enlarging the size and the number of locations at which such goods could be purchased.

3. To satisfy consumers, goods are presently offered at retail in a great variety of stores, featuring an enormous range of goods and services.

4. The future of retailing will be characterized by an increase in franchising, wider use of automation, and ever more shopping centers.

5. Research to prevent unnecessary risk in retailing has expanded in recent years and will gain importance in the future.

REVIEW QUESTIONS

1. Define *retailing* in your own words.
2. Compare the trading post with the general store. How did the two retail institutions differ?
3. What is another name for limited-line store? What contributed to the need for this type of retail enterprise?
4. How many units comprise a chain organization?
5. Discuss some advantages for customers of department-store shopping.
6. The department store offers a wide variety of goods, but so did the general store. Are they basically the same operation? Defend your answer.
7. The mail-order business flourished as soon as it began. What market did mail-order retailers seek to service?
8. Define *branch store*. Why are these stores established?
9. The department store and the supermarket afford the same convenience for customers. Which convenience?
10. What lines are sold in supermarkets in addition to foodstuffs?
11. Discuss what is meant by *leveling off* pertaining to discounters and traditional retailers.

12. By what other name are discounters known?

13. Aside from the typical management responsibilities performed centrally by chain organizations, a rather unusual, important task is often executed centrally. Name and describe the procedure.

14. What attractions do supermarkets hold for their customers?

15. What is the reason for the steady increase in mail-order sales 'aside from new lines of merchandise?

16. For what reasons are individuals attracted to franchising rather than to establishing their own retail stores?

17. How is electronic data processing used by retail management?

18. In order to increase sales, some major controlled shopping centers have altered their physical structures. Describe the procedure and discuss it in terms of sales.

19. How have retail hours changed?

20. Where do vending-machine operators generally achieve their greatest volume?

CASE PROBLEMS

Case Problem 1

Supermarkets continue to grow because of their popularity with the consuming public. Endover, a small city in the northeastern part of the country has seen several supermarket chains establishing units in the community. Large parking fields, competitive prices, and wide assortments of food items have contributed to the supermarkets' success.

While this supermarket boom has taken place, Bill's Grocery has slowly declined. Many of his regular customers have moved away and many have switched to the supermarkets for their needs. Although Bill has thought about closing his doors and bowing to big business, at the present time he still wants to fight. His encouragement comes from travel to other communities where he has witnessed the same supermaket explosion, plus the existence of some small produce stores, delicatessens, and grocers.

On the other hand, his family is trying to persuade him to close his business and take a job with one of his large competitors. With his experience, a job is a certainty.

Question

1. Should Bill fight or switch? Defend your answer.

Case Problem 2

For twenty-five years Steinway Stores have operated as a chain, specializing in hardware and automotive productions. Among the products carried are tires, automotive batteries, car accessories, paint, conventional and power tools, small appliances, and plumbing supplies. Business has been excellent for most of the time. Recently an opportunity has materialized that would direct Steinway Stores into a new field of endeavor.

Bartlett Associates, realtors and developers of large and small shopping centers, have offered the Steinway organization a two-story structure of one hundred thousand square feet. The building plans call for sufficient space for a full inventory of hard goods and soft goods. The location is adjacent to one of Steinway's existing units, the second largest in the chain.

Steinway Stores are interested for a number of reasons. The most important is that if they decide against the new location, a competitor to their already established business could affect the success of this unit.

After a good deal of negotiation, management decides to accept Bartlett's offer and to proceed with the new enterprise. One by no means simple problem facing the executives is how to operate this new store and turn it into a successful venture.

Questions

1. What roads are available to Steinway Stores?
2. If you were to make the decision, how would you operate the new business? (Keep in mind that the merchandise offerings must be expanded past what is in the realm of management's knowledge.)

BIBLIOGRAPHY

Dalrymple, Douglas J., and Donald L. Thompson, *Retailing*. New York: The First Press, 1969.

Davidson, William R., and Alton F. Doody, *Retailing Management*. New York: The Ronald Press Company, 1966.

Diamond, Jay, and Gerald Pintel, *Mathematics of Business*. Englewood Cliffs, N.J.: Prentice-Hall, Inc., 1970.

Gillespie, Karen, and Joseph Hecht, *Retail Management*. New York: McGraw-Hill Book Company, 1970.

Gist, Ronald R., *Management Perspectives in Retailing*. New York: John Wiley & Sons, Inc., 1967.

———, *Concepts and Decisions*. New York: John Wiley & Sons, Inc., 1967.

McGregor, C. H., and Paul Chakonas, *Retail Management Problems*. Homewood, Ill.: Richard D. Irwin, Inc., 1970.

McNair, Malcolm P., and Eleanor G. May, *The American Department Store 1920–1962*. Cambridge, Mass.: Harvard University Press, 1963.

Markim, Rom J., *The Supermarket: An Analysis of Growth, Development, and Change*. Pullman, Wash.: Washington State University Press, 1968.

Pintell, Gerald, and Jay Diamond, *Retailing*. Englewood Cliffs, N.J.: Prentice-Hall, Inc., 1971.

Rachman, David J., *Retail Management Strategy*. Englewood Cliffs, N.J.: Prentice-Hall, Inc., 1970.

Stockman, Lynn H., *The Smaller Independent Men's-Wear Store*. Chicago: Hart, Schaffner & Marx, 1967.

Wingate, John W., and Joseph S. Friedlander, *The Management of Retail Buying*. Englewood Cliffs, N.J.: Prentice-Hall, Inc., 1963.

SALES PROMOTION

14

INTRODUCTION

There are about as many different definitions for the term *sales promotion* as there are textbooks concerning this area of marketing. In the context of this chapter, *sales promotion* refers to such mass communications media as advertising, special promotions, display, and publicity. Personal selling, which some might consider logical to include as part of sales promotion, will be discussed independently in Chapter 15. The primary reason for this separation is that the forms of promotion presented here, contrary to those in personal selling, appeal to groups rather than to individuals.

Marketers, as we have learned earlier, spend about as much in the marketing of goods as they do in their manufacture. Often the costs of marketing exceed those of actual production. A large portion of the marketing dollar goes for promotion of the product. This is not only true for new products but also for established ones.

BUDGETING

The actual sum a company should spend for adequate promotional coverage constitutes a problem that continues to plague even the most sophisticated marketers. Agreement is unanimous among knowledgeable marketers that in order to bring a successful product into being it must be promoted, but the amount to set aside and the method to employ in establishing the amount is not standard procedure. Unfortunately, most budgets are made by executives who are not directly involved in day-to-day expenditures. This often leads to unrealistic budgeting. Many barometers are used. Among the most popular are:

Percentage-of-Sales Method

In this approach, companies use a percentage of the past year's sales in determining the amount to be set aside for promotion. Some companies vary this technique by substituting an average of several previous years' sales instead of just the previous year. Although this may be thought of as a logical base upon which to set the budget, many promotion experts con-

TABLE 14–1

PROMOTIONAL COSTS AS PERCENTAGE OF SALES OF CONSUMER GOODS: BY INDIVIDUAL COMPANIES

Note the wide variations in the promotional mixes used by different firms. Compare the cosmetics firm (no. 3) and the insurance company (no. 62). Also note the variations in total promotional appropriations. A paint company (no. 12) devoted 27 percent of sales to promotion, while the promotion budget of an appliance company (no. 43) was only 8 percent of sales. How do you account for these differences?

Number	Type of Product	Advertising Budget[a]	Advertising	Sales Promotion	Sales Force
1.	Toiletries and proprietaries	A	30.0	4.0	10.0
2.	Package goods	AA	25.0	8.0	8.0
3.	Cosmetics	C	24.0	5.0	7.0
4.	Cosmetics	AAA	22.0	2.0	10.0
5.	Housewares	B	20.0[b]	—[b]	3.5
6.	Perfumes and cosmetics	B	16.0	3.0	21.0
7.	Drug sundries	A	14.0	3.0	5.0
8.	Drugs	A	12.0	8.0	7.0
9.	Books	A	11.0	6.0	5.0
10.	Food	AAA	11.0	6.0	—
11.	Mail order	AAA	10.5	0.2	0.3
12.	Paints	B	10.0	2.0	15.0
13.	Housewares	B	10.0	2.0	6.0
14.	Beer	AA	9.5	6.4[e]	—
15.	Food and feed	AAA	8.1	3.2	6.1
16.	Food	AAA	7.0	5.0	3.0
17.	Food	AAA	7.0	4.5[e]	—[e]
18.	Small housewares	B	6.0	1.3	12.5
19.	Appliances	AAA	5.0	1.0	—
20.	Soft drinks	B	5.0	3.0	1.0
21.	Soft goods	C	5.0	6.0	12.0
22.	Nonferrous metals	AA	5.0[c]	—[c]	—
23.	Salt	C	5.0[c]	—[c]	—
24.	Packaged grocery products	AAA	4.8	0.7	1.2
25.	Beverages	A	4.6	1.4	—
26.	Tool manufacturing	C	4.0[c]	—[c]	10.0
27.	Paper converting	C	4.0	4.0	—
28.	Soft goods, textiles	A	4.0	1.0[f]	17.0
29.	Tires, foam rubber	A	4.0	4.0	—
30.	Pianos	C	4.0	0.3	5.0
31.	Chemicals	D	3.5	1.0	—
32.	Automotive parts	C	3.5	—	10.3
33.	Photographic equipment	C	3.3[c]	—	3.0
34.	Food	A	3.5	1.7	6.0
35.	Appliances	A	3.0	3.0	—
36.	Textiles	B	3.0	0.7	3.6
37.	Shoe manufacturing	A	3.0	0.3[f]	4.5
38.	Marketing cooperative—fresh produce	C	3.0[c]	—[c]	10.0
39.	Baby foods	A	2.7	2.6	6.0
40.	Hand tools	B	2.5	0.9	7.1

TABLE 14–1 (cont.)

Number	Type of Product	Advertising budget[a]	Advertising	Sales Promotion	Sales Force
41.	Home furnishings	B	2.5	2.0	6.0
42.	Power tools	C	2.5	—	—
43.	Appliances	A	2.5	1.5	4.0
44.	Airline	AA	2.2	0.7	—
45.	Building materials	A	2.2	1.9	4.8
46.	Liquors	A	2.0	—	—
47.	Basic metals	A	2.0	1.0	—
48.	Heating and air conditioning	A	2.0	0.5	4.5
49.	Soft goods	C	2.0	2.5	4.5
50.	Floor coverings	A	2.0[c]	—	—
51.	Plumbing and heating	A	2.0[c]	—	—
52.	Shoe manufacturing	D	2.0[c]	—	5.3
53.	Steel equipment	C	2.0[c]	—	16.0
54.	Transportation	AA	1.8	0.2	6.0
55.	Building materials	AA	1.5	0.7	8.0
56.	Automotive	D	1.5	—	3.0
57.	Rubber	C	1.5	1.5	4.5
58.	Rubber products	C	1.3	1.0	—
59.	Water pumps	D	1.3	1.3[f]	5.0
60.	Photographic equipment	B	1.3	0.7	3.0
61.	Food	A	1.0	0.3	—
62.	Insurance	A	1.0	0.5	17.5
63.	Textiles	B	1.0	1.0	0.5
64.	Petroleum	C	1.0	—	—
65.	Retail food chain	AAA	1.0[c]	—[c]	—
66.	Oil	A	0.7	0.3	—
67.	Petroleum	A	0.6	0.3	—
68.	Domestic pumps and water systems	C	0.6	1.0	—
69.	Over thirty industries	A	0.5	1.5	—
70.	Glass manufacturing	A	0.5	0.2	—
71.	Steel manufacturing	D	0.2	0.5	0.5
72.	Iron and steel	D	0.1	—	—
73.	Aluminum	B	0.1	0.1	—
74.	Building industry	A	0.1[d]	—[d]	—[d]

Note: Dash (—) indicates data not given.
[a] AAA—$10,000,000 and over; AA—$5,000,000–9,999,999; A—$1,000,000–4,999,999; B—$500,000 –999,999;C—$100,000–499,999; D—under $100,000.
[b] Advertising, sales promotion and marketing research combined.
[c] Advertising and sales promotion combined.
[d] Advertising. sales promotion. marketing research, and sales force combined.
[e] Sales promotion, marketing research, and sales force combined.
[f] Sales promotion and marketing research combined.
Source: Dale Houghton, "Marketing Costs: What Ratio to Sales?" *Printers' Ink.* Feb. 1, 1957, pp. 54–55.

sider the system to be illogical. Advertising men believe that sales result from advertising and other promotional devices, rather than the opposite. Expenditures for promotional purposes should not be decided as a result of sales. Certain companies who effectively use the percentage-of-sales ap-

TABLE 14–2

PROMOTIONAL COSTS AS PERCENTAGE OF SALES OF INDUSTRIAL GOODS: BY INDIVIDUAL COMPANIES

Sales force expenditures are typically much higher than advertising appropriations. In the promotional mix, marketers of industrial goods usually emphasize personal selling to a much greater degree than firms selling consumer products. Why? Compare this table and Table 14–1; note that the total promotional budget for industrial products is typically a smaller percentage of sales than that for consumer goods.

Number	Type of Product	Advertising Budget[a]	Advertising	Sales Promotion	Sales Force
1.	Paint	D	10.0	—	—
2.	Road construction and agricultural	D	4.0[b]	—[b]	7.0
3.	Industrial fasteners, steel shelving, and shop equipment	B	2.8	—	—
4.	Office equipment	C	2.5[c]	—[c]	—
5.	Instrument	C	2.0	0.9	9.0
6.	Tool manufacturing	C	2.0[c]	—[c]	10.0
7.	Paper converting	C	2.0	2.0	—
8.	Instruments and controls	C	2.0[b]	—[b]	15.0
9.	Electrical control	C	1.8	3.8	—
10.	Metalworking machinery	C	1.8	0.2	—
11.	Graphic arts	C	1.5	0.5	16.0
12.	Metalworking	C	1.5[c]	—[c]	5,0
13.	Metal cutting tools	C	1.2	—	5.6
14.	Industrial machinery	D	1.0	2.0	7.0
15.	Package grocery products	B	1.0	0.9	4.8
16.	Metal product—foundry and machining	C	1.0	0.8	5.5
17.	Automotive parts	C	1.0	0.5	4.5
18.	Building materials	B	1.0	0.3[d]	4.0
19.	Nonferrous metals	A	1.0[c]	—[c]	—
20.	Die cutting	D	1.0	—	10.0
21.	Basic metals	AA	1.0	—	—
22.	Aluminum	A	0.8	0.4	—
23.	Petroleum	B	0.8	0.3	3.0
24.	Chemicals and plastics	A	0.8	—	—
25.	Chemical and food processing, steel mill, and construction equipment	A	0.7	0.2	6.0
26.	Iron and steel	A	0.6	—	—
27.	Hand tools	C	0.5	0.2	2.4
28.	Materials handling	B	0.5	0.5	—
29.	Soft goods—textile	C	0.5	—	12.0
30.	Automotive	D	0.5	—	0.5
31.	Plate steel fabrication	D	0.4	0.5	0.5
32.	Foundry	C	0.3	—	—
33.	Iron and steel	C	0.3	—	—
34.	Rubber products	D	0.3	—	—
35.	Photographic equipment manufacturing	D	0.2	—	—
36.	Food and feed	C	0.1	0.3	2.5

TABLE 14–2 (cont.)

Number	Type of Product	Advertising Budget[a]	Advertising	Sales Promotion	Sales Force
37.	Chemicals	B	0.1	—	—
38.	Glass manufacturing	D	0.1	—	—
39.	Oil	C	0.1	—	—
40.	Aircraft	C	0.1	—	—
41.	Heavy manufacturing and aircraft accessories	C	0.1	—	9.3
42.	Manufacturing conveyors and pneumatic tube systems	C	—	—	—
43.	Building industry	C	—	—	—

Note: Dash (—) indicates data not given.
[a] AAA—$1,000,0000 and over; AA—$5,000,000–9,999,999; A—$1,000,000–4,999,999; B—$500,000–999,999; C—$100,000–499,999; D—under $100,000.
[b] Advertising, sales promotion and marketing research combined.
[c] Advertising and sales promotion and marketing research combined.
[d] Sales promotion and marketing research combined.
Source: Dale Houghton, "Marketing Costs: What Ratio in Sales?" Printers' Ink, Feb. 1, 1957, p. 24.

proach in budget determinations have found that it makes more sense to use anticipated sales as a base than previous sales figures. The latter technique seems to be most logical in that it takes into consideration company growth and the value of sales promotion in achieving this growth.

Units-of-Sales Method

Instead of basing a budgetary decision on total dollars, some companies expend sums for the promotion of their goods based on the number of individual units of merchandise they sold in the past year (or hope to sell in the coming year). A determination is then made as to how much an individual article will cost to promote. This sum is then multiplied by the total units of production to arrive at the actual budget.

Task Method

Use of this technique requires complete research of the product and its potential markets. The company using this method defines its objectives, such as the number of units to be sold, total sales, and profit expectation. After careful consideration of the costs involved to reach these objectives, a budgetary figure is reached. Sometimes called the task-and-objective method, this technique is considered by many marketers to be the soundest approach in the determination of the promotion allocation.

Although businesses can get scientific in the planning of the budget, some organizations leave the amount to be spent for the promotion of goods to chance. Unsophisticated approaches like whim or whatever amount happens to be available at the time is sometimes the deciding factor. Little logic is associated with this kind of thinking, but there are businessmen who will confide that this is the tactic used by their companies. Little can be said for the validity of such an approach.

ADVERTISING

Advertising as defined by the American Marketing Association is "any paid-for form of nonpersonal presentation of the facts about goods, services, or ideas to a group." A breakdown of the definition and comparison with the other areas of sales promotion makes it more easily understandable. Publicity is free and advertising is paid for; display actually shows the goods, whereas advertising only tells the facts about them; and selling (as noted, considered by some to be included as a sales-promotion activity) is personal, but advertising is nonpersonal or to a group.

By and large, companies feel that the greatest return for the promotion dollar comes as a result of advertising. Hence, advertising warrants and is afforded the lion's share of the promotion budget by most marketers.

Marketers make use of two classifications of advertising: product and institutional. The former stimulates the market regarding the product or services, whereas the latter is designed to create a proper attitude toward the seller and to build good will.

The Major Marketing Advertisers

The marketing institutions responsible for the majority of advertising are manufacturers and retailers. Although the media employed by both groups are the same (the amount of emphasis in each of the media will differ), the messages they convey are not. Manufacturers make every effort to arouse the customer's desire to purchase their product. Where or how the purchase is made is often immaterial. Retailers, on the other hand, concentrate their efforts on convincing the public to buy products from them. With the tremendous amount of competition at both marketing levels, manufacturers and retailers alike expend enormous sums to garner their share of the market. It is estimated that marketers are spending today about twenty billion dollars a year for advertising.

Advertising Agencies

Although companies often have their own advertising staffs, the advertising agency plays the major part in the advertisement of goods and services. The agency is an independent business charged with responsibility of the preparation of ads and the selection of appropriate media for presentation. Remuneration generally comes from the media. This is usually 15 percent of the cost of the ad. If a company goes directly to the media to place an ad, the cost will be the same as that charged by the agency. The agencies actually receive a better price for advertising space or time because of their purchasing power. Thus, the cost of employing an agency to carry out the advertising task virtually does not contribute any additional expense to marketers.

Advertising Media

The advertising media available to marketers include newspapers, magazines, radio, television, direct mail, hand-distributed circulars, signs and billboards, car cards, and shopping publications. Few companies utilize all media. A discussion of each type follows to indicate the various advantages of each classification for the marketer.

NEWSPAPERS. There are two distinct types of newspapers for the promotion of goods and services. They are the consumer newspapers (the ones we read as consumers) and the trade papers, which are carefully scrutinized by business men.

Both types of papers are directed to specific audiences; when properly executed, both reap the rewards sought. From this point, *newspaper advertising* is to mean the consumer newspapers. Traditionally, retailers spend the larger part of their promotional dollar on advertising. Patronized by retailers are the giant dailies such as the *New York Times,* the *Miami Herald* and the *Chicago Sun Times.* Not neglected but nonetheless not as widely used in terms of overall dollars are the publications that cover smaller, local areas. Most newspapers have numerous data on hand to enable the advertisers to determine which newspaper is best suited for their needs.

Of the advantages of newspaper advertising the following are most significant:

1. The newspaper's offerings are so diversified that they appeal to almost every member of the family. For example, a young adult, not prone to newspaper reading, might be attracted by an advertisement while looking for the television section.

2. Although advertising space might be considered costly upon initial examination, closer inspection shows its cost to be lower per reader than the cost of all other media.

3. The newspaper can be examined at leisure and therefore its life is longer than that of broadcast advertising. A moment away from the television set means that the commercial will not be seen.

4. Being brought home by the working members of the household (many read the newspapers on the train ride home) or delivered by newspaperboys, the newspaper is available simply and on a daily basis.

Newspaper advertising also has its disadvantages.

1. Longer distance from the stores sometimes prevents the interested reader from shopping the advertised merchandise.

2. The life of the message may only be for a very short time. Sometimes it is for only part of the ride home.

3. The quality of the stock (paper) used often limits the attractiveness of the item being offered for sale. For this reason, color is rarely used.

Advertising Rates. The rates charged for space vary according to size of the advertisement, location (placement), circulation, and newspaper in which the ad is placed. Although it is common practice to sell space on a full-page, half-page, and so on arrangement, the cost is actually figured on a line basis. The number of lines multiplied by the cost per line indicates the cost of the space. The cost for the same ad in two newspapers may vary considerably. To find the true value, that is the cost per reader, the milline rate formula is applied as follows:

$$\frac{\text{rate per line} \times 1{,}000{,}000}{\text{circulation}} = \text{milline rate}$$

If the rate per line is forty cents and a paper's circulation is four hundred thousand, then the milline rate is:

$$\frac{.40 \times 1{,}000{,}000}{400{,}000} = \$1$$

By applying this formula to the various newspapers' rates and circulation, an advertiser can determine whether a higher line rate might actually cost less per reader.

As indicated earlier, in addition to the cost per line in newspapers, the costs vary according to placement or position of the ad. The least-expensive method of advertising placement is called "ROP" or "run of paper." This means that the advertisement will be placed at the discretion of the newspaper. "Regular position" guarantees that a store's advertisements will be placed in the same position all the time. It is costlier than ROP, but readers eventually know where to find a store's advertisements. "Preferred position," the most costly, locates the advertisement in the most desirable spot in the newspaper for that particular ad. The position may be adjacent to a pertinent newspaper column. For example, men's sporting goods' advertisements would be more effective if placed next to a sportswriter's daily column. This positioning guarantees exposure to the appropriate readers.

Taking all these factors into consideration, a retailer is often wise to run a smaller advertisement positioned in the best location in a newspaper with a larger circulation than a larger ad without these important features. After careful examination of all the variables, the actual rate per line might not be the most important consideration.

CONSUMER MAGAZINES. On an overall basis, the magazine is extensively used by marketers, although the retailing segment is not a major user. Magazines' trading areas generally extend beyond the bounds of the retailer's trading area. Thus the cost per reader, of those actually able to patronize the retail store, is very high. Stores are usually involved in advertising promotions that are planned in considerably less time than is necessary to meet the magazines' advertising deadline. Stores like Saks Fifth Avenue and Lord & Taylor do spend some money on magazine advertising, but this can be considered as an effort to gain prestige.

Magazine advertising may not be the retailers' medium, but it is the one consistently employed by manufacturers. The magazine has many advantageous features for them. First, the life of a magazine is longer than that of any other written publication. It therefore can be passed from household to household, enabling it to reach many more readers than the actual subscriber. Second, each magazine has a clearly defined audience. Thus, specific markets are easy to reach. The Rolls Royce manufacturer can advertise in a magazine that boasts an affluent readership. Magazines specializing in sports, hobbies, travel and theater, for example, will appeal to manufacturers of merchandise that is of interest to their particular readers. Third, magazines frequently offer to their advertisers markets more limited than their general circulation by running ads only for specific regions. For example, marketers wishing only to appeal to the northeastern part of the country may do so. In this case, the cost is less than for full coverage.

TELEVISION. Television has accounted for the greatest growth as an advertising medium. With the vast number of receivers in operation today, marketers can easily and quickly reach a very large audience. For almost every product the visual impression on television cannot be duplicated by any of the media. With the popularity of color (and the increase in color sales) marketers continue to expand their television-advertising budgets. Only the actual in person viewing of the product coupled with expertise in personal selling can be more effective in the promotion of a product. The high cost has restricted the use of television to the giants of the marketing industry. Manufacturers of automobiles, household products, such as detergents and toothpaste, public utilities, such as Bell Telephone, and foods are principal users for purposes of advertising.

RADIO. The very nature of the ratio today has changed its position in advertising. Once the family congregated around the radio for its entertainment, but its attention has shifted to television. Thus, the radio-listening audience is now generally relegated to the automobile driver, the housewife tending to her household chores, and the teen-age market.

Although the medium is perhaps not so frequently employed any more by national advertisers, it still is an excellent outlet for the small, local advertiser who wants to cover his own market but cannot afford the high cost of television. The teen-age segment of the population is an avid listening audience. Whether it is in automobiles, at the beaches, or just at home, the teen-ager spends a good deal of time listening to the radio. Marketers of teen-age clothing, records, entertainment places (discotèques), and so on are able to get their messages across to their potential customers through radio at a cost that is compatible with their advertising budgets.

Broadcast advertising, in comparison with the other media, has been sparingly used in retailing. Some firms do invest a small portion of their sales-promotion dollars in these media. Since the costs are very high and the audiences are spread across the country, advertisers do not sponsor entire programs; instead they make use of a spot commercial either when a station identifies itself during program changes or as one of a great number of sponsors on various shows. By using the media in this way costs are minimized and messages are restricted to that segment of the viewing and listening audiences that is pertinent to the particular store. Spot commercials generally only go to preselected local audiences. This type of advertising is generally employed by stores wishing to announce special one-day sales, special events, or news of that nature.

DIRECT ADVERTISING.   Direct advertising is delivery of advertising materials like merchandise brochures, sale announcements, letters, catalogs, booklets, and circulars by means of the mail or hand distribution.

Marketers, both large and small, extensively use direct advertising. Among many of the benefits derived from the practice are:

1. Direct advertisements are often included in billing statements of both manufacturers and retailers. The manufacturer might send to the wholesaler or retailer a brochure that features new items. Retailers similarly whet their customers' appetite in this fashion. Without additional delivery expense the advertisement can be distributed.

2. The company can appeal to a particular group of people. Mailing lists can be compiled from names of satisfied customers or purchased from commercial list houses that categorize the population according to classifications as occupation, income, education, religious background, and so on.

3. Direct advertisements, in comparison with the other media, afford the advertiser the prospect's undivided attention. The periodicals contain many advertisements, in one issue, that tend to vie for the prospect's eye.

4. Costs of direct advertising can be as varied as the budget allows. This is not true for newspaper, magazine, radio, and television rates. A simple message, for example, about a change in the manufacturer's discount allowances, can reach the customer at minimal expense via a postcard.

A serious disadvantage of direct advertising is that some pieces go straight into the wastebasket without being read. Another of the pitfalls is poor maintenance of mailing lists. If these lists are not continuously updated, a percentage of the mail will not be delivered. The main reason why it is necessary to alter the list is that customers may move. With guaranteed postage, the post office will return all undeliverable mail to the sender. Thus, if the company makes use of this service, it can easily clean up its mailing list. The method employed is the printing of Form 3547 on the mailing piece, which requires the postman to make the adjustment. Businesses often, in an attempt to solicit new customers, prepare a mailing addressed to "occupant." This directs mail to a particular address but to no particular person. This system is used, for example, when a new company begins operation and wishes to announce its opening.

BILLBOARDS. Marketers make relatively little use of billboard advertising. Billboards are permanently painted, or covered with prepared advertisements that can be changed frequently, or they offer an illuminated and often animated presentation. Billboard space is generally available on a rental basis. The cost is dependent on size and location of the billboard. It is inexpensive to advertise in this manner, as the cost per observer is little, but the audiences attracted are usually moving quickly (in an automobile, for example) and are not selected on any scientific basis. Magazines, on the other hand, have particular audiences and a company can select the most appropriate one. The billboard medium does not allow for such precise selection. The reader is aware of the billboard for only a limited period, so that the message must also be brief. Although there are certain disadvantages to billboard advertising, marketers do find it more or less valuable for the promotion of certain goods and services, such as automobiles, gasoline, motels, and restaurants.

CAR CARDS. Travelers on public transportation witness a great number of advertisements during their rides. Colorful posters or cards occupy a great deal of space on train and bus walls. With the great number of riders using public transportation daily, businesses make extensive use of this form of advertising. Cigarette manufacturers, loan companies, local retail shops, and entertainment establishments like theaters spend large sums on this medium.

In New York City, a producer of Broadway plays might select a railroad from a nearby suburb in which to place car-card advertisements, in order to gain new, distant audiences.

Car-card space is purchased in runs; full, half, quarter, and often double runs. A full run would place one card in each car of a train. A half run would place one card in every other car, and so on.

Messages must be brief, printed in color, and lettered sufficiently large to be seen by most pople in the car. Since passengers usually remain in one place for an entire trip, careful planning is necessary to guarantee a maximum amount of exposure.

INDEPENDENT SHOPPING PUBLICATIONS. In many cities advertisers have been publishing independent periodicals primarily for the purpose of retail advertisements. The *Pennysaver* is an example of such a publication. It is almost completely devoted to the advertisement of the local retail store. It is extremely attractive for this segment of retailing in that it is less expensive than regular newspaper or broadcast advertising and reaches a clearly defined market in which the store's customers live. These publications are either mailed to prospects in a particular area or hand-delivered to the home, free of charge. Their success can be evidenced by the increasing number of shopping publications now in print. The *Pennysaver* is very successful on Long Island. Local merchants find it their best and least-expensive advertising investment.

Advertising Effectiveness

The effectiveness of its advertising is vital to the growth of the company. Evaluating the effectiveness is usually the task of the marketing-research department or of an outside research agency.

Although it is important to receive advice from experts concerning the effectiveness of advertising, this source alone is not sufficient for a truly scientific measurement.

Advertisements and their effectiveness may be measured at three distinct periods: prior to publication, while shown to the potential market, or after presentation.

There are number of tests to measure effectiveness. They are:

1. *Sales-results tests,* which try to measure the sales volume that will directly result from the advertising compaign that is being tested.

2. *Readership tests* (sometimes known as recall tests), which involve showing all or part of an advertisement to the reader in an attempt to have him recall all or part of the ad, such as the sponsor's name.

3. *Coupon measurement.* Some ads include coupons that readers are asked to return to the advertiser if they are interested in more information, a free sample, and so on. Count of the returned coupons shows whether or not the ad was read.

4. *Comparison measurements,* which use consumer panels to select the best possible ads for a company.

Only scientific measurement will guarantee the effectiveness of advertising, which is both expensive and valuable to the marketer.

SPECIAL PROMOTIONS

In addition to the mentioned advertising media, marketers spend considerable sums on special promotions. Although events as the Macy-sponsored Thanksgiving Day parade would be prohibitive in terms of cost for most firms, the use of a special demonstration to attract customers may be within a company's reach.

Fashion Shows

The display of fashions on live models has been a regular sales-promotion device for manufacturers as well as retail stores. Executives may express the opinion that the presentation of a fashion show is primarily for prestigious purposes; however, companies do achieve immediate business from them. Only watch the women rise from their chairs to rush over to the racks of clothing after an Ohrbach's showing of European fashions to realize the instant success of the show in terms of sales. Retail-store buyers likewise spend a great deal of time attending the season's openings, both here and abroad, in preparation of their buying needs. Even if a fashion show does not result in immediate sales, it is valuable in that it exposes fashion merchandise to potential buyers in a lively and exciting manner unobtainable through any other medium. With properly conceived and executed production appetites are likely to be whetted for future motivation.

Demonstrations

Demonstrations are not new to businessmen. What can better sell typewriters than to show how they can be utilized? Business shows dramatize the use of the computer by demonstrating the remarkable data it can instantaneously sort and feed to executives. These demonstrations are often a result of the combined efforts of manufacturers, wholesalers, and retailers. Some are only one-day events, whereas others are major special events, requiring large space and a number of demonstrators. A major demonstration jointly sponsored by manufacturer and retailer took place at Gimbels in New York for the promotion of Corning ware, that is, Pyroceram cooking utensils, manufactured by Corning Glass. Food was prepared before the prospective customers' eyes, and whoever was interested could taste it. Also shown was that the utensils could easily be transferred from extreme cold to extreme heat without breakage and that it was simple to clean the Corning ware. Closed-circuit TV showed the product's resistance to breakage by presenting a brief film entitled *Bull in a China Shop,* in which the Corning ware was knocked over without resulting damage. The cooperation of the involved companies guaranteed a more successful event. Store sales increased, which meant reorders and increased sales for the manufacturer.

Sampling

A method of promoting sales very closely related to demonstrating is to attract prospective customers through the use of samples. Sampling is similar to demonstrating in that it shows the customer how to actually use the merchandise. The major difference between the two methods is that in the one case the merchandise is used by a company representative and in the other by the customer personally. The decision on whether to sell by demonstration or sample is based on the characteristics of the merchandise. Expensive merchandise that requires skill to operate is sold by demonstration.

Products that can be inexpensively sampled, and the use of which requires no previous training, can be very effectively sold by means of samples.

The importance of the sample method is that it allows the customer to actually touch the product. Depending on the merchandise, sampling can effectively take place in the store or in the customer's home. Food products, stationery, candies, and yard goods are generally given out by salespeople in the stores. Soap powders, razor blades, and swatches of material for shirts, bedclothes, sheets, and a variety of other uses are frequently mailed to the customer's home. As long as the cost of the sample is relatively low, sampling is a very effective way to sell merchandise and get publicity.

Premiums

Premiums, that is, the process of giving special merchandise (products that are not regularly offered for sale) as an inducement to buy goods, have been very popular during the past ten years. The premiums may be awarded for single transactions (a box of Ivory flakes with each Jantzen girdle bought), or for multiple transactions (a drinking glass for each twenty gallons of gasoline purchased). Premiums may be free, as in the previously mentioned cases, or not free, in which case the buyer is offered the premium at substantial savings, for example, a one-dollar pair of nylon stretch stockings for fifty cents plus one coupon from a Kraft cheese package. Whatever the premium plan—and there is a constantly growing variety of plans— when properly handled, premiums offer an important means of stimulating sales.

Trading Stamps

Trading stamps have lost much of their popularity, but they are still used as an inducement to buy. Stamps are given at the time merchandise is purchased. The rate varies, but the general practice is ten stamps for each dollar. In slow periods, double the regular number of stamps is offered as means of further motivation. Stamps are pasted in books and redeemed for premium merchandise that may be inspected in catalogs, or even more closely at redemption centers. Presently it is estimated that 15 percent of the total retail sales are made by customers at stores featuring stamps.

The cost of trading stamps to the retailer is about two-hundredths to three-hundredths cent per stamp, plus the time involved in handling. This can be a fairly high cost to large-volume stores, but the use of trading stamps builds sales volume by attracting customers who might otherwise shop at a competitive store.

To the consumer, trading stamps offer a means of savings to get premium merchandise in a somewhat painless fashion. That the books of stamps have a definite value has been proven by many studies, which show the books to have a value of $3.21 in traditional stores or $2.82 in discount stores.

The question most often raised among customers of stores that feature trading stamps is "am I paying for these stamps in terms of higher prices?" The answer, of course, is yes. On the other hand, the customer pays for all store promotions (such as advertising) with no questions asked.

Whether or not a store should handle trading stamps is a problem that requires careful analysis. However, it is likely that of two otherwise equal stores, the one handling trading stamps will attract more customers.

DISPLAY

Display, unlike advertising, is a visual presentation of the goods to be sold. Manufacturers play an important role in the preparation of point-of-purchase display materials for the retail outlets to whom they sell. In some industries, for example, the liquor industry, manufacturers (or wholesale distributors) take care of display services. Displaymen travel from store to store to put up the displays. Other manufacturers make the display materials, complete with easy-to-follow instructions and photographs, available to the retailer. For example, Russell Stover, manufacturer of packaged chocolates, prepares such a package. To the new marketing student, the displaying of merchandise might seem to be the sole responsibility of the retailer. This is not true because the manufacturer, in order to sell merchandise, must make certain that his outlets are successful. By becoming involved in display, he is improving the visual presentation of his product to the consumer.

Nevertheless, the retailer plays the major role. For many years retailers have considered windows (and counters) to be silent salesmen. With the growing practice of self-selection in stores throughout the country, greater emphasis is now placed on display, or visual merchandising, than ever before.

The display must attract the attention of the buying public. This may be achieved by exciting use of color, dramatic lighting effects, or motion. The great annual event at Lord & Taylor's in New York at Christmastime (dancing dolls in the window, or a live Santa coming down the chimney) is an example of an in motion display.

In addition to attracting attention, a satisfactory display must hold the individual's interest much the same as a newspaper or magazine advertisement. It is not enough to stop the reader, it must make him investigate further. Interest is held by the timeliness of the display, the appeal of the merchandise, or the information contained in the message on the accompanying show card.

Next, the display must be exciting enough to arouse the desire to further examine the merchandise (by asking to see it, try it on, and so on. Marketers have long argued over whether display creates or arouses desires. They should settle for the awakening of the individual's desire to purchase.

When the window display achieves these ends, the customer will enter the retail store. Then, either creative interior displays will take over or perhaps the salesperson will answer those questions still unanswered by window display alone.

PUBLICITY

According to the American Marketing Association, "publicity is the nonpersonal stimulation of demand for a product, service, or business unit by planting commercially significant news about it in a published medium or obtaining favorable presentation of it upon radio, TV, or stage that is not paid for by the sponsor."

The issue is promotion without cost. For example, a new automobile might be produced that is so outstanding that the local newspaper or automotive magazine will review it. A retail store's holiday parade might get attention on a television news broadcast. The larger companies employ public-relations men who are charged with the responsibility of preparing releases about their offerings that might attract the media and, therefore, customer interest. The free publicity a business receives is not always kind, and could work adversely. For example, recent newspaper coverage of the effect of disposable containers on the environment could hurt the sales of a company making use of this type of package.

IMPORTANT POINTS IN THE CHAPTER

1. Sales promotion refers to such mass communications media as advertising, special promotions, display, and publicity. Personal selling is excluded, since its appeal is to individuals, whereas the others appeal to groups.

2. Promotoin budgets are based on three measurements. They are percentage of sales, units of sales, and task to be performed.

3. Newspapers receive the largest part of the retail-advertising dollar; magazines account for the largest part of the manufacturer's advertising allocation.

4. Television is presently accounting for the fastest growth in advertising.

5. Manufactures spend large sums for special promotions such as fashion shows, demonstrations, samples, premiums, and trading stamps.

6. *Display* is the visual presentation of goods to be sold. Although retailers play the major role in the display of merchandise, manufacturers become involved in the preparation of point-of-purchase display materials for retailers.

7. Publicity, unlike the other forms of promotion, is free. It comes as the result of effective advertising, display, or special promotions.

REVIEW QUESTIONS

1. What other forms of sales promotion are there besides advertising?
2. On what bases do companies plan their advertising budgets?
3. Discuss the term *task method*.
4. Define *advertising*. How does advertising differ from personal selling?
5. In what principal way does retail advertising differ from that engaged in by the manufacturer?
6. How does the advertising agency receive its remuneration?
7. Which of the advertising media is used most commonly by retailers? What advantage does this medium offer to retail stores?
8. Determine the milline rate if the rate per line is forty cents and the newspaper's circulation is four hundred thousand.
9. Differentiate between *ROP* and *preferred position* in newspaper advertising.
10. Why do manufacturers generally limit their newspaper advertising expenditure? Why do they extensively invest in magazine advertising?
11. Which of the media has accounted for the greatest growth in recent years? Why?
12. For what reasons do marketers invest in direct-mail advertising?
13. Billboard advertising is infrequently used by marketers. Why?
14. Define: *full run, half run*.
15. Which marketing institution uses the sampling method in the promotion of new products? What characteristic must a product have in order to be promoted via this method?
16. Discuss the importance of trading stamps in marketing.
17. Cite some examples (other than those in the chapter) of the use of premiums in the promotion of goods.
18. How do display and advertising differ?
19. To what extent do manufacturers become involved in display?
20. Define *publicity*. How does it differ from the other sales-promotion techniques?

CASE PROBLEMS

Case Problem 1

Childcraft, Inc. has just started business as manufacturers of a full line of toys. Areas of concern, such as the number of different items to produce, the prices to charge for each item, and the consumer market to be reached, have been discussed. In fact, just about all the pertinent questions relating to the marketing of a new line have been examined, and plans are under way for the start of production.

Mr. Funk, marketing manager for Childcraft, has been unable to come to a decision concerning the promotion of the line. Specifically, he is uncertain about where and how to promote the line and about exactly how much should be set aside for the promotional budget.

The company is new, so it would be impossible to make use of past company experience. Also, budgeting is difficult, since the firm's newness eliminates the percentage-of-sales and unit-of-sales methods for the determination of an appropriate budget.

Questions

1. Where should Mr. Funk look for help in deciding how to promote the line?
2. Where would you suggest that Childcraft should advertise? Why?
3. Which technique should be used in determining the promotion budget? Discuss the areas to be investigated.

Case Problem 2

David's Department Store has been in operation for twenty years. It is a conventional-type business, with a main store located in a downtown shopping area and five branch stores in suburban shopping centers. For the past few years, David's has suffered a steady decline in business. The problem seems to be attributable to the number of discount operations that have opened in competition to David's.

Since the store is service-oriented, management has decided that it would be both inappropriate and unprofitable to lower prices in order to regain lost sales.

Mr. Clements, senior vice-president in charge of operations, has charged the store's promotion departments with the responsibility of reattracting old customers and motivating new business.

Questions

1. Which promotion departments should be involved in the new assignment?
2. Since price cannot be stressed, what should their advertising appeal to?
3. What kinds of special events could the store plan in order to attract customers?

BIBLIOGRAPHY

Belair, R. O., "How to Promote a New and Unknown Product," *Marketing Insights,* March 3, 1969.

Bond, Edward L., Jr., "The Future of the Advertising Agency Business," *Marketing Insights,* April 8, 1968.

Boyd, Harper W., Jr., and Sidney J. Levy, *Promotion: A Behavioral View.* Englewood Cliffs, N.J.: Prentice-Hall, Inc., 1967.

Buchanan, Dodds I., "A New Look at 'Old' Advertising Strategy," in Ralph L. Day, *Concepts for Modern Marketing.* Scranton, Pa.: International Textbook Co., 1968.

"Industrial Ads in the Conglomerate Year of 1968," *Marketing Insights,* April 7, 1969.

Kernan, Jerome B., and James U. McNeal, "The Closest Thing to Measuring Advertising Effectiveness," in Ralph L. Day, *Concepts for Modern Marketing.* Scraton, Pa.: International Textbook Co., 1968.

Kleppner, Otto, *Advertising Procedure.* Englewood Cliffs, N.J.: Prentice-Hall, Inc., 1966.

Littlefield, James A., and C. A. Kirkpatrick, *Advertising: Mass Communication in Marketing.* Boston: Houghton Mifflin Company, 1970.

McGarry, Edmond, "The Propaganda Function in Marketing," in Robert J. Holloway and Robert S. Hancock, *The Environment of Marketing Behavior.* New York: John Wiley & Sons, Inc., 1969.

Sales Promotion Calendar. New York: National Retail Merchants' Association, Sales-Promotion Division (published annually).

Sandage, Charles H., and Vernon Fryburger, *Advertising Theory and Practice.* Homewood, Ill.: Richard D. Irwin, Inc., 1967.

Tillman, Rollie, and C. A. Kirkpatrick, *Promotion: Persuasive Communication in Marketing.* Homewood, Ill.: Richard D. Irwin, Inc., 1968.

Wheatley, John J., *Measuring Advertising Effectiveness.* Homewood, Ill.: Richard D. Irwin, Inc., 1969.

Wright, John S., Daniel S. Warner, and Willis L. Winter, Jr., *Advertising.* New York: McGraw-Hill Book Company, 1971.

PERSONAL
SELLING

15

INTRODUCTION

When marketing management's attention is focused on sophisticated aspects of present-day marketing (research, computer applications), personal selling is too often treated as the company's stepchild. However, whether it is selling for a manufacturer, showing a wholesaler's complete line, or approaching the customer in a retail store, salesmanship is extremely vital to today's business organization. The lifeblood of the distribution of goods is still in the hands of the trained salesman. Paying attention to the other functions in the marketing mix, such as product and price, and not to personal selling, can lead to the failure of even the most promising product.

Often a person considering a marketing career must begin at a lower level before he can gain a position of authority like sales manager, marketing-research director, or transportation manager. To make a career in marketing, a salesman's job is the usual port of entrance. Only perfect preparation will make the salesman sufficiently effective to go out and turn prospects into purchasers and purchasers into regular customers. Without regular customers and their continuous orders the company will soon run out of prospective buyers. Satisfied customers, who demonstrate their satisfaction through repeat business, are the end result of effective selling.

Among the objects of salesmanship considered to be the most important in marketing are the customer, product and competitive knowledge, pricing policies and practices, prospecting, planning the sales presentation, handling customer objections, and closing the sale. Prior to a discussion of these key points, those qualities necessary for successful careers in personal selling will be examined.

PERSONAL QUALITIES FOR THE SALESMAN

Too often management insufficiently stresses the importance of the salesman's ability. When two companies offer similar or exactly the same merchandise (as is possible through two wholesalers), the impression projected by the salesman might influence the prospective customer. The image of the company is usually generated by contact with the salesman. It should be kept in mind that, in most instances, the salesman is the sole representative with whom buyers negotiate. To the prospect the salesman *is* the company. In order to make certain the company is to be properly represented marketers most carefully scrutinize their sales staffs and adequately prepare them for the prospective buyers.

Appearance

Initially, the only tool for the salesman, upon meeting the prospect, is appearance. It is of paramount importance that the impression is satisfactory. When the two parties are to meet for the first time, appearance is about the only factor (aside from possible advance knowledge about the merchandise) that the buyer can measure and by which he can be motivated. It is unlikely that shoddy dress will be well received.

Enthusiasm

Being enthusiastic should not be confused with being pushy or overly aggressive. If the salesman dominates the prospective customer, the transaction (if it does materialize) might not really be appropriate. The wrong merchandise might be ordered, which could prove to be a misfortune for the customer. This could lead to termination of a business relationship that otherwise could have been fruitful to both parties. Being enthusiastic, on the other hand, often transfers from the salesman to the customer. Proudly displaying and demonstrating a line of merchandise in a real and stimulating manner often meets wtih a warm reception.

Voice and Speech

To be able to project the voice sufficiently and to use proper diction is a must for successful personal selling. This does not mean that professional training is essential for a proper sales demonstration. Care should be exercised as to the words the salesman chooses to use. Proper speech is certain to produce an image that should make the buyer more attentive and receptive.

Tact

Being tactful is essential to all levels of selling, but in particular to retailing. The retail salesman's job is helping to satisfy the customer's needs. Should he allow the customer to purchase something that he knows is wrong, even though the customer wants to make the purchase? Allowing this purchase to be made might lead to the possible loss of future business. On the other hand, his suggestion that the buyer's choice is a poor one might be an affront. Tact must be used not to offend the customer by trying to dissuade this particular purchase and by directing him to goods that are more appropriate. Tactfulness comes only with caution and experience.

Self-Discipline

Losing patience is very possible for almost every salesman. Prospective customers' personalities and attitudes are not all the same. A salesman must remember that if he is to be successful, he must control his emotions even when the situation seems intolerable. Abusing the customer will only lead to loss of sales. The individual who is easily excited by the shortcomings of others should not pursue a salesman's job.

In addition to the previously mentioned essentials for good salesmanship, a prospective salesman should show initiative, sincerity, cheerfulness, knowledge, and resourcefulness. Although it seems unusual for all people interested in sales positions to possess all these qualities, the more they have, the greater their chances for success.

ESSENTIAL KNOWLEDGE FOR SELLING

In addition to knowing his customer (no two customers are exactly alike!) the salesman must have knowledge in three specific areas: his company, his product, and competing companies. Only when armed with this knowledge can he make an effective sales presentation.

Company Knowledge

It is safe to assume that the prospective customer is most often interested in what is being offered for sale, but it is presumptuous for any salesman to believe that only he has the goods that can adequately satisfy the customer's needs. Merchandise from one wholesaler will probably come from others as well. Also, at the retail level, the same merchandise is certainly available at different outlets. Even the manufacturer's creations are offered in forms similar enough to accommodate the most discriminating buyer. Consequently, often the company itself, its background, and its policies rather than the specific goods appeal to buyers. Among the points which might be stressed during a presentation are the growth and development of the company; its merchandising practices, such as policies regarding merchandise returns and allowances; credit arrangements; key personnel involved; production features; discounts and other price advantages; and service facilities such as repair depots. The characteristics of the company to be stressed can be determined individually for each prospect. For example, a buyer might be sold on the merchandise but could have doubts about punctuality of deliveries. For this purchaser an overview of production facilities and shipping practices, coupled with the elaboration of key people involved in the specific activities, might overcome the uncertainties. Likewise, if a salesman is representing a wholesaler whose goods are the same as those of three other local wholesalers, he might stress the fact that his company has the best credit policy. Whatever the situation, delving into the background of a company can supply the answer that is often needed to make the sale.

Product Knowledge

To successfully sell any merchandise without prior product knowledge is rather difficult for the salesman. To sell goods or services in a manner that will gain the customer's confidence, an understanding of what is for sale is required. The inability to answer specific product questions tends to make salesmen bluff or avoid the queries. The extent of product knowledge needed to complete a sale varies according to the complexity of the goods. For example, salesmen of technical objects (dentist's apparatus, lease of computer equipment) must be better acquainted with their products than representatives selling paper supplies to retail stores. Similarly, the manufacturer's salesman must generally be better informed than the retail salesman, simply because the former's customers are certainly more knowledgeable about products than the latter's. Specifically, salesmen must be prepared to discuss the product's construction, the serving that is required, the justification of its price, the manner in which the product will exactly meet the buyer's needs, and perhaps other uses for the product that would make it more salable. A closer examination of these points should clarify their importance.

Meeting the buyer's needs is of utmost importance. For example, the salesman representing a manufacturer of a new type of paint, stucco paint, (which, when applied, gives a three-dimensional look to the wall) must have at his fingertips information that will make other, conventional paint used to achieve this effect seem obsolete. The salesman must extract, from all the information that is available to him, the knowledge that his customer (the retailer) can in turn use on his customer (the ultimate consumer). By simply putting the pertinent information in a logical order and presenting it in comparison to the paint that is now used, the salesman can approach the prospective customer with confidence. Many manufacturers supply their salesmen with training manuals that include this type of information in similar arrangements.

This clear and logical information will enable the salesman to present a factual and meaningful demonstration.

The manufacturing processes often make the difference between closing a sale and losing a sale. Single-needle tailoring (an example of fine sewing) might prove to be the deciding point for the prospect. A knowledge of steel and its advantages over wood is probably a must for the salesman

COMPARISON STUDY FOR THE ACHIEVEMENT OF TEXTURED WALLS

Stucco Paint		*Conventional Paint*
1. No base application		1. Application of plaster (irregulary applied)
2. Regular brush or roller		2. Specially designed roller or brush to apply paint over plaster
3. One-step application		3. Two-step application
4. Fast drying		4. Plaster must dry before painting can begin

trying to promote steel tennis rackets. Being able to knowledgeably discuss the manufacture of fiberglass boats and the advantages over wooden boats would certainly be necessary for the salesman of fiberglass vessels. Whether the product is food, machinery, fashion merchandise, or general office supplies, a knowledge of the product's materials and construction will make for a more convincing presentation.

Servicing and facilities for servicing are factors that often turn prospects into buyers. Buyers of machinery, either consumers or industrial purchasers, are concerned with servicing. Factors such as the number of centers for servicing, the costs involved, the expertise of the service departments, and the company's promptness in answering service calls are extremely important to buyers. All things being equal, the company providing the best service will most likely make the sale. The consumer can easily understand this when considering the purchase of an automobile. Cadillacs can be purchased at a variety of agencies, at prices that almost always are identical. The consumer is therefore influenced by something other than cost. Frequently, this is the service afforded by the particular agency.

Aside from remembering the price, the salesman should be able to justify it. The recitation of "you get what you pay for" is not likely to satisfy the industrial purchaser or, for that matter, the shopper in a retail store. Most frequently, the salesman relies upon the quality aspect in justifying price. The distributor of a line of television receivers, whose price might be higher than the rest of the market, might justify the costs by indicating that his line boasts a handwired chassis or that the cabinets are hand-rubbed for additional beauty. The recitation of the product's salient features and the translation of those features into user's benefits is the most intelligent manner in which to convince the buyer that the price is warranted.

Most products are only usable for that function for which they were intended. In some cases, a salesman might promote the sale of his line of merchandise by being able to suggest additional uses for the products. The vacuum cleaner that can also be used as a spray-painting device and the power drill that adapts as a polisher or buffer are examples of promotion of a product for its different uses.

The area of product knowledge to be stressed depends on the individual buyers. The salesman, through study and experience, can quickly determine which to use in his presentation.

The Competition

Rarely will a salesman have the opportunity of approaching a prospective buyer who has not either actually purchased from the salesman's competition or heard about it. Buyers of consumer and industrial goods are knowledgeable individuals who are highly paid to carry out their jobs. They seldom make purchases without being fully aware of the entire market for the goods that they purchase. They must be familiar with such factors as prices, delivery, services, and quality. Keeping this in mind, it is unlikely that a salesman can successfully sell to one of these prospects without thoroughly knowing his competition. Much merchandise is sold merely by underscoring the advantages gained by purchasing from one particular company rather than the competition. Every salesman must be prepared to offer some of these advantages. Although price can be an important factor, not every company offers the lowest price. It is the salesman's job to be prepared with that point that beats the competition. Presenting misinformation regarding the competitor's company or product to the buyer is dangerous. In addition to the fact that misrepresentation is unethical and dishonest, it is also risky. It could prove disastrous for a salesman to alter the truth in order to sell his product, since buyers are experts in their fields and are generally aware of prices, availability of merchandise, and quality. The buyer who hears false information from a salesman will lose confidence and will not purchase. Even if he were fooled once by the less-than-truthful salesman, repeat business will not be forthcoming.

Salesmen who are prepared, either through formal college education, on-the-job training, or actual experience, will concur that there is no substitute for knowledge; the effort made in acquiring this knowledge will be reflected in sales.

PROSPECTING

The difficulty encountered in finding customers varies. The retail store prospects primarily through advertising or some other form of promotion, such as display. Many retail customers just walk into stores as a routine matter. In the case of manufacturer's and wholesaler's salesmen, prospecting is different. The ease or difficulty encountered by these sales representatives is affected by such factors as size of the market, location of customers, cost of the product, and competition.

Salesmen use a variety of prospecting techniques. Some are dictated

by management, others are just left to the skill and ingenuity of the salesman. Among those methods most frequently employed are:

Cold Canvass

The salesman using this method merely tries to approach every user
of the product in his territory (salesmen are assigned specific geographic
areas in which to sell). For example, those carrying a line of household
tools (hammers, screwdrivers, and so on) would call upon every store that
sells that merchandise. This method is time consuming in that every prospective customer is approached indiscriminately. For example, some might be
credit risks, whereas others might not have a need for the goods. Although
some businesses frown upon using the cold-canvass method, other companies
have enjoyed enormous success with it. Occasionally, the salesman who practices other prospecting techniques will cold canvass if extra time is available
in a particular workday.

Leads

This technique gives the salesman some indication that specific purchasers might need the product. Rather than just knocking on any door,
the salesman has names of prospects that have been supplied to him. Leads
come from a variety of sources, for example, company advertising, sales
managers, and friends. Many companies advertise in trade journals that are
religiously read by purchasing agents. Purchasers whose interests have been
aroused by a particular advertisement might call the company for more
information or for specific contact with a sales representative. This is an
excellent type of lead, since the prospective customer has taken the initiative
to reach the seller. Sales managers often supply leads for which sales can
be consummated. For example, the sales manager of an automobile agency
might, as a routine matter, check his agency's service department. By determining important indicators such as frequency and magnitude of repairs and
age of the automobile, he can very often suggest to salesmen the names of
customers who might be in need of a new vehicle. In the insurance business,
in particular, salesmen selling auto and life insurance find an excellent
source of leads through friends.

Commercial List Houses

There are numerous organizations whose principal business it is to
compile lists and supply them to customers for a fee. These lists are arranged
according to the needs of prospective customers. Thousands of different
kinds of lists are available to salesmen. For example, the Rolls Royce Agency,
looking for an affluent clientele, might purchase from a commercial house a
list of names of people with achievements earmarking them as good prospects.

Other methods employed by salesmen are the endless chain approach, in which a salesman secures the names of prospects from someone to whom he has just made a sale (this is used frequently in door-to-door selling); making use of credit-agency directories, such as the one published by Dun & Bradstreet that lists businesses according to classification and also provides credit ratings; the use of exhibitions such as the Boat Show presented annually at the New York Coliseum, which serves as a place to get names of interested customers who can be followed up at other times; and the use of spotters who might cold canvass to gather names of good prospects for the regular salesmen.

Besides selection of the most appropriate methods for prospecting, the characteristics of good prospects must be determined by marketers. Among those deemed essential by most knowledgeable salesmen are the following:

1. Does the prospect have a need for the product or service?

2. Is the company considered a good credit risk? Since most transactions are based on credit (at the wholesaler's and manufacturer's levels), an appropriate line of credit (determined generally through affiliation with credit-rating agencies such as Dun & Bradstreet and Credit Exchange) is necessary.

3. Is the prospect you are about to approach actually the buyer? It is necessary to ascertain whose responsibility it is to purchase for a company before the actual contact is made. It is not unusual for the inexperienced salesman to show his line to an individual only to find he does not have the authority to buy. This can be a great waste of time. Most large companies have tables of organization from which it can be found which person is responsible for purchasing.

After careful consideration of the foregoing points, the salesman is ready to approach the customer.

APPROACHING THE CUSTOMER

The approach differs depending on whether the customer enters the salesman's establishment (as is the case in retail selling) or the salesman contacts the customer (as is generally the case in wholesale sales). Whichever the situation, the salesman's attitude must be conducive to purchasing. Customers should be greeted with a friendly smile. The grumpy-looking salesman is certain to put the customer into a poor frame of mind. The greeting used to begin a conversation is most important. One should not begin with a question that might bring a negative response. For example, in the retail store, approaching a customer saying "May I help you?" might bring a reply of "No." Although this is typical of retail-store selling, it is a poor way to begin a sales presentation. Preferably a salesperson might begin by saying, "Good morning, I'm Mr. Smith. I'd like to help you with your purchasing needs." This approach is less likely to receive a negative reaction. Another desirable approach is to strike up a conversation regarding an article of merchandise that a shopper is examining. For example, "That chair is as comfortable as it is good-looking. Why don't you try it?" When a customer approaches you for help, the greeting is less difficult because your assistance is sought. A mere "good afternoon" is sufficient. Even "May I help you?" is acceptable, since the fact that the customer approaches you will not bring the earlier-mentioned possibility of a "no" response.

At this very early point in the sales demonstration it is time to determine the shopper's needs. Certainly approaching the customer who is examining an item gives the salesperson an idea of what is desired. If the customer is not studying the merchandise, determination of what is needed is a little more difficult. Some brief questions (which become second nature with experience) pertaining to style, color, size (if applicable), and so on will guide the salesperson in the selection of appropriate merchandise. Keeping in mind what the store has available for sale, the salesman is now ready to show the merchandise to the customer.

Salesmen working on the wholesale level generally arrange for an appointment in advance of their arrival. The actual initial approach is then prearranged.

PRESENTING THE MERCHANDISE

The actual presentation is the most important aspect of the salesman's job. Whether the approach used is memorized (although generally unconvincing, that is done by some major marketers) or planned according to a carefully conceived outline, the salesman should have with him all the materials necessary to close the sale. In the retail store the actual merchandise available for sale is shown to the prospective customer. Together with good selling technique, this is all that is necessary to successfully complete the sale. Representatives of manufacturers or wholesalers have a number of aids that can be used to dramatize their products. In many cases salesmen carry lines of actual samples, but the nature of some goods does not permit this. For example, the computer salesman cannot possibly carry an actual large piece of data-processing equipment with him. When actual presentation of the goods is impossible and for reasons like inaccessibility the prospect cannot come to the salesman's showroom to see the goods, other selling aids are necessary. Even where the goods are available for buyer examination, the very size of the order often warrants additional sales aids. Some regularly used aids are:

Models of the actual merchandise
Photographs

Copies of advertisements of other customers

Charts or graphs to show sales growth

Manuals giving all the pertinent information about the product in a logical order

Films—used, for example, by advertising agencies to show commercials that they have prepared for other accounts

Testimonials of satisfied customers

Whatever the product, the salesman should offer strong selling points in a manner inoffensive to the prospect. The day of the hard-sell approach is part of marketing history. Buyers are too knowledgeable to be taken in by fast-talking salesmen.

HANDLING OBJECTIONS

Prospects indicate that they are possibly ready to become customers in a number of ways. Questions as, "What is the completion date for delivery?", "Is there a cash discount?", or "Are other colors available?" may conceivably signal the salesman that a sale is imminent. These are but a few of the indications that a prospect might become a customer. Even after spending time in the consideration of making a purchase the buyer might hesitate and raise objections. These objections might be excuses telling the salesman that the buyer is not going to buy, or they might be sincere objections that need further clarification and overcoming. Whatever the foundation of the objections, the salesman must overcome them to close the sale.

Most common in nature are objections about price, poor delivery, unsatisfactory product features, and comparison with a competitor's offerings. The experienced salesman is prepared to handle these objections and does so in a number of ways. One method most frequently used by experienced salesmen is that which agrees with the customer's objection but to which is quickly added a new selling point. For example, Mr. Walters expresses interest in Style #4863 but declares, "The price is high." The salesman handling the objection in the manner described might reply, "Yes, but the high standard of construction will guarantee tremendous sales potential." Instead of saying "yes, but" to handle objections, other words such as the following might be used:

1. "Certainly, but have you considered . . ."

2. "You're right, Mr. Adams, however, have you examined . . ."

3. "One of my other accounts felt exactly as you do, but he finally bought from us because . . ."

4. "It is a little longer than our usual delivery period, but . . ."

The aforementioned statements are only suggestions. Experience affords the salesman a wealth of statements from which he can choose.

Another method employed in handling objections is to ask the customer questions. In this way a salesman can separate excuses for not buying from real objections. Examples of some questions to use are:

1. "What's wrong with the range of colors, Miss Foster?"

2. "What is your objection to the typewriter?"

3. "What would you consider an appropriate price for electric coffee makers?"

Still another technique to be used, but with caution, is to deny the objection. The salesman must be absolutely certain of his information when employing this method. For example:

Customer's Objection	Salesman's Response
1. "I don't believe we will have it in time for our sale."	"I will guarantee delivery."
2. "The Acme Company sells it for $1.25 less than your price."	"Our company always sells that item at a price lower than the Acme Company."
3. "I don't believe the colors will be appropriate to coordinate with the shoe buyer's purchase."	"The colors have been carefully dyed to ensure perfect coordination."

When employing this last technique, only accurate information should be offered to the customer. Any misinformation can lead to mistrust and possible loss of future business from the buyer.

CLOSING THE SALE

When the salesman feels that he has answered all the prospect's questions and satisfied him to the best of his ability, closing the sale should be attempted. Inexperienced salesman ask how you know that it is the exact time to close, but this knowledge comes from experience. There are signals that may serve as a guide; from there on, experience takes over. It should be understood that the buyer will rarely say "you've sold me, I'm ready..."

Some of the signals are:

"How long will it take for special orders?"

"Can I have an additional thirty days in which to pay the bill?"

"When can I expect the merchandise to be delivered?"

"If these items don't sell, will you change them for other numbers?"

"Is the guarantee for one year?"

When the salesman recognizes what he believes to be the opportune moment, he should proceed to close the sale. Choosing the right words at this time might seem difficult to the student of marketing. Using the question, "Are you ready to buy?" is certainly not the correct approach. The use of questions and statements such as these prove to be effective in trying to close the sale:

"Shall we send it express or airfreight?"
"Which would you like, style #602 or #605?"
"Will that be delivered to the stores or to your warehouse?"
"When would you like it delivered?"
"After this week these items go back to their original prices."
"This is the last day for immediate delivery. Later orders will take four weeks."

Even the most experienced salesman sometimes finds that he has not chosen the appropriate time to close the sale. It might take several attempts before a sale is finalized. Marketing students should keep in mind that not every prospect is really a customer and also that not every buyer can be satisfied with their firm's offerings. The buyer's refusal to purchase should be evaluated in terms of what he says. For example, a definite "no" might indicate that the buyer cannot be satisfied. Reactions such as "I'd like to see other styles" or "No, I'm still uncertain" are signals that perhaps more salesmanship is necessary. Whatever the degree of negativism, a seasoned salesman should not give up after the first attempt to close has not been successful. The number of times to try to close is questionable. Too few attempts might let the customer slip away. Too many tries might tend to make the buyer feel he is being high pressured. The right number of times, before giving up, will eventually be realized through experience.

After making an unsuccessful attempt a salesman must be able to proceed again to a point that will result in success. In order to do this he must keep some information in reserve that will perhaps whet the buyer's appetite. For example,

"If you purchase today you will be entitled to a 5 percent discount."
"This is the last day of our special offer; tomorrow the price will go up 10 percent."

In retail selling, if consecutive attempts to close are unsuccessful and it is felt that the customer still might purchase the product, some salesmen resort to something called a T. O. or turnover method. This technique involves turning the customer over to a more prestigious department member, such as the manager or buyer. Customers might respond more affirmatively to these people and thus the department will benefit.

It is important to remember that even if a buyer does not purchase at this time, he is still a prospect for future business. Courtesy is extremely important to guarantee that the customer can again be approached. It is at this time that many companies lose their favorable image. A disagreeable or disgruntled salesman can be disastrous in terms of customer satisfaction.

Customers who have just purchased an appliance frequently are offered service contracts at less than the customary price.

PROMOTING FUTURE BUSINESS

Upon completion of the sale the resourceful salesman takes the opportunity to guarantee the customer's future purchases. Experienced salesmen seek to establish a reputation that will encourage other transactions. Spending a few extra moments with the buyer at this time will promote good will needed for future business.

SALESMEN'S COMPENSATION

Salesmen are remunerated in a variety of ways. To select the one that will achieve the greatest motivation for salesmen while at the same time guaranteeing customer satisfaction is no simple task for marketers. Each method has its advantages and disadvantages and should be carefully examined by management before subscribing to it.

Straight salary is probably the most widely used method of compensation in retail stores. It simplifies the company's bookkeeping, but it does not provide incentive.

Salary plus commission guarantees a regular income plus a commission for incentive. The commission is usually small.

Straight commission is generally restricted to manufacturer's and wholesaler's salesmen. This system does not guarantee anything to the salesman. His earnings are largely in keeping with his own ability and the desirability of the product he sells. Most companies advance a salesman a sum each pay period. This is known as a "draw against commission." It is actually an advanced estimate of commissions until the time the salesman's commissions are tabulated. At that point, the difference between the monies drawn and those earned are compared. The salesman then either receives the difference or owes it to the company.

The quota bonus plan is an arrangement under which the salesman receives a commission on everything he sells over and above a pre-determined amount. Sales managers are often paid on a variation of this method. They receive a bonus for sales (of their entire staff) in excess of an established quota for a period.

Variations and combinations of all these methods are common. It is the job of management to find the one that best serves the particular company.

IMPORTANT POINTS IN THE CHAPTER

1. Personal qualities such as proper appearance, enthusiasm, good voice and speech, tact, and self-discipline are essential for an individual in order to become a good salesman.

2. To be successful, the salesman must be well-informed concerning his company's background, the product, and the competition.

3. Prospecting (the method used to find new customers) techniques vary. Among the most common methods are cold canvass, leads, use of commercial lists, endless-chain approach, and use of credit-agency directories.

4. When approaching a customer, proper opening statements should be used. In a retail store, "May I help you?" should be avoided, since it might bring a negative response.

5. If the merchandise is unavailable for presentation during the sale, substitutes should be used, for example, scale models, photographs, advertisements, manuals, charts, and films.

6. Customer objections are handled in a variety of ways. The most common methods are the "yes, but..." technique, questioning the customer, or denying the objection.

7. If the salesman is unsuccessful in closing the sale, numerous additional attempts should be made. The salesman should hold some important features about his product in reserve to be used if repeated closing attempts are necessary.

8. Salesmen are compensated in a number of ways. Most common are straight salary, salary plus commission, straight commission, and quota bonus plan.

REVIEW QUESTIONS

1. To which types of jobs can that of salesman lead?
2. Being tactful is absolutely necessary for good salesmanship. Why?
3. Does enthusiasm mean a person must employ theatrical tricks?
4. How can a salesman's enthusiasm or lack of enthusiasm play an important role in salesmanship?
5. Is proper appearance still important for the salesman?
6. Discuss the various facts the salesman should know concerning the product.
7. Aside from product knowledge, what must a wholesaler's salesman generally impress upon prospective customers in order to make a sale?
8. How important is it to be truthful when discussing your competitors with your customers?
9. Which method of prospecting requires the least amount of investigation? How effective is it?
10. Salesmen find lists to be extremely helpful in prospecting. By whom are lists prepared?
11. Is it the salesman's job to justify price? Why?
12. Why does the salesman, calling at his customer's place of business, usually have an easier job at introduction than the retail salesman?

13. Which approach is considered improper in retail selling? Why?

14. What are some of the aids used by salesmen to make their presentations more meaningful?

15. Can the computer salesman demonstrate his product at the prospect's office? If not, how does he overcome this?

16. Is it ever appropriate to deny the customer's objections? If so, when?

17. Describe the questioning technique of handling objections.

18. What is the quota bonus method of remuneration?

19. Define *T.O.* When is it used?

20. Draw against commission is a method used to compensate salesmen. Describe this method and indicate which types of salesmen are often paid this way.

CASE PROBLEMS

Case Problem 1

Lime-Light, Inc. is a wholesaler specializing in light bulbs, lighting fixtures, and lamps. Its goods are specifically for consumers' use, although occasionally it does sell bulbs for use in offices and showrooms. Lime-Light has been in this business for ten years and carries merchandise produced by several leading manufacturers. The merchandise it sells to retail-store buyers can also be purchased from other wholesale sources.

Recently, Stuart Klar was hired as a salesman to represent Lime-Light in the New York metropolitan area. Although he was inexperienced in wholesale sales (he only worked briefly as a retail shoe salesman), his appearance and enthusiasm convinced the sales manager that he could do the job.

After studying the line, learning the important features, memorizing and practicing closing techniques, and so on, he started to make appointments with prospective buyers. He presented himself in a manner that was well received by the buyers, but he was not able to complete many sales.

Perhaps a self-evaluation of his responses to objections raised by the buyers would shed light on the problem. The most common objections raised were:

Buyers' Objections	Klar's Responses
1. "Your prices aren't better than those of the competition."	"No. But we aren't higher."
2. "The services offered by your company seem inadequate."	"We offer the same as the other companies."
3. "You probably won't deliver on time."	"We always deliver on time."

Questions

1. Do you believe Klar's responses are sincere?

2. Would you respond differently? How would you answer each objection?

3. Are there any additional points Klar might make to be more convincing? Discuss.

Case Problem 2

Steve Clements was just hired as a salesman by the Reputable Life Insurance Company. Mr. Clements's experience prior to this job has been in retailing (as a part-time salesclerk while going to college) and in wholesaling (as a salesman for a paper-and-twine dealer). In both of these jobs he was able to show his product, highlight its important features, and ultimately make his share of sales.

What perplexes Mr. Clements at this time is that because of the very nature of his present product, he has nothing to really show the prospective customers. In his retail job he could allow customers to try on the merchandise. In his wholesale job, the paper bags could be tested and evaluated.

Questions

1. Is it possible to dramatize an insurance salesman's presentation?
2. What aids would you use if you were Mr. Clements?

BIBLIOGRAPHY

Baker, Richard M., Jr., and Gregg Phifer, *Salesmanship: Communication, Persuasion, Perception*. Boston: Allyn & Bacon, Inc., 1966.

Cash, H. C., and W. J. E. Crissy, *The Psychology of Selling*. Flushing, N.Y.: Personnel Development Associates, 1957–1962.

Crissy, W.J.E., and Robert M. Kaplan, *Salesmanship: The Personal Force in Marketing*. New York: John Wiley & Sons, Inc., 1969.

Gwinner, Robert F., and Edward M. Smith, *Sales Strategy: Cases and Readings*. New York: Appleton-Century-Crofts, 1969.

Haas, Kenneth B., and John W. Ernest, *Creative Salesmanship: Understanding Fundamentals*. Beverly Hills, Calif.: Glencoe Press, 1969.

Johnson, H. W., *Creative Selling*. Cincinnati, Ohio: South-Western Publishing Co., 1966.

Kirkpatrick, C. A., *Salesmanship: Helping Prospect Buy*. Cincinnati, Ohio: South-Western Publishing Co., 1966.

Pederson, Carlton A., and Milburn D. Wright, *Salesmanship: Principles and Methods*. Homewood, Ill.: Richard D. Irwin, Inc., 1970.

Reynolds, William H., "The Fail-Safe Salesman," in Ralph L. Day, *Concepts for Modern Marketing*. Scranton, Pa.: International Textbook Co., 1968.

Russell, Frederic, Frank Beach, and Richard Buskirk, *Textbook of Salesmanship*. New York: McGraw-Hill Book Company, 1969.

Shockey, Ralph, "Selling is a Science," *Department Store Economist*. April, 1965–January, 1966.

Thompson, Joseph W., *Selling: A Behavioral Science Approach*. New York: McGraw-Hill Book Company, 1966.

Webster, Frederick E., Jr., "The Industrial Salesman as a Source of Market Information," in Robert J. Holloway and Robert S. Hancock, *The Environment of Marketing Behavior*. New York: John Wiley & Sons, Inc., 1969.

Wingate, John W., and Caroll A. Nolan, *Fundamentals of Selling*. Cincinnati, Ohio: South-Western Publishing Co., 1964.

THE COMPUTER AND MARKETING

16

INTRODUCTION

The production requirements of World War II resulted in a surge of growth for American industry. The continuing prosperity of the postwar years led to a near-constant period of business expansion. Throughout this time, technological advances led to improved production and marketing methods, which kept pace with the steadily increasing demands of the consuming public. However, since most businessmen consider office procedures to be a necessary evil, resulting neither in profits nor in cost reduction, this era of commercial growth and production improvement saw practically no change in clerical procedures. Around 1950, our larger industrial organizations had grown to a point at which the paper work required to support their business activities was such that their poorly equipped office staffs were unable to keep pace. The bottleneck was so great that further business growth was threatened. Management was faced with the alternative of developing new office techniques or slowing down the industrial growth rate. The decision was to spend money.

THE COMPUTER

As is frequently the case with industrial problems, when the necessity is joined with money required to solve the problem, the solution can be found. In this instance, the solution was the computer; expensive, difficult to change over to, with practically no trained personnel available to operate, but capable of handling an unbelievable amount of data. In short, the computer was the perfect answer to the paperwork bottleneck.

It is not the purpose of this book to fully explain computers; however, no understanding of its capabilities can be achieved without a brief explanation of the workings of an electronic data-processing system. The devices use electrical impulses that can be added, subtracted, or stored. Since it is possible to store electrical impulses, the machine may be said to have a memory. That is, the computer can be instructed to perform an operation at some future time. Then, when the operation is required, it can fulfill its instructions. For example, the computer can be instructed to multiply the hours Fred Smith works by two dollars, his hourly rate of pay.

Then, at the end of any week, when told the number of hours Fred worked, it can compute his week's earnings.

The electrical circuitry of a computer is enormously complicated. Its capabilities on the other hand are quite simple. It can add, subtract, transfer from one location to another, and store. Nothing more. It is essentially a moron, with one redeeming feature. It can perform these operations in millionths of a second. Thus, although it cannot even multiply but must use repeated addition as a substitute (it computes 3×4 as $4 + 4 + 4$), it can find the product of two ten-digit numbers in a fraction of a second. A further illustration of computer speed is that it can print the results of its computations at the rate of better than nine $8\frac{1}{2} \times 11$ pages per minute. It is this blinding speed that has made the computer the perfect tool for handling massive amounts of data.

Business uses of the computer began in the offices. As we shall see, it was quickly adapted to other business functions in which instant, accurate information is vital. Before going into other applications of computers, let us briefly discuss the historical development of computers.

History and Development

In 1812 an English mathematician named Charles Babbage designed his "difference engine." This machine was so far ahead of its time that the technical requirements for its manufacture constituted unsolvable problems. The device could do everything but work. It could not even be built.

It was not until the late 1880s that a workable, practical data-handling machine was constructed. It happened at that time because it was needed. The situation was this: the laws of the United States require that a census be taken every ten years to serve as a basis of reapportioning seats in the House of Representatives. By 1880 the population of the country had grown so rapidly that it was not until 1887 that the 1880 census had been completely tabulated. It was obvious that the 1890 census could not be completely analyzed in the required ten years. At this time, Dr. Herman Hollerith, a statistician with the Census Bureau, developed the punched card and the machinery necessary to handle it. (The punched card is so widely used today that it is called Hollerith card.) Needless to say, the 1890 census was tabulated by Hollerith in record time and at a considerable financial saving. From then on, data processing was off and running. By 1896 Hollerith organized the Tabulating Machine Company to manufacture and market the machines and cards. Through a series of mergers, the Tabulating Machine Company has become the International Business Machines Corp. (IBM), currently the world's leading producer of data-processing equipment. From the time that Hollerith proved the value of data-processing machines, their use in industry has grown steadily. This growth, coupled with technical improvements in the speed and adaptability of computers, has brought us to a point at which large establishments, to keep their competitive place in industry, find the use of the conputer an absolute necessity.

The Computer and Marketing

Among the various areas of American businesses that turned to electronic data processing, marketing was one of the slowest. There are several reasons for this:

1. The company that originally acquired a computer for clerical reasons generally found itself with a small data-processing installation that was unable to handle the increased capacity required by the solution of marketing problems. Any increase in the size of a data-processing system is generally extremely expensive.

2. Trained programmers and other specialists that are required to develop the procedures needed to solve marketing problems are in short supply.

3. Top-level management is likely to give higher priorities to the problems of the financial and accounting departments that to the more intricate problems posed by marketers.

4. Marketing problems are complicated. For the computer to operate effectively, the information that is to be put into the computer must be absolutely complete and accurate. Such information is not always available in a form that can be used by a computer. Getting this information into usable shape may be expensive and time consuming.

Despite these formidable obstacles, the use of the computer in marketing is increasing rapidly. Polls taken of computer-using firms indicate a constantly growing use of the computer for marketing decision making. Some of the reasons for this trend are:

1. Technological advances in the electronic data-processing field, which have led to better usage of computers in terms of getting information into and out of the system with a minimum of effort and training.

2. The fact that because the high cost problem was overcome vital decision-making information is made quickly available by computerized installations. For example, a large ladies' wear chain rented a computer for inventory control. One day the buyer of ladies' sweaters decided he would like to know which sizes were most popular. This is a simple computer problem and the information was readily available. Then he wanted to know about the popularity of various colors, and he was given the answer. Then he wondered if bright colors were better in small sizes than in large. This goes on and on, until the buyer is so well equipped with information that he can perform with far greater efficiency. At this point it is foolish to compare the cost of the computer with the salaries of the clerks it replaced, since the information the device supplies is far more important than the job for

which it was originally installed. This, incidentally, is also an example of why computers that were purchased to work six hours a day are now working twenty-four hours a day.

3. The insistence of top-level management that the constantly growing investment in electronic data processing produce a greater return in more business areas.

4. The desire to match the considerable competitive advantage of the firms that use electronic devices for the solution of marketing problems.

5. The emergence of the managerial scientist on the business scene.

To sum up, efficient marketing depends upon information. Much of the necessary knowledge has always been available in the records, but analyzing such mountainous records and producing timely, accurate informational summaries have not been possible until now.

MANAGERIAL SCIENCE

Managerial science, sometimes known as systems analysis, is a new body of knowledge built around the computer. The systems analyst, when arriving on the scene, found that the computer was used chiefly in order processing, billing, bookkeeping, sales-performance analysis, and inventory control; in other words, essentially as a high-powered bookkeeper. Realizing that the computer is capable of far more sophisticated applications, the systems analyst approaches marketing problems armed with two principal weapons: the mathematical model and the data bank.

The Mathematical Model

No aircraft-manufacturing company would consider going into the production of a new airplane without first building a series of scale models of alternative designs that could be tested under a variety of conditions. For this purpose two types of models are constructed. The first is a wind tunnel designed to be a replica of the actual world, in which a number of different situations may be adjusted. The second is a series of variations of the particular airplane that is planned. In this way, several changes in the basic design can be tested in various actual flying conditions and decisions can be made on the most suitable design.

As is the case with an aircraft model, marketing models are pictures of the part of the real world in which the marketer is interested. Such models are mathematical representations that consist of a series of mathematical equations. In this way, the effect of any change in the makeup of the mathematical formulas cas be studied in terms of its results. For example, a change in the price portion or the formula can be used to determine the effect of the price change on sales, and the best price at which to offer an item may be selected.

The procedure for setting up a marketing model is this:

The actual description of the customers is taken from the company's records or other sources. This information is programmed and fed into the computer. After this has been done, the particular product or marketing scheme that has been determined by means of surveys and consumer testing is programmed and fed into the machine as well. The interaction of the product models on the customer's models may be used to answer questions about the expected volume at different selling prices, the effect of various packaging plans on sales, projected profits, the success of the product with several classes of customers, and so on.

Pillsbury is one of the most aggressive users of electronic data processing in the solution of marketing problems. Before putting their new brownie mix on the market, a series of computerized tests were developed by a marketing research team that included an economist, a home economist, and a statistician as well as data-processing personnel. This team programmed 120 models of their own recipes, competitor's recipes, and home recipes that had been sent in by housewives. Instead of constructing a computerized model of the buying public, the 120 recipes were given to one thousand housewives in nine cities. The preferences of the housewives were segragated in a manner that gave the company information on the choices of the marketing segments (by economic standing, number of children, and so on). Six months and 300 mathematical formulas later the company was able to market the recipe that, based on the information supplied by the computer, had the best chance of success.

Data Banks

The computer is essentially a tool for the near-instantaneous manipulation of large masses of data. The success or failure of the model depends on the size and accuracy of the information fed into the computer. A data bank is a mass of data in a form that may be fed into a computer, which can be used for a specific purpose. For example:

1. Northrup & King uses a data bank consisting of 250,000 farmers that are mailed new seed offerings twice a year.

2. Charles Pfizer, a major drug manufacturer, uses a data bank of physicians that indicates the type of practice, type of prescription they use, amount of drugs used, and locality.

3. The Metromail Division of Metromedia, Inc. offers a list of about one million households in the largest thirty cities. The list is classified into annual income groupings of eighty-five hundred to ten thousand dollars, ten thousand to fifteen thousand, fifteen thousand to twenty-five thousand, and over twenty-five thousand dollars. The individuals on the list may also be selected according to fifty-four different occupations and seventy-four different industries, buying habits, leisure activities, and other factors.

4. In 1968, to help promote its new MARK III luxury car, the Lincoln-Mercury Division of Ford was able to send a direct mail piece to fifty-five thousand homes that had annual incomes of over twenty-five thousand dollars and owned a higher-than-medium-priced car for less than one year. Responses from the mailing were sent to the local dealers as leads. The list was purchased from the data banks of Metromedia's Metromail Division.

AREAS OF APPLICATION

The computer's uses are by no means limited to the construction of models for the solution of marketing problems. A fully integrated data-processing system is used throughout the many divisions of a marketing enterprise. A good rule of thumb for deciding whether or not to use a computer for clerical-type work depends on the answers to the following questions:

1. Is the volume of work large enough?

2. Is the work similar enough to make the programming feasible?

If the answer to these two questions is affirmative, an electric data-processing system can not only do the work at a great savings in time but also have the capability of producing reports that are vital to managerial decision making.

As we have seen, the computer, originally installed as a kind of superclerk, has come into its own as a vital information source. For example, effective retailing, particularly in high-fashion merchandise, depends on prompt, accurate data. Since the computer is an excellent source of such information, the marriage between retailing and the computer is certain to be a happy one.

So that you may fully appreciate the value of the computer as an informational device, the next portion of this chapter will be devoted to specific retailing applications of electronic data processing.

Inventory Control for a Department Store

In retailing, the merchandise inventory on hand is probably a store's most important asset. In dollars, it requires a very large part of the enterprise's capital. In terms of profits and losses, the makeup of the inventory is critical. Having the wrong merchandise is disastrous. Having the correct merchandise but too little quantity loses sales. Too much of the right merchandise results in markdowns. In addition to this, a large store has an inventory of thousands of items, frequently kept at a large number of locations. The problems of inventory control are so vast in a large organization that decisions on what to buy, how much to buy, when to buy, and from whom to buy require a considerable amount of up-to-data information. These problems match perfectly with the capabilities of the computer:

1. Its capacity is so huge that it can collect data from many departments and locations.

2. Its speed is so great that it can process an enormous amount of data rapidly.

3. It has the ability to print out reports in easily understood form.

It must be borne in mind that the computer cannot think out a problem by itself, but it can follow instructions to a point where the results would be the same if it did or did not think. For example, the computer by itself does not know whether or not the inventory is low. However, it can be programmed so that when 80 percent of the stock previously on hand has been sold, it can type a reorder of those sizes, styles, and colors that sold most effectively. Thus, the result is the same as it would have been if the machine could think.

Since the end product of the computer is the informational report, it is vital that the computer be given all information necessary to construct such a report. Basically, the required information consists of the merchandise on hand, the merchandise sold, and the merchandise on order. Moreover, to be usable, the data must be presented to the computer in a language it can understand. The following is the input necessary to the computer for comprehensive merchandise-inventory control. (It should be pointed out that many department stores are moving toward the following systems, but that most stores have considerably less.)

1. Style number	8. Cost
2. Vendor	9. Selling price
3. Sales	10. Color and size
4. On hand	11. Markdowns
5. On order	12. Customer returns
6. Receipts from vendors	13. Shipment to branches
7. Returns to vendor	14. Shipment among branches

From this information, the computer can be instructed to provide, as output, a wide variety of reports at required time intervals. A particular department store furnished its buyers with the following informational reports:

1. Information on sales of high-fashion merchandise every three days. Such reports allow buyers to make decisions on reordering or transferring stock between branches while the style in question is still new, available, and in demand. Since this report is to be used by a buyer for reordering, it would include the following information for each style: price, color, three days' sales, week's sales, sales to date, sales in the various branches, number of pieces on hand, number of pieces on order, date the order is due, and so

forth. In short, all information needed by the buyer to make the reordering decision.

2. Reports on staple-type goods, for example, men's black socks, need not be nearly so detailed or frequent. Since staples do not run "hot," the decision based on the reports is merely to reorder when the number of units on hand falls below a certain level. In many operations, the computer is actually instructed to print out a reorder automatically, whenever the stock on hand falls below a certain level.

3. Weekly unit reports are frequently presented to the buyer, merchandise manager, and department manager of sales for the week, prior week, and month to date, as well as the on hand figure for each style. From this report, trouble spots can be seen earlier and remedial action, such as transfers between branches and promotions, can be taken before markdowns become necessary.

4. A dollar report furnishes information every ten days on the current total inventory, this month's and this year's sales, and markdowns for each store in the chain. From this the buyer can determine trouble spots, the amount of inventory in each store, and the financial success of each store.

5. A monthly report showing the relative importance of each price line in the various units making up the chain. This reports gives a comparison between the prior year's units and dollars of sales and those of the current year. Future merchandising trends for each unit can be established from these monthly reports.

6. The vendor's analysis presents the buyer every six months with information on total purchases, returns, markdowns, and gross profit for each vendor. Excessive returns, markdowns, and so on, turning up in such reports are important for future purchasing.

7. Special reports are constantly flowing from the computer to the buyer in addition to the reports already mentioned. These might include size and color analysis and the aging of the inventory to indicate the amount of time each unit has been in the store. In fact, almost any information that the buyer requests and for which computer time can be found can be produced.

Although large retail establishments have been operating successfully for many years and the computer is relatively new, it is difficult to understand how buyers could ever have performed effectively without them.

Sales Forecasting

Perhaps the most vital marketing decisions, such as those affecting plant expansion, advertising budgets, research and evaluation budgets, and inventory size are dependent on the answers to the questions: Will the sales be up or down next year? At what level will they be five years from now?

As competitive demands become more severe, companies are turning to the computer to produce the informational reports that are necessary to reduce the guesswork in sales forecasting. As is the case in all data-processing applications, the computer brings to the sales-forecasting problem the ability to handle millions of bits of information at lightning speeds. This enables sales forecasting to be broken down into individualized forecasts for each product in the line and each territory in the country by the week, month, season, or year.

In addition, where precomputer analysis was limited to relatively few considerations, data processing permits many factors to be taken into account. This results in a more accurate forecast. For example, prior to the use of computers, sales of cosmetics were based on just two factors: the number of females over fourteen and disposable income. The data-handling capacity of the computer enables present-day sales forecasts in the cosmetics industry to be calculated using six factors; one for each of four female age groups, one for disposable income, and one for the change in disposable income since last year. The result of this increase in the number of factors is a more accurate forecast of future sales.

Direct Mail

The computer has had an enormous impact on direct-mail marketing. This has come about as a result of the following three capabilities of the machine:

1. The computer's tremendous capacity for storing information from which exact combinations can be selected allows the direct-mail piece to be sent to exactly the right prospect. Where in the past a direct-mail piece might have been sent to all homeowners in an area, it may now be sent only to those homeowners who have college-age children.

2. The computer's speed, analytical ability, and report-producing capacity provide means of correctly checking the effectiveness of the direct-mail promotion.

3. The computer's ability to personalize a direct-mail piece will improve upon the chance of success of the direct-mail effort.

The trend in direct mail-lists is toward size and selectivity. Generally, the lists are compiled by specialists into massive data banks that are available for customers. For example:

1. R. L. Polk offers its customers a magnetic tape of all automobile owners including the total dollar value of the cars owned by each family.

2. The Reuben H. Donnelley Corp. controls the Donnelley Quality Index master file that contains fifty million names taken from auto registration lists and telephone directories.

3. By interviewing twenty-four million homeowners, R. L. Polk com-

piles its Household Census List, in which sixteen separate factors are supplied.

The above are merely a few examples of the many data banks that are available. A marketer, with a plan for a direct-mail promotion aimed at a specific segment of the population, is able to pinpoint from these massive lists his likeliest customers. This is one of the reasons why the computer is increasing direct-mail response above the expected 2 percent level. Another effect of better selectivity in direct-mail promotion will be a considerable decrease in the amount of junk mail received by the average householders, since his receipt of promotional mail will be limited to those areas in which the computer has indicated his interest.

Managing Sales

The use of the computer as a selling tool and a means of controlling the sales force has been growing at a rapid rate. Important uses to which computers have been put in the area of sales managements are:

1. Producing leads for salesmen. By matching typical customers against a Dun & Bradstreet data bank of over 650,000 firms, Honeywell Corp. is able to provide each salesman with all the pertinent data concerning the prospects in his territory; the lead is printed out on a 3×5 information card.

2. Pillsbury's Electronic Data-Processing Center counts the number of stores a salesman visits, the frequency of his visits to each account, and his actual sales against the goals set up in advance. Using this information, the sales manager can spot weak salesmen, instances in which too much time is spent with one customer at the expense of other customers, and territories that are either too large or too small for the number of salesmen allotted to them.

3. CIBA, a large drug manufacturer, used a computer to realign its four hundred sales territories according to the doctor count in seven medical specialties. Included in the program was the provision that the salesman's home be included in the territory. As a result of the computer's efforts, no CIBA sales territory has a doctor count that is over 4 percent less than the average.

4. Many companies, particularly supermarket chains, by computerizing their transportation and storage functions, have cut costs through a combination of many small warehouses into relatively located distribution centers.

TIME SHARING

An increasing number of small businesses is taking advantage of computer systems by renting computer time for their needs. Commercial computer centers are springing up throughout the country to service businesses that are interested in obtaining computer output but are too small to afford their own installation. These service companies supply programmers, operators, and computer time on an hourly basis. As a result, the computer, once only available to commercial giants, is now being used by their relatively small competitors. Since this trend is growing steadily, it is vital that all business people familiarize themselves with the capabilities of computers.

Renting computer time from a computer-service company is by no means limited to small businesses. Frequently, large companies, even those with extensive data-processing centers, simply do not have the computer time or specifically trained personnel to perform the highly individual problems that may arise. In such cases computer-service companies are called in.

Another instance of time sharing may occur when the cost of the project is excessive. An example of this may be found among the advertising agencies on Madison Avenue. Compton Advertising, one of the large agencies, approached the Diebold Group, a service company, to construct a model to help in media selection. When Diebold quoted a price of close to five hundred thousand dollars for the work, Compton called in nine other agencies to share the burden.

A little over fifteen years ago the first electronic computer was profitably used by a marketing organization. Since then, more and more commercial organizations have used this modern tool to solve their business problems with great efficiency and speed. Unquestionably, the future will see wider use of computers of all sizes by business organizations of all sizes. Electronic data processing is no longer restricted to use by the industrial giants, but is in general use throughout a wide spread of American businesses. The point is rapidly being reached that any school claiming to train businessmen must make an introductory course in computers a requirement for graduation.

IMPORTANT POINTS IN THE CHAPTER

1. The rapid growth of American business during and after World War II resulted in a bottleneck in the clerical areas that necessitated sophisticated equipment if business were to continue its expansion. Data processing, which was available, was introduced to industry to handle the clerical problems.

2. The importance of the computer lies in its ability to handle huge masses of data at enormous speed. This advantage more than offsets the high cost of the installation and the changeover problems.

3. Since the computer was originally installed as a clerical device, its use as a marketing tool was delayed. This was due to higher priorities for clerical work, lack of computer time, shortage of computer-trained marketing specialists and lack of marketing people trained in computer uses.

4. The increase in computer use as a high-level marketing tool is the result of managerial recognition of the importance of computer informational reports, constant simplification of computer equipment, keeping up with the competition, and arrival on the scene of the managerial scientist.

5. The managerial scientist (systems analyst), by constructing a model of a specific situation through mathematical equations and using immense pools of data (data banks), is able to solve market research problems with considerable accuracy.

6. Computer-service companies rent time and know-how to small companies and do specific jobs for large companies.

REVIEW QUESTIONS

1. Explain the manner in which the need for data processing coincided with the improvement in data-processing procedures.

2. Why did the adaptation of data processing to business functions depend on the growth of business clerical tasks?

3. What sort of business applications lend themselves to electronic data-processing solutions?

4. Give several reasons for the fact that data-processing procedures are more often used for clerical office procedures than for the solution of marketing problems.

5. Explain the rapid growth of use of data processing for the solution of nonclerical marketing procedures.

6. What are the characteristics of a computer that make it such a vital instrument for business?

7. Define and give an example of a *managerial scientist's model.*

8. Define and give an example of a *data bank.*

9. Would highly styled goods require more frequent computer information reports in a department store than staple goods? Why?

10. Why should a business install an expensive control?

11. Indicate several reasons for the computer's success in marketing.

12. What information must be given to a computer if it is to be used for automatic reordering?

13. Is a computer a necessity for a small retailer?

14. Why do most firms eventually run short of computer time?

15. Discuss the cost of a computer in terms of clerical-help savings. Is it important?

16. Computers are widely used in sales forecasting. Explain the advantages of using a computer for such a purpose and give examples.

17. What are the three factors that make electronic data processing an excellent device for direct-mail users?

18. Give examples of the use of data banks in direct-mail promotion.

19. How is a small store, of limited financial resources, able to afford a computer?

20. Discuss several instances in which large marketers with giant computer installations might turn to computer-service companies for help.

CASE PROBLEMS

Case Problem 1

The Medical Sundries Corporation is a jobber of small, relatively inexpensive medical supplies that are used by doctors. Its offerings include in excess of one thousand small items (thermometers, tongue depressers, and so on) which are sold to small surgical-supply jobbers who, in turn, sell them to practicing physicians.

Although salesmen are used, the most important promotion tool is a large, expensive catalog that lists all the company's merchandise and is distributed free to all customers.

Very few of the items offered for sale are unique. The company's success is due to the fact that it maintains a large inventory, which permits it to make immediate delivery on all its cataloged goods.

Management is progressive and up-to-date. Each year, a major portion of profits is reinvested in expanded inventory. Every three years, a new, larger catalog is produced. These policies have resulted in a constant rate of growth in terms of sales, profits, and, of course, inventory.

Obviously, inventory control is vital to the continued success of the business. The goods are kept in bins and on shelves in a large warehouse. At each location, there is a card indicating the catalog number of the merchandise and the minimum quantity at which goods should be reordered. As the foreman walks through the warehouse each day, he lists goods that are to be reordered and passes this information on to the office.

Lately, several costly errors have been made in reordering. It has become apparent that the business has outgrown the old reorder system.

Management has called you in, as a computer expert, to help with the problem of inventory control.

Questions

1. Does the problem lend itself to a computerized solution? Why?

2. What input information would be required by the computer for this inventory-control problem?

3. Suggest some output reports that management might find useful.

Case Problem 2

Downtown New York City is a center of the performing arts. The opera, legitimate theatre, concerts, sports events, off-Broadway theatre, and many other spectator activities offer a constant flow of eagerly sought-after experiences.

Tickets to these performances are frequently sold on a reserved-seat basis to customers who buy well in advance of the date of showing.

Prior to World War II the market for these tickets consisted of residents of New York City plus a few suburbanites. Since the war, the migration to the suburbs has changed all this. The New York City entertainment industry presently draws its customers from a population upwards of twenty million people, spread over hundreds of square miles. The effect on the ticket sales has been significant. Whereas in the past a customer could pick up tickets with relatively little inconvenience, he is now required to fight heavy traffic to make the same purchase. Naturally, ticket sales suffered.

Ticketron, Inc. is the name of a computer-service company that solved the problem.

Questions

1. Can you figure out Ticketron's operation?
2. Why is this a computer problem?

BIBLIOGRAPHY

Alderson, Wroe, and Stanley J. Shapiro, eds., *Marketing and the Computer.* Englewood Cliffs, N.J.: Prentice-Hall, Inc., 1963.

Buescher, Frank J., "Fashion and the Computer," *Department Store Journal,* April, 1966.

Burck, Gilbert, *The Computer Age.* New York: Harper & Row, Publishers, 1965.

"Computers Begin to Solve the Marketing Puzzle," *Business Week,* April 17, 1965.

"Data Processing in the United States," *Retail Business,* November, 1965.

"EDP Breakdown Data Reduces Waste," *Chain-Store Age,* March, 1970.

Ford, James V., "The Impact of Computers on Marketing Management," *Sales/ Marketing Today,* November, 1965.

Godfrey, M. L., *Applying Today's Computer Technology to Advertising and Marketing.* New York: Association of National Advertisers, 1966.

Kaylin, S. O., "Distribution Centers: Special Report on Automation and Data-Processing Systems," *Chain Store,* Executives edition, October, 1965.

"Marketing Harnesses the Computer," Management Bulletin No. 92, American Marketing Association, 1964.

"The Computer Goes to Market," *Sales Management,* September 15, 1966.

"The Surge in Data Processing," *Department Store Economist,* November, 1965.

INTERNATIONAL MARKETING

17

MAINTAINING GOOD WILL IN FOREIGN MARKETS
  Hiring Foreign Nationals
  Investing Profits in Foreign Countries
  Contributing to Worthwhile Causes
  Other Methods
IMPORTANT POINTS IN THE CHAPTER
REVIEW QUESTIONS
CASE PROBLEMS
BIBLIOGRAPHY

INTRODUCTION

When the domestic market of a highly industrialized nation, as the United States, becomes saturated through excessive competition, its producers must turn to foreign markets to insure their continued survival and growth. Since World War II, the world market has increased enormously in terms of population and gross national product, which has had the effect of greatly increasing the importance of foreign markets as a source of sales volume and profits for domestic producers.

Some years ago, foreign trade was generally limited to supplying needs that could not be produced locally. At present, world trade is truly global in nature. Such nondomestic products as German automobiles and Japanese cameras are extremely successful in the United States in the teeth of a highly technical, industrially advanced local competition. Trends indicate a continued expansion in world trade.

Economic Importance of Exports

The growth and importance of world trade to the United States is shown in Table 17–1. In 1969, exports in value of in excess of thirty-seven billion dollars were sent to foreign markets while imports exceeded thirty-six billion dollars. In total, our trade with foreign sources equaled 8 percent of the gross national product of the United States. The Department of Commerce estimates that each one billion dollars of exports results in one hundred thousand jobs in the United States. Based this estimate, foreign exports in 1969 resulted in the employment of nearly four million American workers. It is obvious that foreign trade has an importance to the country far beyond the profits made by any individual producer. Naturally, some industries are more involved with overseas markets than others. For example, some 7 percent of total employment in manufacturing, and 11 percent of the jobs in agriculture, forestry, fisheries, and mining are the result of our overseas markets.

Table 17–2 indicates the percentage of the total production of certain industries that are shipped to foreign markets. For example, 41 percent of all hides, skins, and pelts produced are marketed abroad, as are 35 percent of cotton-farm products. It should be emphasized that Table 17–2

TABLE 17–1

U.S. PORTION OF GROSS NATIONAL PRODUCT OF IMPORTS
AND EXPORTS (IN BILLIONS OF DOLLARS)

	Exports		Imports	
Year	Amount	% of Gross National Product	Amount	% of Gross National Product
1941–1945	10.1	5.6	3.5	1.9
1946–1950	11.8	4.8	6.7	2.7
1955	15.5	3.9	11.4	2.9
1960	20.6	4.2	14.7	2.9
1965	27.5	4.0	21.4	3.2
1969	37.4	4.0	36.1	4.0

Source: U.S. Bureau of the Census.

TABLE 17–2

PERCENTAGE OF DOMESTIC OUTPUT EXPORTED BY THE
UNITED STATES IN 1966

Hides, skins, and pelts	41
Cotton-farm products	35
Medicines	34
Cash grains	29
Pulp-mill products	27
Sewing machines	27
Construction and mining equipment	26
Oil-field machinery	26
Gum and wood chemicals	23

is a partial list. Were it to include all domestic output of which 10 percent of total production (an important amount) is sold in world trade, the list would cover many pages.

Imports

Foreign trade is not limited to exports. Domestic producers may be finding profitable markets overseas, but foreign products are becoming important on the American market as well. The following list of imports will indicate their importance on the domestic market and the strength of the competition they give to American industries:

Japan—TV and radio (Sony), motorcycles (Honda), various cameras
Italy—sewing machines (Necchi), different clothing items
Germany—automobiles (Volkswagen), cameras (Leica)
Holland—petroleum products (Shell), electric razors (Norelco)

In terms of total volume, the United States is by far the largest trader on the global scene. The importance of foreign trade to a country's economy can be measured in terms of the percentage of the nation's imports and exports to total production. Table 17–3 indicates that foreign trade is relatively minor to the total economy of the United States compared to its importance to other countries.

TABLE 17–3

PORTION OF GROSS NATIONAL PRODUCT OF IMPORTS
AND EXPORTS FOR SELECTED COUNTRIES—1966

Country	Percentage of GNP	
	Imports	Exports
United States	4	4
EUROPEAN ECONOMIC COMMUNITY		
Belgium	37	36
France	14	15
Germany (Federal Republic)	19	21
Italy	16	18
Luxemburg	82	79
Netherlands	55	52
CENTRAL AMERICAN COMMON MARKET		
Costa Rica	28	25
Guatemala	19	19
Honduras	30	29
El Salvador	29	26
Panama	40	37
EUROPEAN FREE-TRADE AREA		
United Kingdom	19	18
Denmark	30	29
Norway	42	41
Sweden	25	25
Austria	27	25
Switzerland	30	31

Source: United Nations Yearbook.

CHOOSING AN AREA

There are many factors that must be considered by a company interested in building an export market for its product. The most important of these is the choice of an area that has a satisfactory market demand. This is dependent, in large part, on the stage of economic development of the country in question.

Economic Development

The company that chooses to involve itself in international trade must select the country in which it is to offer its product with great care. The stage of economic development of the various countries of the world can be roughly separated into six groups, each of which has its own unique marketing characteristics. Estimated demand for a company's product is based, in large part, on the economic development of the target market.

THE PRIMITIVE NATIONS.   The first stage involves nations in a economic system based on family-sized farming, hunting, and food gathering. There is no marketing system or wealth accumulation that can be used to purchase imports. Countries such as this may be found in parts of Africa, South America, and New Guinea. Exports to these countries are generally government-sponsored. Such countries are definitely not fertile ground for a marketing program.

THE EMERGING NATIONS.   The second stage includes nations that have progressed somewhat beyond the primitive stage. They may be found throughout Africa and the Middle East. Raw materials such as oil and metals are exported, as are surplus agricultural products. This results in surplus wealth available for imports, but the wealth is concentrated in the hands of a few large landholders, a very small middle class, and the government. The majority of the population is still in the primitive farming stage and not available as a market. The government's wealth is used for large projects (dams, roads, and so on), and the remaining wealth is in too few hands to afford a large enough market for any widespread importing.

THE START OF MANUFACTURE.   The third stage is characterized by the beginning of the processing of the materials that were previously exported in a raw state. Such products as sugar, rubber, oil, and metals are partially processed before export. These preliminary manufacturing processes employ both native labor and technical personnel from more advanced countries. Although the major part of the population may still be involved in non-currency agriculture, those that work in manufacturing are paid in currency that is available to buy imported products. This market may be tapped by exporting to native distributors. Typical of the countries in this phase are Indonesia and the Persian Gulf nations.

THE MANUFACTURE OF CONSUMER GOODS.   The fourth stage is distinguished by the fact that more people are drawn from the farms to jobs in the processing of raw materials, where earnings are paid in currency, so that there is an increasing demand for consumer goods and funds are available for such purchases. Domestic manufacture, particularly in areas requiring small capital, can begin. Textiles, beverages, food, drugs, and other products may be manufactured locally instead of being imported. Frequently, local laws may be passed that encourage such manufacture by restricting competitive imports. Capital goods, such as machinery for local manufacturers, and durable consumer goods, such as automobiles and re-frigerators, must still be imported.

The Manufacture of Capital and Durable Goods.   In the fifth stage of economic progress, a country reaches a point at which the money and demand are sufficient to support the manufacture of capital goods and durable consumer goods. This production may require the importing of raw materials. Although industrialization has begun, the import of foreign products in competition with local industries may be at a very high level. The major economic resources of a country at this stage still rest in the export of raw and semifinished materials.

Exporting Manufactured Products.   The final stage of economic development finds the country a full-fledged manufacturing nation involved in international trade. In such countries all consumers have currency and the demand for imports is great. At this point local production competes with foreign imports.

In assesing the probable demand for its product, the company must fit its merchandise offerings to a foreign market whose stage of economic development, as outlined above, is keyed to the company's product. This includes both the type of product and the method of distribution. For example, nations in the primitive, developing, and early manufacturing stages of economic development would offer insignificant markets to an automobile manufacturer. However, there might be some demand from their more affluent citizens. It would be ridiculous to set up a major exporting system, but a simple export system or local agency might be worthwhile.

As a country progresses economically, its wealth and its demand for manufactured products increase. The foreign exporter wishing to tap this market is faced with increasing competition from local manufacturers. That this need not be a deterrent to successful exporting is evidenced by the fact that the major portion of foreign trade is between highly developed countries. Although specialty items, for example, Swiss watches, are frequently traded between such countries, many other products are successful despite strong, direct, local competition. Typical are German cars and Japanese cameras competing successfully with highly developed products manufactured in the United States.

Political Development

It would be unwise for any American business to expand its foreign operations into any area that is antagonistic to the United States or so unstable politically as not to be able to guarantee the maintenance of peace and lawfulness that are necessary for commercial success. Companies that make this mistake may find themselves helpless in the face of harassment that the local government either cannot or will not halt. Frequently, emerging nations, desperate for economic investment, are not in a position to attract exporters because they are unable to guarantee peace and stability for any appreciable length of time.

Monetary Regulations

Often the monetary restrictions placed on a country by its government are so tight that a foreign company cannot get its investment or profits out of its operation there. Occasionally, a bartering arrangement can be made under which funds can be removed from the country in the form of easily marketable exports. If this is not the case, the company has the choice of waiting for more favorable monetary regulations or investing its profits within its foreign market.

In some cases the monetary standard of a country is so unstable that the value of that country's currency cannot be depended on. For example, Brazil recently devalued its cruzeiro (Brazil's unit of currency) by half. The holder of any contract requiring the payment of a specific number of cruzeiros would have suffered a severe loss. This can be offset by insisting that dealings with a foreign country with an unstable currency be made in dollars, pounds sterling, gold, or any other stable currency.

Habits and Culture

The habits and culture of a country, even that of neighbors, vary considerably. An example of this may be found in the expansion of American-style one-stop supermarket shopping throughout the world. In Buenos Aires, lines begin forming in front of supermarkets at 6 A.M. A Belgian family's evening walk is likely to include a stroll through a nearby supermarket. In Germany, however, the expansion of the one-stop shopping concept was much slower. The German housewife must shop in many specialized stores to complete her marketing. Unlike American women, she does not consider this a chore but a social event, which she is loathe to give up for supermarket shopping. As a result, the expansion of supermarkets in Germany was less spectacular than expected. Other national differences encountered by supermarkets are: in France, higher taxes are imposed on supermarkets than on small shops, and in Italy, there is a political stigma among radicals holding supermarkets as a prime example of American monopolistic practices. (Despite these occasional problems, supermarkets are spreading rapidly throughout Europe.)

Tariffs and Import Quotas

Many governments attempt to improve the competitive position of domestic manufacturers by imposing tariffs (taxes on imports) and quotas (limitations in the amount of imported goods.) Such an act is usually called *protective,* as it serves to protect domestic producers from foreign competition. This practice is most prevalent in developing countries, but it is found among highly industrialized nations as well. In August, 1971, the United States placed a 10 percent tariff on imported merchandise in order to protect American manufacturers from foreign competitors.

It is vital that a company, studying a foreign market for its product, take into account not only the present tariff and quota arrangements of the area but possible future changes in such arragements as well. A seemingly favorable competitive area can suddenly be made unfavorable by a change in a country's tariff or quota system.

Foreign-Market Research

Although it is more important to research foreign than domestic markets, in practice such research is rarely done thoroughly. The problem is expense. Information on population, government regulations, family size and so forth, readily available at small cost on the domestic scene, would be very expensive to gather in many foreign countries. In addition, the foreign market, though large, is split up into many small segments. The cost of researching each area is very high in relation to the total potential volume from that area.

CHOOSING A PRODUCT

One of the most common causes of exporting failure is the inability to properly adjust the product or the company's message concerning the product. This is the result of ineffective market testing or the unwillingness to spend the money required for product adaptation. It is a serious error to assume that a product that is successful in one country will automatically be accepted by a neighbor with a seemingly very similar culture. Successful marketing on the domestic or the foreign scene requires the product to be keyed to customer demand. This may require varying degrees of change in the product or the promotional message.

No Product Adaptation

A few companies are fortunate enough to be able to sell the identical product, with the same promotional scheme, both at home and abroad. Pepsico, with an outstanding export division, is typical of such companies. Pepsico's management probably agrees that a changed promotional message might be beneficial, but they feel that the high volume under the present strategy and the cost of the changes rule out the advantages of such adaptation.

Adapting the Product

Perhaps the best way to emphasize the importance of changing the product to meet foreign requirements would be to list several costly foreign failures of locally successful products. Each of the following failures resulted from faulty foreign-market research.

Campbell's tomato-soup formula was unsuccessful in Britain because the market demand was for a more bitter taste.

General Mills' Betty Crocker division suffered a costly failure in attempting to sell their U.S.-proven fancy frostings and cake mixtures in Britain. Another U.S. company researched the market and found that the

British take cake at teatime and prefer a dry type of pastry that can be held in the left hand while holding a teacup in the right hand. This company was successful in marketing the type of product demanded by the consumers.

Dry soup mixtures are favored in Europe. CPC International imported the Knorr dry-soup line after successful taste tests with canned soups. The product was a domestic failure, perhaps because dry mixtures need twenty minutes of cooking, whereas canned soups have merely to be heated.

Adapting the Message

Some products can do very well in foreign markets but serve a function different from their requirements on the domestic scene. In such cases, the message requires adaptation, whereas the product can be sold unchanged.

Bicycles and motor scooters are a recreational and leisure item at home but an important means of transportation in many foreign countries.

Outboard motors that were designed for and used by hobby boat owners serve admirably as power sources for commercial fishing boats abroad.

Small, powered gardening tools, designed for suburban homeowners, are ideally suited to small farms in less-developed countries.

European dried soups sell well in America, but for making sauces and dips rather than soup.

Product Life Cycle in Foreign Trade

The life cycle of a new product follows a pattern either on the domestic or the foreign scene. However, the factors at work on the product are different in international trade. Studies of the life cycle of products like office machines, motion pictures, synthetic fabrics, electronic goods, and durable consumer goods indicate the following stages in the life of an exported product:

Exclusive U.S. export
Beginning of foreign production
Competition from foreign producers on the world market
Competition from foreign producers on the domestic market

By understanding each of these stages, a domestic exporter may determine the part of the cycle his product is in and plan his action for the next cycle.

EXCLUSIVE U.S. EXPORT.   Since new-product research usually has the purpose of satisfying the domestic market, most American new products are designed for a high-income market. Industry in the United States is highly technical in nature and new products require design and other technical changes to fit consumer demand. As a result, new products, although they can usually be produced more cheaply in low-labor-cost foreign factories, are generally manufactured locally so that necessary changes can be quickly and easily made.

As the product becomes perfected and the domestic market broadens, the goods become available for export. At this time export of the product is an exclusive U.S. activity, which is supplied by large-scale American production. As the export trade to any one area grows, the producers of that area become interested in the product.

BEGINNING OF FOREIGN PRODUCTION. Foreign manufacturers, already familiar with the product, begin manufacture as soon as the demand within their area reaches a level that indicates profitability. Blessed with a fully developed product, the foreign producer's developmental costs are minimized. He has the further advantage of being able to study the demand for the product that has been pioneered by the American exporter.

Considering the savings in labor, shipping, duty, and tariffs, the foreign producer is usually successful in competing with the American exporter on his local market. As yet, the foreign producer is still a small-scale manufacturer whose production costs, despite a low labor cost, exceed the cost of American producers. Although he can compete very successfully with American exporters at home, his expensive small-scale production costs put him at a disadvantage when he is faced with shipping costs and tariffs, and his export trade is negligible.

At this stage of a product's life cycle, American manufacturers, although still dominant on the world market, begin to lose out to local producers in specific areas. Since local manufacture begins when local demand is high, the export loss is likely to occur in the highest-volume foreign markets. The result is a decline in the rate of the product's export growth. The decline accelerates as the number of foreign producers increases. American dishwashers are presently in this stage of the export life cycle.

COMPETITION FROM FOREIGN PRODUCERS ABROAD. When the foreign producers grow in size and experience to a point at which they equal their U.S. competitors, their lower-cost labor market gives them an advantage over American producers on the world market. Shipping and tariff costs are the same. Consequently, when their production problems are solved, lower labor costs give foreign manufacturers a competitive advantage that results in a shrinking of American export volume. The competition faced by American exporters of ranges and refrigerators on the South American markets is evidence of this stage.

At this point, shipping costs and American tariffs protect the domestic market from foreign competitors.

COMPETITION FROM FOREIGN PRODUCERS AT HOME. Foreign manufacturers with newer production facilities and lower labor costs, which offset shipping expenses and U.S. tariffs, can frequently penetrate the American domestic market with considerable success. When this occurs, the United States becomes an importer of the product and the export trade dwindles away. Bicycles are typical of a product in this stage, as are many other consumer durables.

As more and more foreign countries progress to the point at which their technical productive capacity is such that they can produce for export, the life cycle of export goods will shorten. To offset this trend, many exporters are constructing manufacturing plants in foreign countries to take advantage of the lower labor costs available there.

The length of an export product's life cycle depends on the characteristics of the item. For example, luxury items, expensive products, and products designed to save labor have a longer cycle than inexpensive necessities.

CHOOSING AN OPERATION

There are several ways in which a company may set up a foreign-trade operation. Each method has its advantages an disadvantages. The methods run from simple and inexpensive to highly complicated and costly. Many companies begin simply and evolve to the more complicated and expensive operations as their export business grows.

Foreign Agents

Companies whose involvement in foreign trade is on a limited or occasional basis frequently work through foreign agents. Such firms employ an export manager who visits the foreign agent from time to time and contacts him when a particular item of interest to the agent comes up. The use of foreign agents requires very little effort or expense on the part of the exporter. On the other hand, very little control may be exercised over the foreign operation, and tariff must be paid by the exporter.

Company-Owned Sales Branches

As the volume of foreign sales from a particular area grows, a company may replace its foreign agent with a company-owned sales branch. This operation results in the complete control of the sales function and permits more aggressive selling and promotion. The use of a company-owned sales branch requires financial investment, risk, and the responsibility for training and managing a sales staff. The sales staff may consist of home-company personnel who must learn about the market, or of foreign nationals who must learn about the product.

The use of company-owned sales branches offers no savings in the way of shipping costs or tariffs.

Licensing

Another method of penetrating a foreign market is by licensing the production and distribution of a product to a local manufacturer. Under this method, the company must find a local manufacturer interested in the production and distribution of the item. The licensee, for a stipulated fee or perunits cost, has complete control over the product for a stated period of time. The use of licenses involves no financial risks and saves tariffs and shipping costs. It has the political advantage of getting a commercial foothold into countries where U.S. ownership is not permitted, tariffs are very high, or import quotas are too restrictive.

Under a licensing arrangement, the exporter has no control over the manufacturing operation. Many exporters oppose licensing, since they feel it is a short-term operation. They hold that, once the foreign licensee has the technical know-how to produce and distribute the product, he will sever relations with the licenser and retain the business for himself.

Contract Manufacturing

To offset the tendency of licensees to take over the entire business, some companies retain the distribution control but contract out the manufacturing to a local manufacturer. This has the disadvantage of having limited control over the manufacturer. In addition, it is often difficult to find a capable manufacturer, and the management of distribution is often a costly and difficult problem.

Joint Ventures

The total or any part of a foreign operation may be owned by a partnership consisting of the exporter and a foreign firm. Typically, under such a deal the American firm would provide the capital and technical know-how, whereas the foreign firm provides the management, labor, and political clearances. The investment and consequent risk involved in joint ventures is high. In return for this, the amount of control and share of the profits are correspondingly increased.

Wholly Owned Subsidiaries

In areas in which the marketing program has reached the level at which the rewards are such that large investment is indicated, a company may construct a wholly-owned manufacturing facility and distribute through a company-owned organization. This procedure maximizes control, profitability, and risk. Many developing countries offer financial and tax incentives to encourage manufacturing for the resulting job opportunities available to their people.

The wholly owned subsidiary is usually a division of the parent exporter and secondary in importance to the domestic operations.

The International Company

The final step in the evolution of a company's foreign-trade operation is the international company, whose export business is of equal importance to its domestic operations. This requires complete integration of all the company's operations, with manufacturing and distributing facilities throughout the world. The international company's Chicago sales office is not more important than its Bangkok office and its manufacturing facilities in Dallas take no precedence over its equal facility in Milan.

It must be understood that a company may be involved in different export arrangements at its various outposts. Thus, a company with a wholly-owned subsidiary in Belgium may work with foreign agents in an less-developed African nation.

Channels of Distribution

In practice there are five major channels of distribution available to U.S. exporters. They are listed in order of their complexity and cost:

1. Manufacturer—U.S. exporter—foreign importer—foreign wholesaler or retailer—foreign consumer.

2. Manufacturer—foreign importer based in the United States—foreign wholesaler or retailer—foreign consumer.

3. Manufacturer—foreign importer based in a foreign country—foreign wholesaler or retailer—foreign consumer.

4. Manufacturer—foreign wholesaler or retailer—foreign consumer.

5. Manufacturer—foreign consumer.

The choice of the particular distributive channel depends on the estimated market potential, the amount of capital to be risked, and the amount of control the manufacturer wishes to exert over the distributional system.

MAINTAINING GOOD WILL IN FOREIGN MARKETS

Companies that have heavily invested in foreign markets find it important to maintain the good will not only of the users of their products but of all citizens of the countries in which they are involved. The following are some of the ways in which this can be done.

Hiring Foreign Nationals

The National Cash Register Company employs twenty-two thousand people abroad, of whom only six are Americans. This indicates to the countries involved that the company sincerely wants to be accepted, and that it is helping the country's economy by providing employment to its citizens. The National Cash Register Company believes that it is cheaper to teach its product to foreign nationals than to teach foreign culture to American nationals. As a result, foreign nationals selling National Cash Register products to people of their own nationality are able to work with increased effectiveness.

Investing Profits in Foreign Countries

Another method of improving company good will in foreign markets is to build confidence that the operation is permanent rather than for a quick profit. This can be done by investing at least part of the profit in the economic development of the country in which the profit was earned. In some countries such investments are forced by currency restrictions. Whatever the reason, increased investment pays off in good will and the increases in profits that go with it.

Contributing to Worthwhile Causes

In Latin America, there is an extreme shortage in proteins and many essential minerals in most diets. The Quaker Oats Company is working on the production and development of *Incaparina,* a product with nutritional values similar to those found in milk. The product is a difficult one to promote, since its use requires the changing of many eating habits. However, because of its social importance, several Latin American governments are interested in it. If the product is successful, Quaker Oats will make many friends in the area.

TABLE 17–4

U.S. INVESTMENT ABROAD AND FOREIGN INVESTMENT
IN THE UNITED STATES (IN BILLIONS OF DOLLARS)

Year	U.S. Investment Abroad	Foreign Investment in the U.S.
1950	19.0	17.6
1955	29.1	27.8
1960	49.4	41.2
1965	81.2	58.9
1968	101.9	81.1

Source: U.S. Department of Commerce.

Other Methods

Any company that must depend on foreign good will for success must be sure to implant in its American employees a respect for the traditions, customs, and religion of the countries involved. It should support its hosts' economic and cultural development and maintain a high reputation for integrity by honoring all contracts and commitments. There should be no involvement in the countries' politics.

IMPORTANT POINTS IN THE CHAPTER

1. The growth of population and purchasing power of the world has resulted in a market of enormous potential for international trade. The importance of foreign trade to the American economy may be emphasized by pointing out that millions of Americans are dependent on foreign trade for their jobs.

2. Before selecting an area for developing an export trade, careful study must be made of its economic and political development, monetary regulations, habits, culture, and tariff and quota regulations. International market research is important as well as expensive.

3. Although some products can be exported in an unaltered state, many must be adapted to meet the needs of the specific market to which they are sent. Generally, the promotional methods must be adapted too.

4. Products that are exported to foreign markets go through a life cycle consisting of the following stages: exclusive U.S. export, beginning of foreign production, competition from foreign producers on the world market, and competition from foreign producers on the domestic market. High-cost luxury products have the longest life cycle.

5. There are several ways in which a country can set up its foreign-trade operation, that is, by way of foreign agents, company-owned sales branches, licensing, contract manufacturing, joint ventures, and wholly owned subsidiaries. The operation chosen depends on the estimated size of the market, the amount of risk involved, and the amount of control required.

6. It is important that a company having business abroad maintain the good will of the country in which it is a guest. This may be done by hiring foreign nationals, investing profits in the country in which they are earned, contributing to worthwhile projects, showing respect for the country's customs, religion, and traditions, and maintaining a high degree of integrity in both commercial and social activities.

REVIEW QUESTIONS

1. Explain the importance of foreign exports to the economy of the United States.

2. In selecting an area to which to export, a company must carefully study the economic development of the area. Why?

3. Explain the foreign-trade potential of a primitive area. What sort of foreign-trade operation is suited to this kind of territory?

4. Discuss the foreign-trade possibilities of countries whose economic level has reached the manufacture-of-consumer-goods level.

5. Fully developed manufacturing countries offer the highest foreign-trade potential. Why?

6. Explain the success of the Volkswagen on the American market.

7. Why is the state of political development of a country important to a would-be exporter?

8. Discuss the importance of monetary stability in foreign trade.

9. What is the importance of market research in international marketing? What are the difficulties?

10. Why do some products require adaptation to foreign markets?

11. Give examples of products that are successful in foreign markets where they are used for a different purpose than originally intended. Explain the effect of this on foreign advertising.

12. Why do producers who can manufacture new products more cheaply abroad prefer to use local facilities?

13. Discuss the stage in the life cycle of a product in which foreign production begins. Why are American producers able to maintain their foreign markets when foreign production begins?

14. At what point in a product's life cycle do foreign products begin to compete on the American market? Give examples.

15. What characteristics of a product affect the length of its life cycle?

16. Discuss the use of foreign agents in an exporting operation. In what areas would you expect to find agents used?

17. What are the advantages and disadvantages of company-owned sales branches?

18. Define *foreign contract manufacturing*. What are its advantages and disadvantages?

19. Discuss the factors that must be taken into account in making a decision concerning the type of overseas operation to be used.

20. Explain the advantages and disadvantages of staffing an overseas operation with foreign nationals.

CASE PROBLEMS

Case Problem 1

The Yamata Camera Company of Tokyo is one of the larger Japanese camera companies. Included in the company's offerings is a line of consumer cameras that controls about 8 percent of the domestic market. The line is also produced for the American market by an American company on a contract basis. Judging from the size of the American orders, the cameras seem to be selling very well on the American market under the name of the American importer—a large, highly respected firm that aggressively promotes the line.

The contract with the American company will expire in two years and the Yamata Company is faced with the question of renewing the contract or exporting its proven product to the United States under its own label, as other Japanese camera firms do with considerable success. Cost estimates indicate that the cameras could be profitably offered at a price below the amount the American consumer is presently paying. The Yamata Camera Company is financially capable of carrying the operation.

Questions

1. What are the advantages and disadvantages of renewing the contract? Of direct exporting?
2. If the company decides to export, what channels of distribution should it use?

Case Problem 2

The Garden-Aid Corporation is a highly successful manufacturer of a complete line of gasoline-powered garden tools that are sold to American home gardeners. Since World War II the migration of Americans to individually owned suburban houses has created a tremendous demand for the company's product and Garden-Aid is a large-scale, efficient producer.

The success of the powered garden-tool industry has brought many competitors into the field. This has resulted in gradual lessening of sales volume and profits. To retain its place on the industrial scene, Garden-Aid has decided to move into the foreign market.

To date, exports of powered garden tools are very small. Garden-Aid's estimate of foreign demand is so high that competitors are certain to follow Garden-Aid into the international market. To offset future competition in the foreign markets, management has decided to go directly into a large-scale foreign operation at many levels and in many areas. It realizes that each area will require product modification, message modification, and a distribution plan unique to the special problems of the area.

Questions

1. Discuss and give examples of the required product modification, message modification, and channels of distribution for each of the following types of countries.

    a. Primitive nations
    b. Emerging nations
    c. Nations beginning to manufacture
    d. Nations manufacturing consumer goods
    e. Nations manufacturing durable goods

2. Describe the probable life cycle of a powered lawn mower.

BIBLIOGRAPHY

Bennett, Peter D., ed., *Marketing and Economic Development*. Chicago: American Marketing Association, 1965.

"Big, Bigger, Biggest—American Business Goes Global," *New Republic*, April 30, 1966.

Carson, David, *International Marketing: A Comparative Systems Approach*. New York: John Wiley & Sons, Inc., 1967.

Dichter, Ernest, "The World Customer," *Harvard Business Review*, July–August, 1962.

Dowd, Lawrence P., *Principles of World Business*. Boston: Allyn & Bacon, Inc., 1965.

Drucker, Peter F., "Marketing and Economic Development," *Journal of Marketing*, January, 1958.

Fayerweather, John, *International Marketing*. Englewood Cliffs, N.J.: Prentice-Hall, Inc., 1965.

Hess, John M., and Phillip R. Cateora, *International Marketing*. Homewood, Ill.: Richard D. Irwin, Inc., 1966.

Robinson Richard D., "The Challenge of the Underdeveloped National Market," *Journal of Marketing*, October, 1961.

————, *International Management*. New York: Holt, Rinehart & Winston, Inc., 1967.

Root, Franklin R., *Strategic Planning for Export Marketing*. Scranton, Pa.: International Textbook Company, 1966.

Slater, Charles C., "Marketing Processes in Developing Latin American Societies," *Journal of Marketing*, July, 1968.

Stuart, Robert D., "Penetrating the International Market." New York: American Marketing Association, Management Report No. 84, 1965.

"U.S. Business in the New Europe," *Business Week*, May 7, 1966.

Wells, Louis T., "A Product Life Cycle for International Trade," *Journal of Marketing*, July, 1968.

"World Markets Are Still a Lure," *Business Week*, August 7, 1965.

Yoshins, Michael Y., "Marketing Orientation in International Business," *Business Topics*, Summer, 1965.

MARKETING MISTAKES

18

INTRODUCTION

In most marketing books, the various activities involved in the marketing process are considered in great detail. Topics dealing with such research as selection of a test market, investigation of primary data, determination of the price that a new product might warrant, packaging innovations, and so forth, occupy most of the text. What about the mistakes made by small and giant marketers alike? Is every new product successful? Students of marketing might be ignorant of the number of marketing mishaps that are encountered annually. Therefore, we shall now examine some products that were expected to be successful but failed to attract a market. In addition, a general overview will be given of the reasons for product failure.

REASONS FOR PRODUCT FAILURE

Statistics are looked upon with skepticism by many observers. However, it is interesting to know that the New-Products Action Team, Inc., a company specializing in new-product services for consumer package-goods manufacturers, reported that nearly 80 percent of the 9,450 supermarket products introduced into the market in 1968 failed. The findings are comparable to other consumer lines. Among the products included in the study, which proved to be unsuccessful in terms of acceptance were such heavily advertised items as Campbell's Red Kettle soups, Gablinger's beer, Heinz's Happy soups, Hunt's flavored ketchups, Noxzema medicated cold cream, and Vote toothpaste. Although all these products carried the names of industrial giants and were marketed with the aid of the world's greatest experts, they failed to appeal to the consuming public.

Products fail for a number of reasons. According to the previously mentioned survey, the major reason for new-product failure is the lack of a real consumer point of difference. The new products (in the survey) boasted a difference in packaging or formulation, but not really a product difference. However, products do fail for many other reasons as well. We shall explain the major reasons, with specific examples in each category, as reported in the findings of the New Products Action Team, Inc.

Insignificant Product Differences

Many consumer-goods producers try to climb aboard the bandwagon of another manufacturer's successful distribution of a specific product. The mere fact that the new product is just the original in disguise generally leads to the failure of the new product. Container changes, slight formula variation, or presentation of the product in a new form (tablets instead of powders, for example) do not seem to adequately convince the customer to buy the new product. Specifically the following items failed as a result of insignificant product differences:

In 1962 *Duractin,* introduced by Menly and James, was marketed as a painkiller that would provide relief for eight hours. This minor difference (as compared with the other successfully marketed painkillers) proved unimportant to the broad segment of consumers who wanted speedy relief. The cost of failure attributed to the western region alone is estimated at $1,500,000.

An expected threat to the leadership of Heinz's Ketchup was Hunt's introduction of flavored ketchups. Pizza, Hickory, and Steak House ketchups were introduced in 1964. They failed to gain the favor of the consumer market. The cost of the failure was approximately $1,200,000. Although Hunt was clearly a loser in this campaign, DelMonte tried to challenge Heinz with a similar idea. It produced a barbecue ketchup, slightly altering the normal ketchup formula by adding onions to the recipe. That too failed.

One of the most frequent reasons for failure in this category seems to be that old products are presented in new forms. For example, the production of tablets instead of powder, liquids instead of tablets, and aerosols in place of pastes, does not generally prove to be successful. *Formula 409* and *Fantastic,* both highly accepted and profitable household cleansers, were challenged by the introduction of *Easy-Off* household cleanser. The former products were in liquid form, the latter was an aerosol foam. Consumers did not see any advantage in the use of *Easy-Off.* The only difference was in product form. The cost of this failure to American Home Products, Inc., producers of *Easy-Off,* was estimated at $850,000.

Poor Product Positioning

Product positioning is categorized into three areas. Insignificant positioning is defined as the consumer disinterest in the product, confused positioning means that the consumer does not understand the promotional message, and mismatched positioning means that the product's performance does not match the appeal.

INSIGNIFICANT POSITIONING. In most cases this is directly related to insignificant product differences. If a manufacturer produces an unimportant product, it will be reflected in the advertising. In the case of *Easy-Off,* the basis of the advertising campaign was that it was an aerosol foam. Comparative demonstrations showed that *Easy-Off* did not run as the liquid did.

Although consumer recall of the advertising campaign was extremely high, the fact that the product was sold at a small scale was evidence that consumers did not care for it. If the product difference is a real one, the consumer generally will purchase. Examples of gimmickless advertising are Head and Shoulders dandruff shampoo and Nyquil nighttime could remedy.

CONFUSED POSITIONING. This is perhaps best illustrated by Revlon's introduction of *Super Natural* hair spray in the early 1960s. The confusion that led to the eventual loss of millions of dollars was directly related to the words *super* and *natural*. In terms of hair sprays, *super* means *more holding power,* whereas *natural* means *less holding power.* The consuming public, faced with this uncertainty regarding the product, did not purchase it. Although Revlon, in its own defense, said that hair-spray purchases were shifting to lower-priced brands and blamed this as the cause for failure, the confusion left for the consumer to unscramble definitely did not help *Super Natural's* position.

MISMATCHED POSITIONING. This is generally regarded by marketers as the greatest individual problem in advertising communication. *Positioning* a new product means determining the most effective combination of the product's features and consumer appeal. An excellent example of a product that was raised to a level of tremendous success by a change in its positioning is *Right Guard* deodorant. Originally positioned as a man's deodorant in 1963, an advertising change was instituted in later campaigns that claimed it to be "the perfect family deodorant because nothing touches you but the spray itself." Sales increased annually by twenty million dollars. Because of a more effective combination of consumer appeal and product performance, *Right Guard* sales are now at the fifty million dollar mark.

Since there may be many different product characteristics and as many different areas of consumer appeal, the possible appeal–product performance combinations can be almost limitless. The task for marketers is to select the most appropriate combination to insure product success.

No Point of Difference

Most new products—about 80 percent—have a point of difference. If not, the new product fails. There are, however, exceptions. In some markets where the number of consumers is large enough, many products without particular differences are successful. Cigarettes, hair sprays, toilet soaps, and floor waxes are examples. However, when a market is not large enough, the introduction of the same product with a new name is apt to fail. Kaiser withdrew its aluminum foil because it did not provide any advantages over the leaders, Alcoa and Reynolds. In marketing, new products with basically no point of difference to existing products are often referred to as *me-too* products.

Bad Timing

Often too many similar products are introduced at the same time. This can alter a company's successful distribution and constitutes a fourth reason for product failure. Usually the smaller company gets squeezed out of the market first.

A few years ago, consumers witnessed the simultaneous introduction of several new toothpastes and mouthwashes. Perhaps best remembered are Vote, Fact, Cue, and Reef. The combined losses to the producers of these products were estimated at better than forty million dollars. More recently consumers saw a household-cleaner market explosion. Among the seventeen brands that were introduced in a nine-month period were *Easy-Off, Clean & Kill,* and *Whistle.* The estimated losses were between five and seven million dollars.

Presently, explosive situations are much in evidence in the markets for items such as presoaks, phosphate-free detergents, feminine-hygiene deodorants, and sugar substitutes.

Product Performance

With the sophistication of product timing available to marketers today, the percentage of product failures that occur as a result of poor performance is substantially decreasing. Each year more emphasis is placed on prolonged market testing before a company will give the go-ahead for production. This longer testing period affords the producer the chance to uncover product defects.

Although the testing procedures are generally rigorous, products occasionally fail due to unsatisfactory performance that is somehow overlooked during the testing period. In some instances the unique feature of a new product is carefully scrutinized, whereas other product aspects might be less-carefully examined. In 1966 General Foods distributed, nationally, Post cereals containing freeze-dried fruits. The problem that eventually cost General Foods five million dollars was the slow reconstitution of the fruit. By the time the fruit was reconstituted, the cereal became soggy.

Most of the products that fail because of poor performance are food products. Essentially the problem is one of assessing the customer's taste preference. Campbell's Red Kettle and Knorr's dry-soup failures were the result of the taste problem. Consumers, for many years, were purchasers of Lipton's dry soups. Campbell and Knorr were unsuccessful due to their inability to assess their taste appeal in relation to Lipton.

Wrong Market for Company

Although companies may be highly successful with certain product lines, often their ventures into different types of manufacture prove to be disastrous. Marketers sometimes seek to enter markets that do not fall within their capabilities.

Procter & Gamble was unsuccessful when it entered the hair-spray market with *Hidden Magic* and *Winterset/Summerset*. Colgate also met with failure with the introduction of *007* after-shave lotion in 1965. Failures of this nature result from lack of experience necessary to generate a "feel" for certain businesses.

Surveys indicate that companies fail because they try to penetrate a new market, but few marketers readily admit that failure was due to their incomplete understanding of that market.

According to the survey taken by the New Products Action Team, Inc. the percent of failure for each category was:

Insignificant product difference	36%
Poor product positioning	32%
No point of difference	20%
Bad timing	16%
Product performance	12%
Wrong market for company	8%

(Total is more than 100% because some failures were due to more than one reason.)

In addition to the causes of product failures explored, which were based exclusively on new supermarket products, there are others that deserve examination.

Costs

Although this does not happen too often, the costs involved in the production and distribution of a new product may be higher than anticipated. Efficient research should determine the costs of manufacturing, which in turn determine the product's price, but unforeseen variables might surpass the estimate. For example, between the product's inception and the distribution to the customer a period of three years might elapse. Test marketing, at a particular price, might have been completed a year prior to production. From all indications the product, according to the test market, will be successful. After testing the product, the price of raw materials used in its manufacture increases, as do factory salaries (at an unusual rate because of a strike). These two factors would probably necessitate a price rise. The resulting higher price might attract a smaller market than originally expected, leading to smaller sales volume and eventual product failure.

Inadequate Sales Effort

The giants of industry generally have adequate sales forces, but the smaller producers often spend little time in the training of salesmen. Insufficient attention paid to formal training or motivation is frequently the cause of the small manufacturer's product failure. It is not the product that is weak, but the selling job that is ineffective.

Other significant causes of product failure, such as poor market analysis, improper determination of consumer motivation, competition, and distribution shortcomings will be discussed in connection with the material presented in the following section.

FORD MOTOR COMPANY—THE EDSEL

No chapter on marketing mistakes, mishaps, errors, or misjudgments, call them what you may, could be complete without the investigation of Ford's Edsel and the reasons for its failure. The preceding material gave glimpses of many products and the specific reasons for their failure. The following section will present an overview of the Edsel from its inception to its withdrawal from the market by the Ford Motor Company.

The Edsel's Emergence

The idea for the Edsel was conceived in 1948, seven years before the final decision for its production was issued. Henry Ford, grandson of the company's founder, proposed that studies be made for the determination of the feasibility of a new, medium-priced automobile. His initial thinking was that the medium price class would offer the best opporunity for future sales. At that time, the company had a product line consisting of three automobiles, with the Ford responsible for 80 percent of total sales. In order to achieve balance, it was felt that the inclusion of a new medium-price automobile was in order. This would offer the consumer a wider choice and would also permit Ford to compete more effectively with General Motors and Chrysler. Ford, at this point, produced only one medium-priced car, whereas Chrysler and General Motors offered two and three, respectively.

Research at this time was inconclusive and it was not until 1955, after further studies had been instituted, that production of the Edsel was recommended. Preliminary investigation, through the study of automobile registrations, showed a growing trend toward cars in the medium-price field. Additional research, confined to Michigan, showed that when Ford owners traded up, they did not buy the Ford Motor Company's Mercury, its only medium-priced car. Instead, they switched to the other producers. By comparison, when Chevrolet purchasers traded up, 87 percent remained with General Motors and 47 percent of the Plymouth owners moved up to a medium-priced car in the Chrysler Corporation line. Twenty-six percent only of the Ford owners purchased the Mercury. (See Figures 18–1 to 18–3.)

It is also interesting to note (in Figure 18–4) that Ford traders contributed almost as much to General Motors medium-price penetration as did Chevrolet traders themselves.

Corporation loyalty was another factor that convinced Ford to produce a new automobile. Research pointed out, through the investigation of auto registration in the Michigan area, that when an automobile owner decides to buy a new make, the tendency is to buy from the same corporation family. There are nine possibilities of movement (as far as price is concerned) when

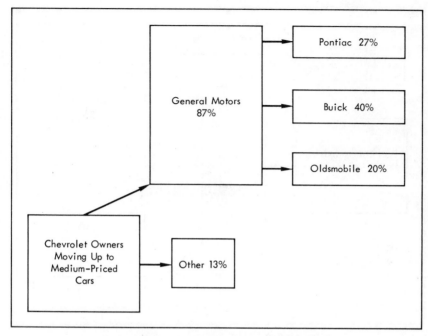

Figure 18–1   Chevrolet owners who traded up

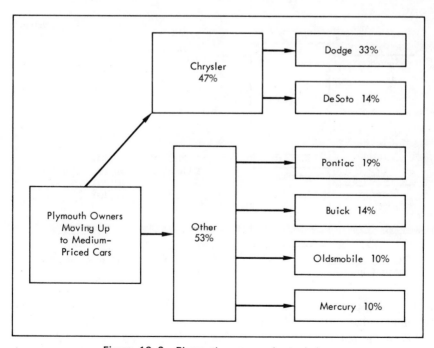

Figure 18–2   Plymouth owners who traded up

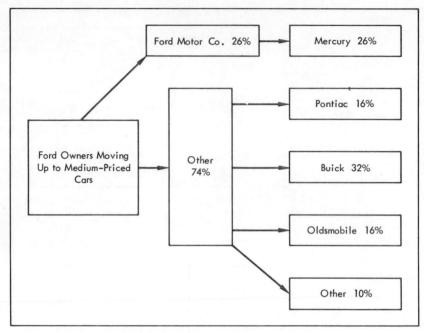

Figure 18–3   Ford owners who traded up

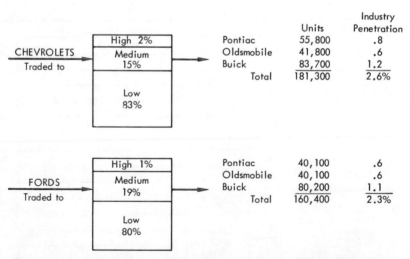

Figure 18–4   Ford traders contribute almost as much to GM medium price penetration as do Chevrolet traders themselves

a new car is purchased. These include movements from low to low, low to medium, and so forth. Ford was interested in retaining the buyer who was no longer interested in purchasing a Ford. Research also showed that the greater the number of products in the line, the greater the corporation loyalty. In the medium-price field, where General Motors had three makes

Categories in which Corporation Loyalty Possible	% of Transactions	Ratio Loyal to Non-Loyal Buying
1. Low–Medium	10.2	2.1–1
2. Medium–Low	9.0	2.3–1
3. Medium–Medium (other makes)	7.0	3.3–1
4. High–Medium	1.2	3.4–1
5. High–Low	1.0	2.2–1
6. Medium–High	.8	2.2–1
7. Low–High	.2	*
Total	29.4%	2.4–1

No Corporation Loyalty Possible		
Low–Low	46.6	
Medium–Medium (same make)	21.2	
High–High	2.8	
Total	70.6%	
	100.0%	

Figure 18–5   Average ratio of corporation loyalty buying to nonloyalty buying = 2.4 to 1

and Chrysler two, Ford only had one make to accommodate loyalty. Figure 18–5 shows, within each of the categories, the ratios of buying another make from the same company against buying a make from a different company. It also shows the percentage of the total industry transactions in each buying category.

When the decision to produce the new car became imminent, the outbreak of the Korean War forced Ford to shelve any immediate plans. At the end of the war, the company authorized new studies to be made by a special Forward Product-Planning Committee. For two years, the committee studied the various possibilities and alternatives. One study undertaken was a forecast of the economy that indicated a rise in the gross national product of more that 135 million dollars by 1965, with the number of cars in operation up twenty million. Additional forecasts were that more than 50 percent of all families in the United States would have incomes in excess of five thousand dollars, compared to 30 percent at that time, and that more than 40 percent of all automobiles would be medium- or higher-priced.

Based on these considerations, the consensus of the committee was that if Ford did not produce a new car, it would be missing out on one of the greatest periods of economic opportunity.

STYLING THE EDSEL.   Conflicting reports concerning the styling of the Edsel are still circulating today. Some at Ford reported that there was not any consumer research done in connection with styling the car. David Wallace, director of marketing research for the Ford Motor Company, indicated the foregoing, whereas Henry Baker, then sales-planning and programming manager, stated in an article that, "since Edsel's consumer research could only give a general idea of the styling principles car buyers prefer, the actual features and form of the car had to be developed in a stylist's ivory tower." From the two executives' points, there seems to be disagreement as to whether or not any consumer research was actually performed. About two years before introduction of the automobile, the model was presented to the Forward Product-Planning Committee, at which time it received an applause comparable to that of Henry Ford's first horseless carriage. Ford Motor Company invested 250 million dollars in plant, equipment, research, and advertising before a single automobile rolled off the assembly line. This made the Edsel the most expensive new-product introduction in history.

Its eventual style, perhaps remembered by millions, featured a novel horse-collar-shaped radiator grille, set in a conventionally low, wide front end. *Newsweek* compared its elegance to that of the Continental.

CREATING THE EDSEL'S PERSONALITY. The Columbia University Bureau of Applied Social Research was commissioned to perform consumer research concerning the personalities of medium-priced cars. Two markets, Peoria, Illinois and San Bernadino, California were selected. Many questions were asked of the consumers concerning their attitudes and opinions. The responses to one question, "Which of these makes do you think might be most appropriate for people in these occupations?" brought forth the conclusion that people do indeed see makes of cars as possessing rather different personalities. Mercury, the Ford medium-priced make, came out as a "white-collar hot rod, not very prestigious."

The key questions that had to be answered were how to satisfy all the variables in order to develop the optimum car personality and to determine which of the market segments were to be considered as prime targets. Attention was focused on the following groups:

1. The young buyers—because it was felt they were more approachable.

2. The thousands of Ford customers who were part of the phenomenon called corporation loyalty.

3. The young marrieds.

The final personality for the Edsel read "The Smart Car for the Younger Executive or Professional on His Way Up."

ADVERTISING THE EDSEL. After considerable investigation of twenty advertising agencies, Foote, Cone, and Belding was selected. Although the agency had billings of seventy-six million dollars in 1955, it had no automobile account. In the nineteen months between the time it got the account and the appearance of the first Edsel advertisement, the agency invested about one million dollars in an office, research, and so forth.

The basis for the advertising campaign was the research that had been done on the personality of the car. The agency felt that it was the best research it had ever seen. The only significant change was to shift the emphasis from *young executive* to *middle-class family* on the way up, since the middle-income family represented a large market. A combination of billboard, magazine, and newspaper advertising was used. No television or radio was incorporated into the campaign. Nor was there any direct consumer research to determine the appeals of the Edsel advertisement.

DISTRIBUTION. Although the usual outlet for a new automobile is handled through the existing company agencies (Mercury is sold by Lincoln dealers), Ford developed a separate dealership organization for the Edsel. They sought twelve hundred dealers. Ford insisted upon knowledgeable and experienced dealers to handle the new car. Since to most dealers this meant switching brands and an outlay of approximately one hundred thousand dollars for a Ford Motor Company dealership, the dealers were extremely hard to find. Under the direction of J. C. Doyle, sales and marketing manager for Edsel, a campaign was started to motivate auto dealers. By the fall of 1957 the quota of twelve hundred dealers was almost met. Not all were exactly what Ford had hoped for, but the number had to be reached. Public relations were entrusted to C. Gayle Warnock. It was his task to get as much publicity for the Edsel as possible. After a short time, the Edsel's description was all over the country. The promotion was so exciting that the public could hardly wait to see the dream car. One of the publicity-team members felt that all the advance publicity might eventually hurt the Edsel; consumers would find out that it was just an automobile, after all, with wheels and an engine like the other cars. Soon after the public was to be disappointed.

INTRODUCTION OF THE NEW AUTO. On September 4, 1957 the Edsel was unveiled in the automobile showrooms. Close to three million people came to see it the first day. Ford executives were satisfied with the day's sales, but after three weeks sales began to lag. As one executive stated, "We started sensing something was not as perfect as we thought."

Failure of the Edsel

Although the plan to bring a new medium-priced car into the market seemed sound (sales trends in the middle 1950s showed an increasing popularity of this price car), the Edsel was a failure. What were the contributing factors? The following are just some of the explanations rendered by Ford executives and the "monday-morning quarterbacks" alike:

1. Operating as a separate division was extremely expensive, which contributed considerably to the impossibly high break-even point. If the Edsel had been merchandised as part of another Ford division, this would not have been the case.

2. The separate dealerships for the Edsel were too hastily assembled. As it turned out, many dealers had insufficient capital and lacked the neces-

sary experience. One reason for the separate dealership was to eliminate the possibility of, for example, a Ford salesman switching the customer to a Ford if a good deal of Edsel opposition was met. However, it is conceivable that the more experienced, established dealers could, in fact, have done a better job.

3. Management had decided that right after the Edsel's introduction the number of Edsels on the road should rise as rapidly as possible. However, there were four series and numerous models, and so the first cars suffered from a number of kinks. The reputation of poor quality acquired this way stayed in the consumers' minds even after the quality controls were later improved.

4. The tremendous amount of publicity showered on the car built it up for the public to a point that was in excess of possible satisfaction. In fact, no car could have lived up to such a high anticipation.

5. The styling could also be considered a mistake. The car's designers sought distinction (research findings did show that medium-priced car buyers sought elegance and luxury), but what they achieved turned out to be a somewhat peculiar automobile. The grille was a constant target for ridicule.

6. The recession of 1958, coupled with Russia's success with Sputnik in the space race, hardly helped the Edsel. It was a poor year for all cars but especially bad for the introduction of a new car.

7. The National Safety Council's stand against advertising of power and speed led to the Automobile Manufacturer's Association decision to stop using auto racing as a promotional device and to deemphasize high performance in advertising campaigns. This decision seriously hampered Edsel's advertising approach to the youthful market it had set out to attract.

8. The timing for such a fancy style was inappropriate. At a time when the consumer's taste was turning to economy cars, compacts, and designs void of decorative chrome and large tail fins, the Edsel was sporting its fancy grille.

9. The market information was already old (sometimes a problem in marketing research), but since it was the only information available, it was used as a basis for production. The information did not really indicate the consumer's feeling at the time of Edsel's actual introduction.

10. "Listening too long to the motivation-research people, who, in their efforts to turn out a car that would satisfy customers' sexual fantasies and the like, had failed to supply reasonable and practical transportation."

Dr. Seymour Marshak, director of Ford's marketing research, blamed the marketing research. It was his contention that the examination of past performance was not really marketing research. Perhaps if there had been continuous research, errors could have been corrected and the introduction could have been postponed for a later date or the idea might have been abandoned altogether.

Marshak's complaint about the lack of sufficient marketing research seems quite appropriate when examining the Edsel's brief history. It is evident that there was no research conducted pertaining to style or price—both extremely important factors in the contemplation of any new product.

The study of a major company's mistake, such as Ford's Edsel, or, for that matter, any of the products mentioned in the chapter, provides students and marketers alike with concrete examples of how and why marketing mistakes are made. Investigation into any marketing mishap may point up the importance of marketing research, and the possibility of disaster to the company because of any carelessness or shortcuts.

IMPORTANT POINTS IN THE CHAPTER

1. Only about 20 percent of the new consumer products manufactured each year is successful. Conspicuously present among the failures are products manufactured by industrial giants.

2. Products fail for a number of reasons. Among the most common reasons for failure are:

    a. Insignificant differences in the product in comparison to those that have already been marketed successfully.

    b. Poor product postitioning, which can be further categorized into insignificant positioning, confused positioning, and mismatched positioning.

    c. No actual point of difference in the new product. An example is Kaiser's failure in the aluminum-foil market because its foil had no advantages over the already successful foils of Alcoa and Reynolds.

    d. Bad Timing.

    e. Product performance does not live up to expectation. This is most relevant in the food industry, although it is not confined to foodstuffs.

    f. The wrong market for the company. When a company's capabilities are inadequate for the marketing of a product because it does not belong to the company's usual line of business, the product often fails.

    g. When the costs of production and distribution exceed anticipation, thus necessitating a price increase, sales volume might fall. This often leads to failure.

h. When the sales force is inadequately prepared and proper presentation of the product to the buyer is impaired, the product might fail.

3. Studies show that the most significant reason for supermarket-type product failure is attributed to insignificant product difference.

4. The Edsel is an excellent example of a major company's product failure. Among the reasons offered for its early withdrawal from the market are:

a. The dealerships were inadequate because they lacked capital and experience.

b. The car's early kinks were not readily forgotten by consumers.

c. The car could not live up to its advance publicity of a dream car and therefore disappointed the market upon arrival on the auto scene.

d. Insufficient marketing research involving style and price.

e. Poor timing. It was introduced when the economy was at a low level and consumers were looking toward economy and compact cars.

5. The study of product failures is essential to underscore the importance of research.

REVIEW QUESTIONS

1. What percent of supermarket products failed in 1968 according to the New Products Action Team, Inc?

2. To what size organization is product failure generally limited?

3. To what major reason did New Products Action Team, Inc. attribute product failure?

4. Some new products fail because they are really old products in a changed container or presented in a new form. Under which major heading are such product failures categorized?

5. Define the term *mismatched product positioning.*

6. To which technical reason was the failure of *Super Natural* hair spray attributed? Describe what this classification of failure means.

7. Differentiate between *insignificant product difference* and *no difference.*

8. What was probably the major reason for the tremendous losses suffered by Vote, Fact, and Cue toothpastes?

9. Why is poor product performance continually decreasing as a reason for product failure?

10. If a manufacturer is successful in the production and distribution of TV's is it likely that he will also be successful in the marketing of frozen foods? Defend your position.

11. When planning the introduction of a new product, costs are generally analyzed with great care. For what reasons, then, might cost be attributed to the product's failure?

12. Do you agree that good products can fail because of inadequate sales efforts? Why?

13. What were initially the main two reasons for the inclusion of a new medium-priced automobile in the Ford family of cars?

14. Define *corporation loyalty*.

15. Which group was charged with the responsibility for determining the feasibility of producing a new medium-priced car for the Ford Motor Company?

16. What kind of research was done in connection with the styling of the Edsel?

17. Describe the prime markets that were to be the aim of the Edsel.

18. For what reasons was the Edsel handled by separate dealerships rather than as part of the existing Ford agencies?

19. What was the reason for Edsel's failure according to Ford's marketing and research director?

20. Why is it important to study product failures?

CASE PROBLEMS

Case Problem 1

For the past twenty-five years Creative Craft, Inc. has been one of the most successful manufacturers of men's dress shirts. It has consistently been a leader in the market catering to the conservatively dressed business executive. The shirts, carefully tailored and manufactured from the finest imported and domestic fabrics, retail at prices that range from eleven to eighteen dollars.

Last year Neil Parker, son of the company's founder, joined the firm. After six months with the company he presented a proposal to his father and to management that in his opinion would enormously increase Creative Craft's overall sales volume. His idea was to create an additional line of mod-type shirts that would appeal to the more modern male. His principal arguments for the new line were that young men were dressing more fashionably—as evidenced by their attire at places where suits and business shirts were standard dress—that young women's fashions had turned to a more casual pants outfit look, and that their regular shirt production was bound to decline once these younger people reached the levels of employment to which Creative Craft catered.

After considerable deliberation the company decided to go after the new market. Prices were to retail from seven to twelve dollars so that the younger, less-affluent male could afford their new product. Creative Craft was to be used as the label for the new line, rather than a new name, since Creative Craft was so well known that it would immediately be recognized in advertisements and in store displays. Similarly, because of their tremendous experience, the same advertising staff and sales force would be used to promote and sell the new line. Production would start at the same plant that produced the regular line of shirts because of the excellent quality control that had been established there.

Soon afterwards production was underway, but although it was evident that other firms were successfully selling mod shirts, Creative Craft's new line never seemed to get off the ground. The stores did not accept the new line enthusiastistically. It was decided that production would cease. The mod line was a flop that amounted to a financial loss of ninety thousand dollars.

Questions

1. In which category would this failure belong according to the general classifications of product failure?
2. Analyzing the situation, what mistakes did Creative Craft make?
3. Could the new product have been successful? How?

Case Problem 2

Clean-Rite, manufacturers of soaps and detergents, decided to promote a new product. Since all existing detergents were either in liquid or powder form and needed measuring when used by the housewife, it was supposed that the new product would capture the market. Clean-Rite's product-research team developed a capsule that would hold the exact amount of detergent necessary for an average washing load. The capsule was similar to those used for vitamins. When adding the capsule—accurately premeasured and filled by the company—to the wash, the shell would disintegrate, thus dispensing the detergent. The advantage to the housewife would be the elimination of measuring the detergent. After sufficient advertising and sales efforts, the new product went into production.

Although the product was enthusiastically received by the stores, house-wives rejected it. It was soon withdrawn, with an estimated loss of $350,000 to Clean-Rite.

Questions

1. Which general classification do you believe accounted for the product's failure?
2. What could have been some of the housewives' complaints?
3. How might the company have prevented such a fiasco from the beginning?

BIBLIOGRAPHY

Angelus, Theodore L., "New Product Payout," *Marketing/Communications,* October, 1969.

———, "Why Most New Products Fail," *Marketing Insights,* May 12, 1969.

Alexander, R. S., "The Death and Burial of Sick Products," in J. Howard Westing and George Albaum, *Modern Marketing Thought.* Toronto: Macmillan Co. of Canada, Ltd., 1969.

Berg, Thomas L., *Mismarketing, Case Histories of Marketing Misfires.* Garden City, N.Y.: Doubleday & Company, Inc., 1970.

O'Meara, John T., Jr., "Selecting Profitable Products," reprinted from *Harvard Business Review* in Charles J. Dirksen, Arthur Kroeger, and Lawrence C.

Lockley, *Readings in Marketing*. Homewood, Ill.: Richard D. Irwin, Inc., 1968.

Reihing, Joseph M., "The Impact of Consumer Research at Ford from the Edsel to the Mustang." Unpublished MBA thesis, Saint John's University, May 25, 1966.

Reynolds, William R., "The Edsel Ten Years Later," *Marketing Insights,* Vol. 2, No. 11 (December 11, 1967).

Stanton, William J., *Fundamentals of Marketing,* 3rd ed. New York: McGraw-Hill Book Company, 1971.

Talley, Walter J., "Profiting from the Declining Product," in Ralph Day, *Concepts for Modern Marketing.* Scranton, Pa.: International Textbook Company, 1968.

Wasson, Chester R., "What Is New about a New Product," in Robert J. Holloway, and Robert S. Hancock, *The Environment of Marketing Behavior,* 2d ed. New York: John Wiley & Sons, Inc., 1969.

A MARKETING APPLICATION

19

INTRODUCTION

Throughout this text, the various traditional approaches to the study of marketing have been employed. Specifically those used were the functional approach (the study of specialized marketing activities, such as buying and selling), the institutional approach (the study of the middlemen and agencies involved in the distribution of goods, such as wholesalers and retailers), and the commodity approach (the study of a product and its movement from its inception to its sale). A more intensified, detailed examination of one particular product can help students to better comprehend marketing in all its functions. Thus, this chapter was included. It might be classified traditionally as the commodity approach to marketing.

SELECTION OF THE PRODUCT

Many products were considered before one was selected. Among the criteria for the product were:

1. It should be a consumer product, which can be easier understood than an industrial product.

2. It should have proven successful, so that its study would be more meaningful.

3. It should be of a consumer-goods classification that students would immediately recognize.

4. It should have very wide appeal.

Many products met these criteria, but the one chosen for thorough analysis was Ford Motor Company's Mustang. A significant reason for the selection was that the Mustang's astounding success came on the heels of the enormous failure by the same company, the Edsel. It is not unusual for companies to have experienced both product successes and failures. To provide a basis for comparison between a successful product and a failure, an overview of the short-lived Edsel and why it failed was presented in Chapter 18.

MARKETING THE MUSTANG

With the Edsel debacle fresh in mind, Ford exercised extreme caution in the development of new automobiles. The Edsel's failure was attributed in part to insufficient marketing research. Therefore, all scientific marketing techniques were employed in the creation of the new car, called the Mustang.

Determining a Market

Before such factors as style, price, and so on could be estimated, it was necessary to determine whether or not there was a market for a new automobile and, if so, what kind of market it would be. In 1959 the auto industry had introduced its compact cars in response to customer demand for economy transportation. Studying its own Falcon and Chevrolet's Corvair, Ford's research team noted certain important facts. Although customers bought the compacts, many were enthusiastically adding accessories to the basic automobile, thus boosting the price and indicating that perhaps economy was not all that was sought. Additional investigation of the Corvair proved that customers wanted luxury features in their compact auto. Chevrolet dressed up the Corvair with bucket seats and some other sporty features and called it the Corvair Monza. This car was a tremendous success in terms of sales. The study of these two cars brought into view that there was an obvious gap to be filled in the automobile industry. Besides this, there was the success of the foreign sports cars to be considered. At a time when it was believed that nothing but economy was wanted by the public, the European sports automobiles were making an impact on the American auto market. From these observations, Ford's marketing research team set out to discover exactly what the consumer wanted. Dr. Seymour Marshak, Ford's marketing research manager, perhaps summed up the situation of the time: "They seemed to want economy, no matter what they had to pay for it."

THE STATE OF THE MARKET. Early in 1961 Ford Motor Company observed with considerable interest a number of new, particularly important, sociological and economic developments in three distinct areas.

First, the World War II babies were entering the automobile market. According to all indications, buyers aged eighteen to thirty-four would account for more than 50 percent of the increase in sales of new automobiles projected for the coming decade. In addition, this market would account for the majority of the purchases of used cars. It was obvious that the young buyers would be a significant factor in the auto market. Research also showed that youth had certain specialized demands about style and performance. For example, studies revealed that 36 percent of all people under twenty-five liked the four-speed floor shift; among those twenty-five only 9 percent preferred to shift gears. Another preference of the younger group was buckets (35 percent of the young people), whereas only 13 percent of the older group liked bucket seats. An interesting early study was conducted by Ford to determine whether or not college students considered bucket seats a hindrance to romance. The results of a survey conducted in eight cities throughout the United States indicated that 42 percent preferred them on first dates in comparison with 15 percent preference of couples going steady. It was evident that the young people were seeking an automobile with a sporty flair.

A second development that was affecting the market was education. In addition to the expectation of more young people in the market, there was the certainty that they would be better educated. In 1960 there were 3.5 million students enrolled in colleges. The prediction for 1970 was double that figure. Bearing this in mind, the company had to be prepared to appeal to a better-educated buyer. Ford's market research showed consistently that college graduates purchase significantly more automobiles than less-educated people. (A study taken in 1964 substantiates this point. Nineteen percent of the population had some college education; this segment of the population bought 46 percent of all the new cars sold in the United States that year.) Aside from the statistics showing a correlation between car purchasing and education, people, in general, were becoming more sophisticated through the enormous influence of television.

A third factor leading to Ford's decision to produce the Mustang was the tremendous increase in the number of multiple-car buyers. In 1959 more than one million families owned more than one car, a number which research men believed would increase in the 1960s. In 1964 multiple-car owners exceeded thirteen million; by 1967 two million families owned three automobiles.

The increasing affluence of the consumer contributed to this growth in multiple-car ownership. Market research went on to predict that this increase in affluence was to continue. This forecast, too, had been substantiated in the last decade and family earnings are expected to keep rising. Women also played an influential role in multiple-auto ownership. Studies showed that the number of women drivers had grown for the period from 1956 to 1962 by 53 percent. They demanded a second car for themselves, and research indicated the type of automobiles they desired. They were interested in ease of parking and handling, a smaller size (because only the first car in the family must be capable of transporting the entire family) and attractive styling.

From the foregoing extensive research, it was obvious to the Ford Motor Company that the ordinary automobile would not suffice. Two criteria, essential to the success of the new car, stood out. The car had to be attractive, with a distinct personality, and the price had to be appropriate for the potential young market.

Creation of the Style

A task force of Ford designers, engineers, and product planners intially set down the concept of an experimental sports car. It was a two-seater, obviously inappropriate for appeal to a mass market. Ford learned with the two-passenger Thunderbird that the market for two-passenger automobiles is too limited to ensure the volume needed to make the new car a success. Research indicated that Ford could not expect to exceed 40,000 units a year for two-passenger models, whereas the figure for a four-passenger auto was as high as 150,000.

A prototype of the original Mustang (see Figure 19–1) was placed on exhibition at the Watkins Glen Grand Prix in the fall of 1962, creating tremendous excitement. Subsequent showings at various colleges drew enormous, enthusiastic crowds. This reaction of admiration coupled with the research statistics regarding potential sales of four-passenger models led Ford to believe that it had the right insights into the production of its new car. The incorporation of the flair of the original two seater-into a four-seater could create a car for both personal and family use that would deal with potential success. While extensive market research continued, spot information and detailed results flowed into Lee Iacocca's (Ford Motor Company vice-president and general manager of the Ford division) office, where they were questioned, challenged, and digested. In those days it was called the T–5 project and it was the topic of brainstorming for the entire executive staff. As various T–5 versions came off the drawing boards, market research looked at them through the eyes of consumer panels asking, Which automotive company would produce a car like this? How much do you think such a car would cost? What don't you like about it? Would you buy it? What would you use it for?

Figure 19–1

Time was a factor at this point because Ford wanted an automobile ready for display at the World's Fair that was scheduled to open in April, 1964. It was felt that this setting would provide a dramatic showcase for the première showing of the Mustang.

A crash program was initiated to arrive at an acceptable design. Designers of the corporate-projects studio, the Ford studio and the Lincoln-Mercury studio were given dimensions and desirable features as indicated through research and were asked to engage in open competition, with a two-week limit, for the presentation of clay models of their design ideas. Seven designs were submitted and reviewed at the end of the two-week period. One model stood out distinctly, although many of them were considered to be excellent. After continuous study the Ford planners felt that the car—distinguished by a sportly air—that was produced by the Ford studio (see Figure 19–2) was the one. In order to satisfy themselves that they chose the best model, selected groups of potential customers were invited to inspect the seven models. Careful observations of reactions were recorded and an analysis was made of the opinions expressed. The response confirmed management's decision to produce the design of the Ford studio. It was felt, at this time, that this model supplied what the market lacked.

Figure 19–2

The next step was to prove out the engineering feasibility of the project. The car stood up well under these tests.

It was determined that the Mustang would offer a wide selection of options and engines. This enabled the automobile to satisfy a large variety of tastes. The luxury buyer could satisfy himself with a number of extras, whereas the young buyer, with a more limited budget, would be able to afford the standard Mustang and would still be satisfied because of its sporty appearance.

Pricing

Having determined through research that the fastest-growing, best-spending segment of the car-buying public consisted of sixteen- to twenty-four-year olds, high-school and college students, young marrieds, and young working people, the most important question to be answered was how much this group was willing to pay for the car. It was Seymour Marshak's (marketing research manager) contention that these people would still have low earning power. He felt that a car was needed that would offer the performance and flair of the highly successful Thunderbird and a price tag in the vicinity of the Falcon.

The price was established along lines similar to those used to set the price for the Model-T Ford when it was originally introduced. That is, first determine what the potential customer is willing to pay for the car, then develop the specifications around that price.

Marketing research asked customers how much they were willing to spend on a new automobile. The studies were conducted among young people and young marrieds, the target market as earlier indicated. Tabulation and analysis of the data collected indicated that the price could not exceed twenty-five hundred dollars. Bearing this in mind, production was organized to create an automobile in that price class.

Consequently, the Mustang was to be priced in an area of the industry that accounted for 22 percent of sales. This figured to almost 2 million units annually. At this price, it was also within a two to three hundred dollar range of an area that accounted for 63 percent of the industry. In terms of units, this meant 4.5 million, based on 1963 figures.

Ford, after weighing and measuring the many pricing factors, decided to sell the Mustang as a one-standard model for $2,368, F.O.B. Detroit. The price included many features that are often extras on automobiles, such as bucket seats, padded instrument panel, full wheel covers, wall-to-wall carpeting, cigarette lighter, turn signals, heater, front armrests, and seat belts.

The specifications for the Mustang that evolved from the marketing research data were as follows:

WEIGHT: Not more than 2,500 lbs
LENGTH: Not more than 180 inches
ENGINE: Peppy six-cylinder
SEATING: Four passengers, bucket seats
PERSONALITY: Demure enough for churchgoing, racy enough for the drag strip, and modish enough for the country club.

Continuous Market Analysis

The research did not cease with the decision to produce the Mustang. There was a continuous study of the potential market. Ford made a series of studies to make sure it was on the right track.

Early in 1963, it conducted a study to check its evaluations of the impact of car sizes and related features on prospective new-car buyers. In February and March additional pricing studies were made. These were rechecked with further special pricing studies in August.

Studies to select a name came in mid-1963. These were put off because it was deemed unnecessary to select a name until the actual production of the automobile was completed. Several marketing-research studies were used to determine the name of the new car. John Conley of the J. Walter Thompson Advertising Agency collected six thousand names from the Detroit public library. After conducting consumer research to check the image that certain names convey, the list was narrowed to a few finalists. These were Colt, Bronco, Mustang, Puma, Cheetah, and Cougar. Cougar was to be the new automobile's name. It was not until near the end that it was discovered that this name belonged to and was controlled by another company.

The name that Henry Ford wanted, *T-Bird III,* was not acceptable to the other executives. The name *Mustang* was finally chosen by the executive group because of its image established in the consumer-research studies. A spokesman for the J. Walter Thompson Agency stated, "it had the excitement of the wide open spaces and was American as all hell."

In September, 1963, a special styling clinic was conducted to recheck the styling decision. It had occurred to the Ford people that, although the Mustang was developed primarily to fit the young and multiple-automobile market, it was sufficiently exciting to attract additional prospects from other segments of the consumer market. Accordingly, when a prototype of the Mustang was completed, fifty-two couples who had preteen children and who owned a single standard-size automobile were selected at random to come to the Ford studio in small groups to see the new car. Although their immediate reactions were enthusiastic in every respect, the observers agreed that the car was impractical for their own needs. When, however, they were asked to estimate the selling price of the Mustang, most of the couples made guesses that were in excess of a thousand dollars higher than the intended selling price. Upon being told of the actual price, by and large, they changed their viewpoints. Second looks seemed to bring to the surface many reasons why the car was really practical for their needs, after all.

Curiously, none of the fifty-two couples in this aspect of the research questioned the car's performance or handling. The car had a performance look about it and that seemed to be sufficient.

These and other studies helped Ford to pinpoint the buying attitudes toward which a marketing campaign could be aimed. Approval had already been given to the car's styling, it possessed a performance look, the low price appealed to couples with children, who were not previously considered part of Mustang's market, and the wide complement of options made the car suitable for luxury-, sport-, or economy-oriented prospective customers.

The continuous analysis of the market did, indeed, provide wider horizons for the Mustang than originally anticipated.

Promotion of the Mustang

Introduction day was scheduled for April 17, 1964, approximately three years after the actual planning of the Mustang began. This is considerable lead time, in terms of most products; however, it is not uncommon in the automobile industry, where it is essential to determine the needs of the market several years in advance.

Four days prior to the public's introduction to the Mustang, a special press preview took place in the Ford Pavillion at the New York World's Fair. The immediate reaction of the press was enthusiastic. Besides just showing the new automobile to the press, Ford did something that was rather innovative. One hundred twenty-four reporters were paired and given Mustangs, complete with rally instructions, that took them 750 miles to Detroit. This activity turned the reporters' original enthusiasm into delight, which was soon expressed by the members of the press in their respective publications. The generous praise that ensued in an example of the publicity that can result from an effective promotional campaign. Cover stories were provided by *Time* and *Newsweek,* with *Life* and *Look* carrying editorials concerning the new car.

On April 16 the Mustang was shown, simultaneously on the three major television networks, to twenty-nine million homes. This was the first time that a major automotive company was on all networks at the same time.

On the following day the Mustang announcement, shown in Figure 19–3, was printed in more than twenty-six hundred newspapers in approximately twenty-two hundred markets. The theme that was used "Presenting the Unexpected"...was underscoring the *unexpected* in styling and low price. Similar to the technique used in catalogs, the ad listed just what the purchaser would recived for $2,368 and what options could be added. The ad was evaluated by the million-market newspapers' reports as having achieved the highest readership score recorded by a full-page color advertisement. It should be noted that successful ads are not just accidental happenings. An enormous amount of effort went into the creation of the ads that

Figure 19–3

Figure 19-3 (cont.)

were used by Ford for the Mustang's introduction. With the help of the J. Walter Thompson Advertising Agency these ads shown in Figure 19–4, 19–5, and 19–6 were designed; they were used in the World's Fair Guide, 1964, the *Ladies Home Journal,* and *Look* magazine, respectively. These ads emphasized design, performance, and price.

In addition to the regular newspaper ads, a special announcement directed to the female market was run on the women's pages the same day. This ad highlighted the "Tiffany award for excellence in design" that had been bestowed upon the Mustang, the first automobile that ever was the recipient of such an award. Since Tiffany meant, to most women, the epitome of elegance, the tie-in was extremely effective. It was estimated that 75 percent of all households in the United States were covered through the newspaper medium.

In an effort to capture the attention of as large a part of the reading public as possible, a Mustang announcement was placed in twenty-four of the nation's largest circulated magazines. The total circulation of these magazines was 68 million. Ford used two- and four-page color spreads to introduce its new automobile to the public.

Although TV, radio, newspapers, and magazines are considered to be the most important advertising media for the introduction of automobiles, Ford felt that no group or promotional device should be neglected in this campaign. The publishing and distribution of a 48-page Mustang introduction-plans book recapped the advertising and merchandising plans for the local dealers. It also provided local agencies with a plan to capture their own areas. Included in this package were registration lists of owners of late-model Fords and competitive automobiles. This provided a list of prospects who might be potential purchasers. In order to capitalize on direct-mail advertising, three million color postcards were sent to the dealers for further distribution. It was also suggested, in the plans book, that pre-introduction parties be hosted for such groups as service-station and independent-garage operators. Word-of-mouth advertising from this group would provide other valuable means of getting the message to the consumer.

Dealer showrooms were provided with a variety of Mustang pictures, mobiles, window-trim material, and posters (See Figure 19–7) to be used to attract the customer at the point of purchase.

To culminate the promotional campaign, Ford dealers were given materials for use in a "Win-a-Mustang" contest. With this device, the agencies were able to obtain the names of over three million potential customers who could be followed up after the initial introductory excitement died down.

The major emphasis in the promotion of the Mustang was exposure to as many people as possible. To achieve this, Mustangs were placed at fifteen major airport terminals from New York to San Francisco and at

FORD MUSTANG HARDTOP

New Ford Mustang–$2368* ^{f.o.b.} Detroit

This is the car you never expected from Detroit. Mustang is so distinctively beautiful, it's the first car to receive the Tiffany Award for Excellence in American Design.

*Yet Mustang carries a suggested retail price of just $2368–f.o.b. Detroit, not including destination charges from Detroit, options, state and local taxes and fees, if any. Whitewall tires are $33.90 extra.

At $2368, Mustang includes luxuries like bucket seats, vinyl upholstery, wall-to-wall carpeting as standard equipment. *And* there's a fabulous range of reasonably priced options!

See Mustang while you're at the Fair . . . and ride Walt Disney's incredible *Magic Skyway* at the beautiful Ford Pavilion.

TRY <u>TOTAL PERFORMANCE</u>
FOR A CHANGE!

Mustang · Falcon · Fairlane
Ford · Thunderbird

Figure 19–4

This is your car, the Mustang. As gentle a car
as you ever drove. So elegant it makes every other car
anywhere near its low price look homemade.
Mustang is amazingly easy to handle. Moves as light
and sure as a very good dancer.
Parks on a penny. If you're thinking about
a new car this year, think about this one.
Mustang.

TRY TOTAL PERFORMANCE
FOR A CHANGE!

FORD

Mustang · Falcon · Fairlane · Ford · Thunderbird

RIDE WALT DISNEY'S MAGIC SKYWAY AT THE   FORD MOTOR COMPANY'S WONDER ROTUNDA · NEW YORK WORLD'S FAIR

Figure 19–5

New Ford Mustang

$2368 *f.o.b. Detroit

This is the car you never expected from Detroit. Mustang is so distinctively beautiful it has received the Tiffany Award for Excellence in American Design ... the first time an automobile has been honored with the Tiffany Gold Medal.

You can own the Mustang hardtop for a suggested retail price of just $2,368—f.o.b. Detroit. *This does not include destination charges from Detroit, options, state and local taxes and fees, if any. Whitewall tires are $33.90 extra.

Every Mustang includes these luxury features unavailable—or available only at extra cost—in most other cars: bucket seats; wall-to-wall carpeting; all-vinyl upholstery; padded instrument panel; and full wheel covers. Also standard: floor-shift; courtesy lights; sports steering wheel; front arm rests; a 170 cu. in. Six, and much more.

That's the Mustang hardtop. With its four-passenger roominess and surprisingly spacious trunk, it will be an ideal car for many families. Yet Mustang is designed to be designed by you. For instance, the trip to the supermarket can be a lot more fun when you add convenience options like power brakes or steering, Cruise-O-Matic transmission, push-button radio, 260 cu. in. V-8.

Or, you can design Mustang to suit your special taste for elegance with such luxury refinements as: air conditioning; vinyl-covered roof; full-length console; accent paint-stripe, and convertible with power top.

If you're looking for action, Mustang's the place to find it, with a 289 cu. in. V-8; 4-speed fully synchronized transmission; Rally-Pac (tachometer and clock) and other exciting options.

For an authentic scale model of the new Ford Mustang, send $1.00 to Mustang Offer, Department B-1, P.O. Box 35, Troy, Michigan. (Offer ends July 31, 1964)

TRY TOTAL PERFORMANCE
FOR A CHANGE!

FORD

Mustang · Falcon · Fairlane · Ford · Thunderbird

RIDE WALT DISNEY'S MAGIC SKYWAY AT THE FORD MOTOR COMPANY'S WONDER ROTUNDA, NEW YORK WORLD'S FAIR

Figure 19–6

A totally new kind of total performance car

Figure 19–7

seventy high-traffic locations in major cities across the country. Mustangs were on display in two hundred Holiday Inns, either in the lobbies or in their main entrances. Even people traveling by automobile at the time of introduction, who might not be exposed through the other media, were given glimpses of the Mustang on billboards in approximately 170 markets.

Introduction Day

With all aspects of the promotion meshing together, introduction day, April 17, 1964, saw Ford dealers literally swamped with traffic. Approximately four million people visited Ford dealerships to see the Mustang.

Within four months, more than one hundred thousand Mustangs were sold, making it one of the top five automobiles in sales volume.

IMPORTANT POINTS IN THE CHAPTER

1. The study of marketing traditionally encompasses any of three approaches: the functional, the institutional, and the commodity approach. The study of the Mustang employs the commodity approach.

2. Before any attention could be paid to style or price, Ford executives first determined whether or not they had a market for a new automobile.

3. The market in the early 1960s had three important areas for Ford to consider. First, millions of World War II babies were coming of age and would become potential automobile users. Second, the

certainty of a better-educated public, and third, the tremendous increase in the number of multiple-car buyers.

4. The ultimate style of the Mustang evolved from an original two-seater concept, which was deemed inappropriate for mass appeal.

5. The price was determined by first finding out what the potential buyer would pay and then developing specifications around the price.

6. After it was decided to produce the Mustang, additional research continued. Such areas as car sizes, pricing, and names were studied.

7. Promotion of the Mustang employed the broadcast and periodical media, coupled with a number of special events, such as introduction at the World's Fair, a 750-mile drive by the press, and a consumer contest.

8. Introduction day attracted an enormous amount of potential buyers; one hundred thousand cars were sold in the first four months.

REVIEW QUESTIONS

1. Define *the functional approach* to the study of marketing.
2. How does the institutional approach differ from the commodity approach?
3. Prior to the study of style and price, what did Ford investigate?
4. What did the study of the Corvair teach the Ford executives?
5. Initially it was thought that which market would account for the 50 percent increase in automobile sales in the sixties?
6. Why did Ford study the attitude of college students toward bucket seats?
7. Why was the certainty that the future would see a better-educated population an important factor for Ford management?
8. Aside from style, what characteristics were preferred by the potential female market for automobiles?
9. Discuss how the style of the Mustang was chosen.
10. For what reason was the original early design of Ford's new car scrapped?
11. The options and types of engines of the Mustang were to be extensive. Why?
12. Pricing was set along lines similar to those used for the Model-T Ford. Which system was employed?
13. Describe the "personality" of the Mustang, according to Ford.
14. How was the name *Mustang* finally selected?
15. Research showed that the Mustang would attract still another market besides the young and multiple-automobile one; which market?
16. What unusual role did the press play in Mustang's introduction?

17. What "first" did Ford engage in when introducing the Mustang on TV at a time that television was already considered commonplace for automobile advertising?

18. Which advertising agency engineered Mustang's campaign?

19. How were automobile drivers made aware of the Mustang at its time of introduction?

20. Discuss the importance of the "Win-a-Mustang" contest for dealers.

BIBLIOGRAPHY

Booth, Gene, "Developing the Mustang: Styling," *Car Life* (special ed.), pp. 11-16.

Boyd, Robert, "The Mustang—A Planned Miracle," *Detroit Free Press,* December 6, 1964.

Bronn, Robert, "The Careful Breeding of a Mustang," *Sales Management,* Vol. 94, No. 1 (January 1, 1965).

Marshak, Seymour, Text of Speech before the Regional New-Products Marketing Conference of the Detroit Chapter of the American Marketing Association, March 17, 1966. (Dr. Marshak is marketing-research director for the Ford Motor Company.)

"The Mustang—A New Breed Out of Detroit," *Newsweek,* Vol. 63, No. 16 (April 20, 1964).

Reihing, Joseph M., "The Impact of Consumer Research at Ford from the Edsel to the Mustang." Unpublished Master's thesis, Saint John's University, May, 1966.

APPENDIX:
MARKETING DEFINITIONS

The following is a glossary of marketing terms that has been prepared by the Committee on Definitions of the American Marketing Association.[1]

A

Accessories– See **Equipment.**

Advertising– Any paid form of non-personal presentation and promotion of ideas, goods, or services by an identified sponsor. It involves the use of such media as the following:

> Magazine and newspaper space
> Motion pictures
> Outdoor (posters, signs, skywriting, etc.)
> Direct mail
> Novelties (calendars, blotters, etc.)
> Radio and television
> Cards (car, but, etc.)
> Catalogues
> Directories and references
> Programs and menus
> Circulars

This list is intended to be illustrative, not inclusive.

Comment. Advertising is generally but not necessarily carried on through mass media. While the postal system is not technically considered a "paid" medium, material distributed by mail is definitely a form of presentation that is paid for by the sponsor. For kindred activities see **Publicity** and **Sales Promotion.**

Advertising Research– See **Marketing Research.**

Agent– A business unit which negotiates purchases or sales or both but does not take title to the goods in which it deals.

---

[1] Ralph S. Alexander, Chairman, and Committee on Definitions of the American Marketing Association, "Marketing Definitions," 1960.

Comment. The agent usually performs fewer marketing functions than does the merchant. He commonly receives his remuneration in the form of a commission or fee. He usually does not represent both buyer and seller in the same transaction.

Examples are: broker, commission merchant, manufacturers agent, selling agent, and resident buyer.

The Committee recommends that the term Functional Middleman no longer be applied to this type of agent. It is hardly logical or consistent in view of the fact that he performs fewer marketing functions than other middlemen.

Assembling– The activities involved in concentrating supplies or assortments of goods or services to facilitate sale or purchase.

Comment. The concentration involved here may affect a quantity of like goods or a variety of goods. It includes the gathering of adequate and representative stocks by wholesalers and retailers.

Automatic Selling– The retail sale of goods or services through currency operated machines activated by the ultimate-consumer buyer.

Comment. Most, if not all, machines now used in automatic selling are coin operated. There are reports, however, of promising experiments with such devices that may be activated by paper currency; machines that provide change for a dollar bill are already on the market.

Auxiliary Equipment– See **Equipment.**

B

Branch House (Manufacturer's)– An establishment maintained by a manufacturer, detached from the headquarters establishment and used primarily for the purpose of stocking, selling, delivering, and servicing his product.

Branch Office (Manufacturer's)– An establishment maintained by a manufacturer, detached from the headquarters establishment and used for the purpose of selling his products or providing service.

Comment. The characteristic of the branch house that distinguishes it from the branch office is the fact that it is used in the physical storage, handling, and delivery of merchandise. Otherwise the two are identical.

Branch Store– A subsidiary retailing business owned and operated at a separate location by an established store.

Brand– A name, term, sign, symbol, or design, or a combination of them which is intended to identify the goods or services of one seller or group of sellers and to differentiate them from those of competitors.

Comment. A brand may include a brand name, a trade mark, or both. The term brand is sufficiently comprehensive to include practically all means of identification except perhaps the package and the shape of the product. All brand names and all trade marks are brands or parts of brands but not all brands are either brand names or trade marks. Brand is the inclusive general term. The others are more particularized.

See also **National Brand** and **Private Brand.**

Brand Manager– See **Product Management.**

Brand Name– A brand or part of a brand consisting of a word, letter, group of words or letters comprising a name which is intended to identify the goods or services of a seller or a group of sellers and to differentiate them from those of competitors.

Comment. The brand name is that part of a brand which can be vocalized—the utterable.

Broker– An agent who does not have direct physical control of the goods in which he deals but represents either buyer or seller in negotiating purchases or sales for his principal.

Comment. The broker's powers as to prices and terms of sale are usually limited by his principal.

The term is often loosely used in a generic sense to include such specific business units as free-lance brokers, manufacturer's agents, selling agents, and purchasing agents.

Buying Power– See **Purchasing Power.**

C

Canvasser– See **House-to-House Salesman.**

Cash and Carry Wholesaler– See **Wholesaler.**

Chain Store–

Chain Store System– A group of retail stores of essentially the same type, centrally owned and with some degree of centralized control of operation. The term Chain Store may also refer to a single store as a unit of such a group.

Comment. According to the dictionary, two may apparently be construed to constitute a "group."

Channel of Distribution– The structure of intra-company organization units and extra-company agents and dealers, wholesale and retail, through which a commodity, product, or service is marketed.

Comment. This definition was designed to be broad enough to include (a.) both a firm's internal marketing organization units and the outside busines units it uses in its marketing work and (b.) both the channel structure of the individual firm and the entire complex available to all firms.

Commercial Auction– An agent business unit which effects the sale of goods through an auctioneer, who, under specified rules, solicits bids or offers from buyers and has power to accept the highest bids of responsible bidders and, thereby, consummates the sale.

Comment. The autioneer usually but not always is a paid employee of an auction company which is in the business of conducting auctions.

Commission House (sometimes called Commission Merchant)– An agent who usually exercises physical control over and negotiates the sale of the goods he handles. The commission house usually enjoys broader powers as to prices, methods, and terms of sale than does the broker although it must obey instructions issued by the principal. It generally arranges delivery, extends necessary credit, collects, deducts its fees, and remits the balance to the principal.

Comment. Most of those who have defined the commission house state that it has possession of the goods it handles. In its strict meaning the word "possession" connotes to some extent the idea of ownership; in its legal meaning it involves a degree of control somewhat beyond that usually enjoyed by the commission merchant. Therefore the phrase, "physical control," was used instead.

The fact that many commission houses are not typical in their operations does not subtract from their status as commission houses.

Commissary Store– See **Industrial Store.**

Commodity Exchange– An organization usually owned by the member-traders, which provides facilities for bringing together buyers and sellers of specified commodities, or their agents, for promoting trades, either spot or futures or both, in these commodities.

Comment. Agricultural products or their intermediately processed derivatives are the commodities most often traded on such exchanges. Some sort of organization for clearing future contracts usually operates as an adjunct to or an arm of a commodity exchange.

Company Store– See **Industrial Store.**

Consumer Research– See **Marketing Research.**

Consumers' Cooperative– A retail business owned and operated by ultimate consumers to purchase and distribute goods and services primarily to the membership—sometimes called purchasing cooperatives.

Comment. The Consumers' Cooperative is a type of cooperative marketing institution. Through federation, retail units frequently acquire wholesaling and manufacturing institutions. The definition confines the use of the term to the cooperative purchasing activities of ultimate consumers and does not embrace collective buying by business establishments or institutions.

Consumers' Goods– Goods destined for use by ultimate consumers or households and in such form that they can be used without commercial processing.

Comment. Certain articles, for example, typewriters, may be either consumers' goods or industrial goods depending upon whether they are destined for use by the ultimate consumer or household or by an industrial, business, or institutional user.

Convenience Goods– Those consumers' goods which the customer usually purchases frequently, immediately, and with the minimum of effort in comparison and buying.

Examples of merchandise customarily bought as convenience goods are; tobacco products, soap, newspapers, magazines, chewing gum, small packaged confections, and many food products.

Comment. These articles are usually of small unit value and are bought in small quantities at any one time, although when a number of them are bought together as in a supermarket, the combined purchase may assume sizeable proportions in both bulk and value.

The convenience involved may be in terms of nearness to the buyer's home, easy accessibility to some means of transport, or close proximity to places where people go during the day or evening, for example, downtown to work.

Cooperative Marketing– The process by which independent producers, wholesalers, retailers, consumers, or combinations of them act collectively in buying or selling or both.

D

Dealer– A firm that buys and resells merchandise at either retail or wholesale.

Comment. The term is naturally ambiguous. For clarity, it should be used with a qualifying adjective, such as "retail" or "wholesale."

Department Store– A large retailing business unit which handles a wide variety of shopping and specialty goods, including women's ready-to-wear and accessories, men's and boy's wear, piece goods, small wares, and home furnishings, and which is organized into separate departments for purposes of promotion, service and control.

Examples of very large department stores are Macy's, New York, J. L. Hudson Co. of Detroit, Marshall Field & Co. of Chicago, and Famous, Barr of St. Louis. Two well-known smaller ones are Bresee's of Oneonta, New York, and A. B. Wycoff of Stoudsburg, Penn.

Comment. Many department stores have become units of chains, commonly called "ownership groups" since each store retains its local identity, even though centrally owned.

The definition above stress three elements: large size, wide variety of clothing and home furnishings, and departmentization. Size is not spelled out in terms of either sales volume or number of employees, since the concept keeps changing upwards. Most department stores in 1960 had sales in excess of one million dollars.

Direct Selling– The process whereby the firm responsible for production sells to the user, ultimate consumer, or retailer without intervening middlemen.

The Committee recommends that when this term is used, it be so qualified as to indicate clearly the precise meaning intended (direct to retailer, direct to user, direct to ultimate consumer, etc.).

Comment. The phrase "firm responsible for production" is substituted for "producer" in the old definition so as to include the firm that contracts out some or all of the processes of making the goods it sells direct, for example the drug house that has its vitamin pills tableted by a contractor specializing in such work.

Discount House– A retailing business unit, featuring consumer durable items, competing on a basis of price appeal, and operating on a relatively low markup and with a minimum of customer service.

Discretionary Fund– Discretionary income enlarged by the amount of new credit extensions, which also may be deemed spendable as a result of consumer decision relatively free of prior commitment or pressure of need.

Comment. These are the definitions of the National Industrial Conference Board, which publishes a quarterly Discretionary Income Index Series. Discretionary Income is calculated by deducting from disposable personal income (a.) a computed historical level of outlays for food and clothing; (b.) all outlays for medical services, utilities, and public transportation; (c.) payment of fixed commitments, such as rent, home owner taxes, net insurance payments, and installment debt; (d.) homeowner taxes; and (e.) imputed income and income in kind.

Discretionary Income—That portion of personal income, in excess of the amount necessary to maintain a defined or historical standard of living, which may be saved with no immediate impairment of living standards or may be as a result of consumer decision relatively free of prior commitment or pressure of need.

Disposable Income– Personal income remaining after the deduction of taxes on personal income and compulsory payment, such as social security levies.

Comment. This is substantially the Department of Commerce concept.

Distribution– The Committee recommends that the term Distribution be used as synonymous with Marketing.

Comment. The term Distribution is also sometimes used to refer to the extent of market coverage.

In using this term marketing men should clearly distinguish it from the sense in which it is employed in economic theory, that is, the process of dividing the fund of value produced by industry among the several factors engaged in economic production.

For these reasons marketing men may be wise to use term sparingly.

Distribution Cost Analysis– See **Marketing Cost Analysis.**

Distributor– In its general usage, this term is synonymous with "Wholesaler."

Comment. In some trades and by many firms it is used to designate an outlet having some sort of preferential relationship with the manufacturer. This meaning is not so widely used or so standardized as to justify inclusion in the definition.

The term is sometimes used to designate a manufacturer's agent or a sales representative in the employ of a manufacturer.

Drop Shipment Wholesaler– See **Wholesaler.**

E

Equipment– Those industrial goods that do not become part of the physical product and which are exhausted only after repeated use, such as Machinery, Installed Equipment and Accessories, or Auxiliary Equipment.

Installed Equipment includes such items as boilers, linotype machines, power lathes, bank vaults.

Accessories include such items as gauges, meters, and control devices.

Auxiliary Equipment includes such items as trucks, typewriters, filing cases, and industrial hoists.

Exclusive Outlet Selling– That form of selective selling whereby sales of an article or service or brand of an article to any one type of buyer are confined to one retailer or wholesaler in each area, usually on a contractual basis.

Comment. This definition does not include the practice of designating two or more wholesalers or retailers in an area as selected outlets.

While this practice is a form of Selective Selling, it is not Exclusive Outlet Selling.

The term does not apply to the reverse contractual relationship in which a dealer must buy exclusively from a supplier.

F

Fabricating Materials– Those industrial goods which become a part of the finished product and which have undergone processing beyond that required for raw materials but not as much as finished parts.
Comment. Examples are plastic moulding compounds.

Facilitating Agencies in Marketing– Those agencies which perform or assist in the performance of one or a number of the marketing functions but which neither take title to goods nor negotiate purchases or sales. Common types are banks, railroads, storage warehouses, commodity exchanges, stock yards, insurance companies, graders and inspectors, advertising agencies, firms engaged in marketing research, cattle loan companies, furniture marts, and packers and shippers.

Factor– (1.) A specialized financial institution engaged in factoring accounts receivable and lending on the security of inventory.
(2.) A type of commission house which often advances funds to the consigner, identified chiefly with the raw cotton and naval stores trades.
Comment. The type of factor described in (1) above operates extensively in the textile field but is expanding into other fields.

Factoring– A specialized financial function whereby producers, wholesalers, and retailers sell their accounts receivable to financial institutions, including factors and banks, often on a non-recourse basis.
Comment. Commercial banks as well as factors and finance companies engage in this activity.

Fair Trade– Retail resale price maintenance imposed by suppliers of branded goods under authorization of state and federal laws.
Comment. This is a special usage of the term promulgated by the advocates of resale price maintenance and bears no relation to the fair practices concept of the Federal Trade Commission; nor is it the antithesis of unfair trading outlawed by the antitrust laws.

G

General Store– A small retailing business unit, not departmentized, usually located in a rural community and primarily engaged in selling a general assortment of merchandise of which the most important line is food, and the more important subsidiary lines are notions, apparel, farm supplies, and gasoline. These stores are often known as "country general stores."
Comment. This is roughly the Bureau of the Census usage.

Grading– Assigning predetermined standards of quality classifications to individual units or lots of a commodity.

Comment. This process of assignment may be carried on by sorting. This term is often defined so as to include the work of setting up classes or grades. This work is really a part of standardization.

H

House-to-House Salesman– A salesman who is primarily engaged in making sales direct to ultimate consumers in their homes.
Comment. The term Canvasser is often employed as synonymous with House-to-House Salesman. Due to its extensive use in fields other than marketing this usage is not recommended.

I

Independent Store– A retailing business unit which is controlled by its own individual ownership or management rather than from without, except insofar as its management is limited by voluntary group arrangements.
Comment. This definition includes a member of a voluntary group organization. It is recognized that the voluntary group possesses many of the characteristics of and presents many of the same problems as the chain store system. In the final analysis, however, the members of the voluntary groups are independent stores, cooperating, perhaps temporarily, in the accomplishment of certain marketing purposes. Their collective action is entirely voluntary and the retailers engaging in it consider themselves to be independent.

Industrial Goods– Goods which are destined to be sold primarily for use in producing other goods or rendering services as contrasted with goods destined to be sold primarily to the ultimate consumer.
They include equipment (installed and accessory), component parts, maintenance, repair and operating supplies, raw materials, fabricating materials.
Comment. The distinguishing characteristics of these goods is the purpose for which they are primarily destined to be used, in carrying on business or industrial activities rather than for consumption by individual ultimate consumers or resale to them. The category also includes merchandise destined for use in carrying on various types of institutional enterprises.
Relatively few goods are exclusively industrial goods. The same article may, under one set of circumstances, be an industrial good, and under other conditions a consumers' good.

Industrial Store– A retail store owned and operated by a company or governmental unit to sell primarily to its employees.
Non-governmental establishments of this type are often referred to as "Company Stores" or "Commissory Stores." In certain trades the term

"Company Store" is applied to a store through which a firm sells its own products, often together with those of other manufacturers, to the consumer market.

Comment. Many of these establishments are not operated for profit. The matter of the location of the control over and responsibility for these stores rather than the motive for their operation constitutes their distinguishing characteristic.

Installed Equipment– See **Epuipment.**

J

Jobber– This term is widely used as a synonym of "wholesaler" or "distributor."

Comment. The term is sometimes used in certain trades and localities to designate special types of wholesalers. This usage is especially common in the distribution of agricultural products. The characteristics of the wholesalers so designated vary from trade to trade and from locality to locality. Most of the schedules submitted to the Bureau of the Census by the members of the wholesale trades show no clear line of demarcation between those who call themselves jobbers and those who prefer to be known as wholesalers. Therefore, it does not seem wise to attempt to set up any general basis of distinction between the terms in those few trades or markets in which one exists. There are scattered examples of special distinctive usage of the term "Jobber." The precise nature of such usage must be sought in each trade or area in which it is employed.

L

Limited Function Wholesaler– See **Wholesaler.**

Loss Leader– A product of known or accepted quality priced at a loss or no profit for the purpose of attracting patronage to a store.

Comment. This term is peculiar to the retail trade—elsewhere the same item is called a "leader" or a "special."

M

Mail Order House (retail)– A retailing business that receives its orders primarily by mail or telephone and generally offers its goods and services for its sale from a catalogue or other printed material.

Comment. Other types of retail stores often conduct a mail order business, usually through departments set up for that purpose, although this fact does not make them mail order houses. On the other hand, some firms that originally confined themselves to the mail order business now also operate chain store systems. For example, Sears Roebuck and Company and Montgomery Ward and Company are both mail order houses and chain store systems.

Mail Order Wholesaler– See **Wholesaler.**

Manufacturer's Agent– An agent who generally operates on an extended contractual basis; often sells within an exclusive territory; handles non-competing but related lines of goods; and posesses limited authority with regard to prices and terms of sale. He may be authorized to sell a definite portion of his principal's output.

Comment. The manufacturer's agent has often been defined as a species of broker. In the majority of cases this seems to be substantially accurate. It is probably more accurate in seeking to define the entire group not to classify them as a specialized type of broker but to regard them as a special variety of agent since many of them carry stocks.

The term "Manufacturer's Representative" is sometimes applied to this agent. Since this term is also used to designate a salesman in the employ of a manufacturer, its use as a synonym for "Manufacturer's Agent" is discouraged.

Manufacturer's Store– A retail store owned and operated by a manufacturer, sometimes as outlets for his goods, sometimes primarily for experimental or publicity purposes.

Market– (1.) The aggregate of forces or conditions within which buyers and sellers make decisions that result in the transfer of goods and services.

(2.) The aggregate demand of the potential buyers of a commodity or service.

Comment. The business man often uses the term to mean an opportunity to sell his goods. He also often attaches to it a connotation of a geographical area, such as the "New England market," or of a customer group, such as the "college market" or the "agricultural market."

Retailers often use the term to mean the aggregate group of suppliers from whom a buyer purchases.

Market Analysis– A sub-division of marketing research which involves the measurement of the extent of a market and the determination of its characteristics.

Comment. See also Marketing Research. The activity described above consists essentially in the process of exploring and evaluating the marketing possibilities of the aggregates described in (2.) of the definition of Market.

Market Potential (also Market or Total Market)– A calculation of maximum possible sales opportunities for all sellers of a good or service during a stated period.

Market Share (or Sales Potential)– The ratio of a company's sales to the total industry sales on either an actual or potential basis.

Comment. This term is often used to designate the part of total industry sales a company hopes or expects to get. Since this concept usually has in it a considerable element of "blue sky," this usage is not encouraged.

Marketing– The performance of business activities that direct the flow of goods and services from producer to consumer or user.

Comment. The task of defining Marketing may be approached from at least three points of view.

(1.) The "legalistic" of which the following is a good example: "Marketing includes all activities having to do with effecting changes in the ownership and possession of goods and services." It seems obviously of doubtful desirability to adopt a definition which throws so much emphasis upon the legal phases of what is essentially a commercial subject.

(2.) The "economic" examples of which are:

"That part of economics which deals with the creation of time, place, and possession utilities."

"That phase of business activity through which human wants are satisfied by the exchange of goods and services for some valuable consideration."

Such definitions are apt to assume somewhat more understanding of economic concepts than are ordinarily found in the market place.

(3.) The "factual or descriptive" of which the definition suggested by the Committee is an example. This type of definition merely seeks to describe its subject in terms likely to be understood by both professional economists and business men without reference to legal or economic implications.

This definition seeks to include such facilitating activities as marketing research, transportation, certain aspects of product and package planning, and the use of credit as a means of influencing patronage.

Marketing Budget– A statement of the planned dollar sales and planned marketing costs for a specified future period.

Comment. The use of this term is sometimes confined to an estimate of future sales. This does not conform to the general use of the term "budget" which includes schedules of both receipts and expenditures. If the marketing budget is to be used as a device to facilitate marketing control and management, it should include the probable cost of getting the estimated volume of sales. The failure to allow proper weight to this item in their calculations is one of the most consistently persistent and fatal mistakes made by American business concerns. It has led to much of the striving after unprofitable volume that has been so costly.

A firm may prepare a marketing budget for each brand or product or for a group of brands or products it sells or for each group of customers to whom it markets. See also **Sales Budget.**

Marketing Cooperative– See **Producers' Cooperative Marketing.**

Marketing Cost Accounting– The branch of cost accounting which involves the allocation of marketing costs according to customers, marketing units, products, territories, or marketing activities.

Marketing Cost Analysis– The study and evaluation of the relative profitability or costs of different marketing operations in terms of customers, marketing units, commodities, territories, or marketing activities.

Comment. Marketing Cost Accounting is one of the tools used in Marketing Cost Analysis.

Marketing Function—A major specialized activity or group of related activities performed in marketing.

Comment. There is no generally accepted list of marketing functions, nor is there any generally accepted basis on which the lists compiled by various writers are chosen.

The reason for these limitations is fairly apparent. Under this term students of marketing have sought to squeeze a heterogeneous and non-consistent group of activities. Some of them are broad business functions with special marketing implications; others are peculiar to the marketing process. The function of assembling is performed through buying, selling, and transportation. Assembling, storage, and transporting are general economic functions; selling and buying are more nearly individual in character. Most of the lists fail sadly to embrace all the activities a marketing manager worries about in the course of doing his job.

Marketing Management– The planning, direction and control of the entire marketing activity of a firm or division of a firm, including the formulation of marketing objectives, policies, programs and strategy, and commonly embracing product development, organizing and staffing to carry out plans, supervising marketing operations, and controlling marketing performance.

Comment. In most firms the man who performs these functions is a member of top management in that he plays a part in determining company policy, in making product decisions, and in coordinating marketing operations with other functional activities to achieve the objectives of the company as a whole.

No definition of his position is included in this report because there is no uniformity in the titles applied to it. He is variously designated Marketing Manager, Director of Marketing, Vice President for Marketing, Director or Vice President of Marketing and Sales, General Sales Manager.

Marketing Planning– The work of setting up objectives for marketing activity and of determining and scheduling the steps necessary to achieve such objectives.

Comment. This term includes not only the work of deciding upon the goals or results to be attained through marketing activity but also the determination in detail of exactly how they are to be accomplished.

Marketing Policy– A course of action established to obtain consistency of marketing decisions and operations under recurring and essentially similar circumstances.

Marketing Research– The systematic gathering, recording, and analyzing of data about problems relating to the marketing of goods and services. Such research may be undertaken by impartial agencies or by business firms or their agents for the solution of their marketing problems.

Comment. Marketing Research is the inclusive term which embraces all research activities carried on in connection with the management of marketing work. It includes various subsidiary types of research, such as (1) Market Analysis, which is a study of the size, location, nature, and characteristics of markets, (2) Sales Analysis (or Research), which is largely an analysis of sales data, (3) Consumer Research, of which Motivation Research is a type, which is concerned chiefly with the discovery and analysis of consumer attitudes, reactions, and preferences, and (4) Advertising Research which is carried on chiefly as an aid to the management of advertising work. The techniques of Operations Research are often useful in Marketing Research.

The term Market Research is often loosely used as synonymous with Marketing Research.

Merchandising– The planning and supervision involved in marketing the particular merchandise or service at the places, times, and prices and in the quantities which will best serve to realize the marketing objectives of the business.

Comment. This term has been used in a great variety of meanings, most of them confusing. The usage recommended by the Committee adheres closely to the essential meaning of the word. The term is most widely used in this sense in the wholesaling and retailing trades. Many manufacturers designate this activity as Product Planning or Management and include in it such tasks as selecting the article to be produced or stocked and deciding such matters as the size, appearance, form, packaging, quantities to be brought or made, time of procurement, and price lines to be offered.

Merchant– A business unit that buys, takes title to, and resells merchandise.

Comment. The distinctive feature of this middleman lies in the fact that he takes title to the goods he handles. The extent to which he performs the marketing functions is incidental to the definition. Wholesalers and retailers are the chief types of merchants.

Middleman– A business concern that specializes in performing operations or rendering services directly involved in the purchase and/or sale of goods in the process of their flow from producer to consumer. Middlemen are of two types, **Merchants** and **Agents.**

Comment. The essence of the middleman's operation lies in the fact that he plays an active and prominent part in the negotiations leading up to transactions of purchase and sale. This is what distinguishes him from a Marketing Facilitating Agent who, while he performs certain marketing functions, participates only incidentally in negotiations of purchase and sale.

This term is very general in its meaning. It also possesses an unfortunate emotional content. Therefore, the Committee recommends that whenever possible more specific terms be used, such as agent, merchant, retailer, wholesaler.

Missionary Salesman– A salesman employed by a manufacturer to call on customers of his distributors, usually to develop good will and stimulate demand, to help or induce them to promote the sale of his employer's goods, to help them train their salesmen to do so, and, often, to take orders for delivery by such distributors.

Motivation Research– A group of techniques developed by the behavioral scientists which are used by marketing researchers to discover factors influencing marketing behavior.

Comment. These techniques are widely used outside the marketing sphere, for example, to discover factors influencing the behavior of employees and voters. The Committee has confined its definition to the marketing uses of the tool.

Motivation Research is only one of several ways to study marketing behavior.

N

National Brand– A manufacturer's or producer's brand, usually enjoying wide territorial distribution.

Comment. The usage of the terms National Brand and Private Brand in this report, while generally current and commonly accepted, is highly illogical and non-descriptive. But since it is widespread and persistent, the Committee embodies it in this report.

P

Personal Selling– Oral presentation in a conversation with one or more prospective purchasers for the purpose of making sales.

Comment. This definition contemplates that the presentation may be either formal, (as a "canned" sales talk), or informal, although it is rather likely to be informal, either in the actual presence of the customer or by telephone although usually the former, either to an individual or to a small group, although usually the former.

Physical Distribution– The management of the movement and handling of goods from the point of production to the point of consumption or use.

Price Cutting– Offering merchandise or a service for sale at a price below that recognized as usual or appropriate by its buyers and sellers.

Comment. One obvious criticism of this definition is that it is indefinite. But that very indefiniteness also causes it to be more accurately descriptive of a concept which is characterized by a high degree of indefiniteness in the mind of the average person affected by price cutting.

Traders' ideas of what constitutes price cutting are so vague and indefinite that any precise or highly specific definition of the phenomenon is bound to fail to include all its manifestations. If you ask a group of traders in a specific commodity to define price cutting, you will get as many conflicting formulas as there are traders. But if you ask those same traders at any particular time whether selling at a certain price constitutes price cutting, you will probably get a considerable degree of uniformity of opinion. It is precisely this condition which the definition is designed to reflect.

Price Leader– A firm whose pricing behavior is followed by other companies in the same industry.

Comment. The price leadership of a firm may be limited to a certain geographical area, as in the oil business, or to certain products or groups of products, as in the steel business.

Private Brands– Brands sponsored by merchants or agents as distinguished from those sponsored by manufacturers or producers.

Comment. This usage is thoroughly illogical, since no seller wants his brand to be private in the sense of being secret and all brands are private in the sense that they are special and not common or general in use. But the usage is common in marketing literature and among traders. Therefore the Committee presents it in this report.

Producers' Cooperative Marketing– That type of cooperative marketing which primarily involves the sale of goods or services of the associated producing membership. May perform only an assembly or brokerage function but in some cases, notably milk marketing, extends into processing and distribution of the members' production.

Comment. Many producers' cooperative marketing associations also buy for their members. This fact does not subtract from their status as producers' cooperatives; this is especially true of the farm cooperatives.

The term does not include those activities of trade associations that affect only indirectly the sales of the membership. Such activities are the maintenance of credit rating bureaus, design registration bureaus, and brand protection machinery.

Product Line– A group of products that are closely related either because they satisfy a class of need, are used together, are sold to the same customer groups, are marketed through the same type of outlets or fall within given price ranges. Example, carpenters' tools.

Comment. Sub-lines of products may be distinguished, such as hammers or or saws, within a Product Line.

Product Management– The planning, direction, and control of all phases of the life cycle of products, including the creation or discovery of ideas for new products, the screening of such ideas, the coordination of the work of research and physical development of products, their packaging and branding, their introduction on the market, their market development, their modification, the discovery of new uses for them, their repair and servicing, and their deletion.

Comment. It is not safe to think of Product Management as the work of the executive known as the Product Manager, because the dimensions of his job vary widely from company to company, sometimes embracing all the activities listed in the definition and sometimes being limited to the sales promotion of the products in his care.

Product Mix– The composite of products offered for sale by a firm or a business unit.

Comment. Tooth paste is a product. The 50 cent tube of Whosis ammoniated tooth paste is an item. Tooth pastes and powders, mouth washes, and other allied items compose an oral hygiene product line. Soaps, cosmetics, dentifrices, drug items, cake mixes, shortenings and other items may comprise a product mix if marketed by the same company.

Publicity– Non-personal stimulation of demand for a product, service or business unit by planting commercially significant news about it in a published medium or obtaining favorable presentation of it upon radio, television, or stage that is not paid for by the sponsor.

Comment. Retailers use the term to denote the sum of the functions of advertising, display, and publicity as defined above.

Purchasing Power (Buying Power)– The capacity to purchase possessed by an individual buyer, a group of buyers, or the aggregate of the buyers in an area or a market.

R

Rack Jobber– A wholesaling business unit that markets specialized lines of merchandise to certain types of retail stores and provides the special services of selective brand and item merchandising and arrangement, maintenance, and stocking of display racks.
Comment. The Rack Jobber usually, but not always, puts his merchandise in the store of the retailer on consignment. Rack Jobbers are most prevalent in the food business.

Resale Price Maintenance– Control by a supplier of the selling prices of his branded goods at subsequent stages of distribution by means of contractual agreement under fair trade laws or other devices.

Resident Buyer– An agent who specializes in buying, on a fee or commission basis, chiefly for retailers.
Comment. The term as defined above, is limited to agents residing in the market cities who charge their retail principals fees for buying assistance rendered, but there are resident buying offices that are owned by out-of-town stores and some that are owned cooperatively by a group of stores. The former are called *private* offices and the latter *associated* offices. Neither of them should be confused with the central buying office of the typical chain, where the buying function is performed by the office directly, not acting as a specialized assistant to store buyers.
Resident Buyers should also be distinguished from apparel *merchandise brokers* who represent competing manufacturers in the garment trades and have as customers out-of-town smaller stores in search of fashion merchandise. These brokers are paid by the manufacturers to whom they bring additional business, on a percentage of sales basis.

Retailer– A merchant, or occasionally an agent, whose main business is selling directly to the ultimate consumer.
Comment. The retailer is to be distinguished by the nature of his sales rather than by the way he procures the goods in which he deals. The size of the units in which he sells is an incidental rather than a primary element in his character. His essential distinguishing mark is the fact that his typical sale is made to the ultimate consumer.

Retailer Cooperative– A group of independent retailers organized to buy cooperatively either through a jointly owned warehouse or through a buying club.

Comment. Their cooperative activities may include operating under a group name, joint advertising and cooperative managerial supervision.

Retailing– The activities involved in selling directly to the ultimate consumer.

Comment. This definition includes all forms of selling to the ultimate consumer. It embraces the direct-to-consumer sales activities of the producer whether through his own stores, by house-to-house canvass, or by mail order. It does not cover the sale by producers of industrial goods, by industrial supply houses, or by retailers to industrial, commercial, or institutional buyers for use in the conduct of their enterprises.

S

Sales Agent—See **Selling Agent.**

Sales Analysis– A subdivision of Marketing Research which involves the systematic study and comparison of sales data.

Comment. The purpose of such analysis is usually to aid in marketing management by providing sales information along the lines of market areas, organizational units, products or product groups, customers or customer groups, or such other units as may be useful.

Sales Budget– The part of the marketing budget which is concerned with planned dollar sales and planned costs of personal selling during a specified future period.

Sales Forecast– An estimate of sales, in dollars or physical units for a specified future period under a proposed marketing plan or program and under an assumed set of economic and other forces outside the unit for which the forecast is made. The forecast may be for a specified item of merchandise or for an entire line.

Comment. Two sets of factors are involved in making a Sales Forecast; (1) those forces outside the control of the firm for which the forecast is made that are likely to influence its sales, and (2) changes in the marketing methods or practices of the firm that are likely to affect its sales.

In the course of planning future activities, the management of a given firm may make several sales forecasts each consisting of an estimate of probable sales if a given marketing plan is adopted or a given set of outside forces prevails. The estimated effects that several marketing plans may have on Sales and Profits may be compared in the process of arriving at that marketing program which will, in the opinion of the officials of the company, be best designed to promote its welfare.

Sales Management– The planning, direction, and control of the personal selling activities of a business unit, including recruiting, selecting, training, equipping, assigning, routing, supervising, paying, and motivating as these tasks apply to the personal sales force.

Comment. These activities are sometimes but not generally designated Sales Administration or Sales Force Management.

Sales Manager– The executive who plans, directs, and controls the activities of salesmen.

Comment. This definition distinguishes sharply between the manager who conducts the personal selling activities of a business unit and his superior, the executive, variously called Marketing Manager, Director of Marketing, Vice President for Marketing, who has charge of all marketing activities. The usage of this form of organization has been growing rapidly during recent years.

Sales Planning– That part of the Marketing Planning work which is concerned with making sales forecasts, devising programs for reaching the sales target, and deriving a sales budget.

Sales Potential– See **Market Share.**

Sales Promotion– (1.) In a specific sense, those marketing activities, other than personal selling, advertising, and publicity, that stimulate consumer purchasing and dealer effectiveness, such as display, shows and exhibitions, demonstrations, and various non-recurrent selling efforts not in the ordinary routine.

(2.) In retailing, all methods of stimulating customer purchasing, including personal selling, advertising, and publicity.

Comment. This definition includes the two most logical and commonly accepted usages of this much abused term. It is the suggestion of the Committee that insofar as possible, the use of the term be confined to the first of the two definitions given above.

Sales Quota– A projected volume of sales assigned to a marketing unit for use in the management of sales efforts.

It applies to a specified period and may be expressed in dollars or in physical units.

Comment. The quota may be used in checking the efficiency or stimulating the efforts of or in remunerating individual salesmen or other personnel engaged in sales work.

A quota may be for a salesman, a territory, a department, a branch house, a wholesaler or retailer, or for the company as a whole. It may be different from the sales figure set up in the sales budget. Since it is a managerial device, it is not an immutable figure inexorably arrived at by the application of absolutely exact statistical formulas.

Sales Research– See **Marketing Research and Sales Analysis.**

Selective Selling– The policy of selling to a limited number of customers in a market.

Self Selection– The method used in retailing by which the customer may choose the desired merchandise without direct assistance of store personnel.

Self Service– The method used in retailing whereby the customer selects his own merchandise, removes it from the shelves or bulk containers, carries it to a check-out stand to complete the transaction and transports it to the point of use.

Selling– The personal or impersonal process of assisting and/or persuading a prospective customer to buy a commodity or a service or to act favorably upon an idea that has conmercial significance to the seller.
Comment. This definition includes advertising, other forms of publicity, and sales promotion as well as personal selling.

Selling Agent– An agent who operates on an extended contractual basis; sells all of a specified line of merchandise or the entire output of his principal, and usually has full authority with regard to prices, terms, and other conditions of sale. He occasionally renders financial aid to his principal.
Comment. This functionary is often called a Sales Agent.

Service Wholesaler– See **Wholesaler.**

Services– Activities, benefits, or satisfactions which are offered for sale, or are provided in connection with the sale of goods.
Examples are amusements, hotel service, electric service, transportation, the services of barber shops and beauty shops, repair and maintenance service, the work of credit rating bureaus. This list is merely illustrative and no attempt has been made to make it complete. The term also applies to the various activities such as credit extension, advice and help of sales people, delivery, by which the seller serves the convenience of his customers.

Shopping Center– A geographical cluster of retail stores, collectively handling an assortment of goods varied enough to satisfy most of the merchandise wants of consumers within convenient travelling time, and, thereby, attracting a general shopping trade.
Comment. During recent years, the term has acquired a special usage in its application to the planned or integrated centers developed in suburban or semi-suburban areas usually along main highways and featuring ample parking space.

Shopping Goods– Those consumers' goods which the customer in the process of selection and purchase characteristically compares on such bases as suitability, quality, price and style.

Examples of goods that most consumers probably buy as Shopping Goods are: millinery, furniture, dress goods, women's ready-to-wear and shoes, used automobiles, and major appliances.

Comment. It should be emphasized that a given article may be bought by one customer as a Shopping Good and by another as a Specialty or Convenience Good. The general classification depends upon the way in which the average or typical buyer purchases.

See Comment under Specialty Goods.

Specialty Goods– Those consumers' goods with unique characteristics and/or brand identification for which a significant group of buyers are habitually willing to make a special purchasing effort.

Examples of articles that are usually bought as Specialty Goods are: specific brands and types of fancy foods, hi-fi components, certain types of sporting equipment, photographic equipment, and men's suits.

Comment. Price is not usually the primary factor in consumer choice of specialty goods although their prices are often higher than those of other articles serving the same basic want but without their special characteristics.

Specialty Store– A retail store that makes its appeal on the basis of a restricted class of shopping goods.

Standardization– The determination of basic limits or grade ranges in the form of uniform specifications to which particular manufactured goods may conform and uniform classes into which the products of agriculture and the extractive industries may or must be sorted or assigned.

Comment. This term does not include Grading which is the process of sorting or assigning units of a commodity to the grades or classes that have been established through the process of Standardization. Some systems of standardization and grading for agricultural products are compulsory by law.

Stock or Inventory Control– The use of a system or mechanism to maintain stocks of goods at desired levels.

Comment. Such control is usually exercised to maintain stocks that are (a) representative in that they include all the items the customer group served expects to be able to buy from the firm involved, (b) adequate in that a sufficient quantity of each item is included to satisfy all reasonably foreseeable demands for it, and (c) economical in that no funds of the firm are held in inventory beyond those needed to serve purposes (a) and (b) and in that it facilitates savings in costs of production.

Storage– The marketing function that involves holding goods between the time of their production and their final sale.

Comment. Some processing is often done while goods are in storage. It is probable that this should be regarded as a part of production rather than of marketing.

Superette– See **Supermarket.**

Supermarket– A large retailing business unit selling mainly food and grocery items on the basis of the low margin appeal, wide variety and assortments, self-service, and heavy emphasis on merchandise appeal. *Comment.* In its bid for patronage the Supermarket makes heavy use of the visual appeal of the merchandise itself.

The Committee realizes that it would be foolhardy in this day of rapid change to try to indicate how large a store must be to be a Supermarket. At the time of this report the latest figures indicate that the average store recognized by the Supermarket Institute as belonging to the class has annual sales of somewhat under $2,010,000, and that about 45 percent of them sell more than that amount each year. Both of these figures have been changing rapidly and may continue to do so. A Superette is a store, somewhat smaller than a Supermarket, and possessing most of the same characteristics.

T

Trade-Mark– A brand or part of a brand that is given legal protection because it is capable of exclusive appropriation; because it is used in a manner sufficiently fanciful, distinctive, and abritrary, because it is affixed to the product when sold, or because it otherwise satisfies the requirements set up by law. *Comment.* Trade-mark is essentially a legal term and includes only those brands or parts of brands which the law designates as trademarks. In the final analysis in any specific case a Trade-mark is what the court in that case decides to regard as a Trade-mark.

Trading Area– A district whose size is usually determined by the boundaries within which it is economical in terms of volume and cost for a marketing unit or group to sell and/or deliver a good or service. *Comment.* A single business may have several trading areas; for example, the Trading Area of Marshall Field for its store business is different from that for its catalogue business.

Traffic Management– The planning, selection, and direction of all means and methods of transportation involved in the movement of goods in the marketing process. *Comment.* This definition is confined to those activities in connection with transportation that have to do particularly with marketing and form an inseparable part of any well-organized system of distribution. It includes control of the movement of goods in trucks owned by the marketing concern as well as by public carrier. It does not include the movement of goods within the warehouse of a producer or within the store of a retail concern.

Truck Wholesaler– See **Wholesaler.**

U

Ultimate Consumer– One who buys and/or uses goods or services to satisfy personal or household wants rather than for resale or for use in business, institutional, or industrial operations.
Comment. The definition distinguishes sharply between Industrial Users and Ultimate Consumers. A firm buying and using an office machine, a drum of lubricating oil, or a carload of steel billets is an Industrial User of those products, not an Ultimate Consumer of them. A vital difference exists between the purposes motivating the two types of purchases which in turn results in highly signficant differences in buying methods, marketing organization, and selling practices.

V

Value Added by Marketing– The part of the value of a product or a service to the consumer or user which results from marketing activities.
Comment. There is urgent need of a method or formula for computing Value Added by Marketing. Increased attention is being devoted to developing such a formula. At present none of those suggested have gained enough acceptance to justify inclusion in this definition or comment.

Variety Store– A retailing business unit that handles a wide assortment of goods, usually in the low or popular segment of the price range.
Comment. While some foods are generally handled, the major emphasis is devoted to non-food products.

Voluntary Group– A group of retailers each of whom owns and operates his own store and is associated with a wholesale organization or manufacturer to carry on joint merchandising activities and who are characterized by some degree of group identity and uniformity of operation.
Such joint activities have been largely of two kinds; cooperative advertising and group control of store operation.
Comment. A Voluntary Group is usually sponsored by a wholesaler. Similar groups sponsored by retailers do not belong in this category. Groups of independent stores sponsored by a chain store system are usually called "Agency Stores."

W

Wholesaler– A business unit which buys and resells merchandise to retailers and other merchants and/or to industrial, institutional, and commercial users but which does not sell in signficant amounts to ultimate consumers.

In the basic materials, semi-finished goods, and tool and machinery trades merchants of this type are commonly known as "distributors" or "supply houses."

Comment. Generally these merchants render a wide variety of services to their customers. Those who render all the services normally expected in the wholesale trade are known as Service Wholesalers; those who render only a few of the wholesale services are known as Limited Function Wholesalers. The latter group is composed mainly of Cash and Carry Wholesalers who do not render the credit or delivery service, Drop Shipment Wholesalers who sell for delivery by the producer direct to the buyer, Truck Wholesalers who combine selling, delivery, and collection in one operation, and Mail Order Wholesalers who perform the selling service entirely by mail.

This definition ignores or minimizes two bases upon which the term is often defined; first, the size of the lots in which wholesalers deal, and second, the fact that they habitually sell for resale. The figures show that many wholesalers operate on a very small scale and in small lots. Most of them make a significant portion of their sales to industrial users.

INDEX

N–O–P